WITHDRAWN

Arcana Vol. 7
Created by So-Young Lee

Translation - Youngju Ryu
English Adaptation - Barbara Randall Kesel
Copy Editor - Nikhil Burman
Retouch and Lettering - Star Print Brokers
Production Artist - Vicente Rivera, Jr.
Graphic Designer - James Lee

Editor - Bryce P. Coleman
Digital Imaging Manager - Chris Buford
Pre-Production Supervisor - Erika Terriquez
Production Manager - Elisabeth Brizzi
Managing Editor - Vy Nguyen
Creative Director - Anne Marie Horne
Editor-in-Chief - Rob Tokar
Publisher - Mike Kiley
President and C.O.O. - John Parker
C.E.O. and Chief Creative Officer - Stuart Levy

A **TOKYOPOP** Manga

TOKYOPOP and 🔅 are trademarks or registered trademarks of TOKYOPOP Inc.

TOKYOPOP Inc.
5900 Wilshire Blvd. Suite 2000
Los Angeles, CA 90036

E-mail: info@TOKYOPOP.com
Come visit us online at www.TOKYOPOP.com

ISBN: 978-1-4278-0165-4

First TOKYOPOP printing: January 2008
10 9 8 7 6 5 4 3 2 1
Printed in the USA

VOLUME 7
SO-YOUNG LEE

HAMBURG // LONDON // LOS ANGELES // TOKYO

THE JOURNEY THUS FAR...

Having reached the land of Eloam, Inez and Kyrette's paths cross once again. Oddly, though, Kyrette does not seem to recognize her. When asked her name, Inez replies that she is called "Enril," a name she herself has never before heard. Soon, voices from her past, emanating from deep within the Labyrinth of Memories, begin to call to Inez. Finally, the girl succumbs, falling unconscious, into the arms of Yulan, who finds himself confronted by the visage of his own future...

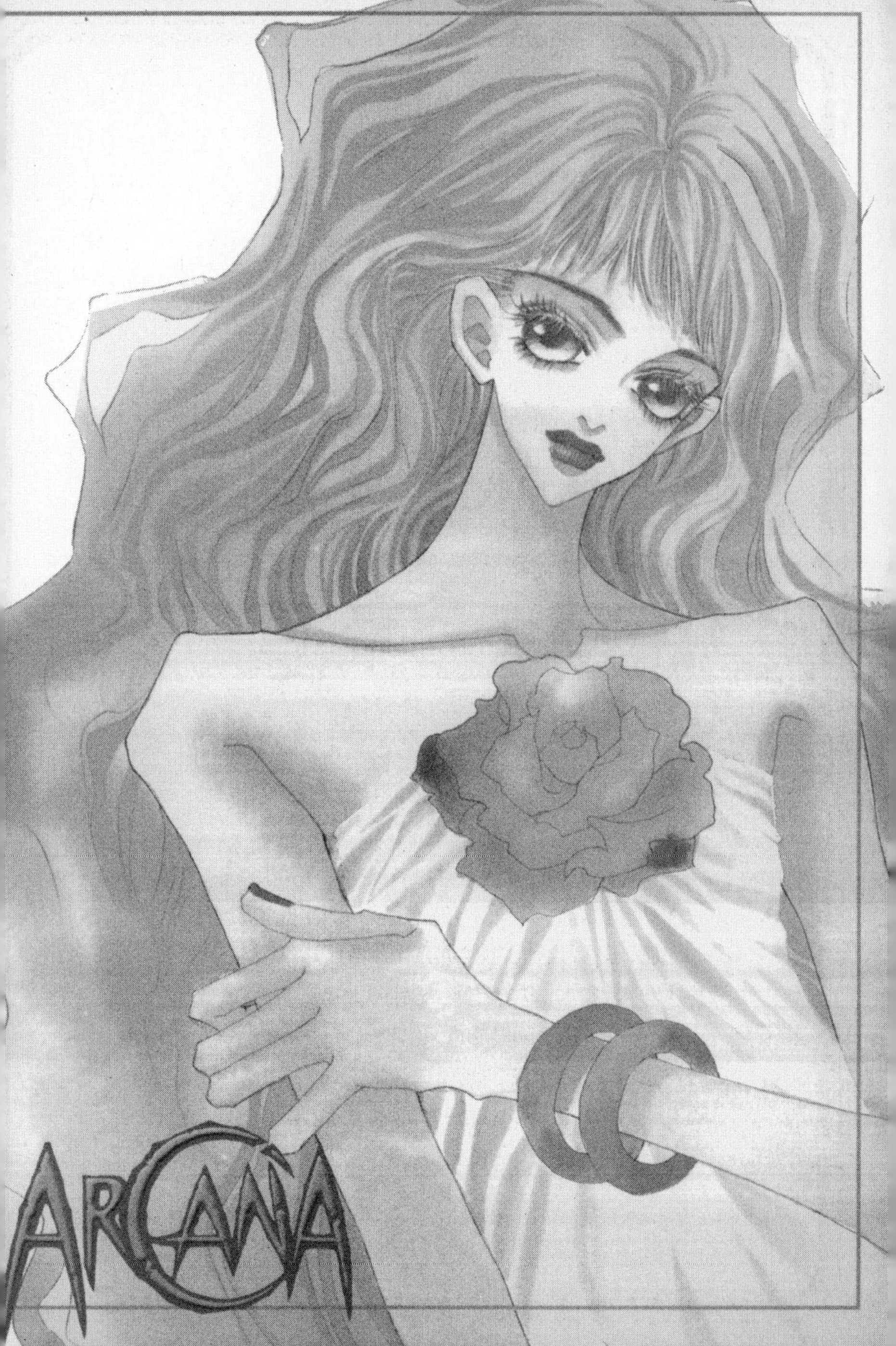
ARCANA

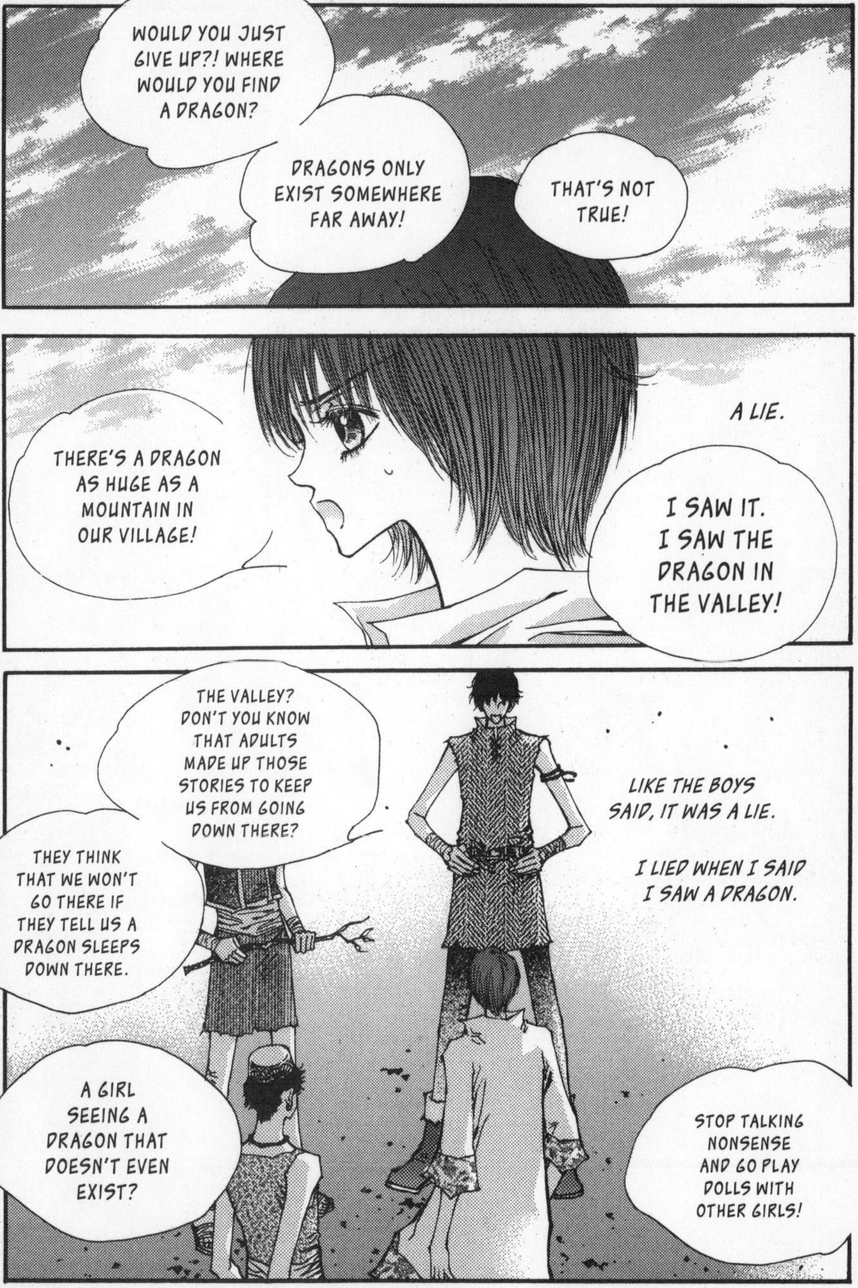
WOULD YOU JUST GIVE UP?! WHERE WOULD YOU FIND A DRAGON?
DRAGONS ONLY EXIST SOMEWHERE FAR AWAY!
THAT'S NOT TRUE!
THERE'S A DRAGON AS HUGE AS A MOUNTAIN IN OUR VILLAGE!
I SAW IT. I SAW THE DRAGON IN THE VALLEY!
A LIE.
THE VALLEY? DON'T YOU KNOW THAT ADULTS MADE UP THOSE STORIES TO KEEP US FROM GOING DOWN THERE?
THEY THINK THAT WE WON'T GO THERE IF THEY TELL US A DRAGON SLEEPS DOWN THERE.
LIKE THE BOYS SAID, IT WAS A LIE.
I LIED WHEN I SAID I SAW A DRAGON.
A GIRL SEEING A DRAGON THAT DOESN'T EVEN EXIST?
STOP TALKING NONSENSE AND GO PLAY DOLLS WITH OTHER GIRLS!

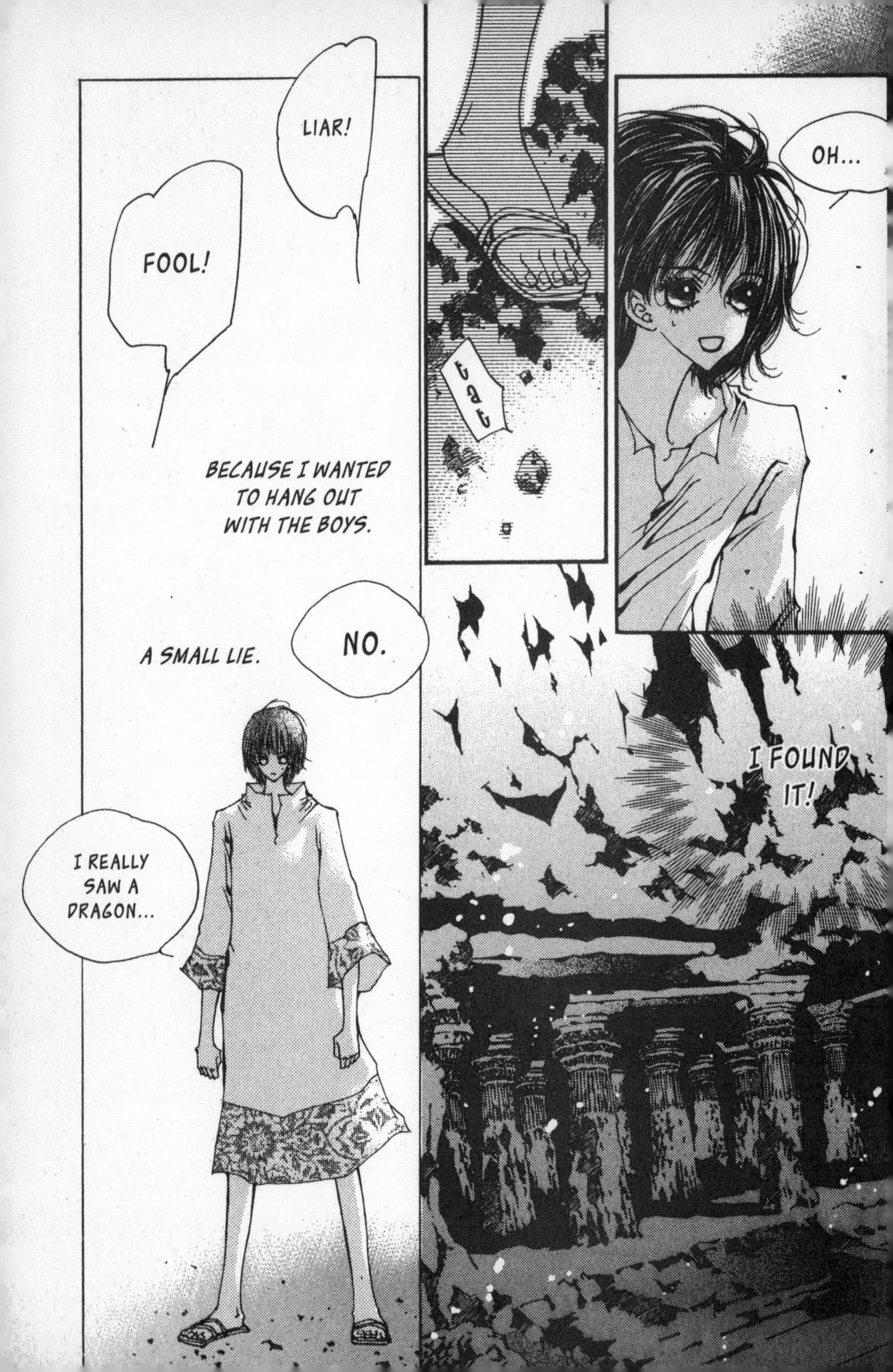
OH...
tat
I FOUND IT!
LIAR!
FOOL!
BECAUSE I WANTED TO HANG OUT WITH THE BOYS.
NO.
A SMALL LIE.
I REALLY SAW A DRAGON...

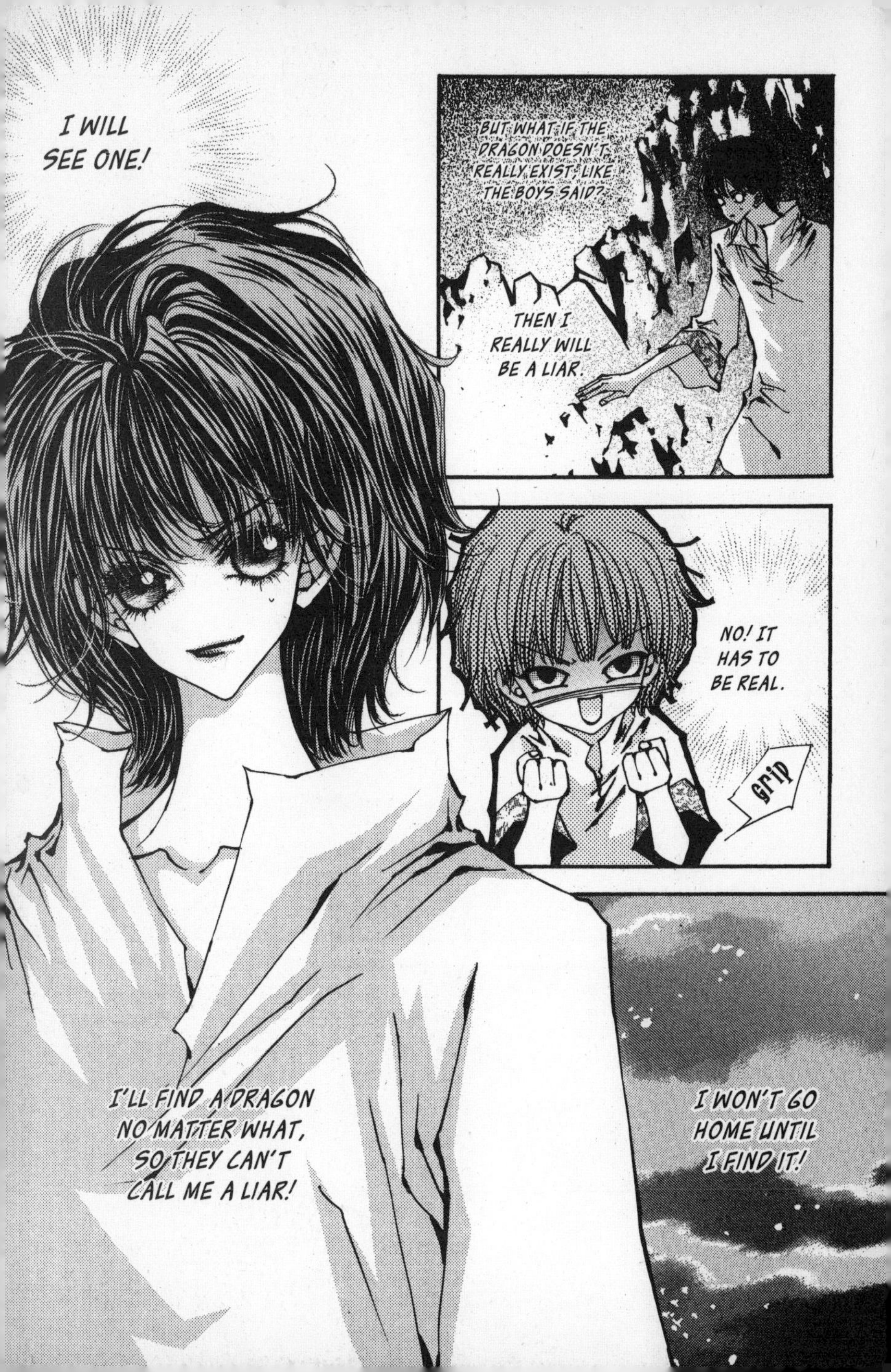
BUT WHAT IF THE DRAGON DOESN'T REALLY EXIST, LIKE THE BOYS SAID?
THEN I REALLY WILL BE A LIAR.
NO! IT HAS TO BE REAL.
GRIP
I WILL SEE ONE!
I'LL FIND A DRAGON NO MATTER WHAT, SO THEY CAN'T CALL ME A LIAR!
I WON'T GO HOME UNTIL I FIND IT!

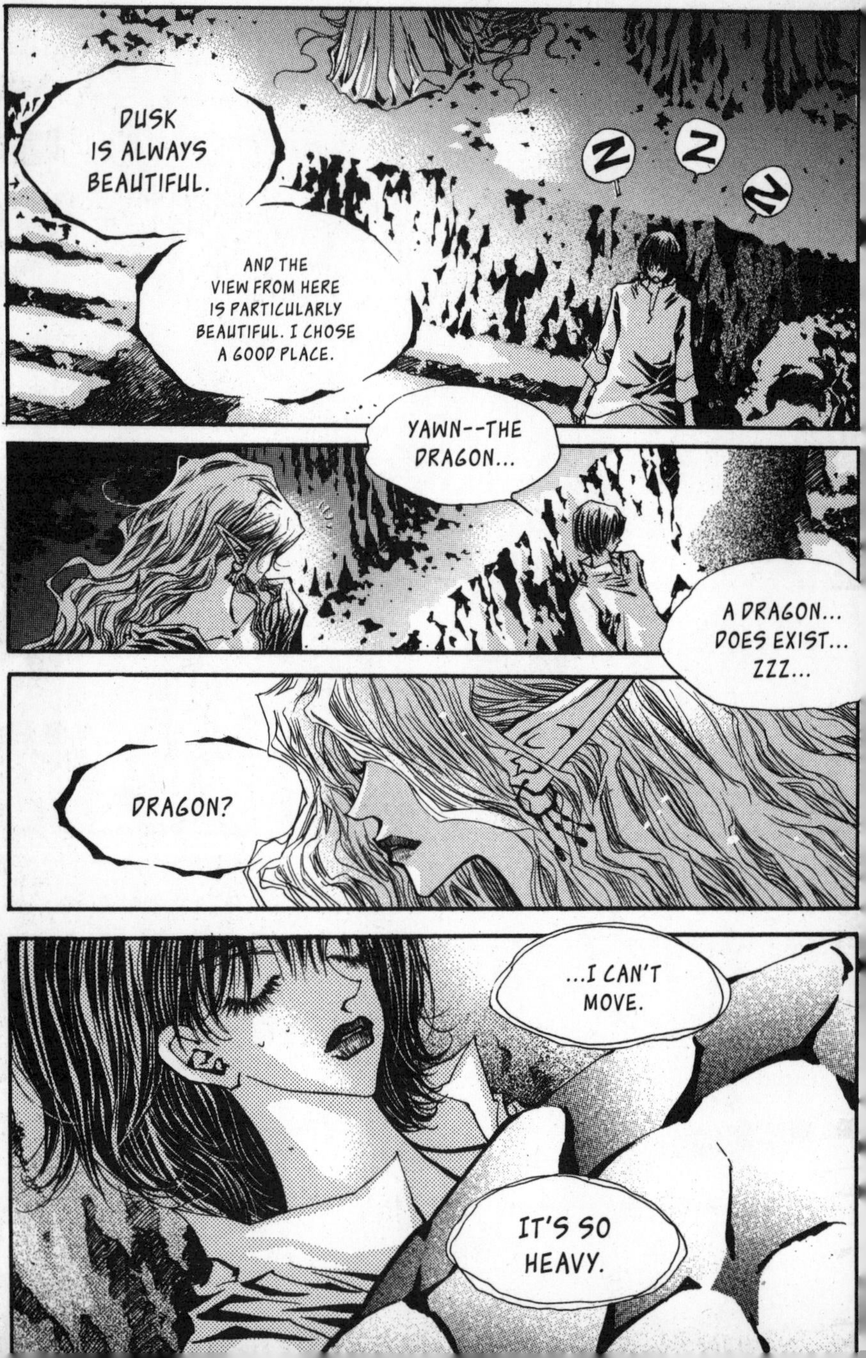
DUSK IS ALWAYS BEAUTIFUL.
AND THE VIEW FROM HERE IS PARTICULARLY BEAUTIFUL. I CHOSE A GOOD PLACE.
Z Z Z
YAWN--THE DRAGON...
A DRAGON... DOES EXIST... ZZZ...
DRAGON?
...I CAN'T MOVE.
IT'S SO HEAVY.

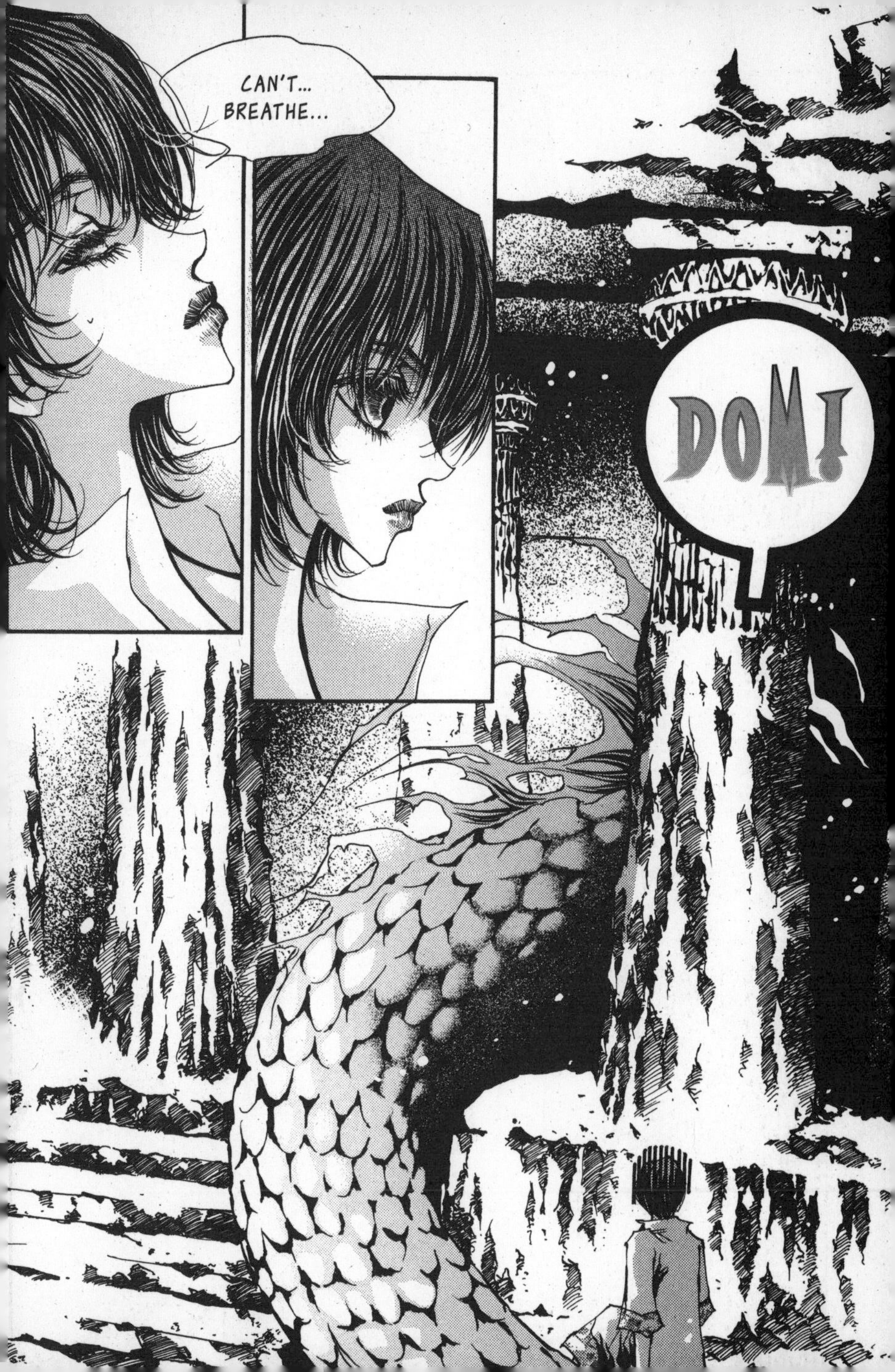
CAN'T...
BREATHE...
DOM!

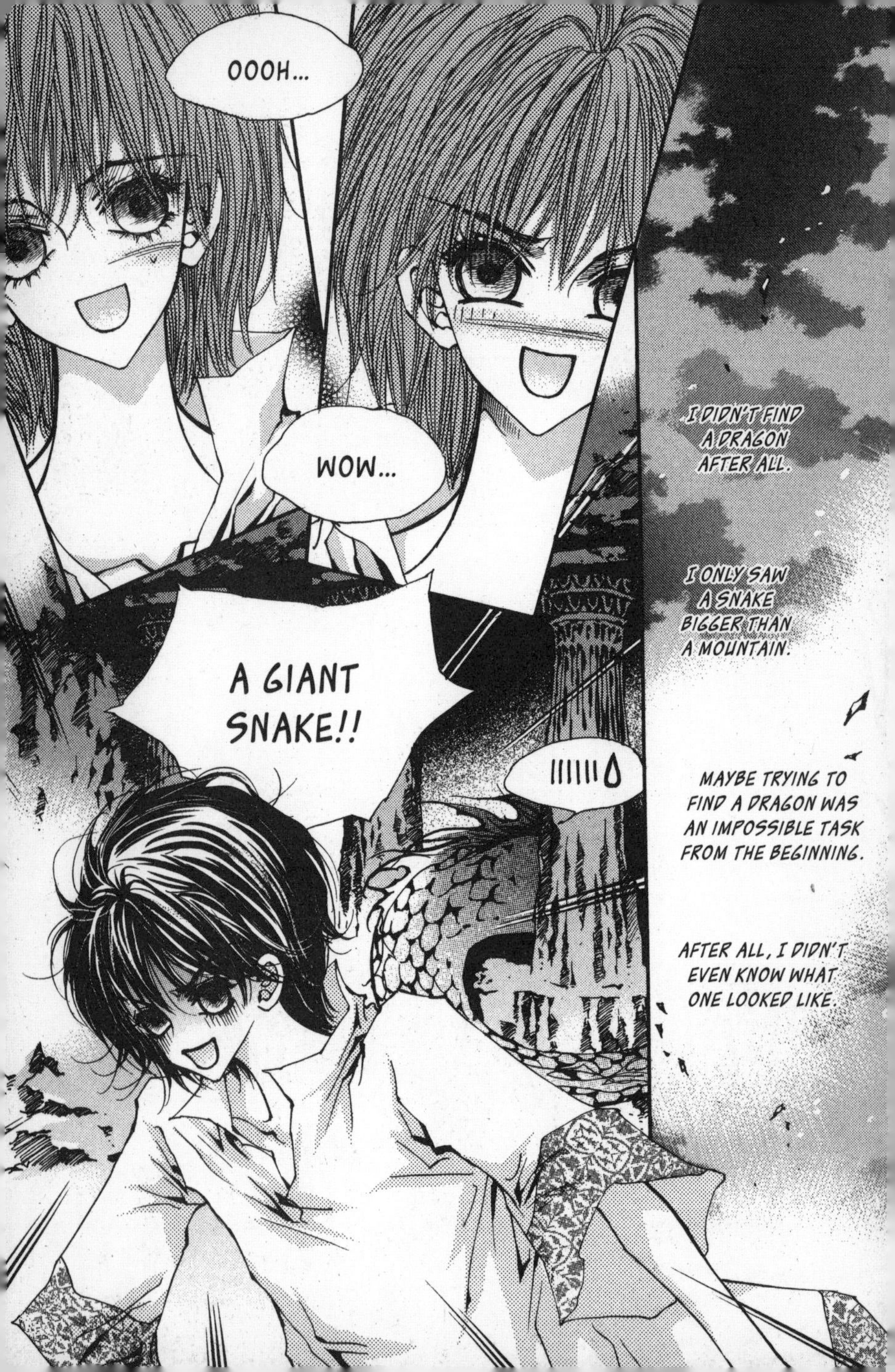
WOW...
OOOH...
A GIANT SNAKE!!
||||||
I DIDN'T FIND A DRAGON AFTER ALL.
I ONLY SAW A SNAKE BIGGER THAN A MOUNTAIN.
MAYBE TRYING TO FIND A DRAGON WAS AN IMPOSSIBLE TASK FROM THE BEGINNING.
AFTER ALL, I DIDN'T EVEN KNOW WHAT ONE LOOKED LIKE.

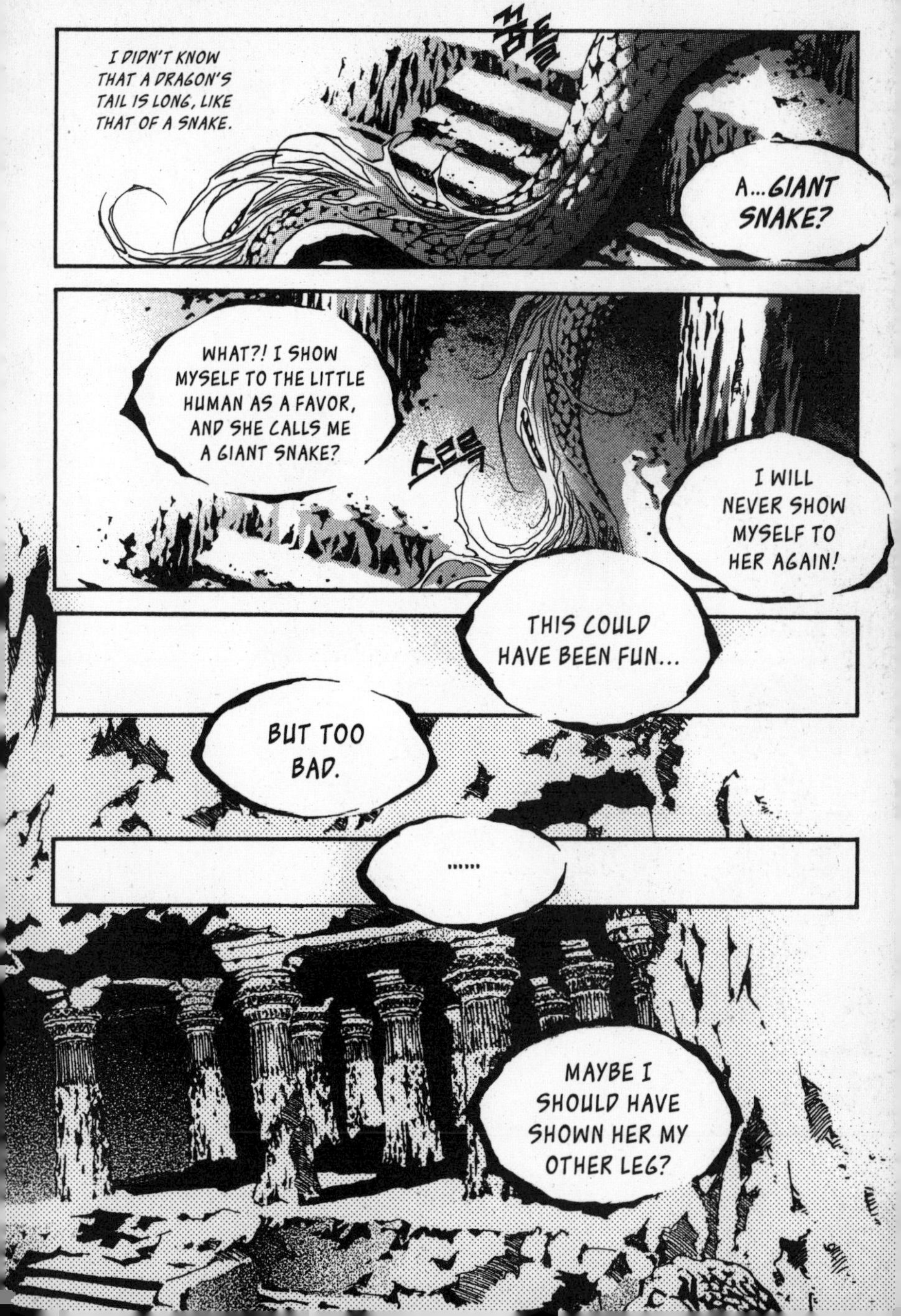
꿈틀
I DIDN'T KNOW THAT A DRAGON'S TAIL IS LONG, LIKE THAT OF A SNAKE.
A...GIANT SNAKE?
WHAT?! I SHOW MYSELF TO THE LITTLE HUMAN AS A FAVOR, AND SHE CALLS ME A GIANT SNAKE?
스르륵
I WILL NEVER SHOW MYSELF TO HER AGAIN!
THIS COULD HAVE BEEN FUN...
BUT TOO BAD.
......
MAYBE I SHOULD HAVE SHOWN HER MY OTHER LEG?

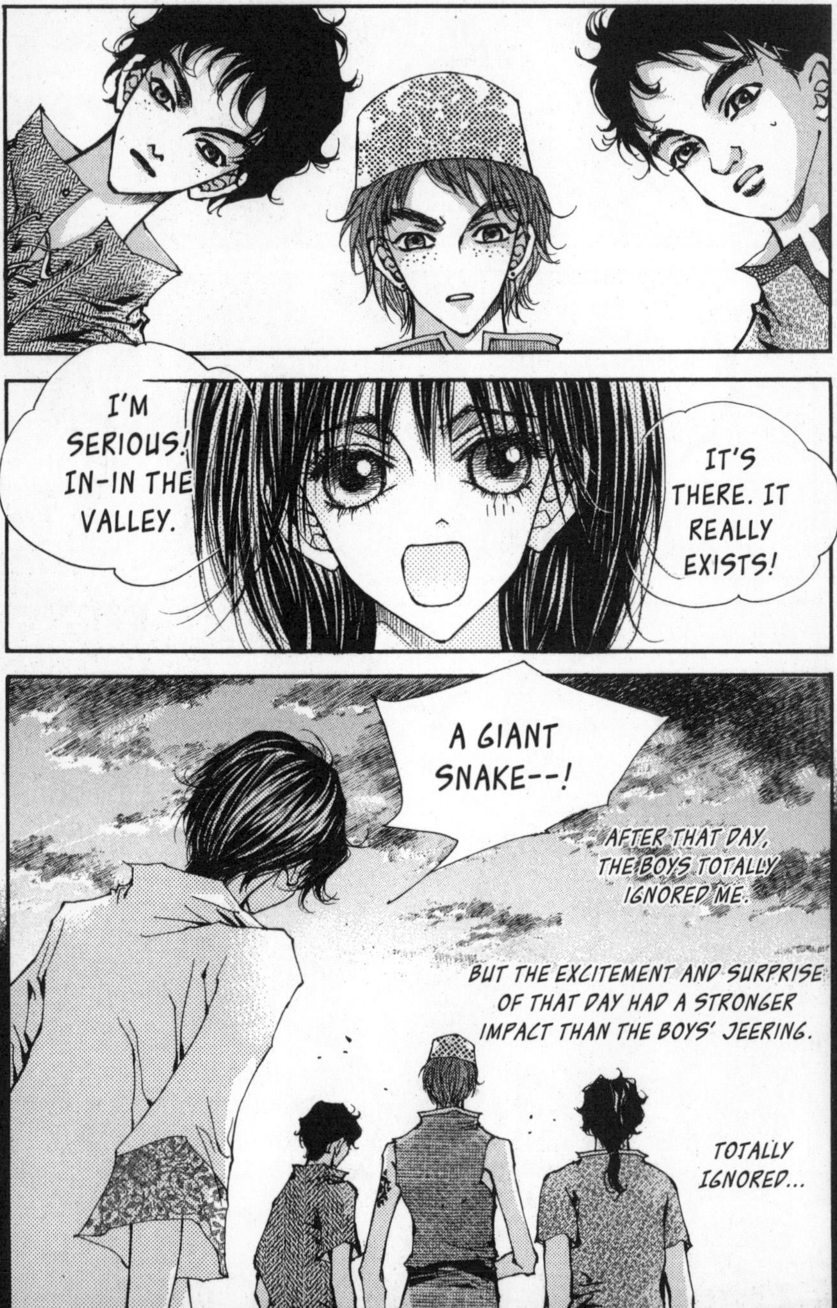

I'M SERIOUS! IN-IN THE VALLEY.
IT'S THERE. IT REALLY EXISTS!
A GIANT SNAKE--!
AFTER THAT DAY, THE BOYS TOTALLY IGNORED ME.
BUT THE EXCITEMENT AND SURPRISE OF THAT DAY HAD A STRONGER IMPACT THAN THE BOYS' JEERING.
TOTALLY IGNORED...

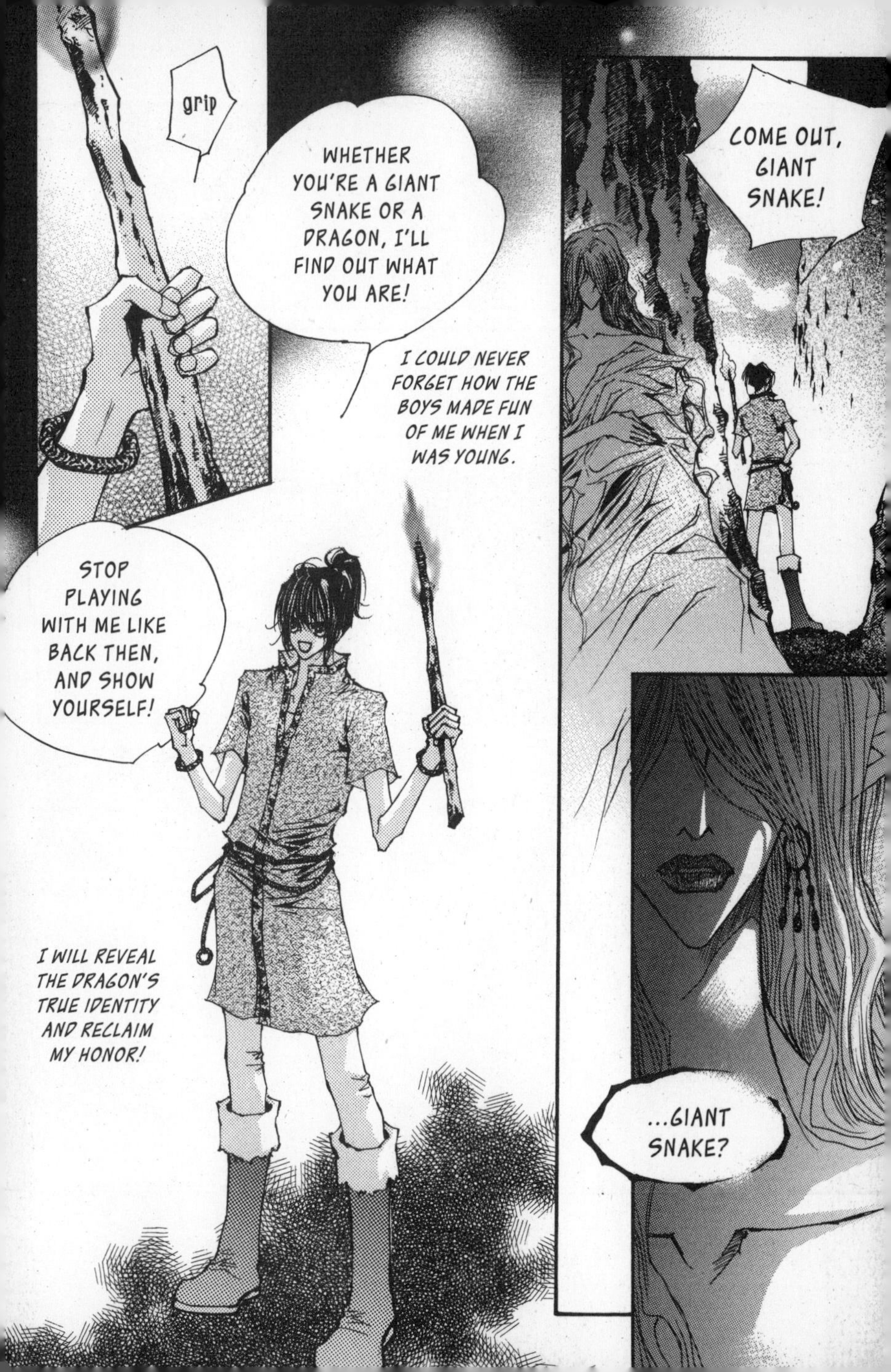
grip
WHETHER YOU'RE A GIANT SNAKE OR A DRAGON, I'LL FIND OUT WHAT YOU ARE!
I COULD NEVER FORGET HOW THE BOYS MADE FUN OF ME WHEN I WAS YOUNG.
STOP PLAYING WITH ME LIKE BACK THEN, AND SHOW YOURSELF!
I WILL REVEAL THE DRAGON'S TRUE IDENTITY AND RECLAIM MY HONOR!
COME OUT, GIANT SNAKE!
...GIANT SNAKE?

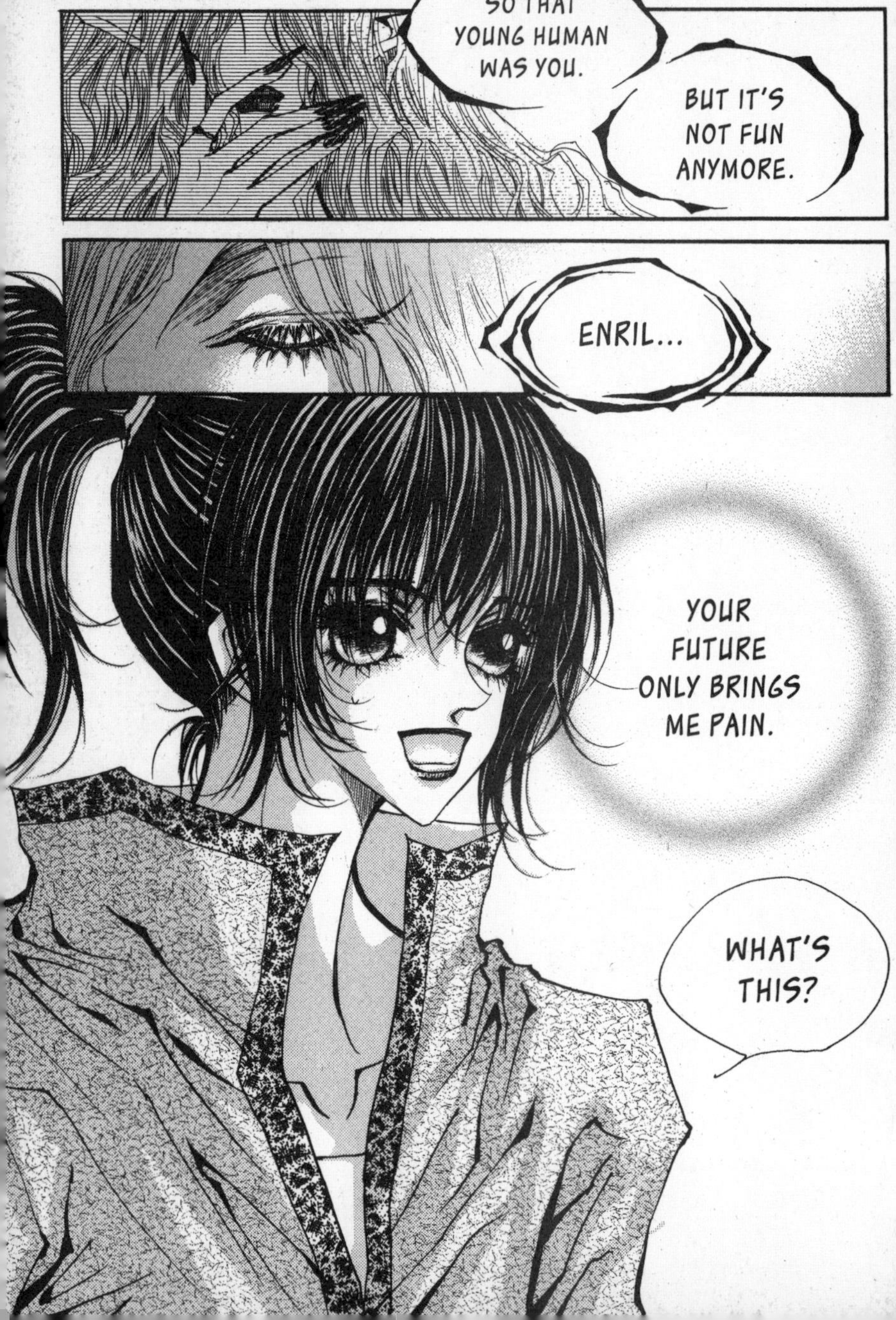
SO THAT YOUNG HUMAN WAS YOU.
BUT IT'S NOT FUN ANYMORE.
ENRIL...
YOUR FUTURE ONLY BRINGS ME PAIN.
WHAT'S THIS?

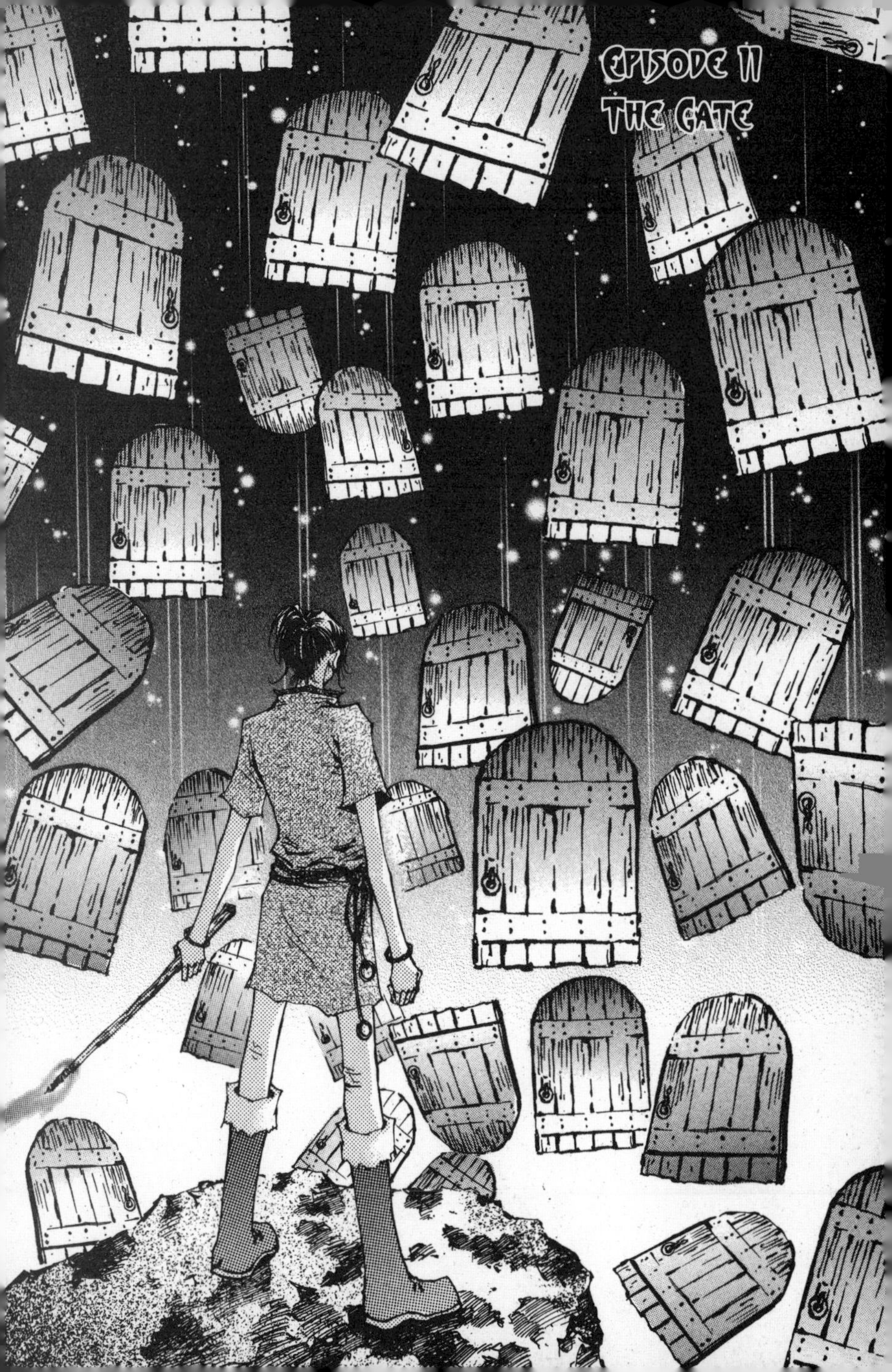
Episode 11
The Gate

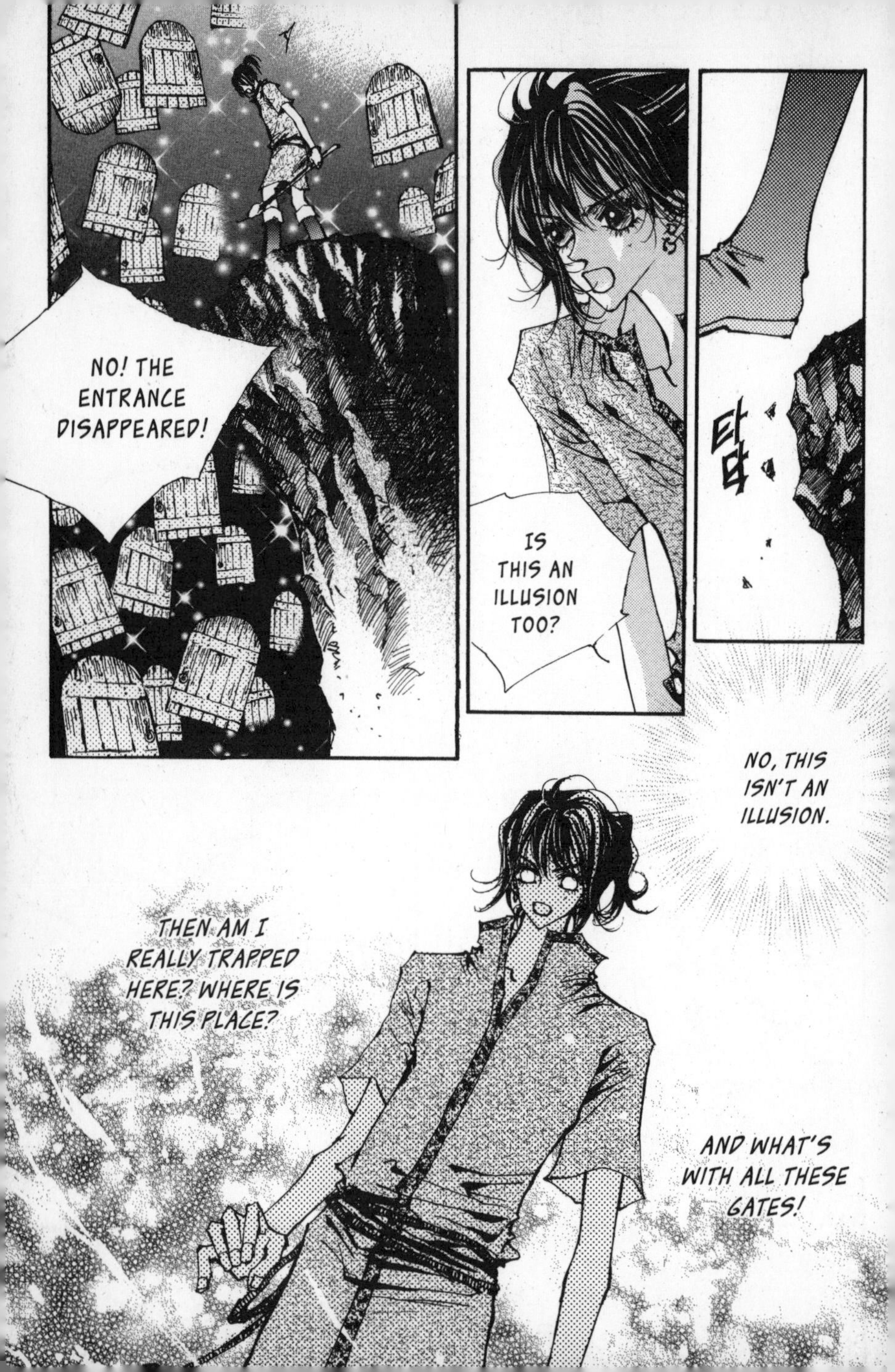
NO! THE ENTRANCE DISAPPEARED!
IS THIS AN ILLUSION TOO?
NO, THIS ISN'T AN ILLUSION.
THEN AM I REALLY TRAPPED HERE? WHERE IS THIS PLACE?
AND WHAT'S WITH ALL THESE GATES!

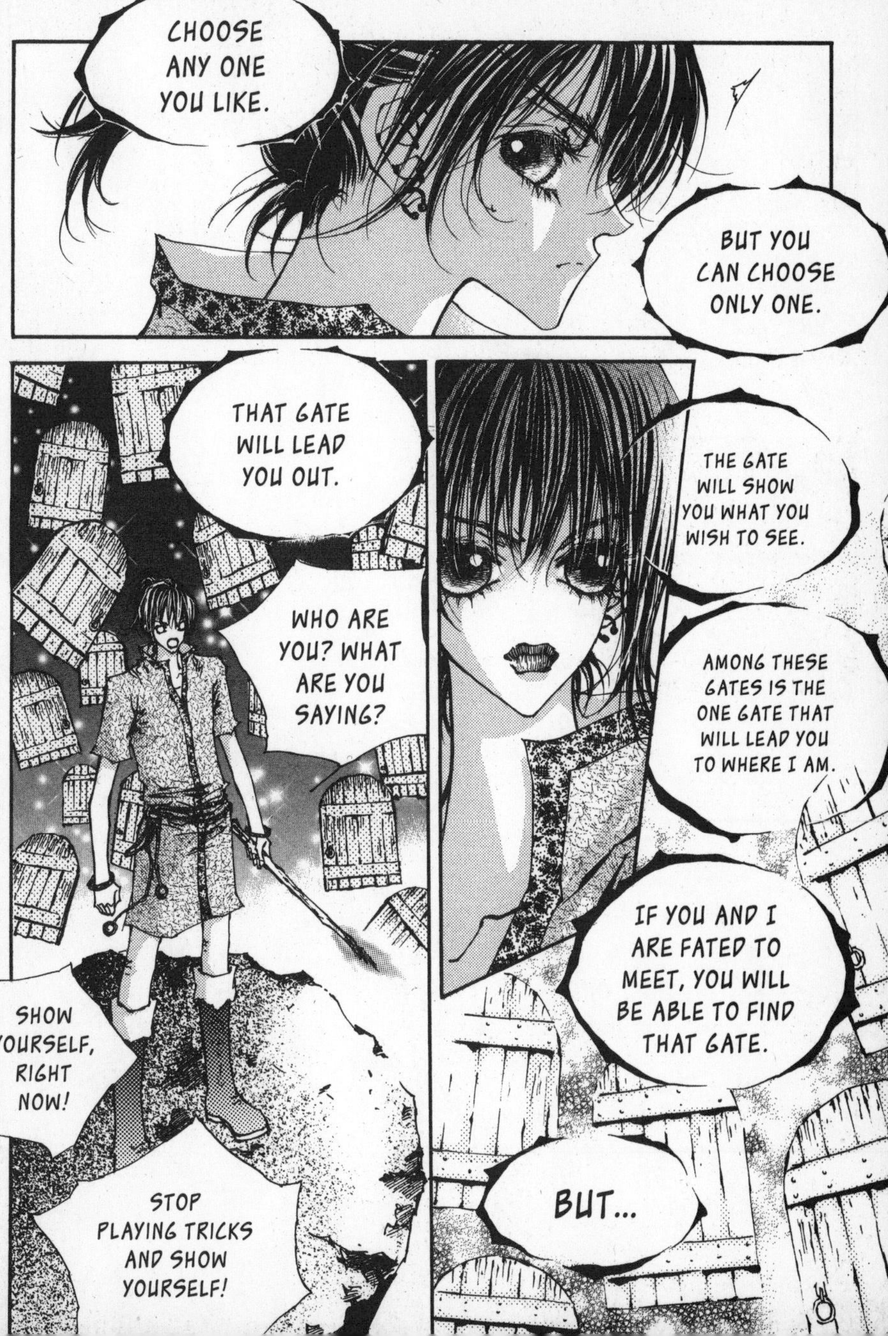
CHOOSE ANY ONE YOU LIKE.
BUT YOU CAN CHOOSE ONLY ONE.
THAT GATE WILL LEAD YOU OUT.
WHO ARE YOU? WHAT ARE YOU SAYING?
SHOW YOURSELF, RIGHT NOW!
STOP PLAYING TRICKS AND SHOW YOURSELF!
THE GATE WILL SHOW YOU WHAT YOU WISH TO SEE.
AMONG THESE GATES IS THE ONE GATE THAT WILL LEAD YOU TO WHERE I AM.
IF YOU AND I ARE FATED TO MEET, YOU WILL BE ABLE TO FIND THAT GATE.
BUT...

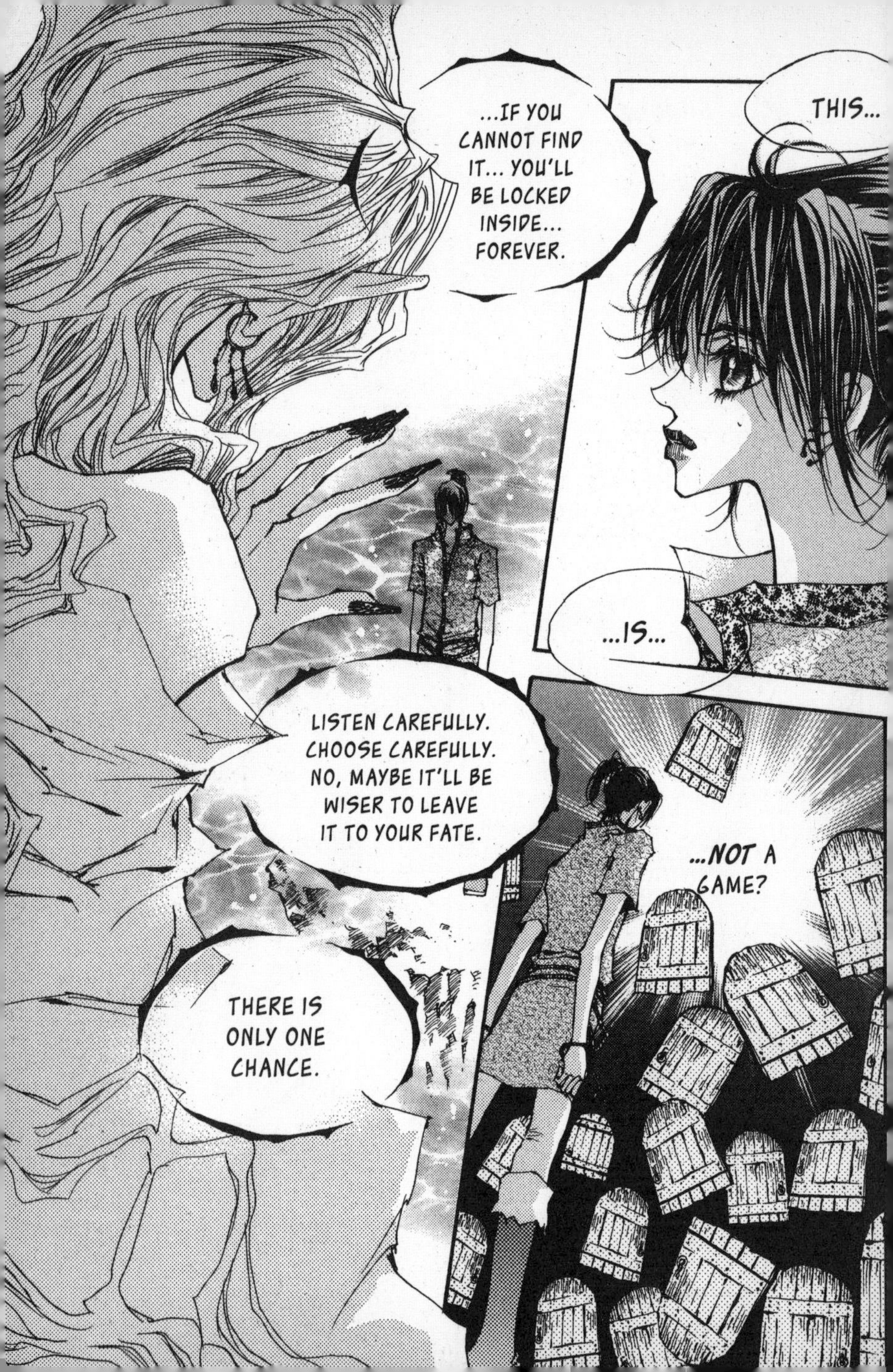
THIS...
...IS...
...NOT A GAME?
...IF YOU CANNOT FIND IT... YOU'LL BE LOCKED INSIDE... FOREVER.
LISTEN CAREFULLY. CHOOSE CAREFULLY. NO, MAYBE IT'LL BE WISER TO LEAVE IT TO YOUR FATE.
THERE IS ONLY ONE CHANCE.

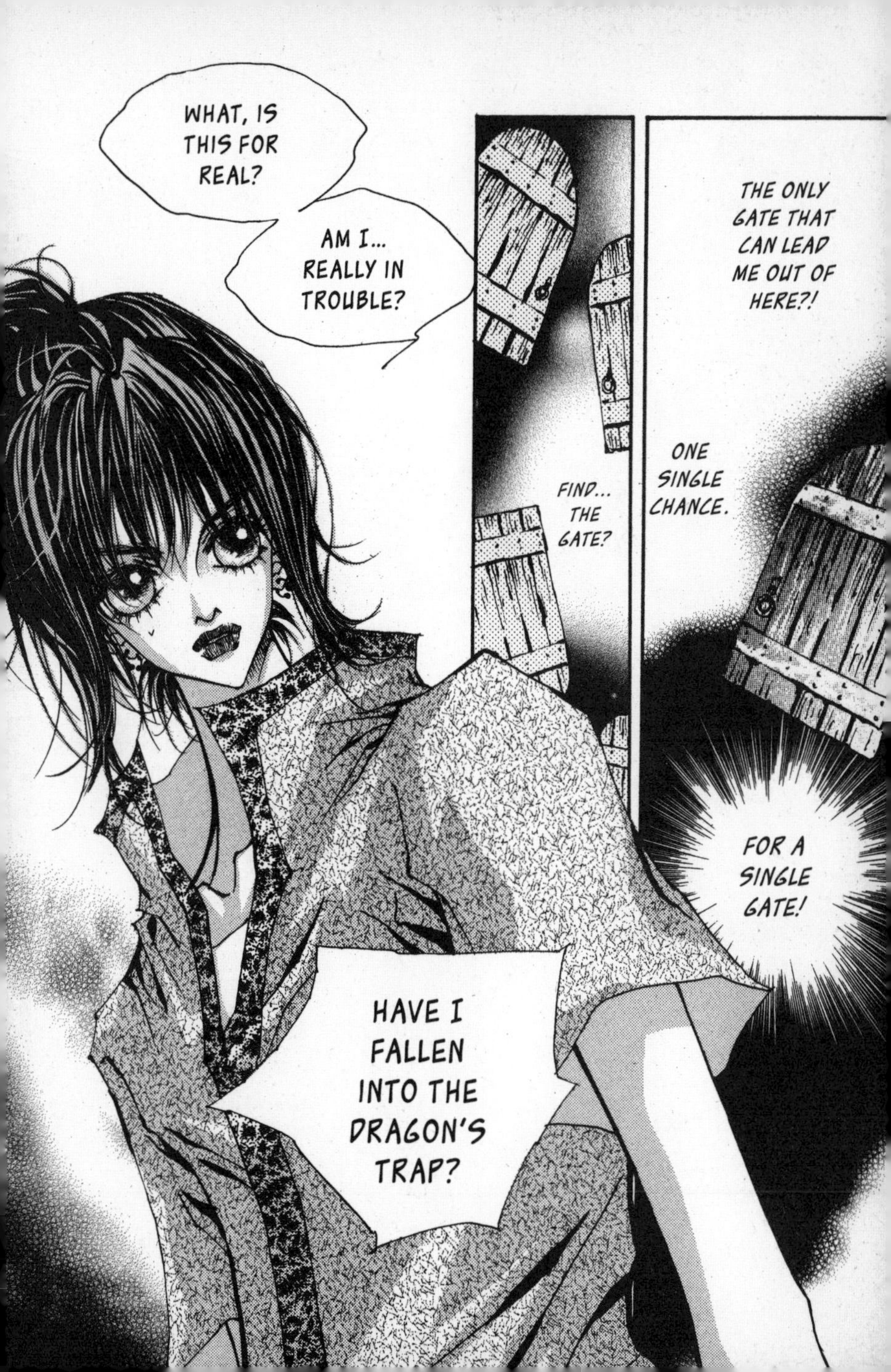
THE ONLY GATE THAT CAN LEAD ME OUT OF HERE?!
ONE SINGLE CHANCE.
FOR A SINGLE GATE!
FIND... THE GATE?
WHAT, IS THIS FOR REAL?
AM I... REALLY IN TROUBLE?
HAVE I FALLEN INTO THE DRAGON'S TRAP?

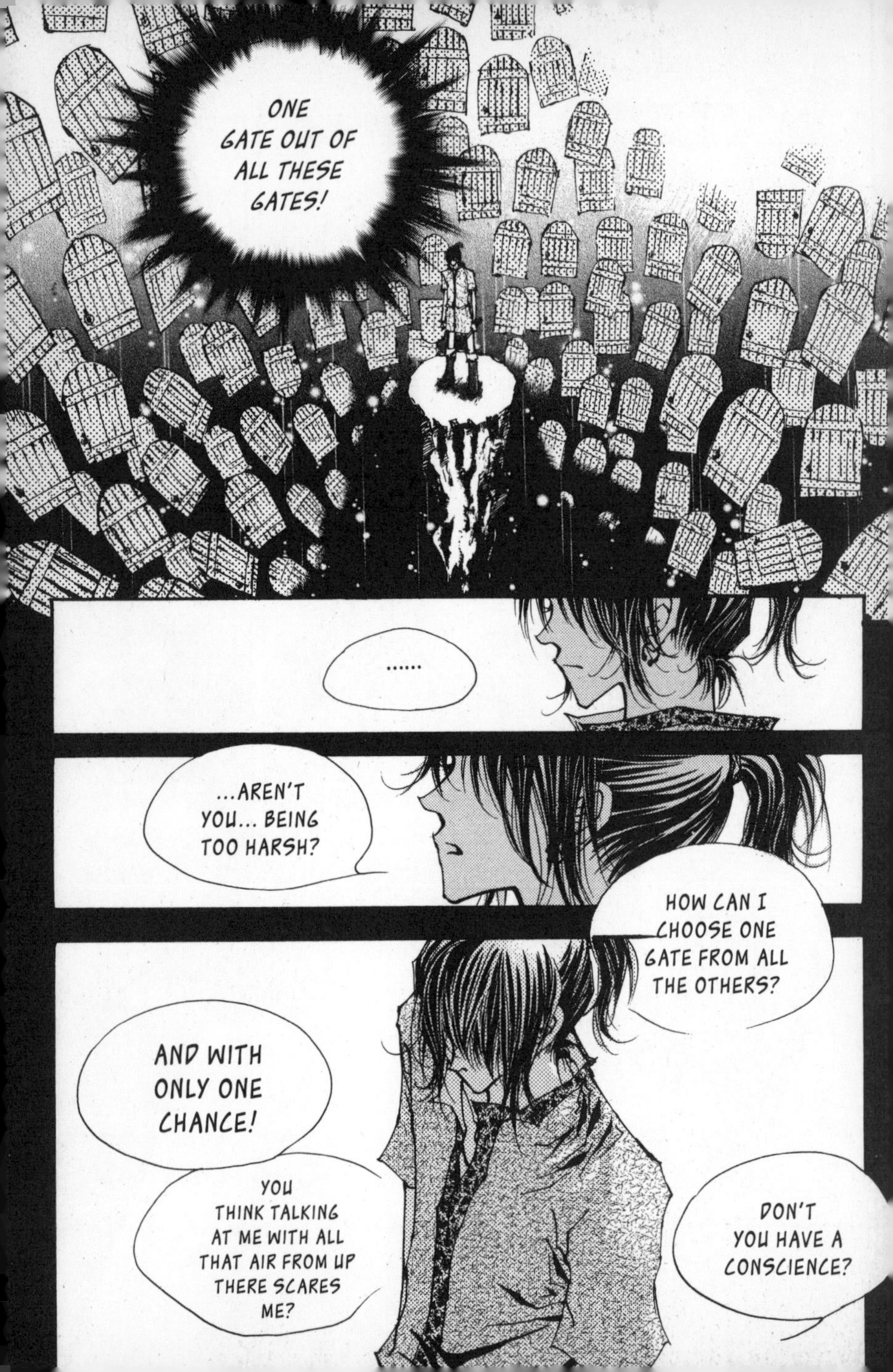
ONE GATE OUT OF ALL THESE GATES!
......
...AREN'T YOU... BEING TOO HARSH?
HOW CAN I CHOOSE ONE GATE FROM ALL THE OTHERS?
AND WITH ONLY ONE CHANCE!
DON'T YOU HAVE A CONSCIENCE?
YOU THINK TALKING AT ME WITH ALL THAT AIR FROM UP THERE SCARES ME?

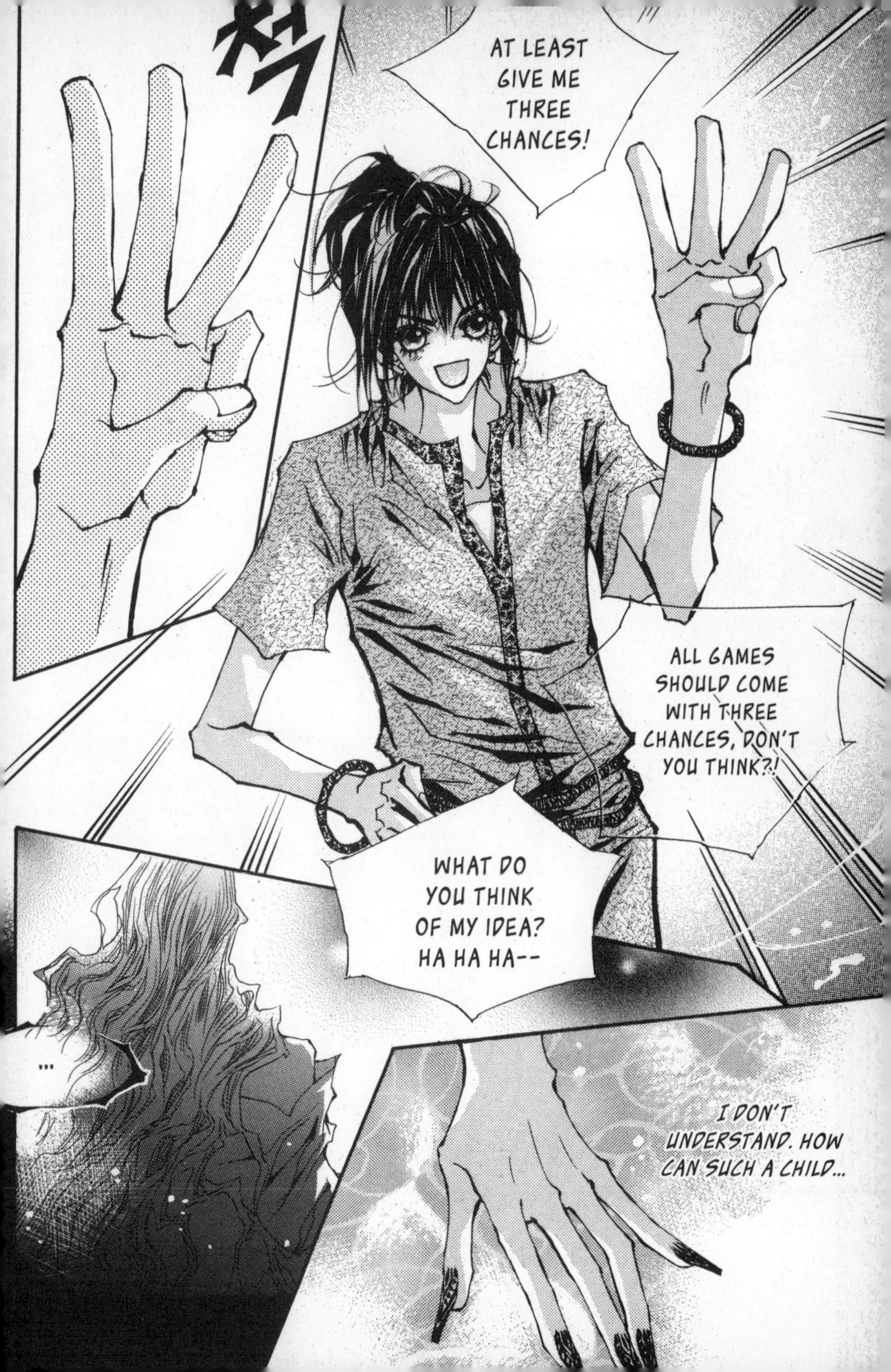
AT LEAST GIVE ME THREE CHANCES!
ALL GAMES SHOULD COME WITH THREE CHANCES, DON'T YOU THINK?!
WHAT DO YOU THINK OF MY IDEA? HA HA HA--
I DON'T UNDERSTAND. HOW CAN SUCH A CHILD...
...

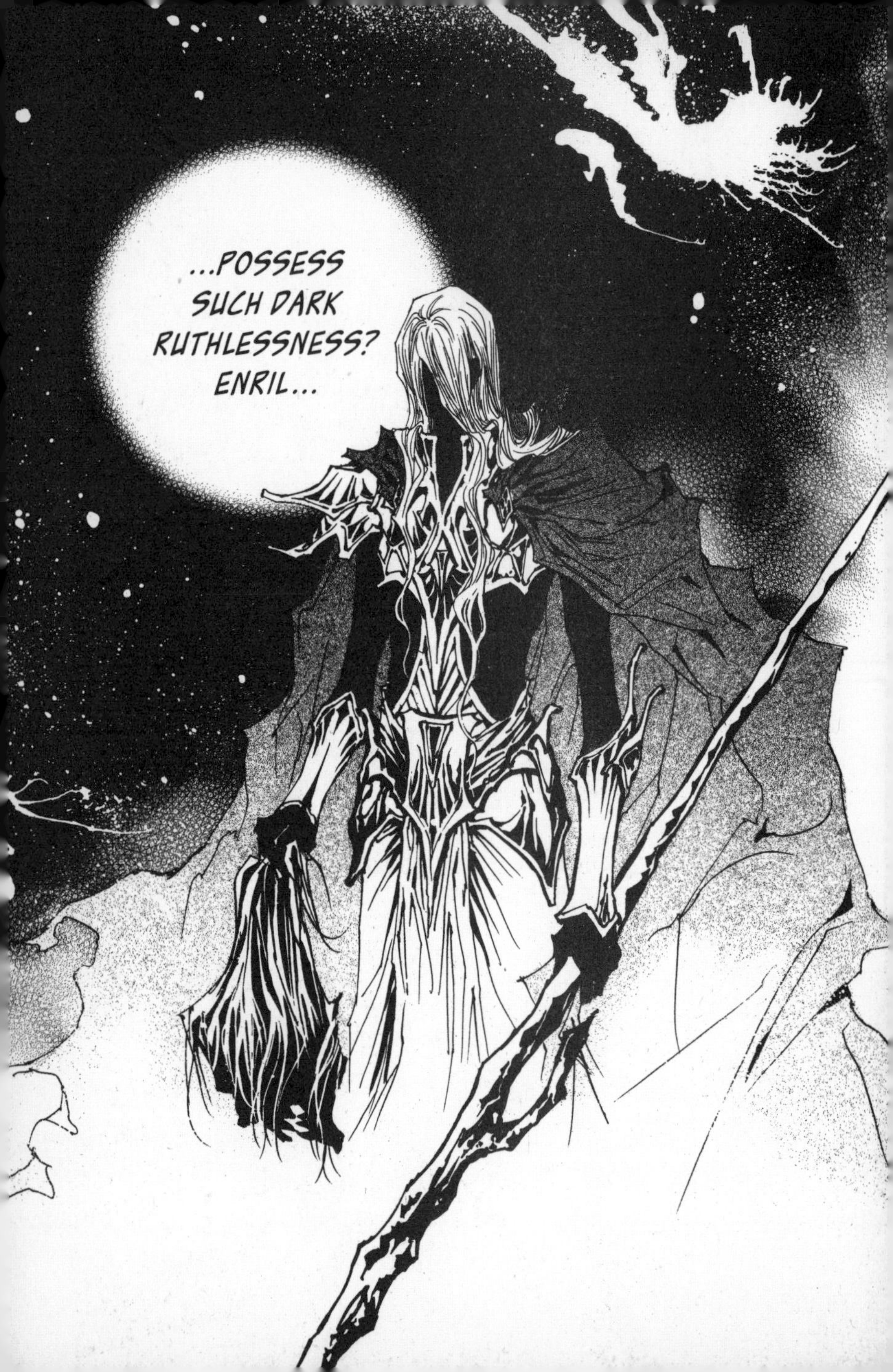
...POSSESS SUCH DARK RUTHLESSNESS? ENRIL...

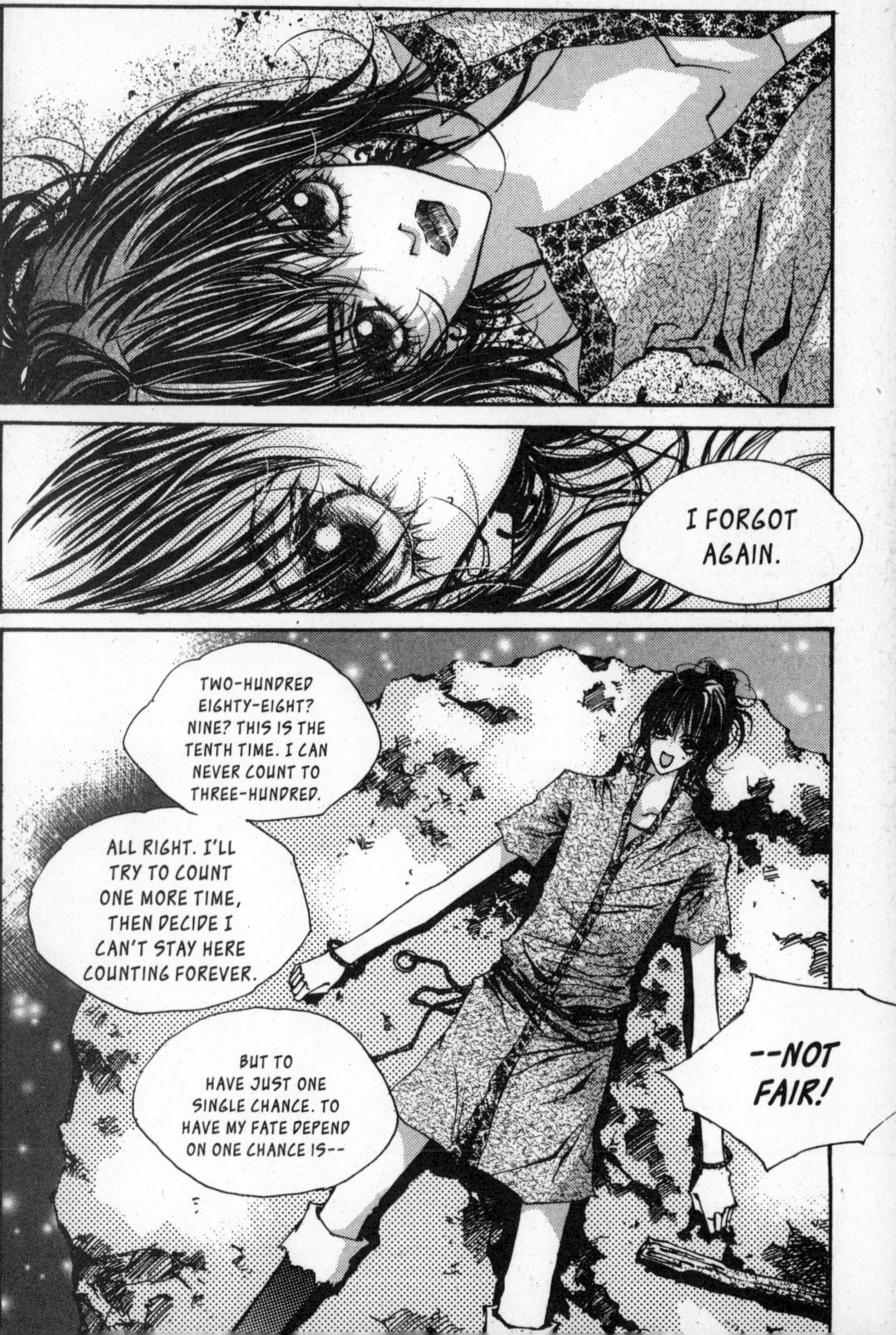
I FORGOT AGAIN.
TWO-HUNDRED EIGHTY-EIGHT? NINE? THIS IS THE TENTH TIME. I CAN NEVER COUNT TO THREE-HUNDRED.
ALL RIGHT. I'LL TRY TO COUNT ONE MORE TIME, THEN DECIDE I CAN'T STAY HERE COUNTING FOREVER.
BUT TO HAVE JUST ONE SINGLE CHANCE. TO HAVE MY FATE DEPEND ON ONE CHANCE IS--
--NOT FAIR!

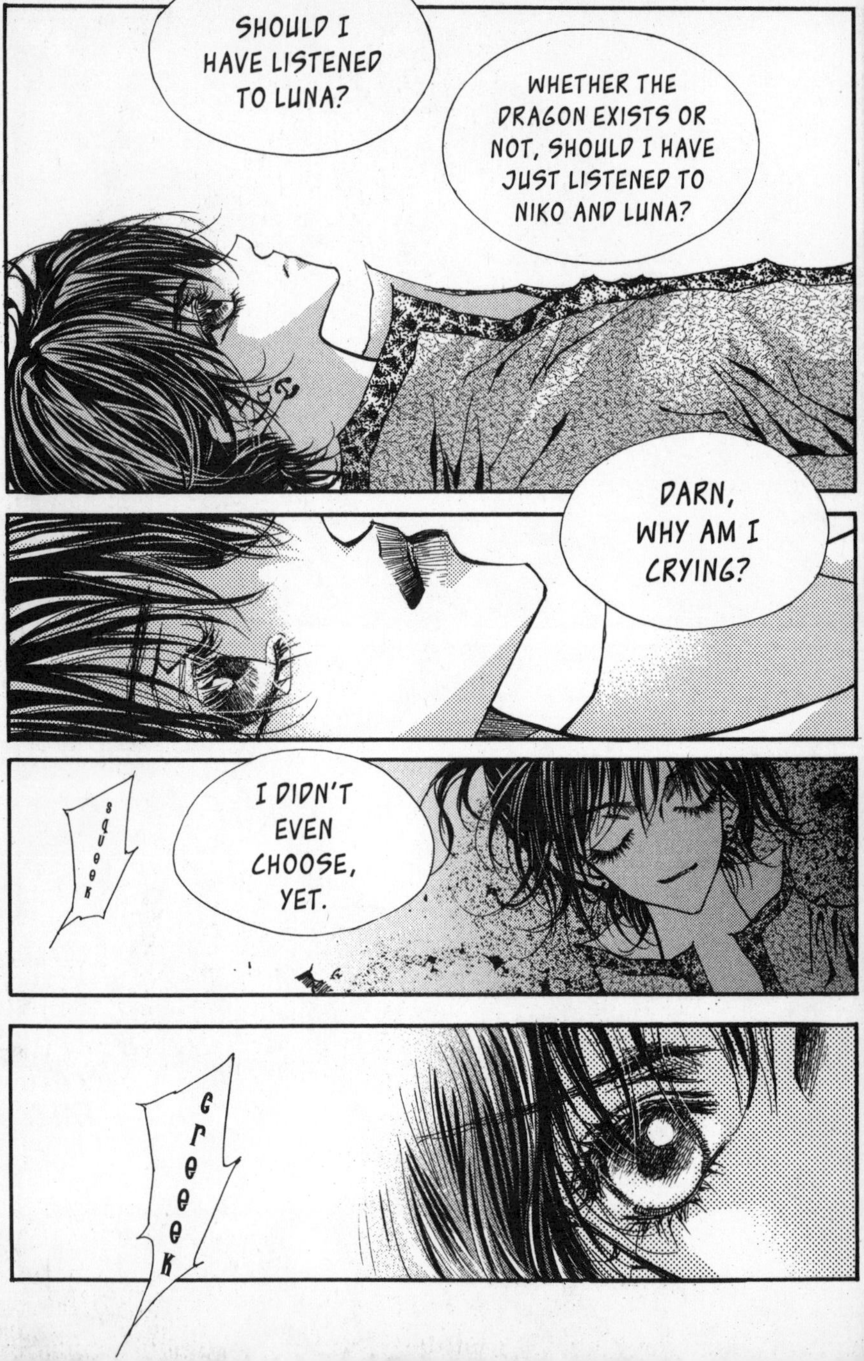
SHOULD I HAVE LISTENED TO LUNA?
WHETHER THE DRAGON EXISTS OR NOT, SHOULD I HAVE JUST LISTENED TO NIKO AND LUNA?
DARN, WHY AM I CRYING?
I DIDN'T EVEN CHOOSE, YET.
squeek
greeek

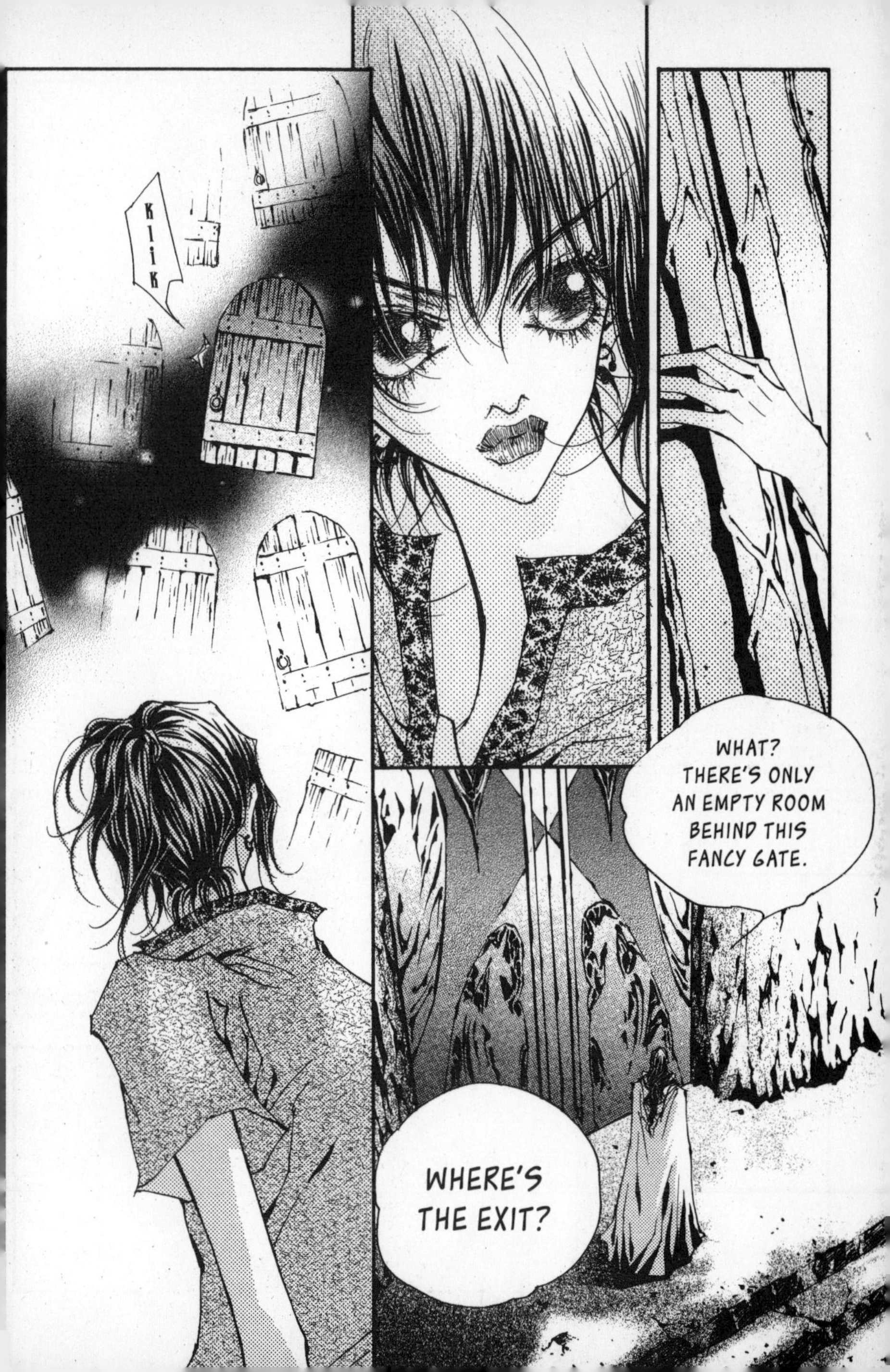
WHAT? THERE'S ONLY AN EMPTY ROOM BEHIND THIS FANCY GATE.
WHERE'S THE EXIT?
KLIK

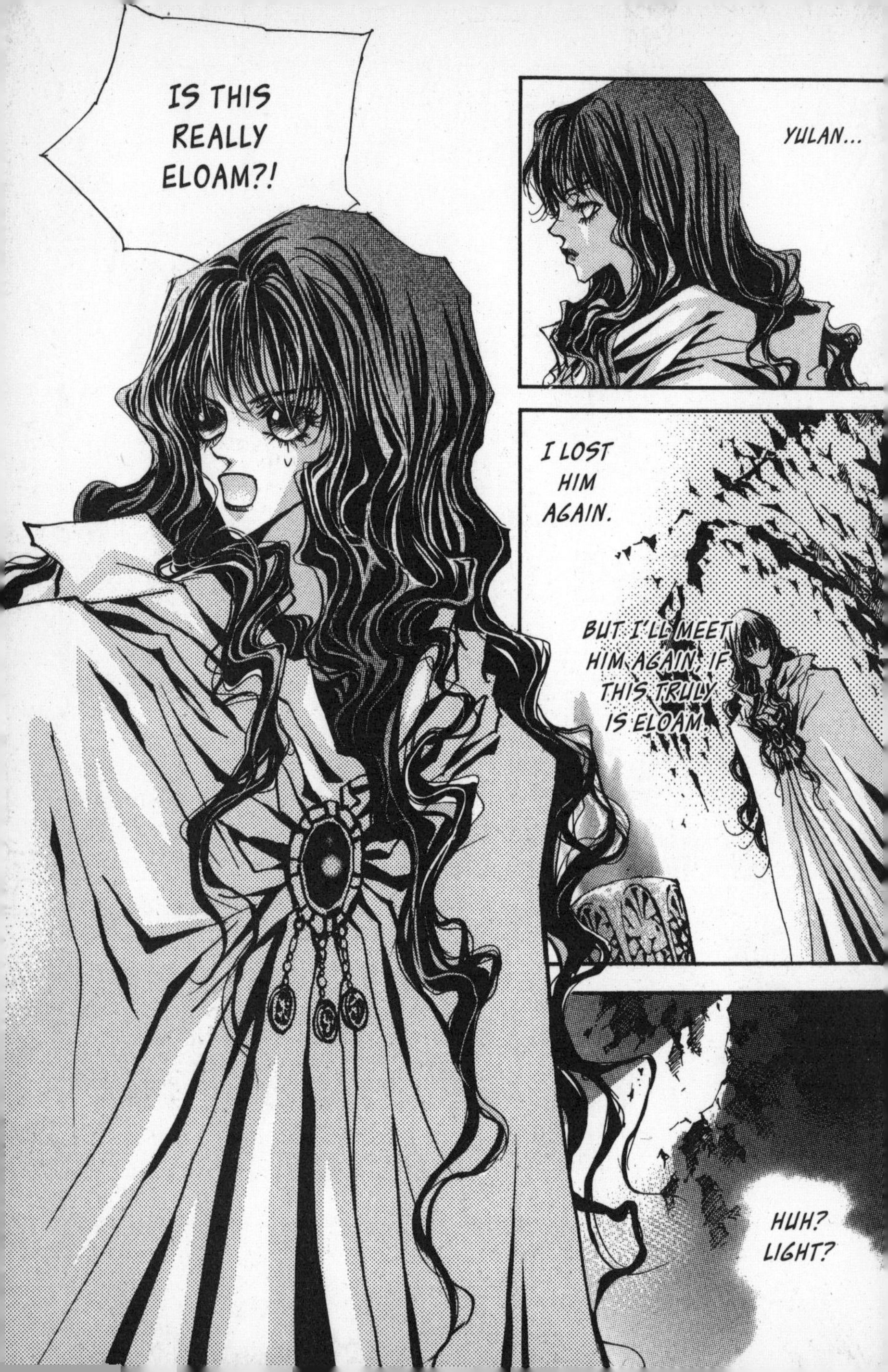
YULAN...
I LOST HIM AGAIN.
BUT I'LL MEET HIM AGAIN, IF THIS TRULY IS ELOAM.
HUH? LIGHT?
IS THIS REALLY ELOAM?!

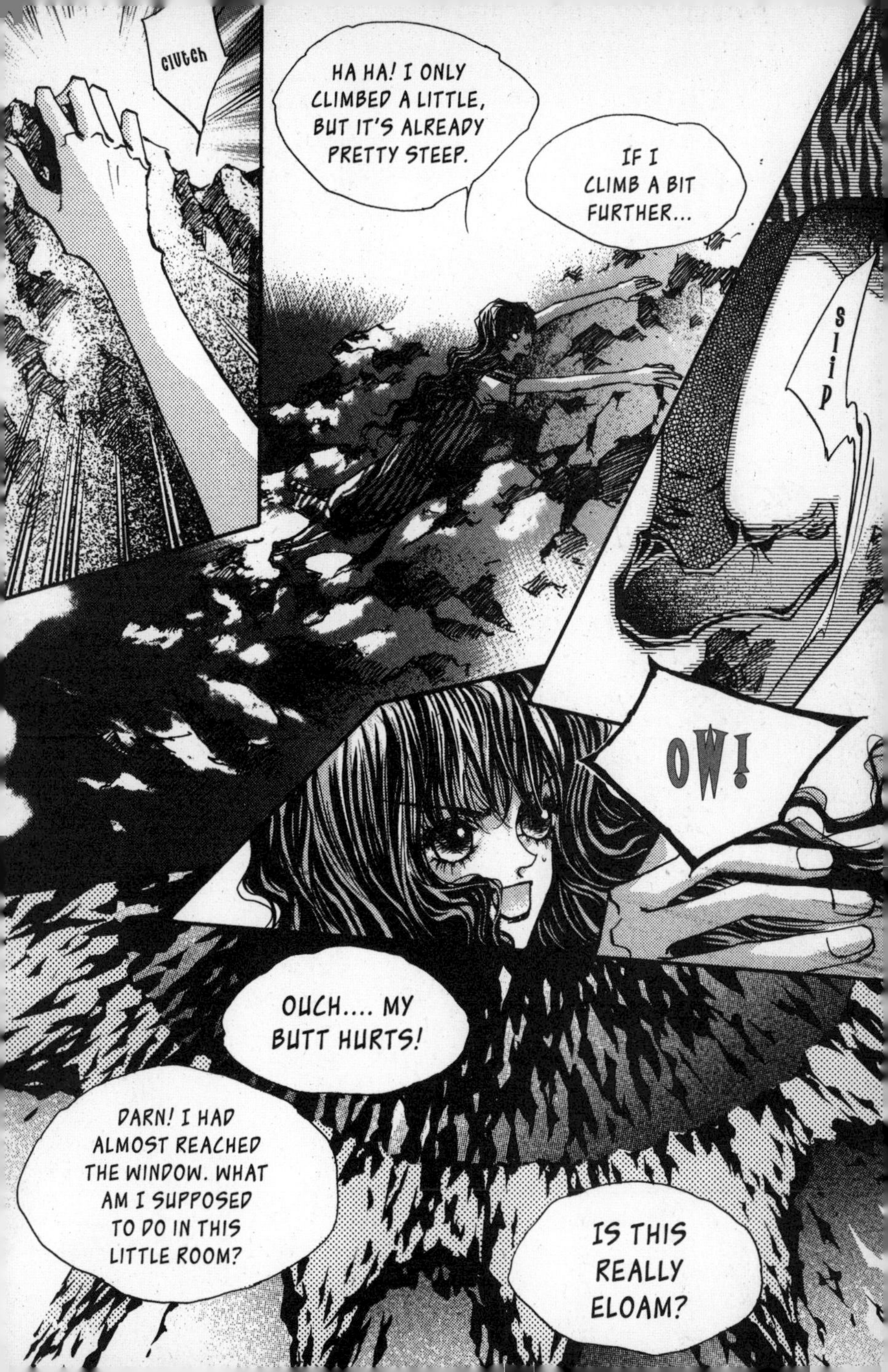
Clutch
HA HA! I ONLY CLIMBED A LITTLE, BUT IT'S ALREADY PRETTY STEEP.
IF I CLIMB A BIT FURTHER...
SLIP
OW!
OUCH.... MY BUTT HURTS!
DARN! I HAD ALMOST REACHED THE WINDOW. WHAT AM I SUPPOSED TO DO IN THIS LITTLE ROOM?
IS THIS REALLY ELOAM?

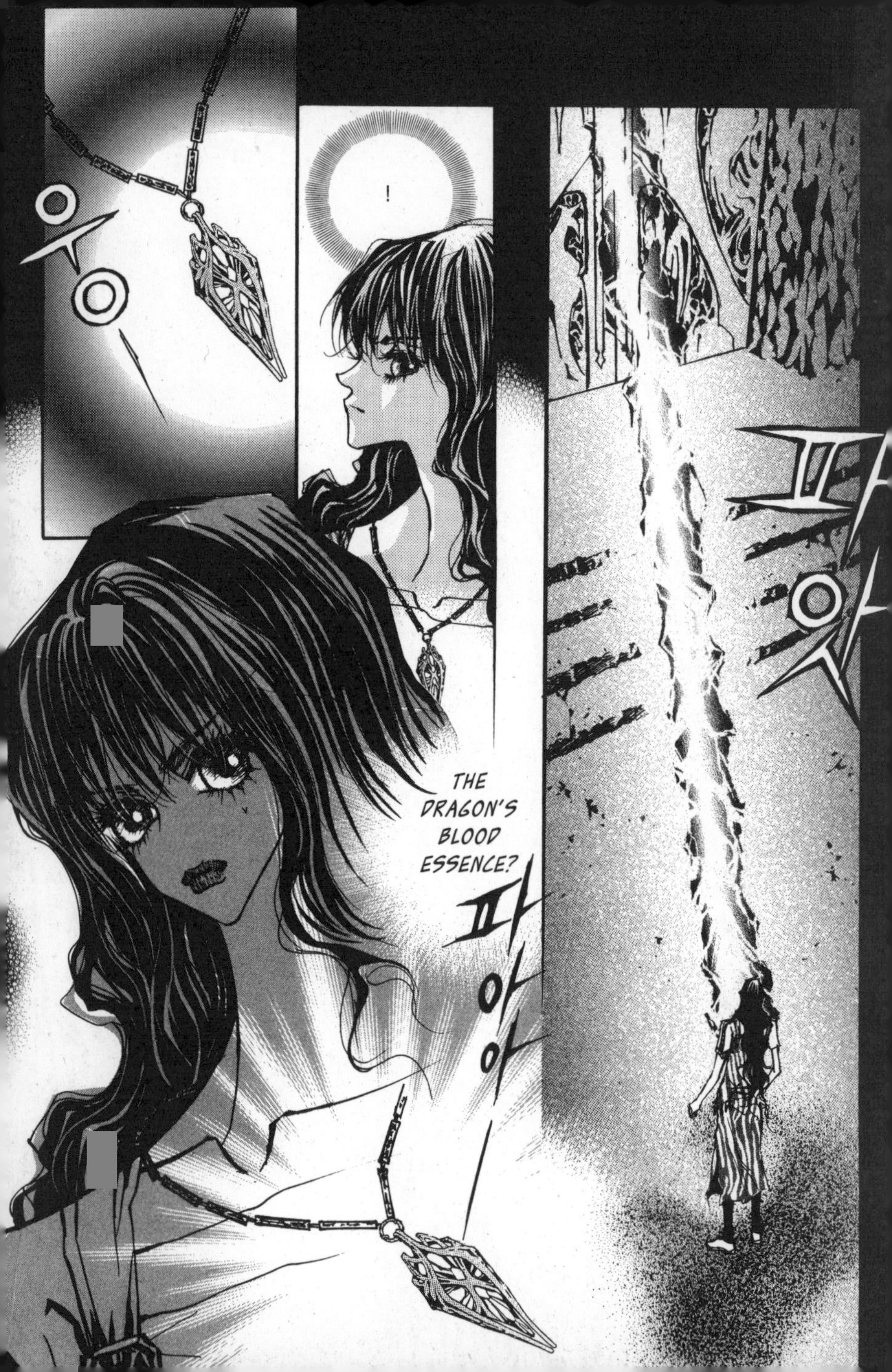
!
THE DRAGON'S BLOOD ESSENCE?

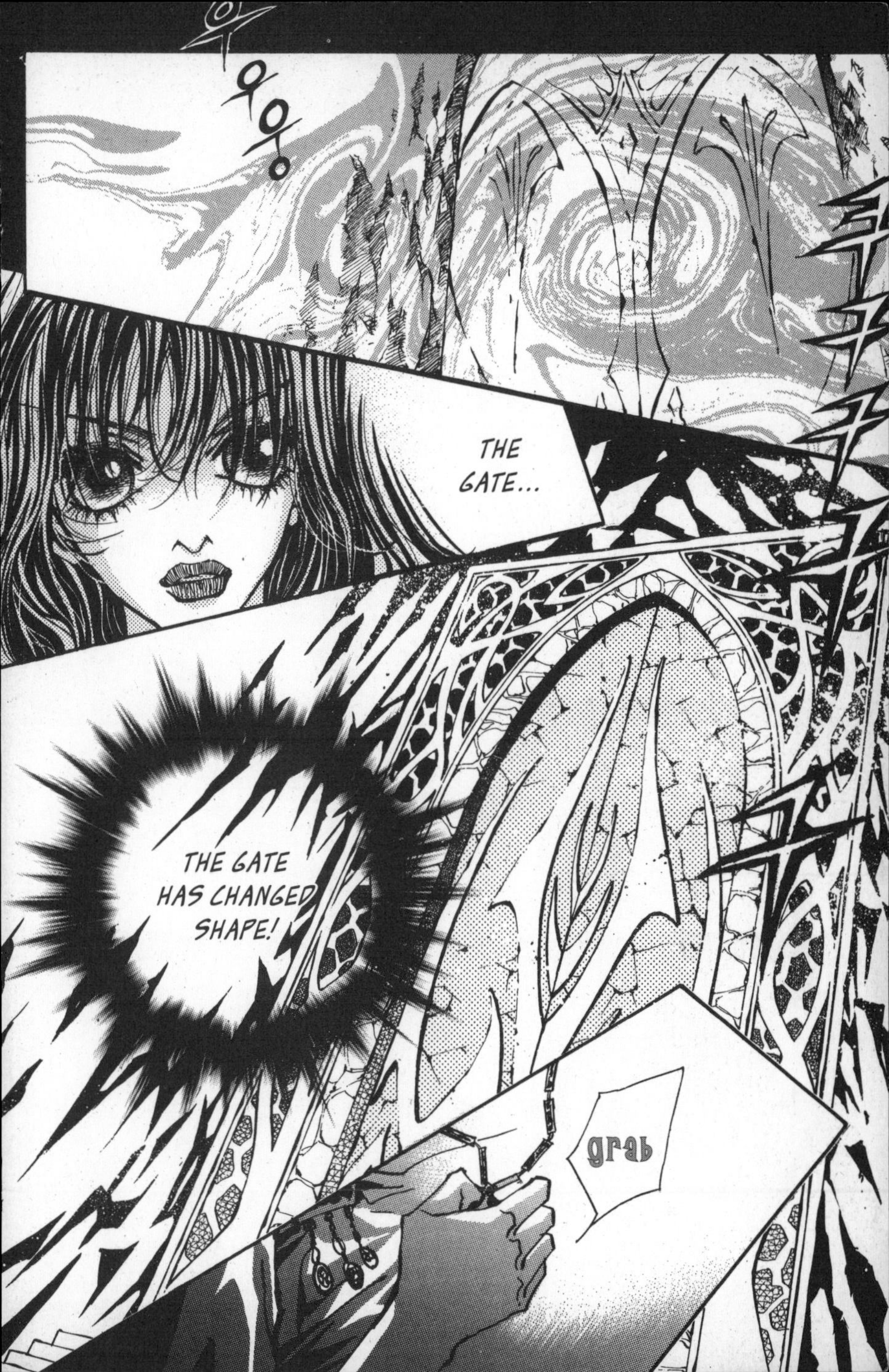
THE GATE...
THE GATE HAS CHANGED SHAPE!
grab

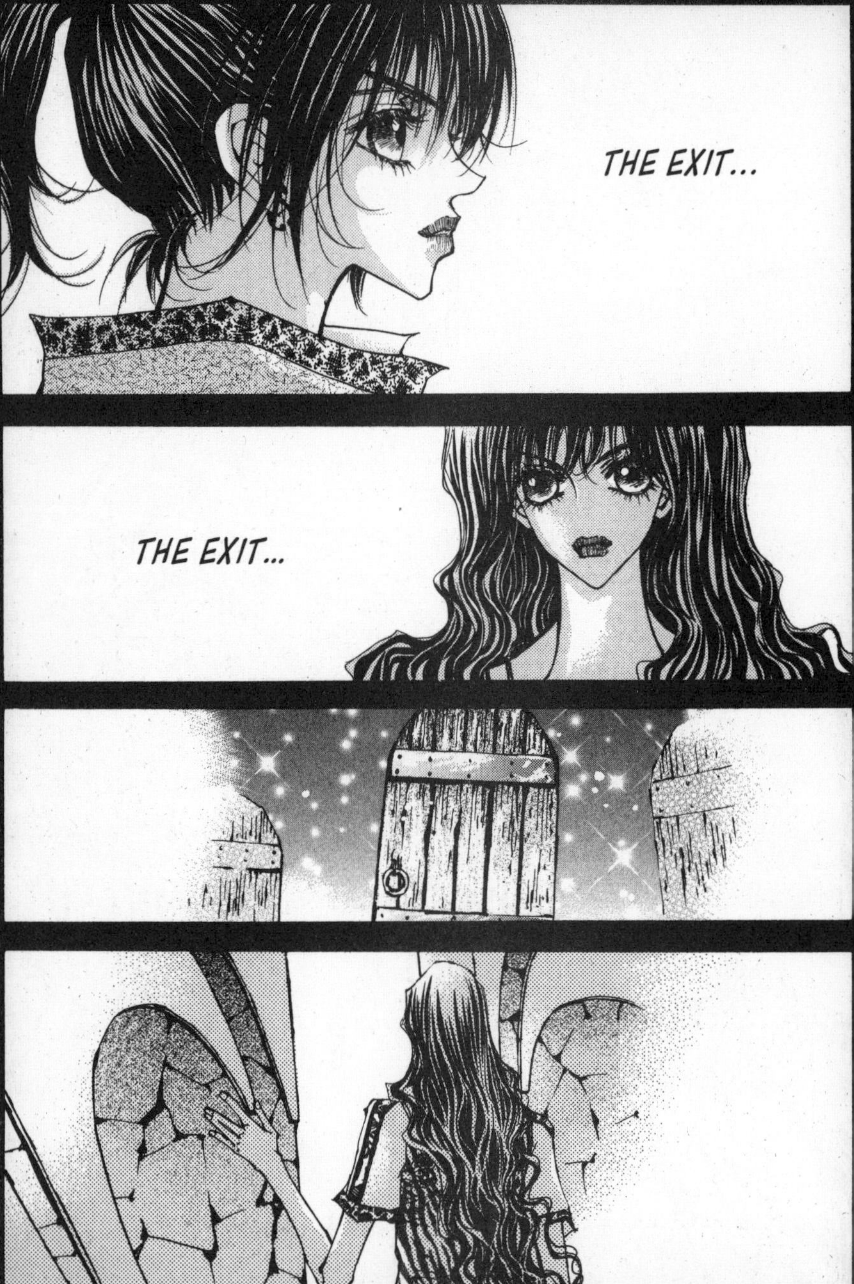
THE EXIT...
THE EXIT...

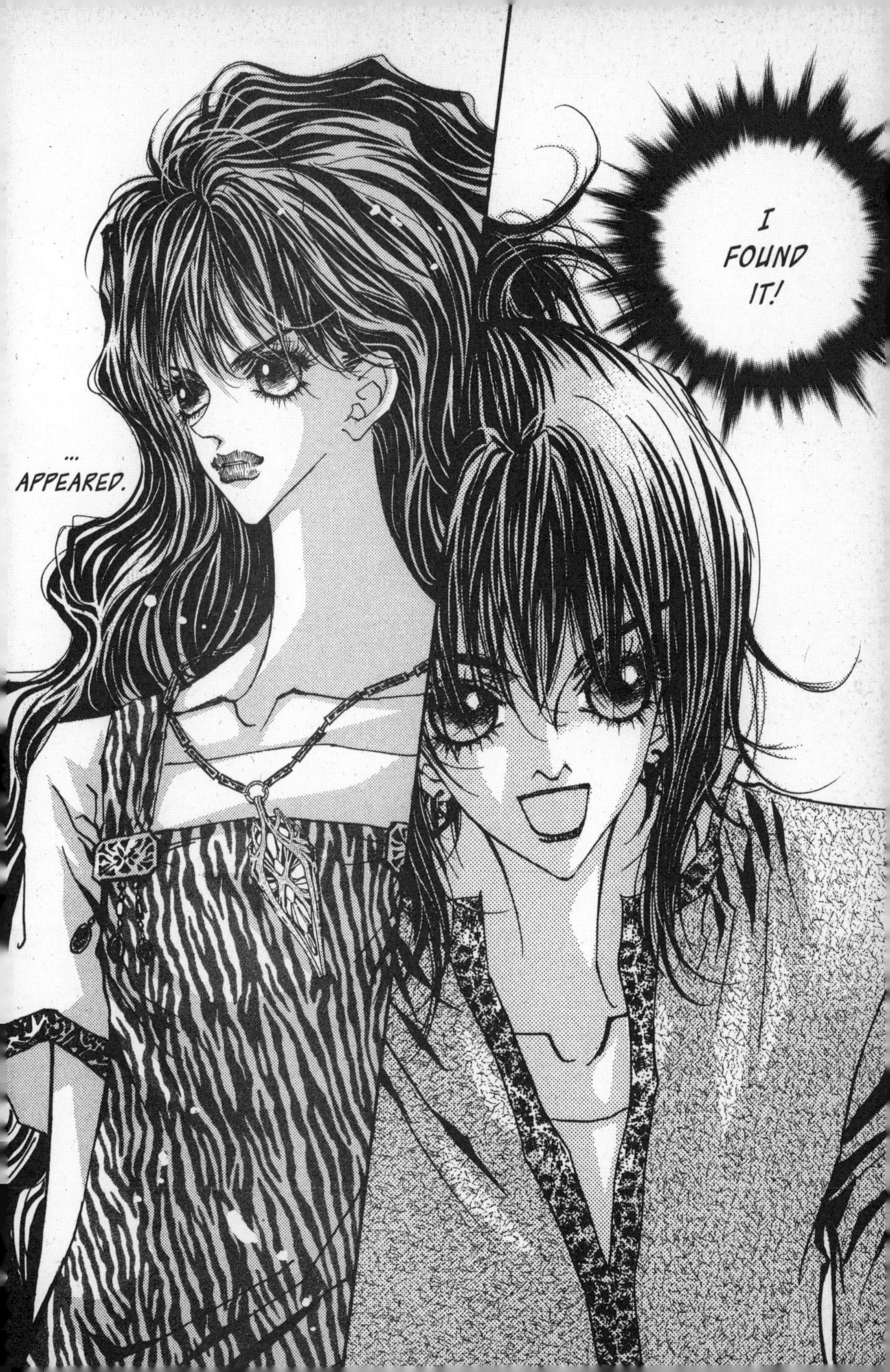
I FOUND IT!
... APPEARED.

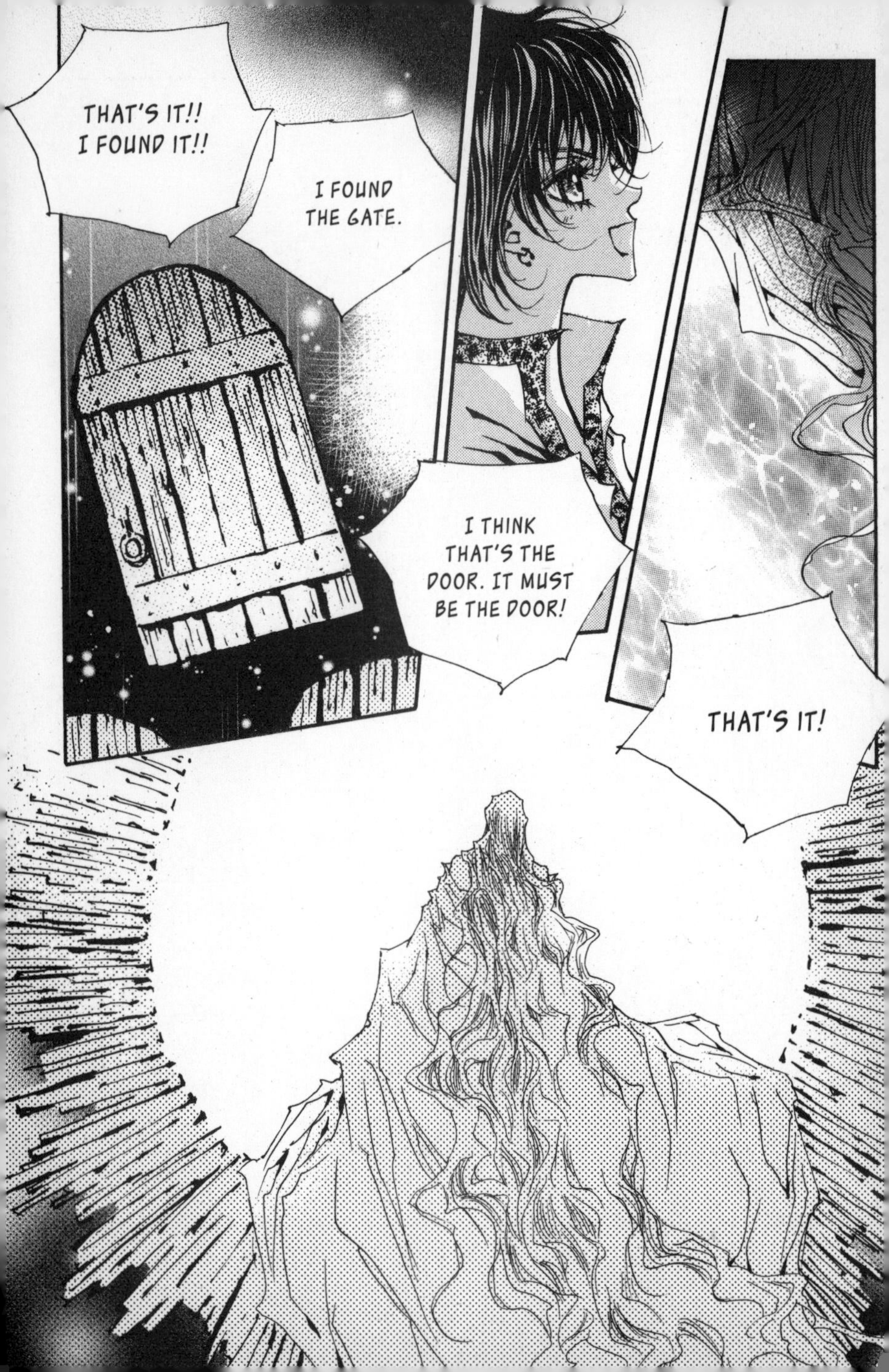
THAT'S IT!! I FOUND IT!!
I FOUND THE GATE.
I THINK THAT'S THE DOOR. IT MUST BE THE DOOR!
THAT'S IT!

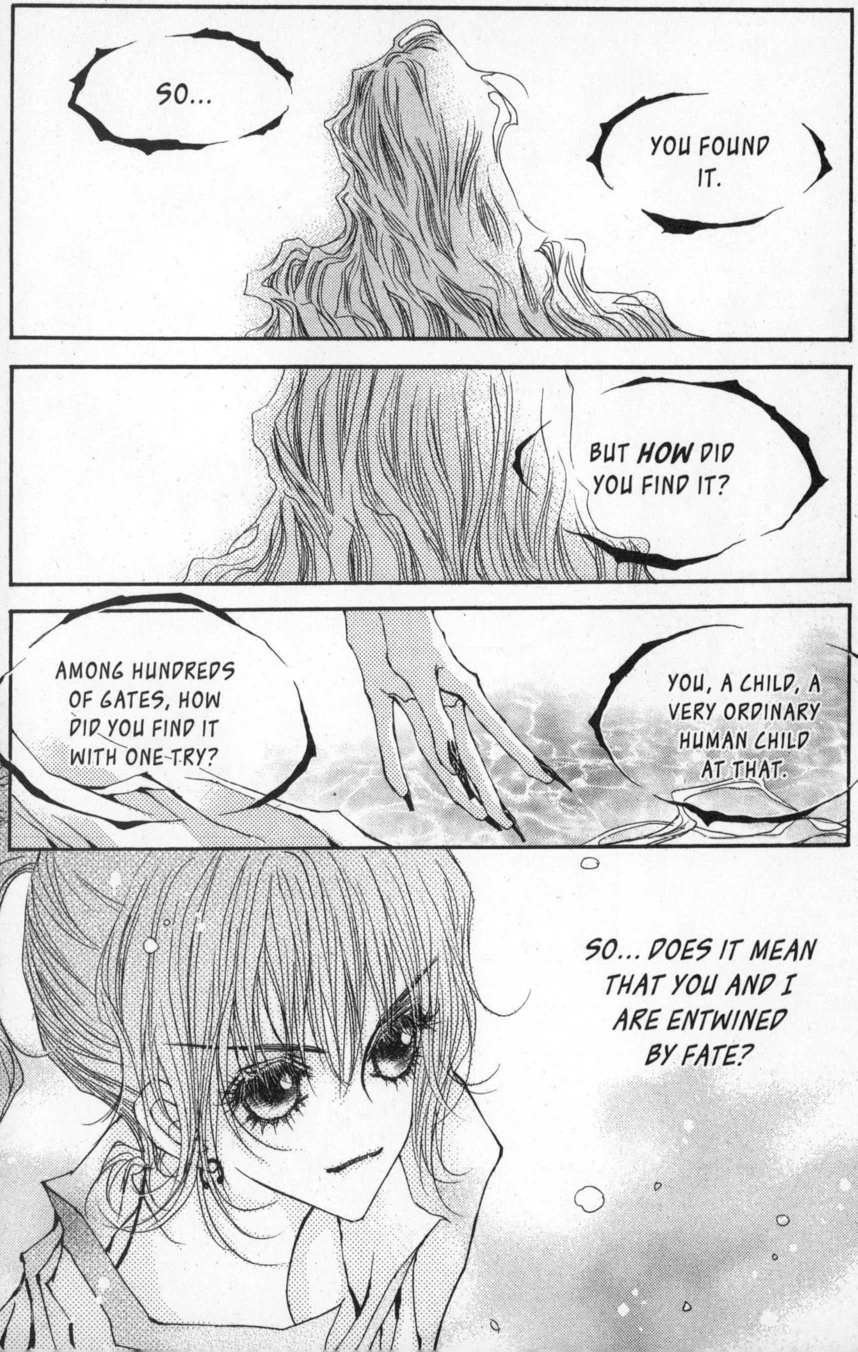
SO...
YOU FOUND IT.
BUT HOW DID YOU FIND IT?
AMONG HUNDREDS OF GATES, HOW DID YOU FIND IT WITH ONE TRY?
YOU, A CHILD, A VERY ORDINARY HUMAN CHILD AT THAT.
SO... DOES IT MEAN THAT YOU AND I ARE ENTWINED BY FATE?

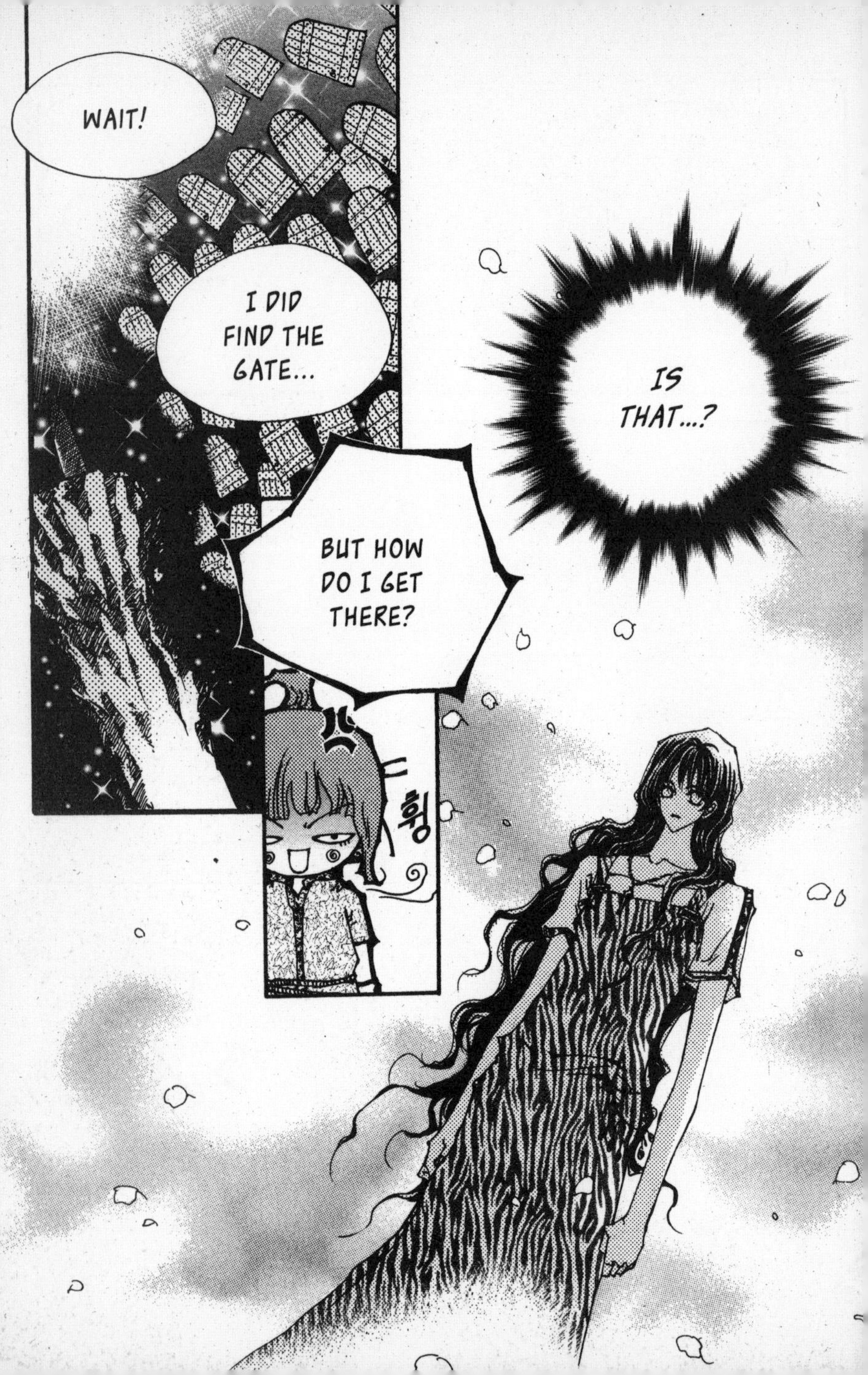
WAIT!
I DID FIND THE GATE...
BUT HOW DO I GET THERE?
휭
IS THAT...?

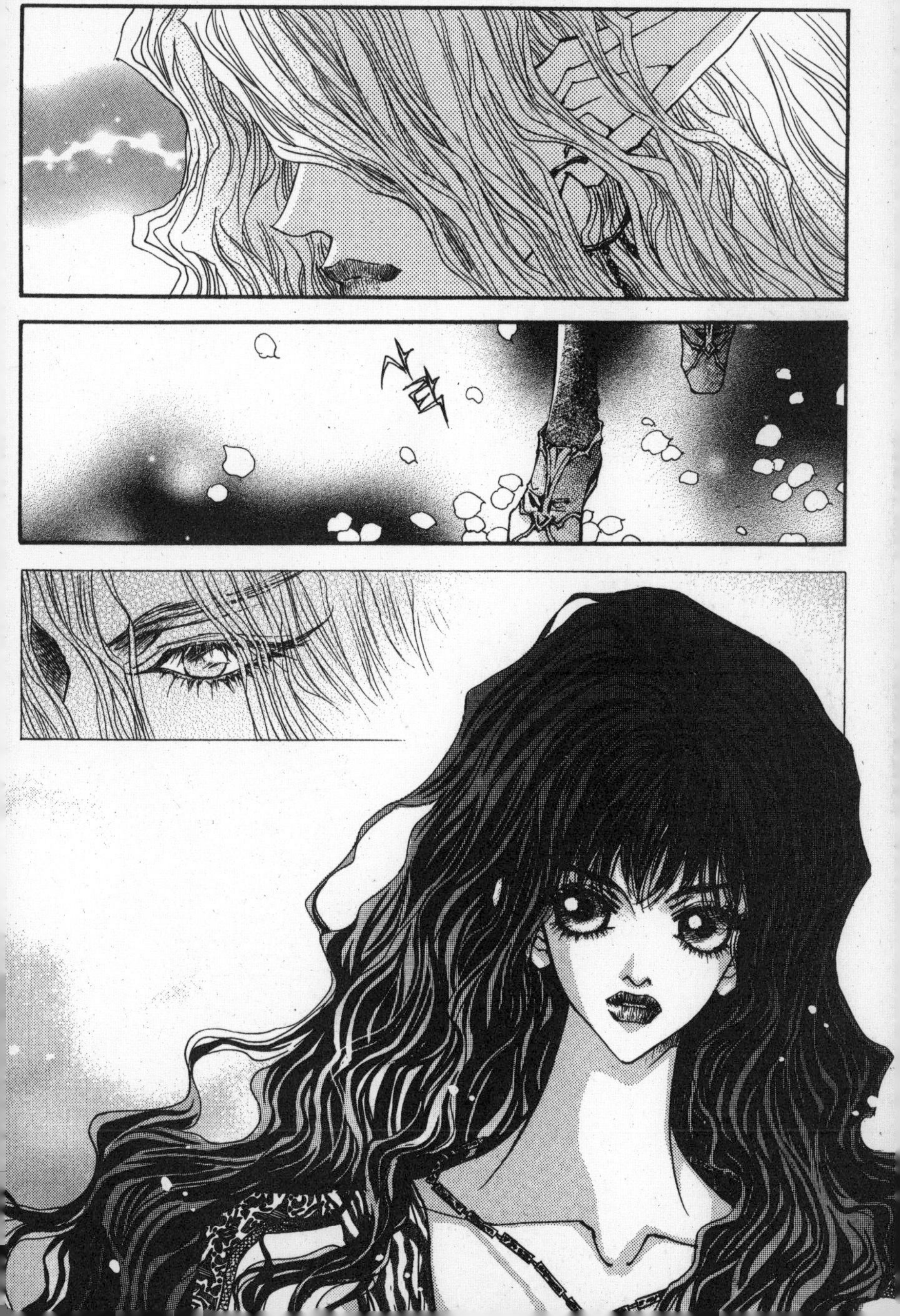

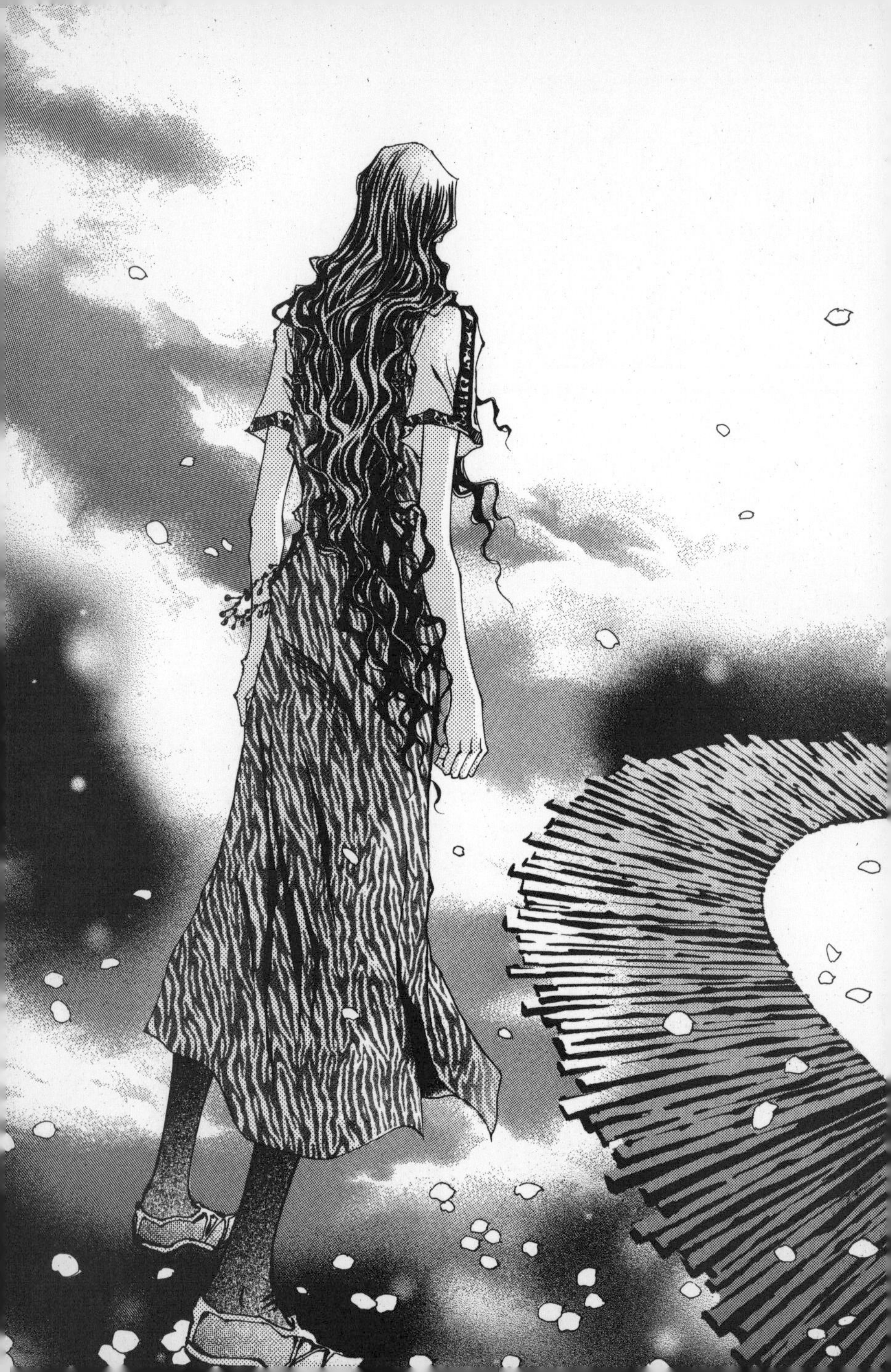

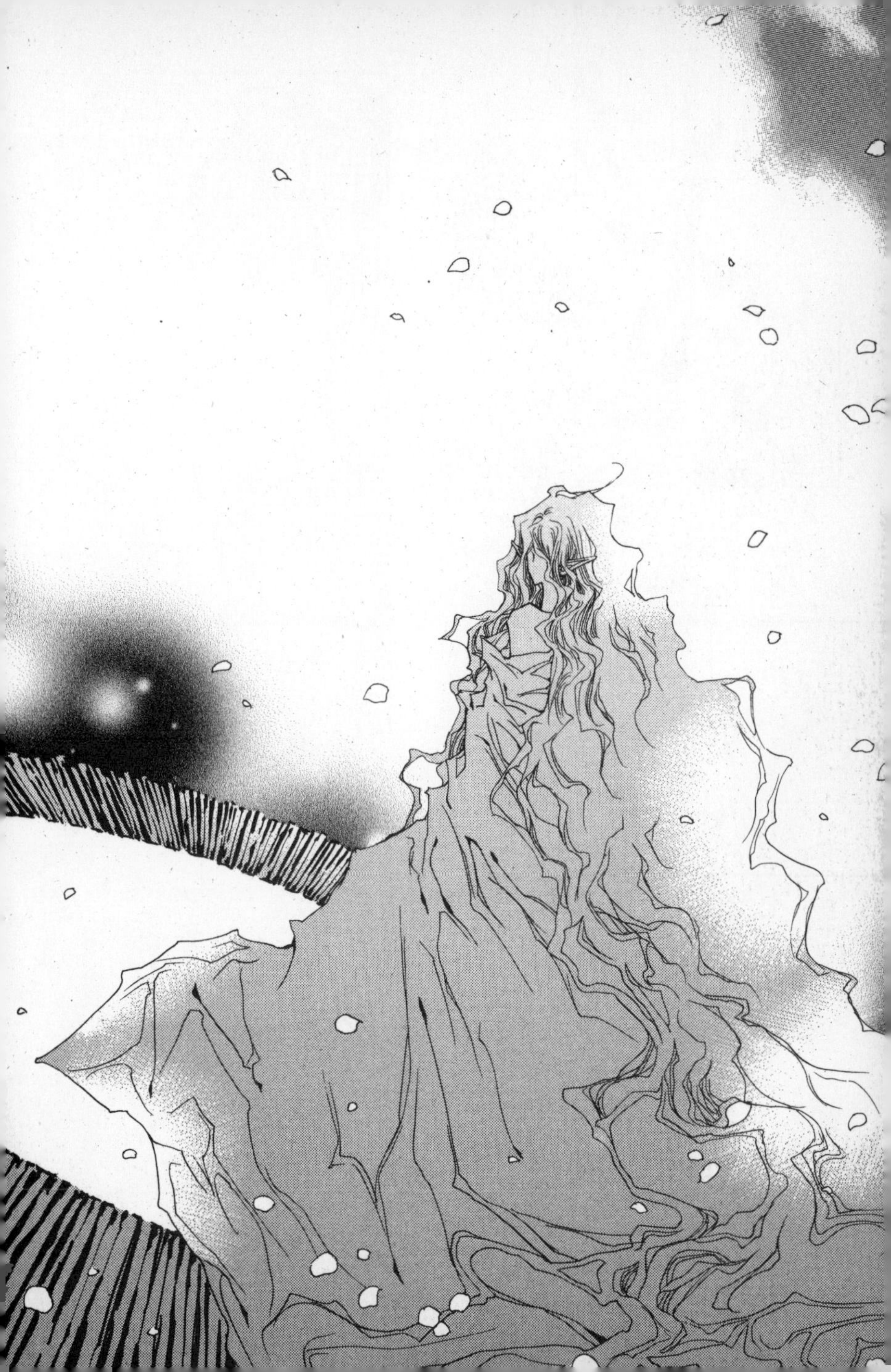

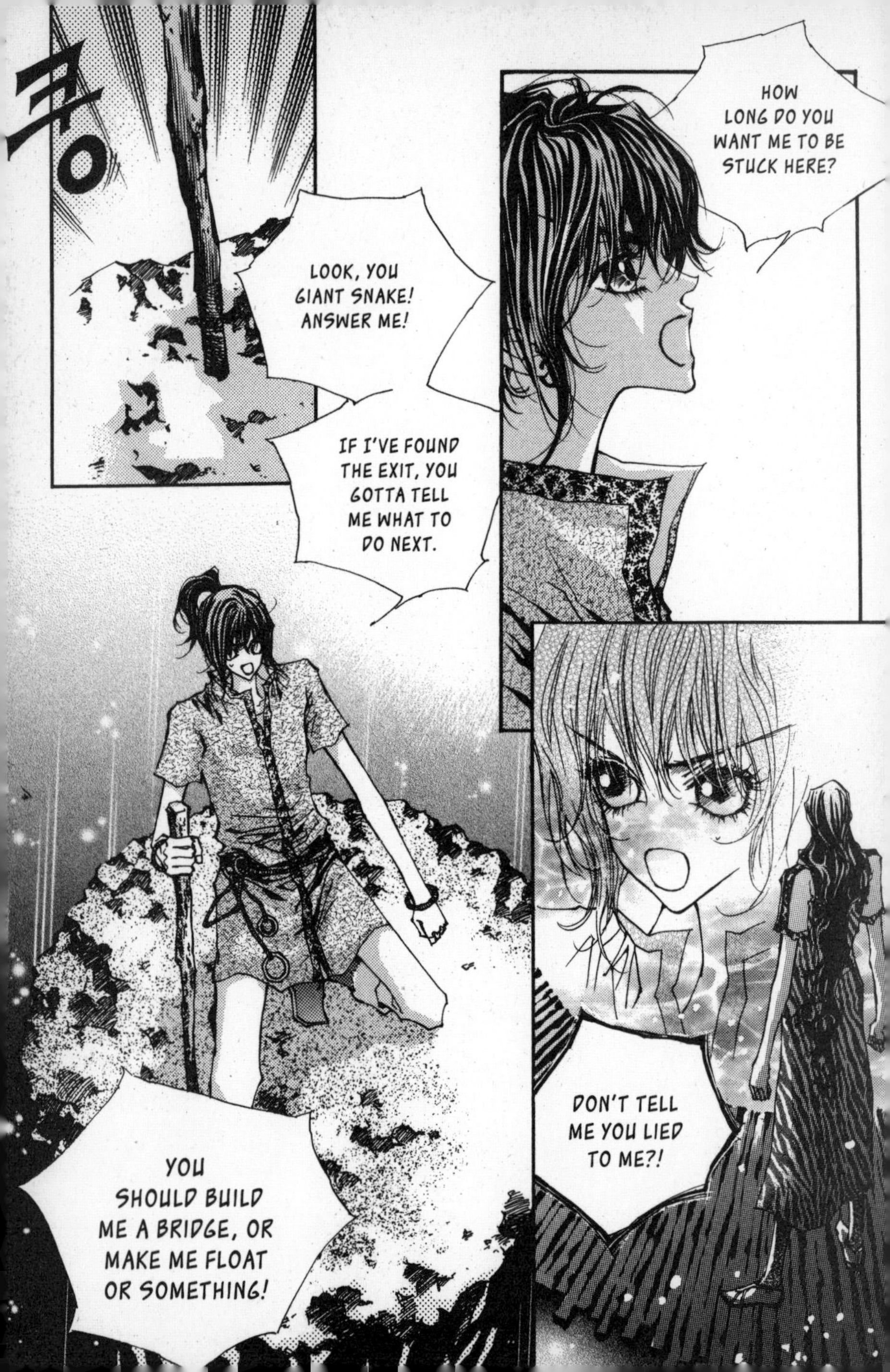

쿵
LOOK, YOU GIANT SNAKE! ANSWER ME!
IF I'VE FOUND THE EXIT, YOU GOTTA TELL ME WHAT TO DO NEXT.
HOW LONG DO YOU WANT ME TO BE STUCK HERE?
YOU SHOULD BUILD ME A BRIDGE, OR MAKE ME FLOAT OR SOMETHING!
DON'T TELL ME YOU LIED TO ME?!

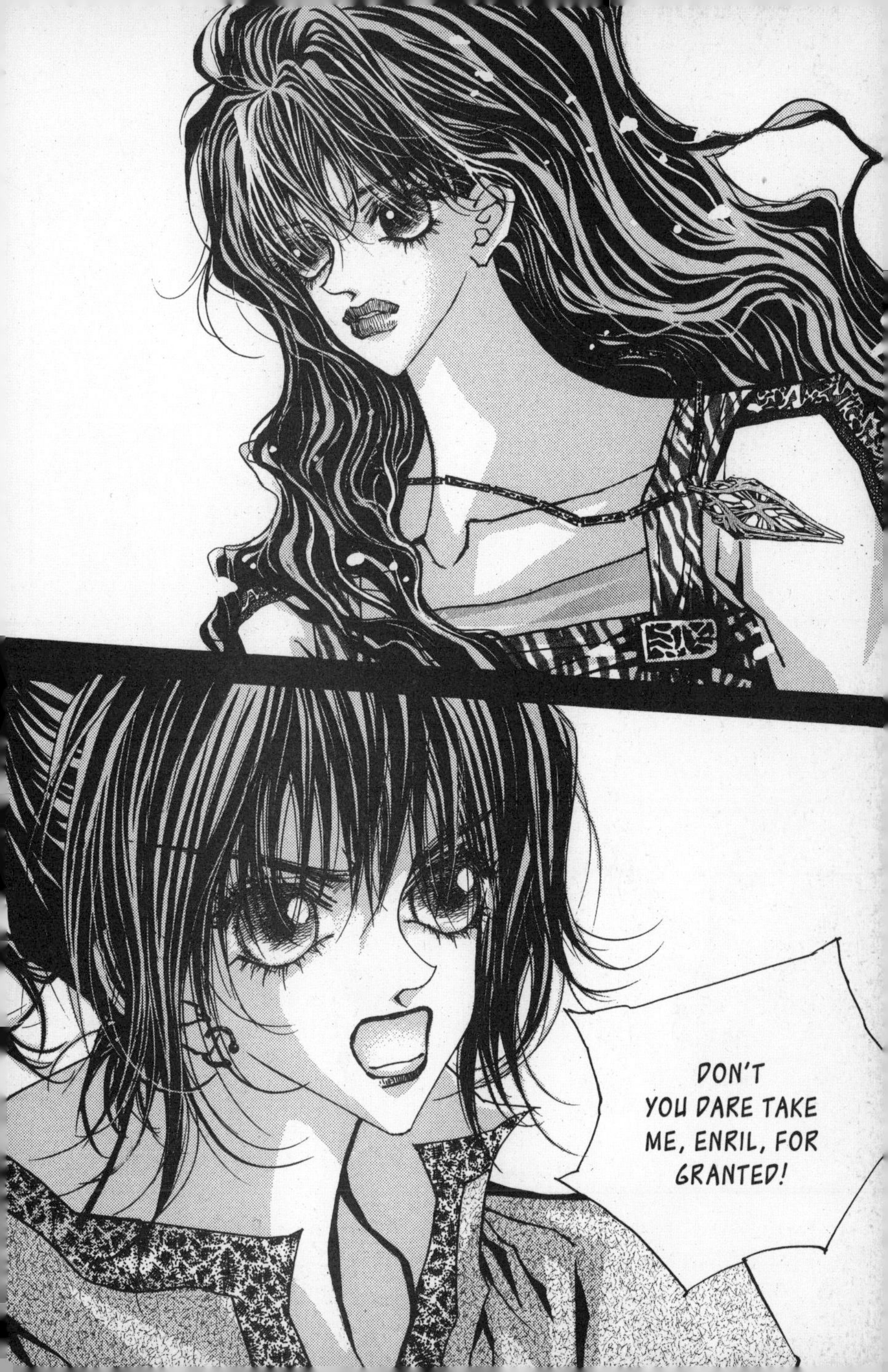
DON'T YOU DARE TAKE ME, ENRIL, FOR GRANTED!

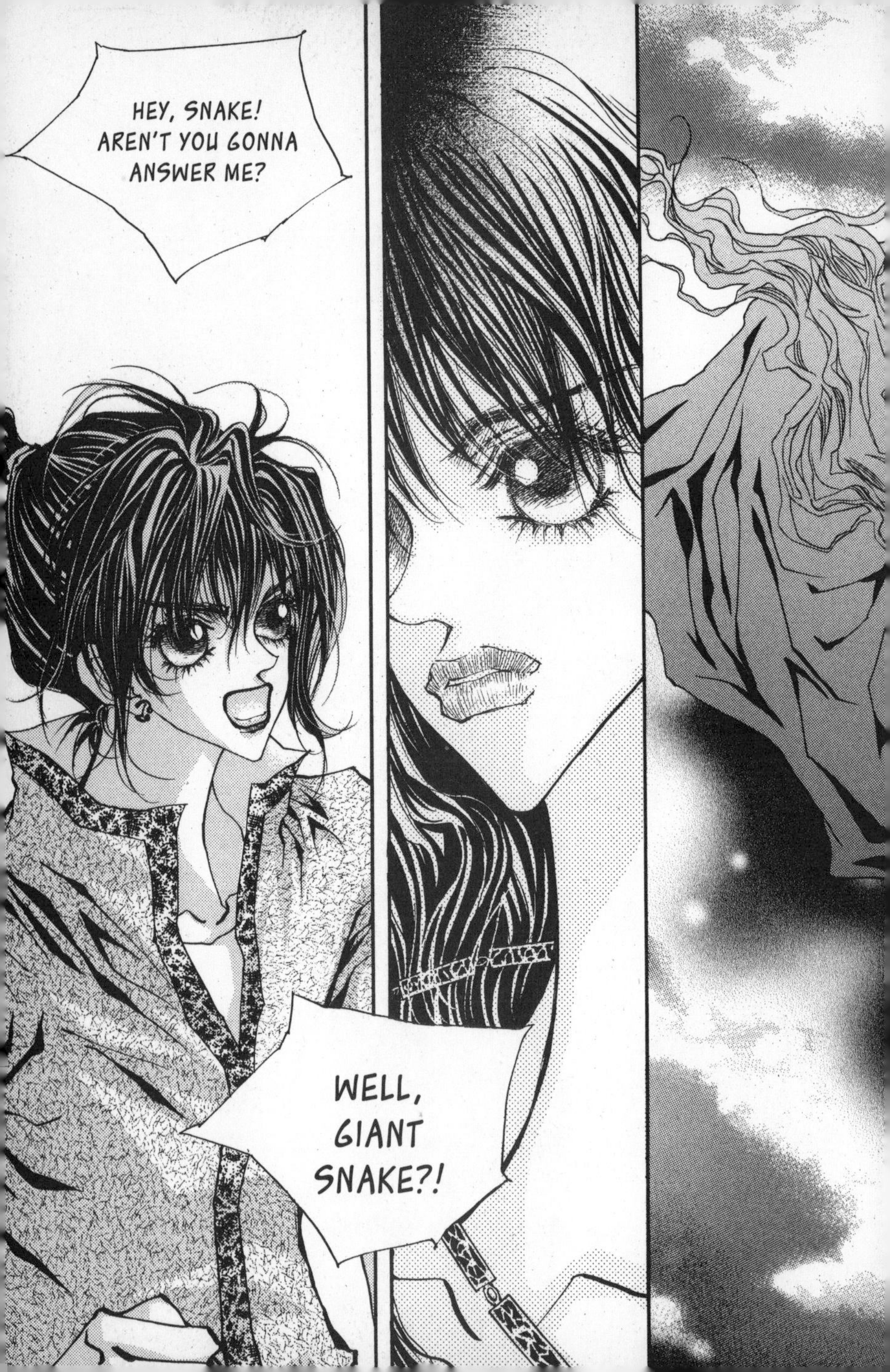
HEY, SNAKE! AREN'T YOU GONNA ANSWER ME?
WELL, GIANT SNAKE?!

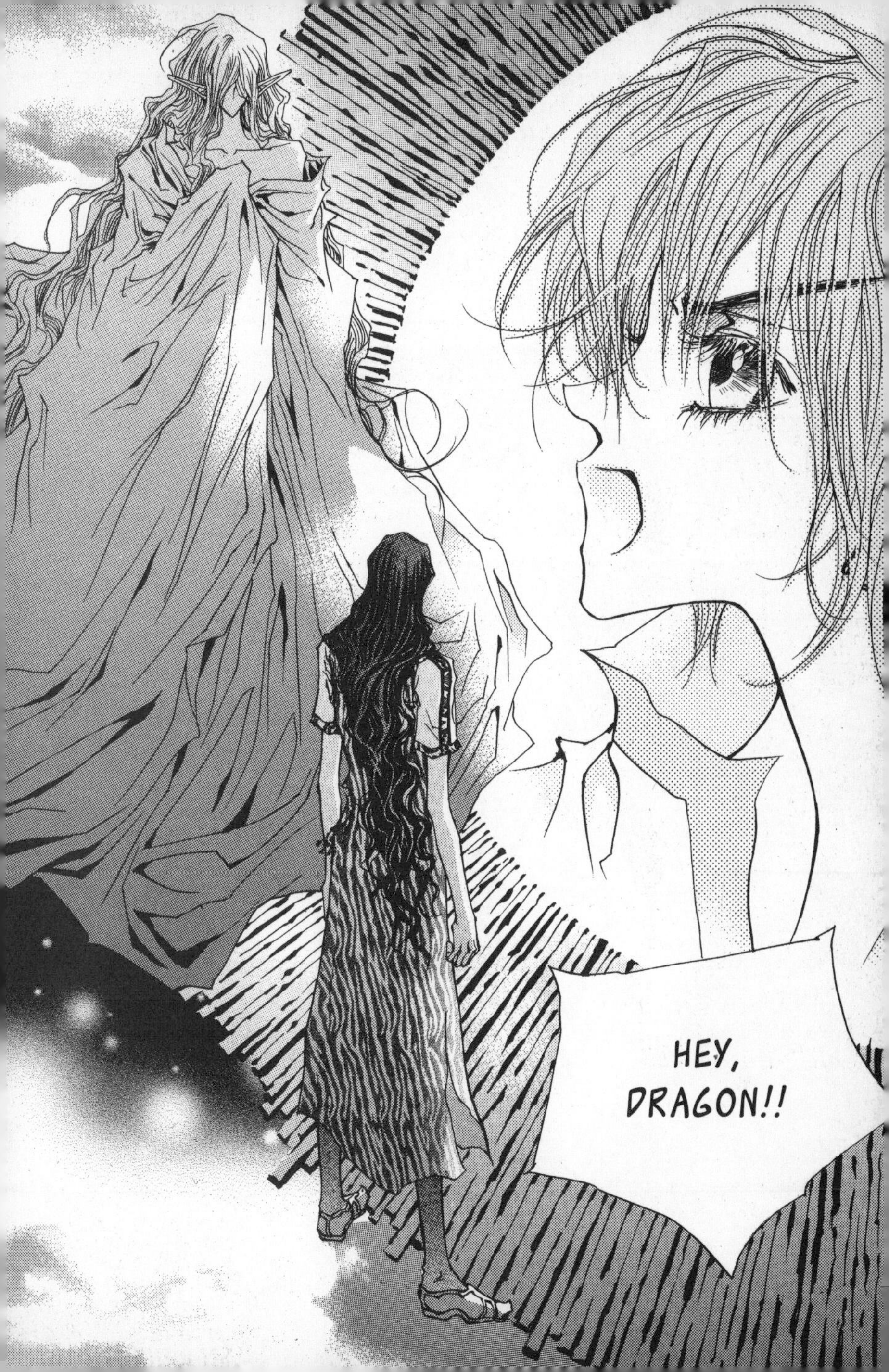
HEY, DRAGON!!

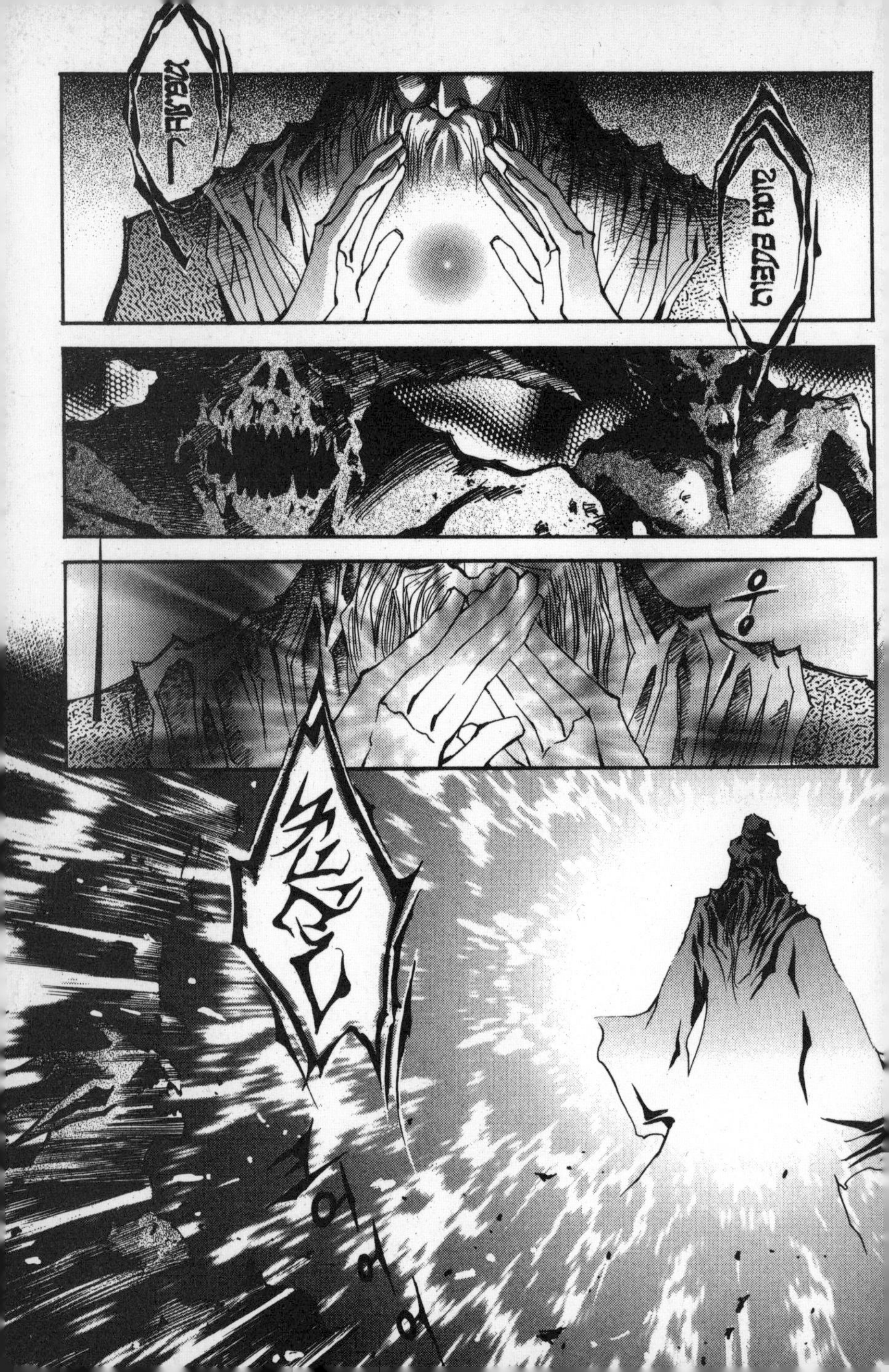

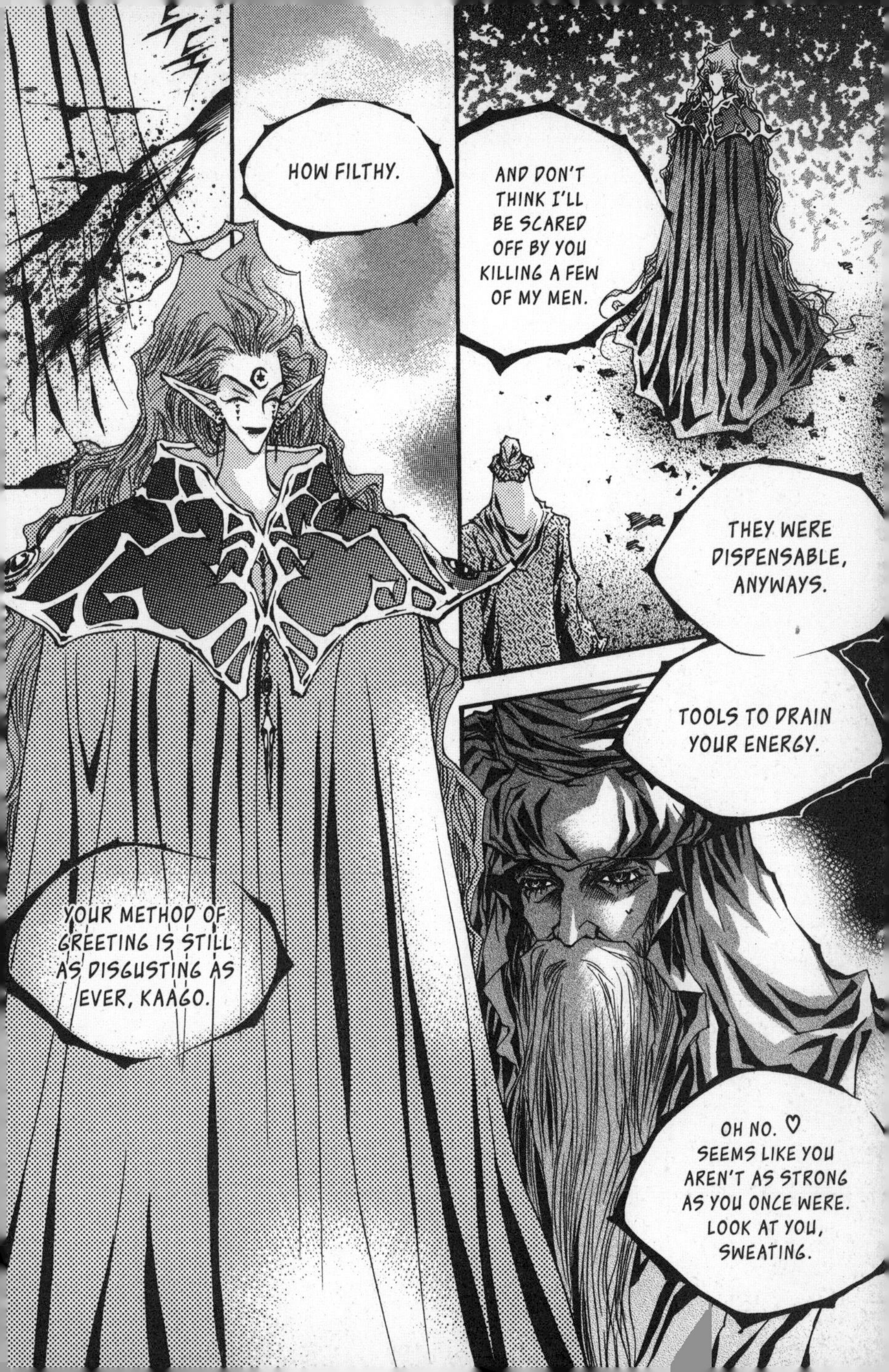
HOW FILTHY.
YOUR METHOD OF GREETING IS STILL AS DISGUSTING AS EVER, KAAGO.
AND DON'T THINK I'LL BE SCARED OFF BY YOU KILLING A FEW OF MY MEN.
THEY WERE DISPENSABLE, ANYWAYS.
TOOLS TO DRAIN YOUR ENERGY.
OH NO. ♡ SEEMS LIKE YOU AREN'T AS STRONG AS YOU ONCE WERE. LOOK AT YOU, SWEATING.

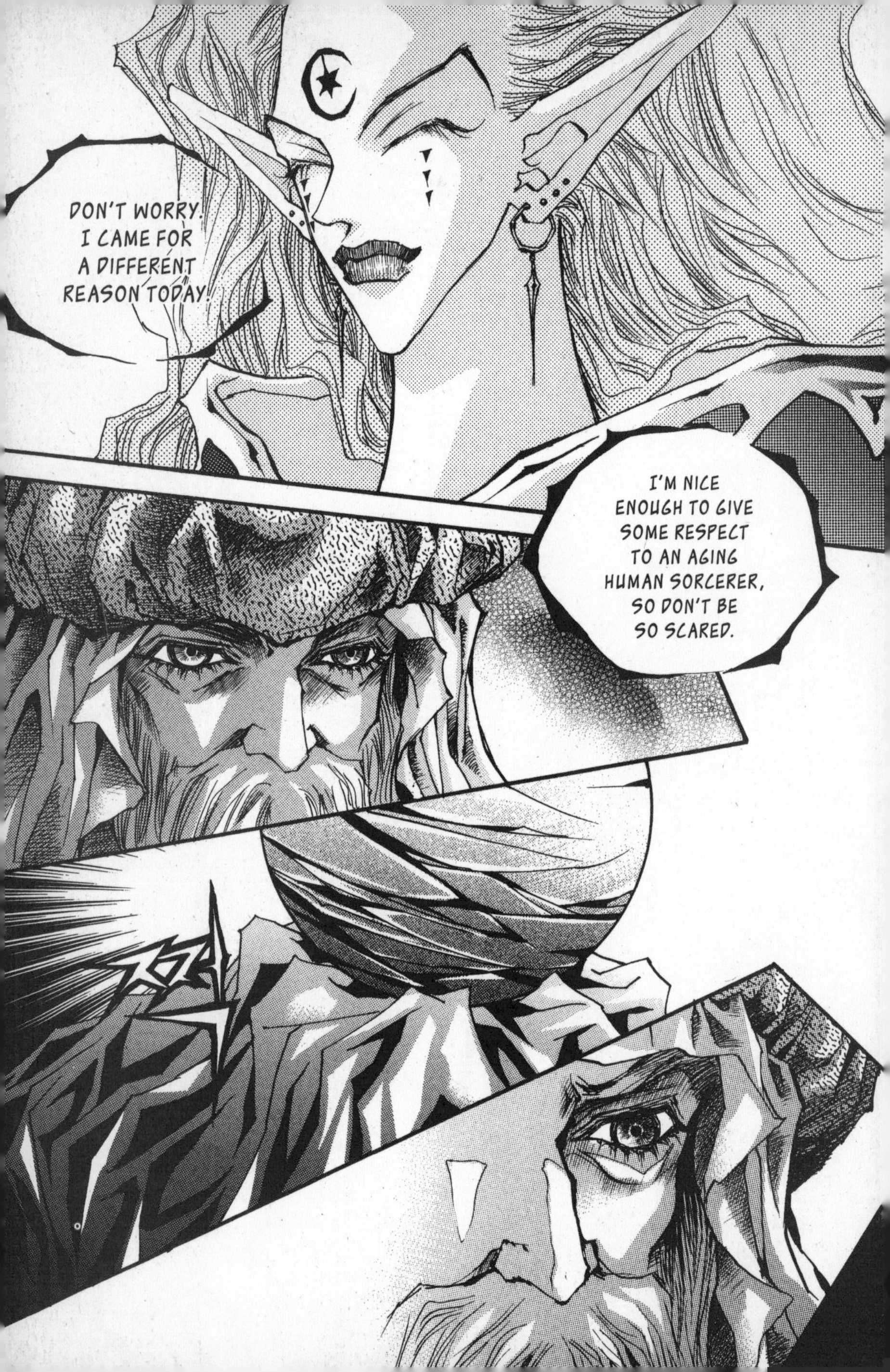
DON'T WORRY. I CAME FOR A DIFFERENT REASON TODAY!
I'M NICE ENOUGH TO GIVE SOME RESPECT TO AN AGING HUMAN SORCERER, SO DON'T BE SO SCARED.

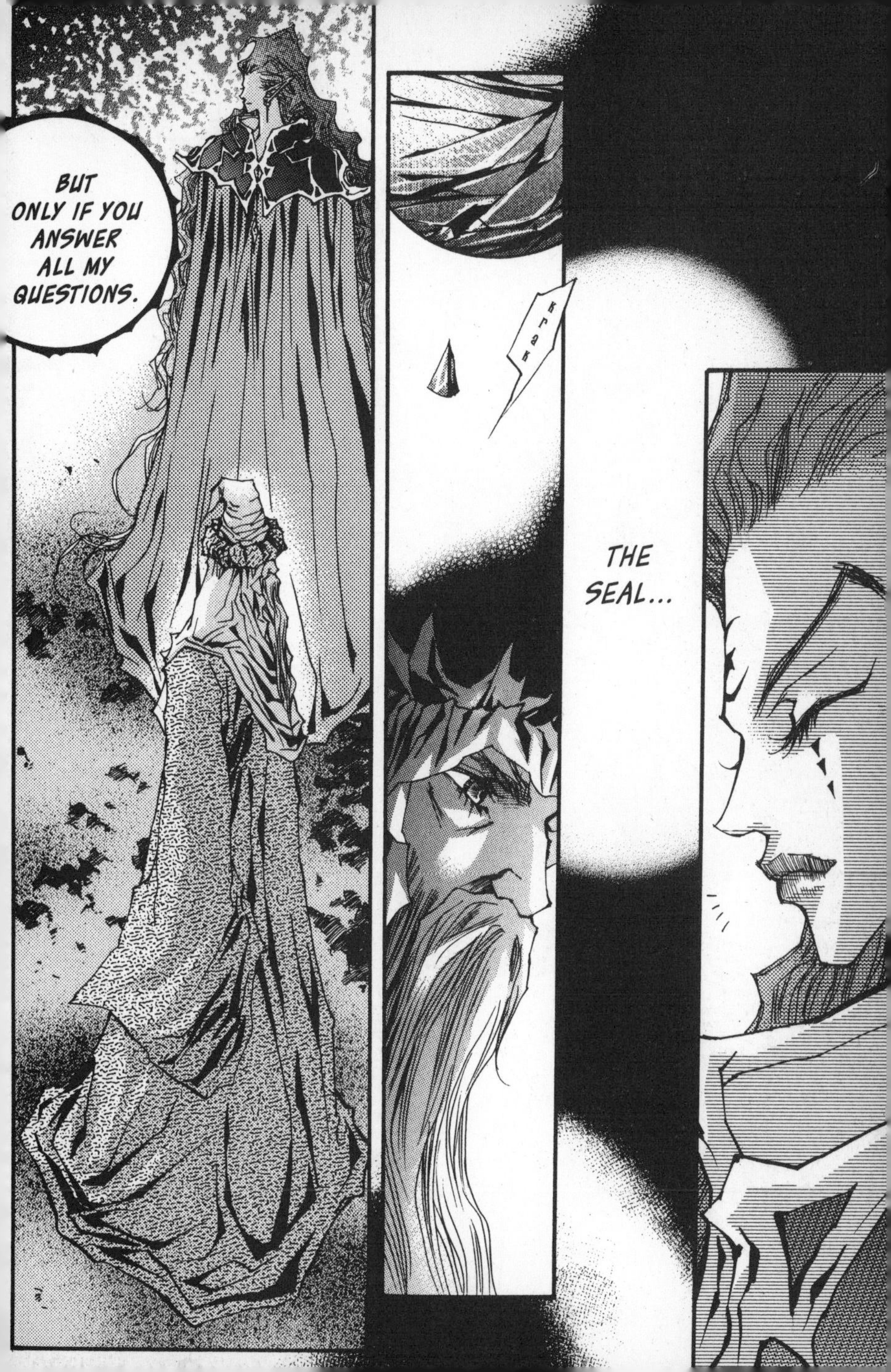
BUT ONLY IF YOU ANSWER ALL MY QUESTIONS.
krak
THE SEAL...

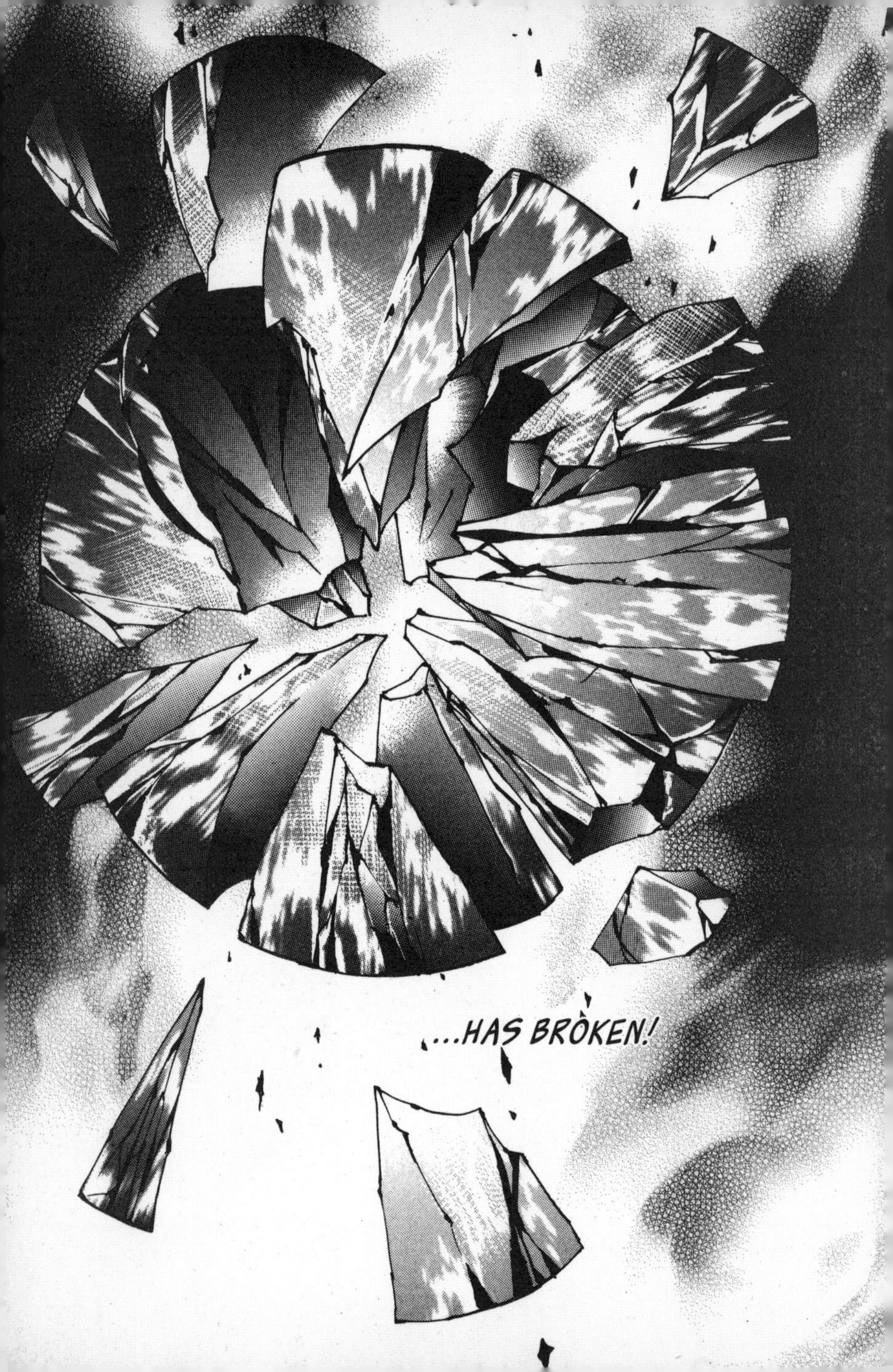
...HAS BROKEN!

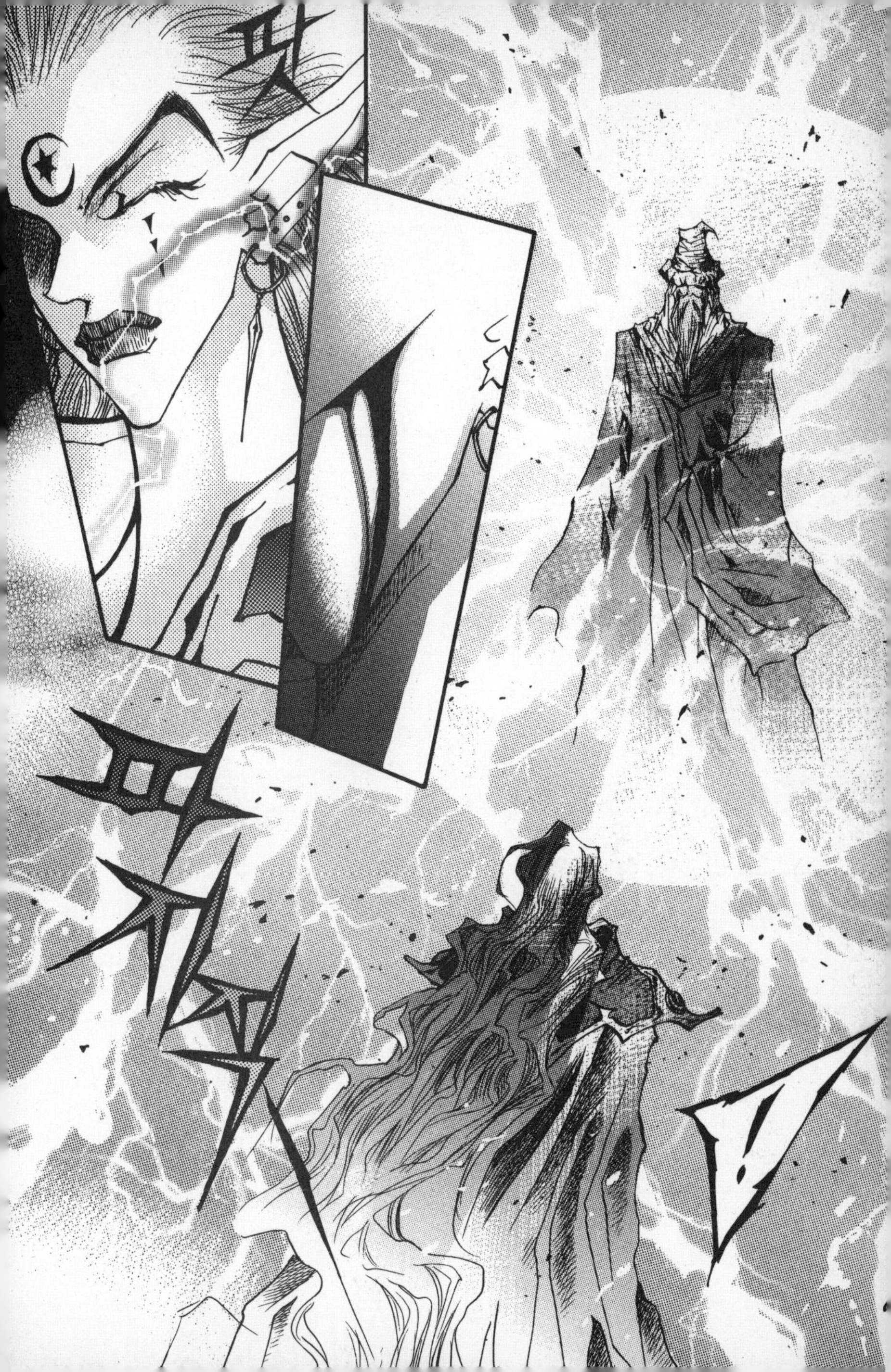
팟
!

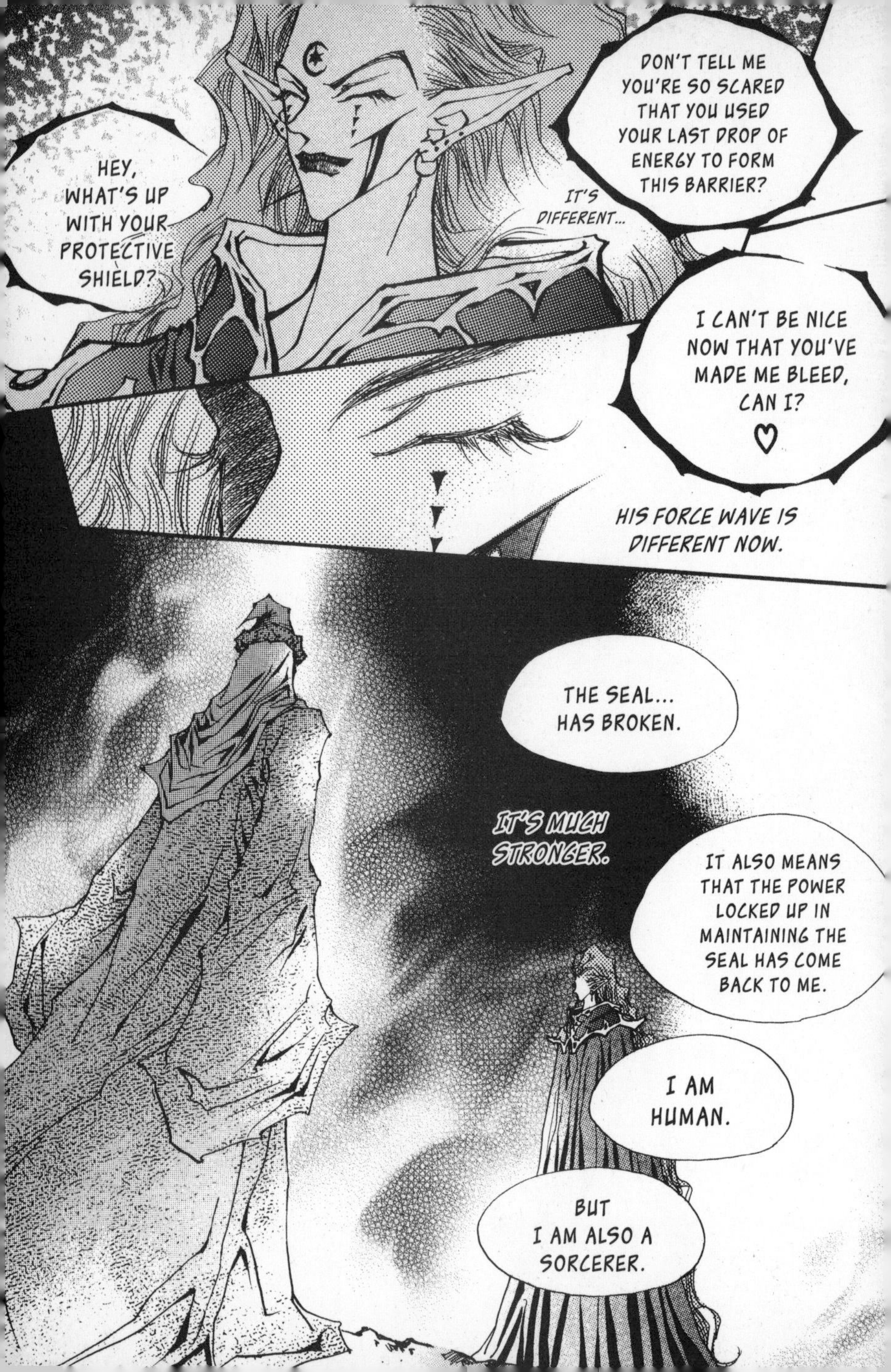
DON'T TELL ME YOU'RE SO SCARED THAT YOU USED YOUR LAST DROP OF ENERGY TO FORM THIS BARRIER?
HEY, WHAT'S UP WITH YOUR PROTECTIVE SHIELD?
IT'S DIFFERENT...
I CAN'T BE NICE NOW THAT YOU'VE MADE ME BLEED, CAN I? ♡
HIS FORCE WAVE IS DIFFERENT NOW.
THE SEAL... HAS BROKEN.
IT'S MUCH STRONGER.
IT ALSO MEANS THAT THE POWER LOCKED UP IN MAINTAINING THE SEAL HAS COME BACK TO ME.
I AM HUMAN.
BUT I AM ALSO A SORCERER.

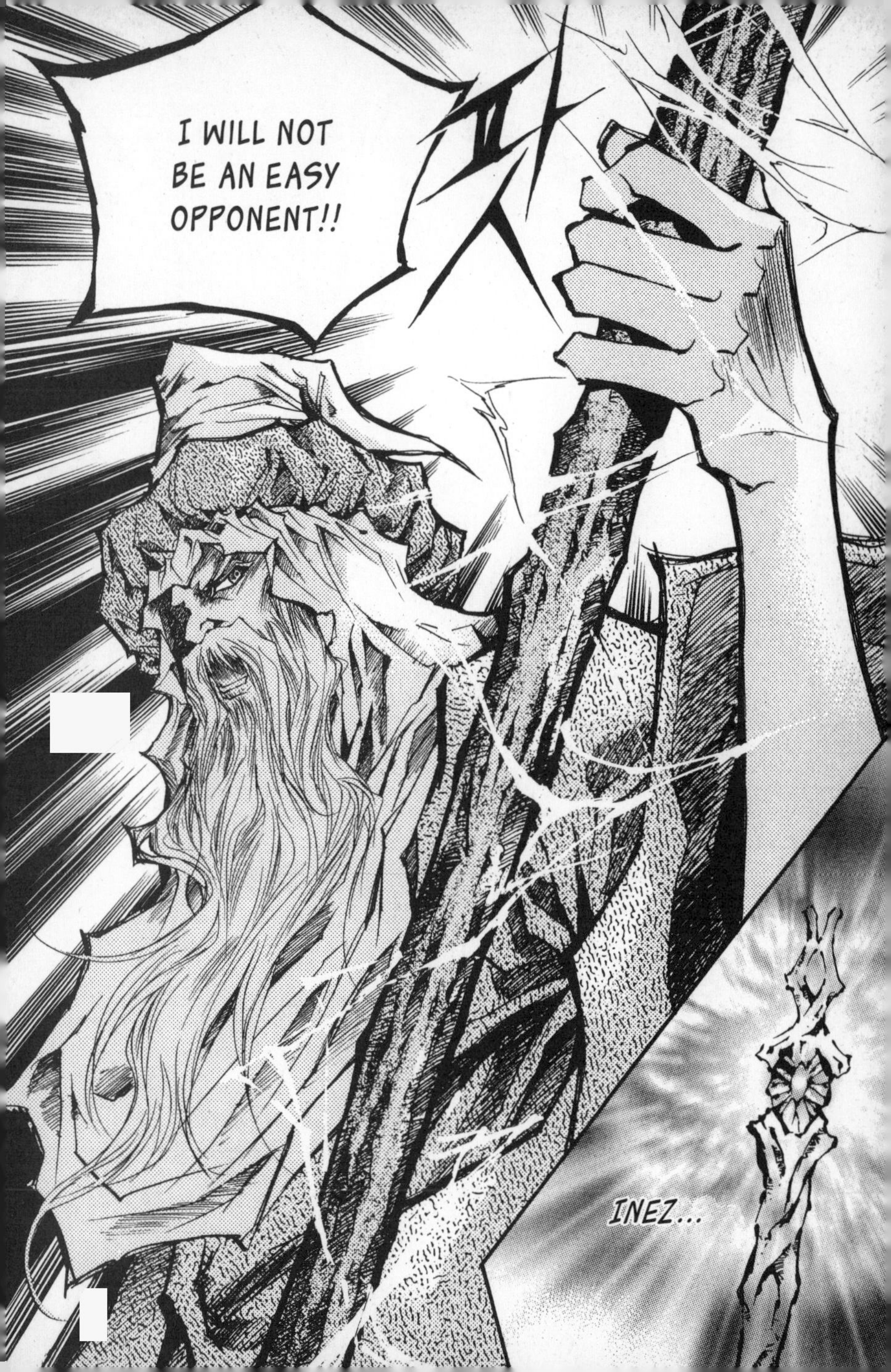
I WILL NOT
BE AN EASY
OPPONENT!!
INEZ...

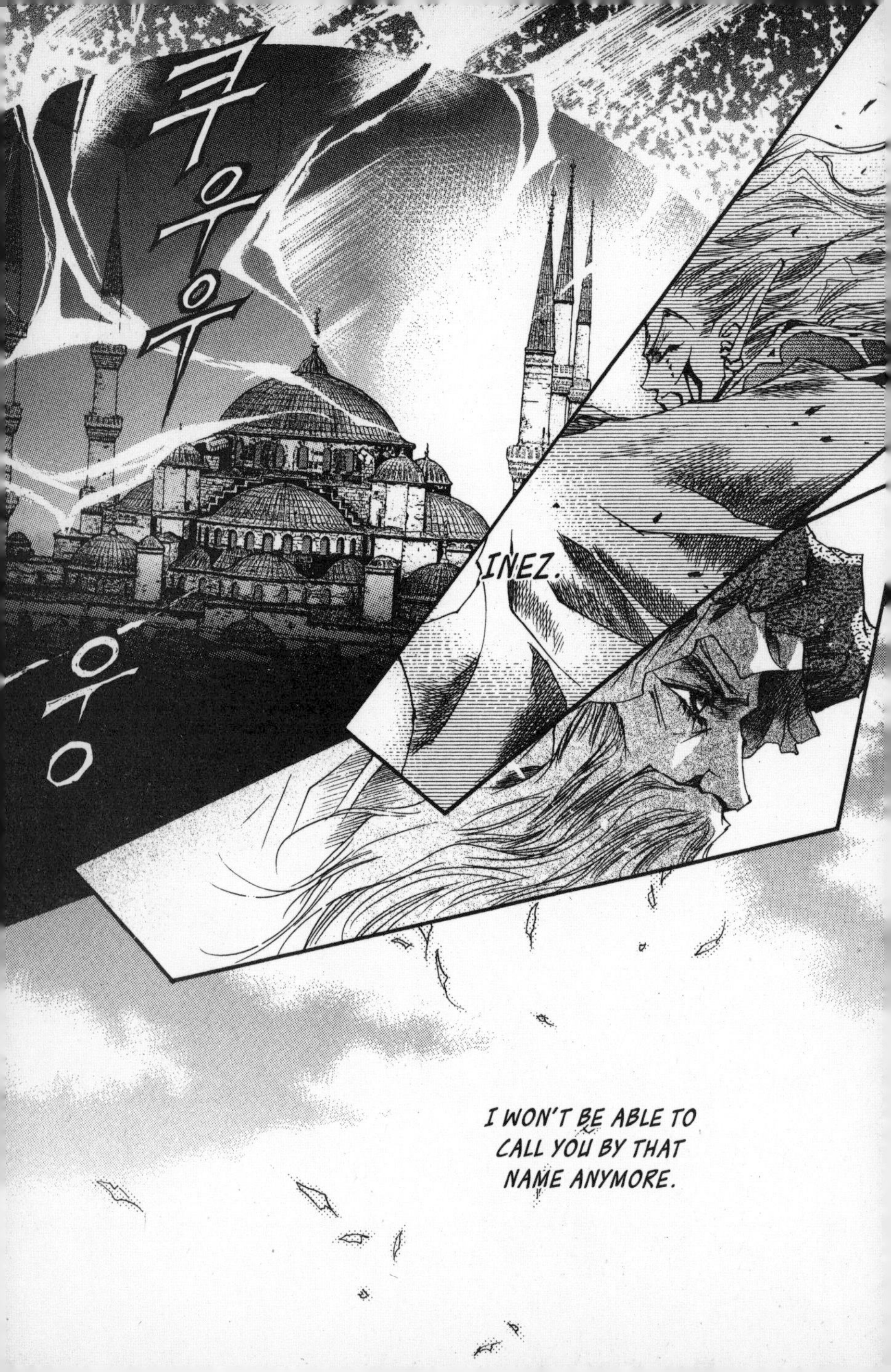
쿠우우우
웅
INEZ.
I WON'T BE ABLE TO CALL YOU BY THAT NAME ANYMORE.

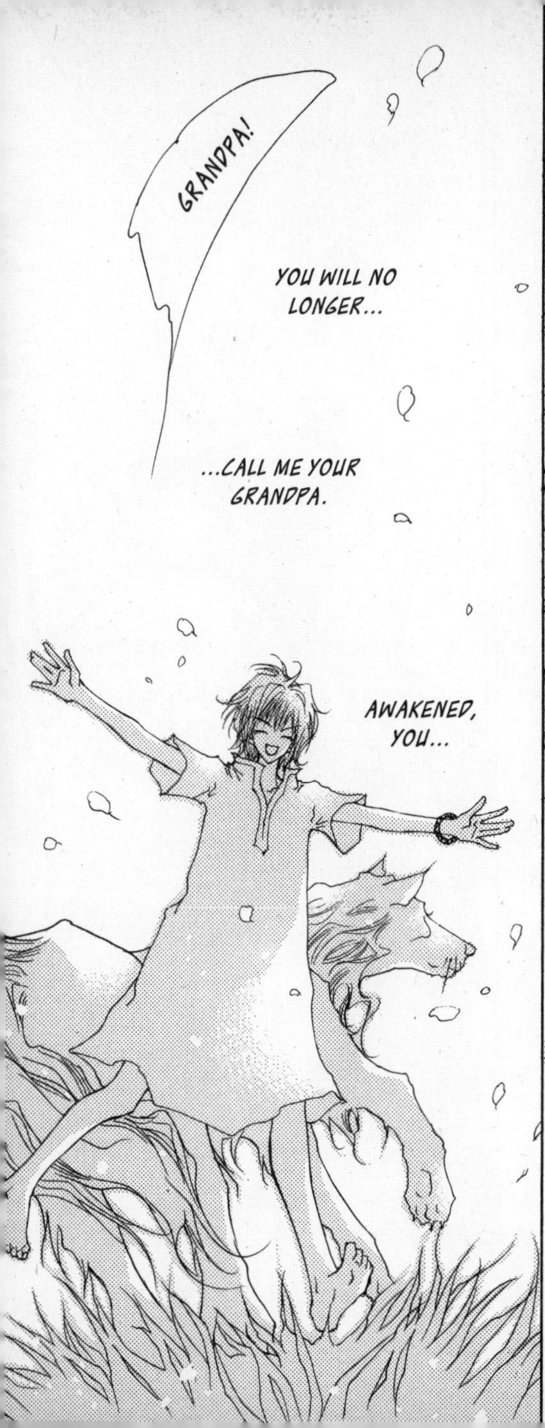
GRANDPA!
YOU WILL NO LONGER...
...CALL ME YOUR GRANDPA.
AWAKENED, YOU...

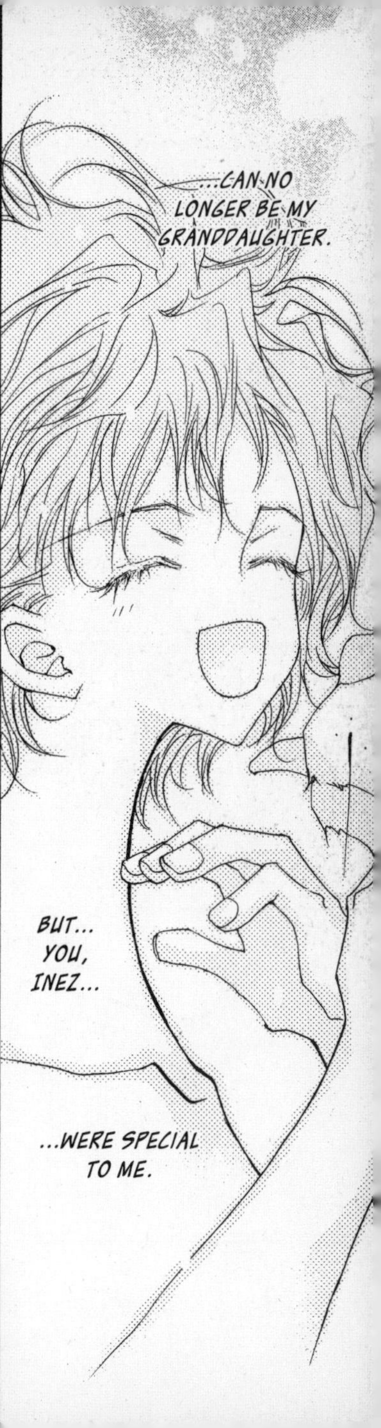
...CAN NO LONGER BE MY GRANDDAUGHTER.
BUT... YOU, INEZ...
...WERE SPECIAL TO ME.

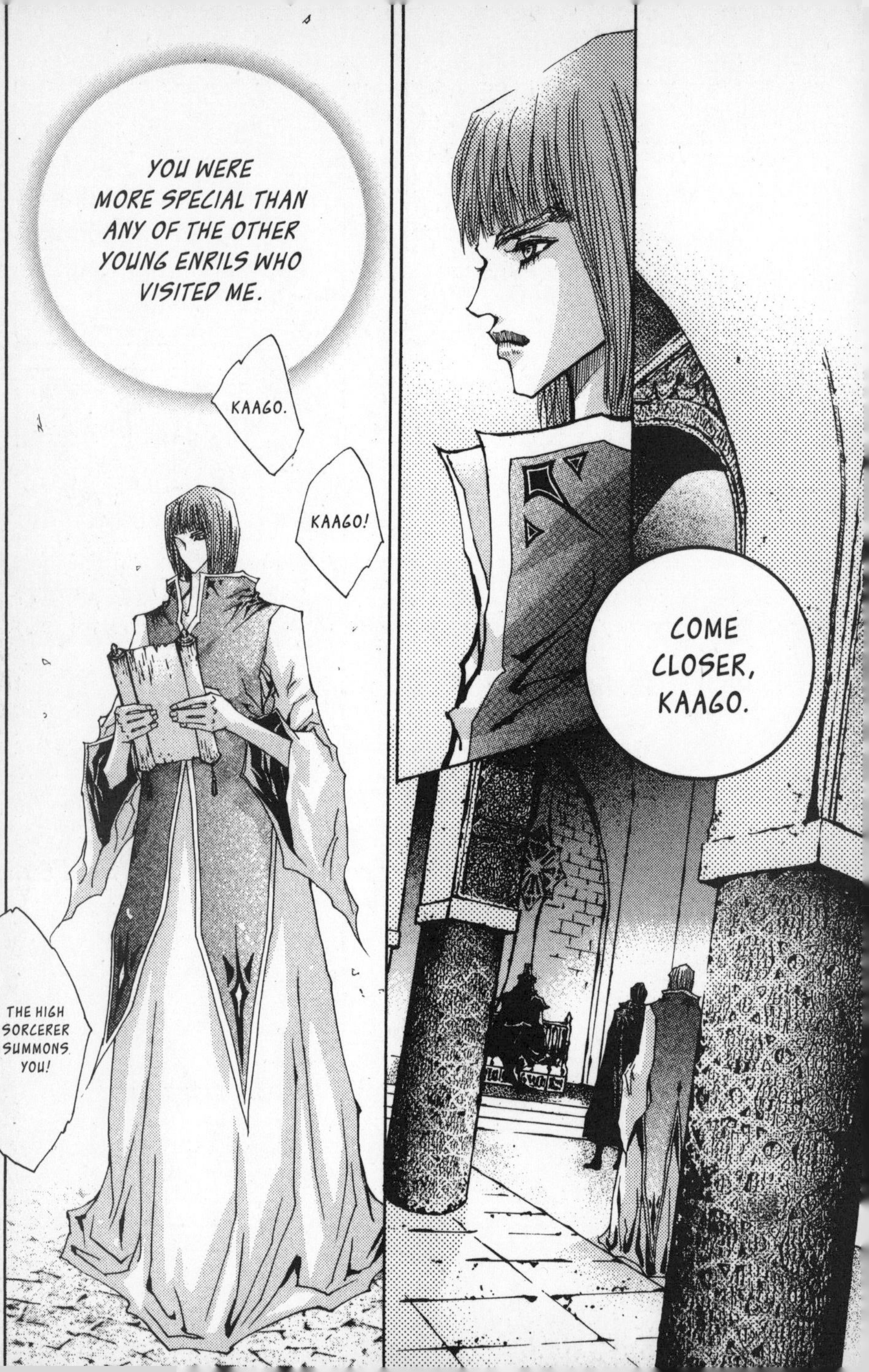
COME CLOSER, KAAGO.
YOU WERE MORE SPECIAL THAN ANY OF THE OTHER YOUNG ENRILS WHO VISITED ME.
KAAGO.
KAAGO!
THE HIGH SORCERER SUMMONS YOU!

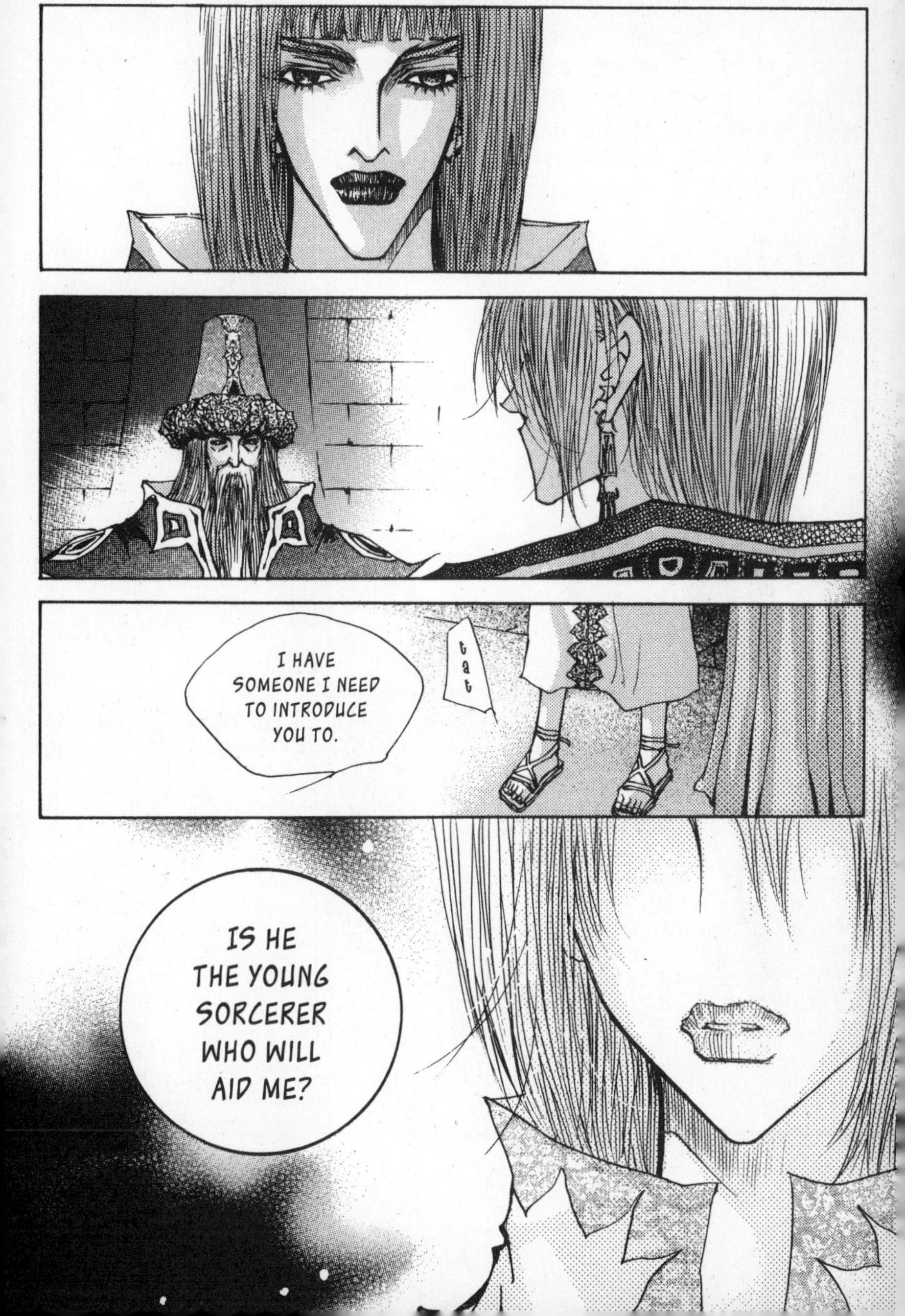
I HAVE SOMEONE I NEED TO INTRODUCE YOU TO.
IS HE THE YOUNG SORCERER WHO WILL AID ME?

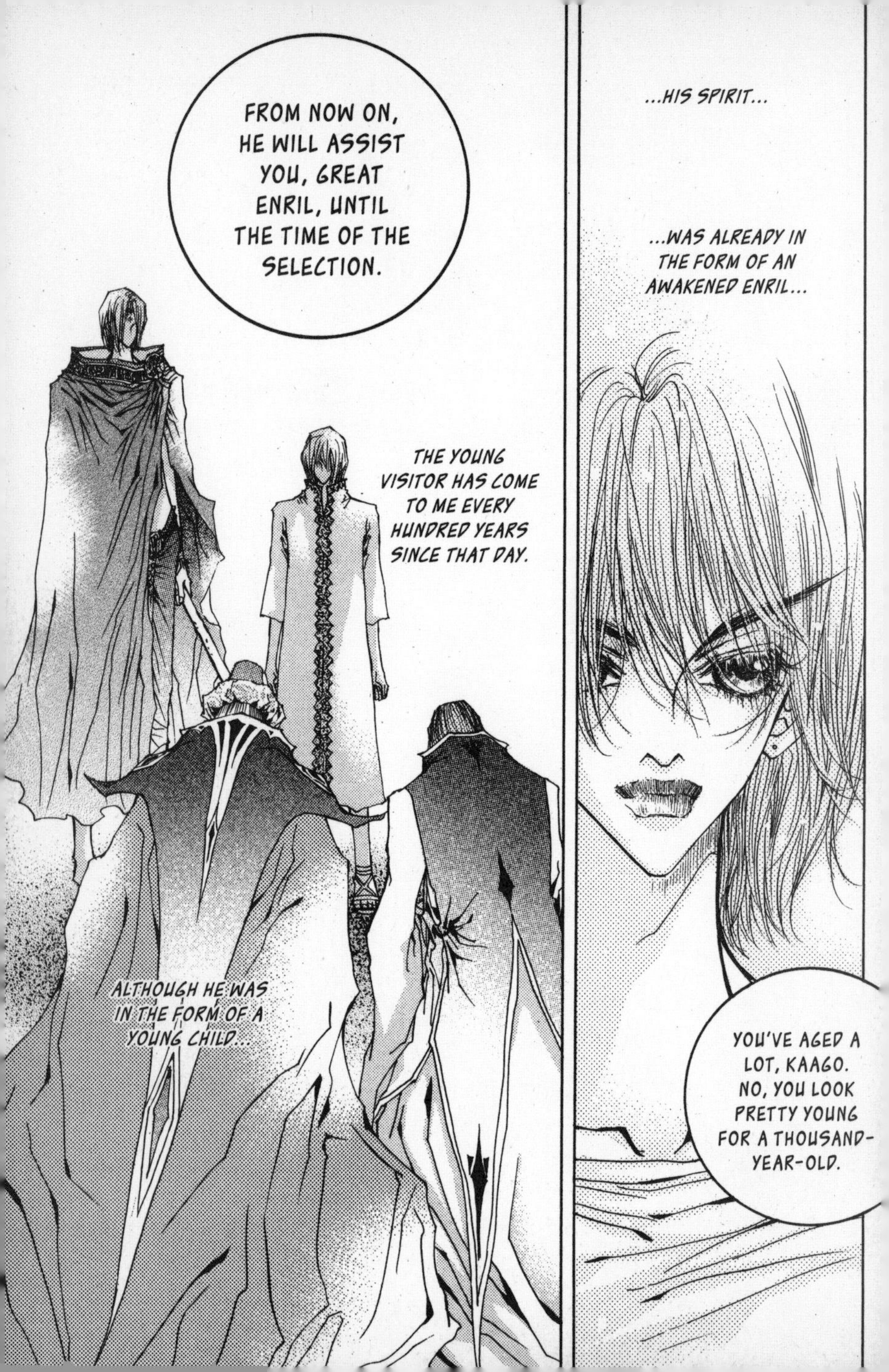
FROM NOW ON, HE WILL ASSIST YOU, GREAT ENRIL, UNTIL THE TIME OF THE SELECTION.
THE YOUNG VISITOR HAS COME TO ME EVERY HUNDRED YEARS SINCE THAT DAY.
ALTHOUGH HE WAS IN THE FORM OF A YOUNG CHILD...
...HIS SPIRIT...
...WAS ALREADY IN THE FORM OF AN AWAKENED ENRIL...
YOU'VE AGED A LOT, KAAGO. NO, YOU LOOK PRETTY YOUNG FOR A THOUSAND-YEAR-OLD.

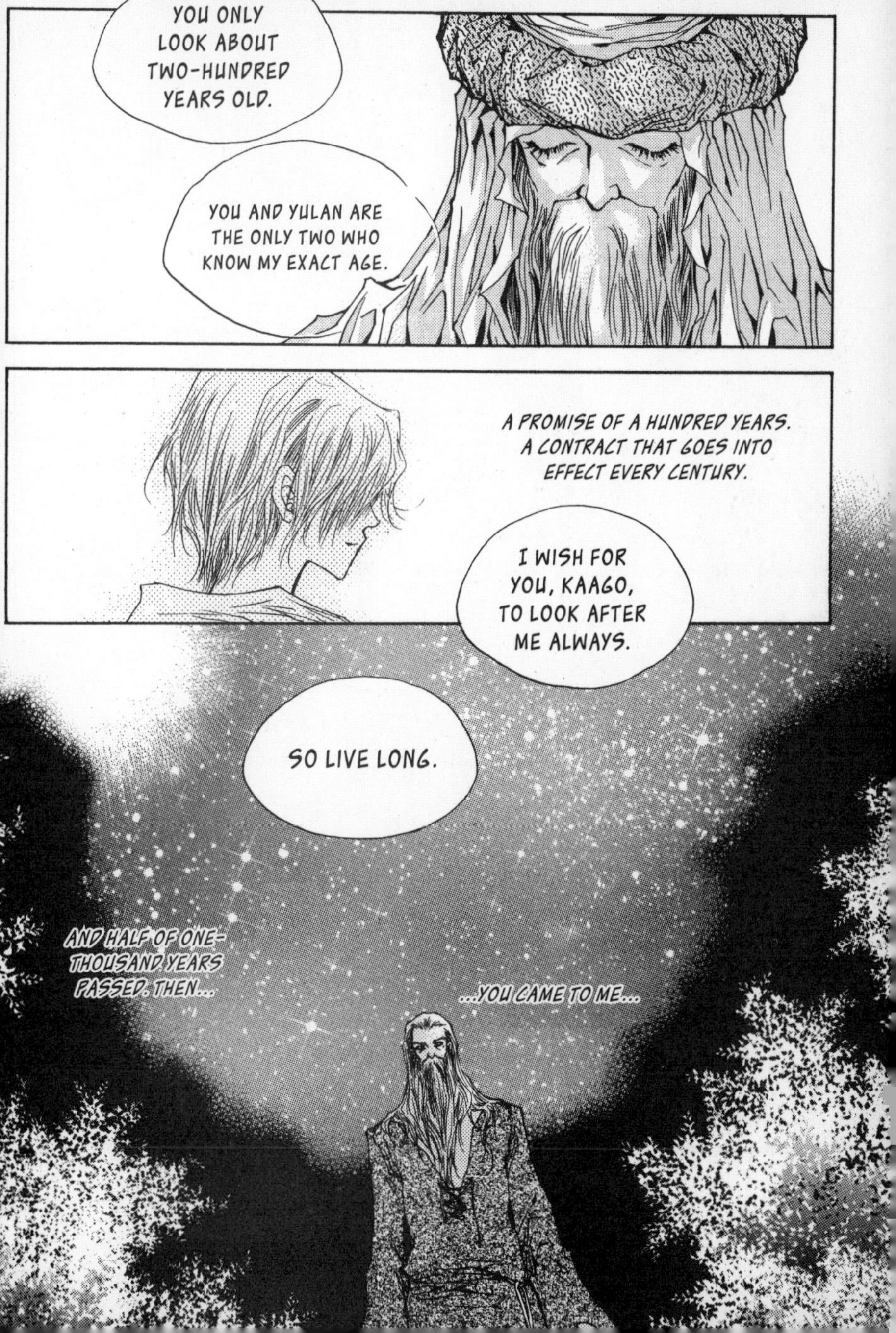
YOU ONLY LOOK ABOUT TWO-HUNDRED YEARS OLD.
YOU AND YULAN ARE THE ONLY TWO WHO KNOW MY EXACT AGE.
A PROMISE OF A HUNDRED YEARS. A CONTRACT THAT GOES INTO EFFECT EVERY CENTURY.
I WISH FOR YOU, KAAGO, TO LOOK AFTER ME ALWAYS.
SO LIVE LONG.
AND HALF OF ONE-THOUSAND YEARS PASSED. THEN...
...YOU CAME TO ME...

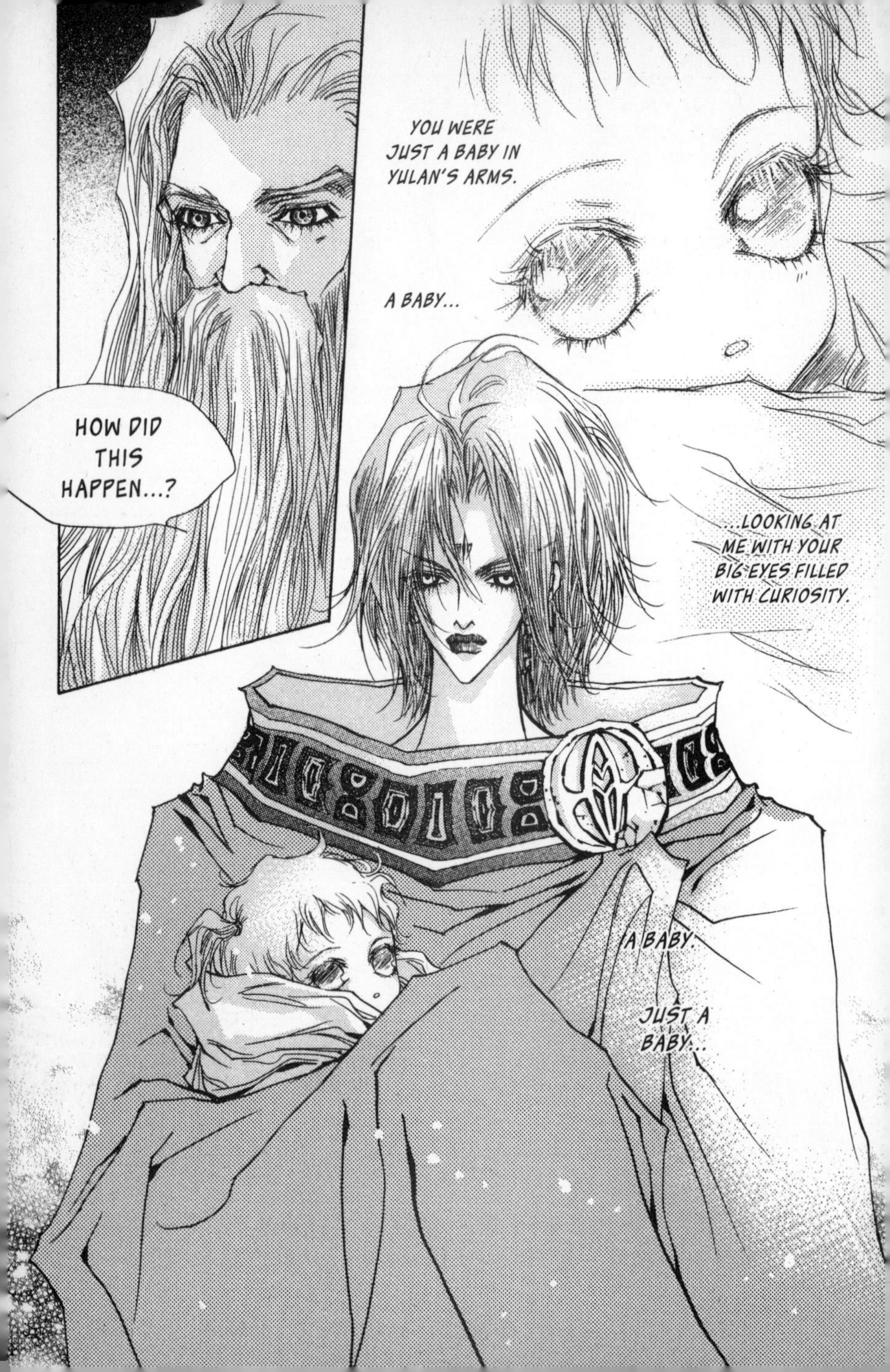
YOU WERE JUST A BABY IN YULAN'S ARMS.
A BABY...
...LOOKING AT ME WITH YOUR BIG EYES FILLED WITH CURIOSITY.
HOW DID THIS HAPPEN...?
A BABY.
JUST A BABY...

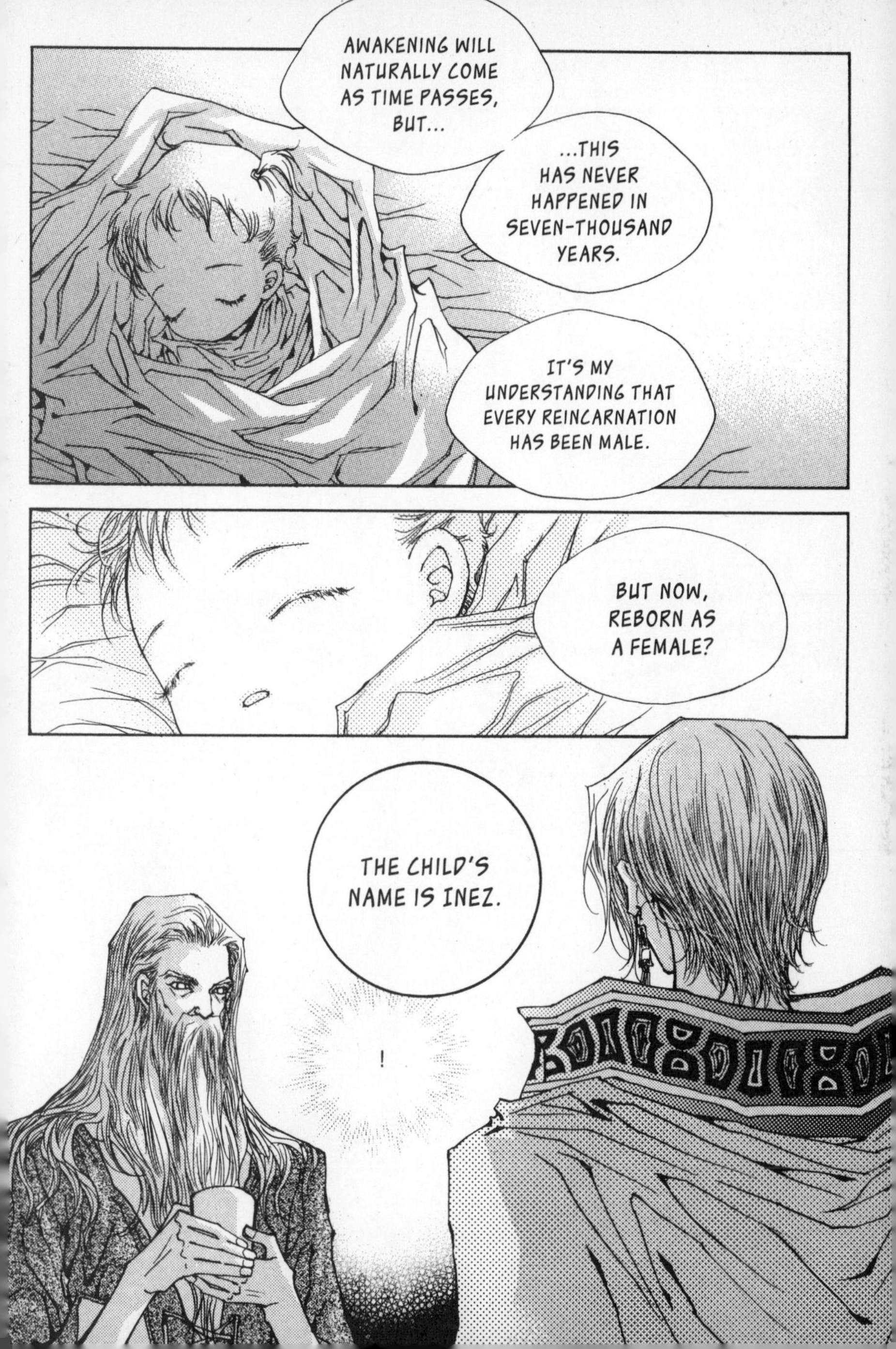
AWAKENING WILL NATURALLY COME AS TIME PASSES, BUT...
...THIS HAS NEVER HAPPENED IN SEVEN-THOUSAND YEARS.
IT'S MY UNDERSTANDING THAT EVERY REINCARNATION HAS BEEN MALE.
BUT NOW, REBORN AS A FEMALE?
THE CHILD'S NAME IS INEZ.
!

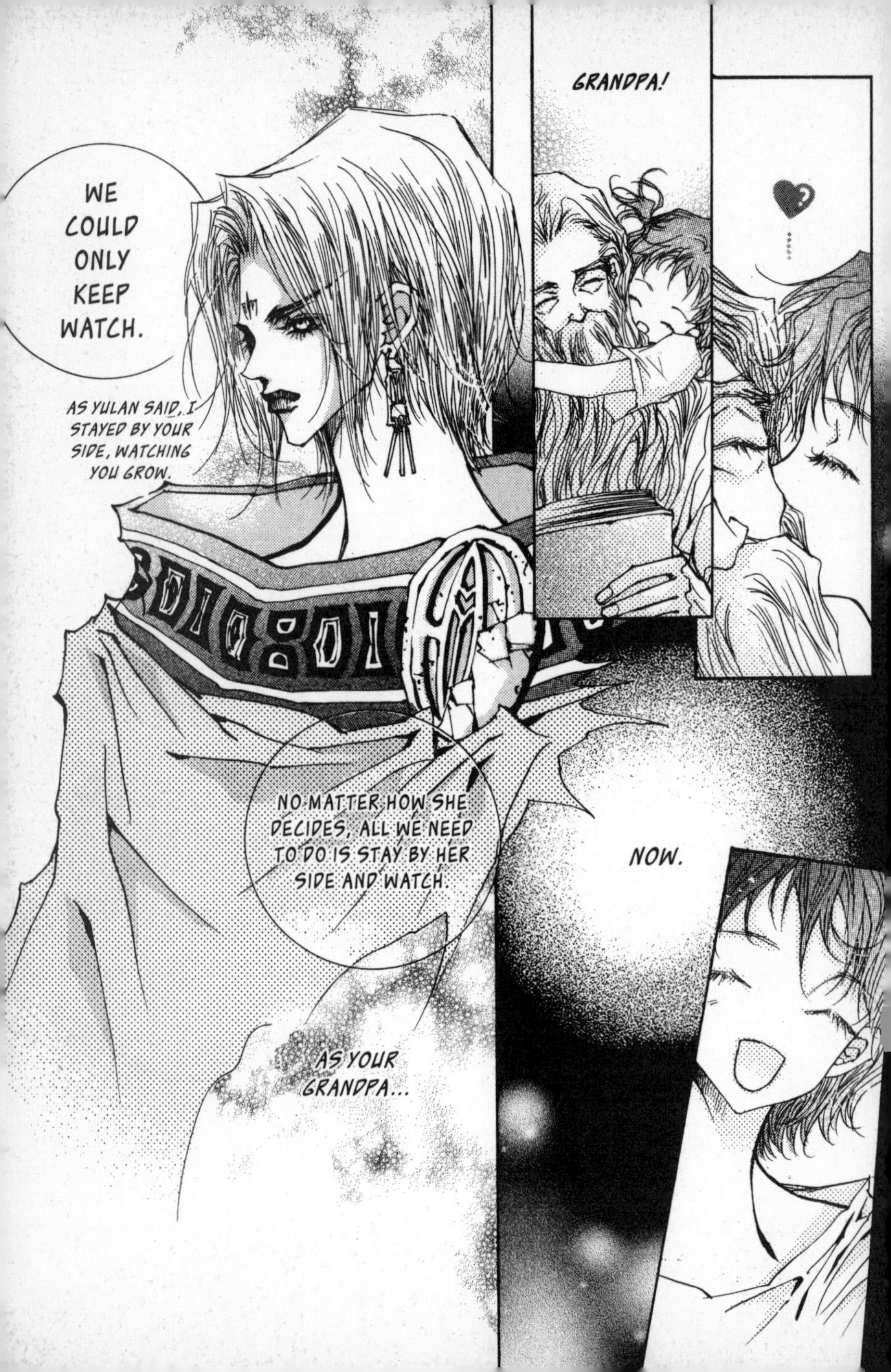
GRANDPA!
NOW.
WE COULD ONLY KEEP WATCH.
AS YULAN SAID, I STAYED BY YOUR SIDE, WATCHING YOU GROW.
NO MATTER HOW SHE DECIDES, ALL WE NEED TO DO IS STAY BY HER SIDE AND WATCH.
AS YOUR GRANDPA...

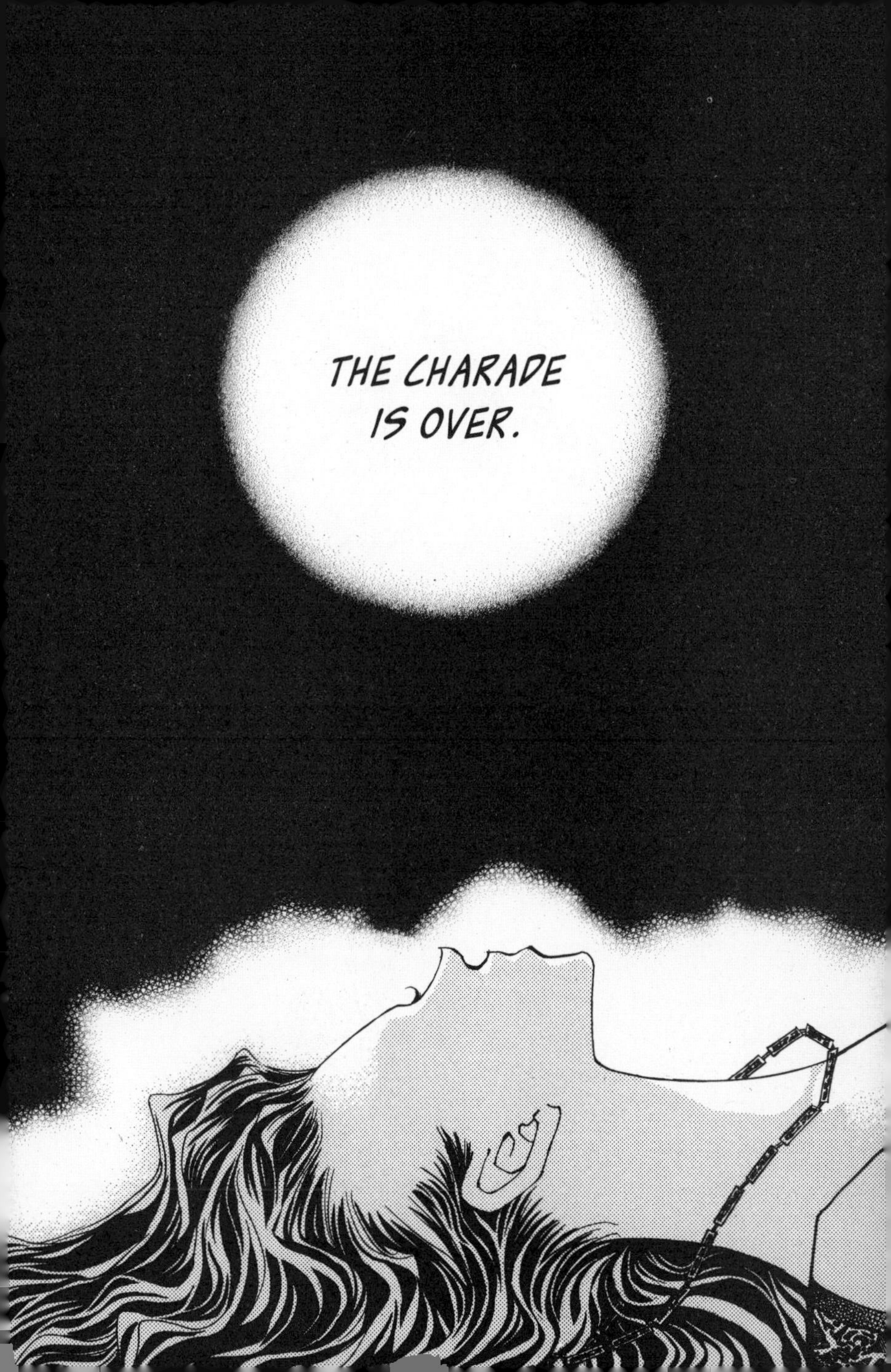
THE CHARADE IS OVER.

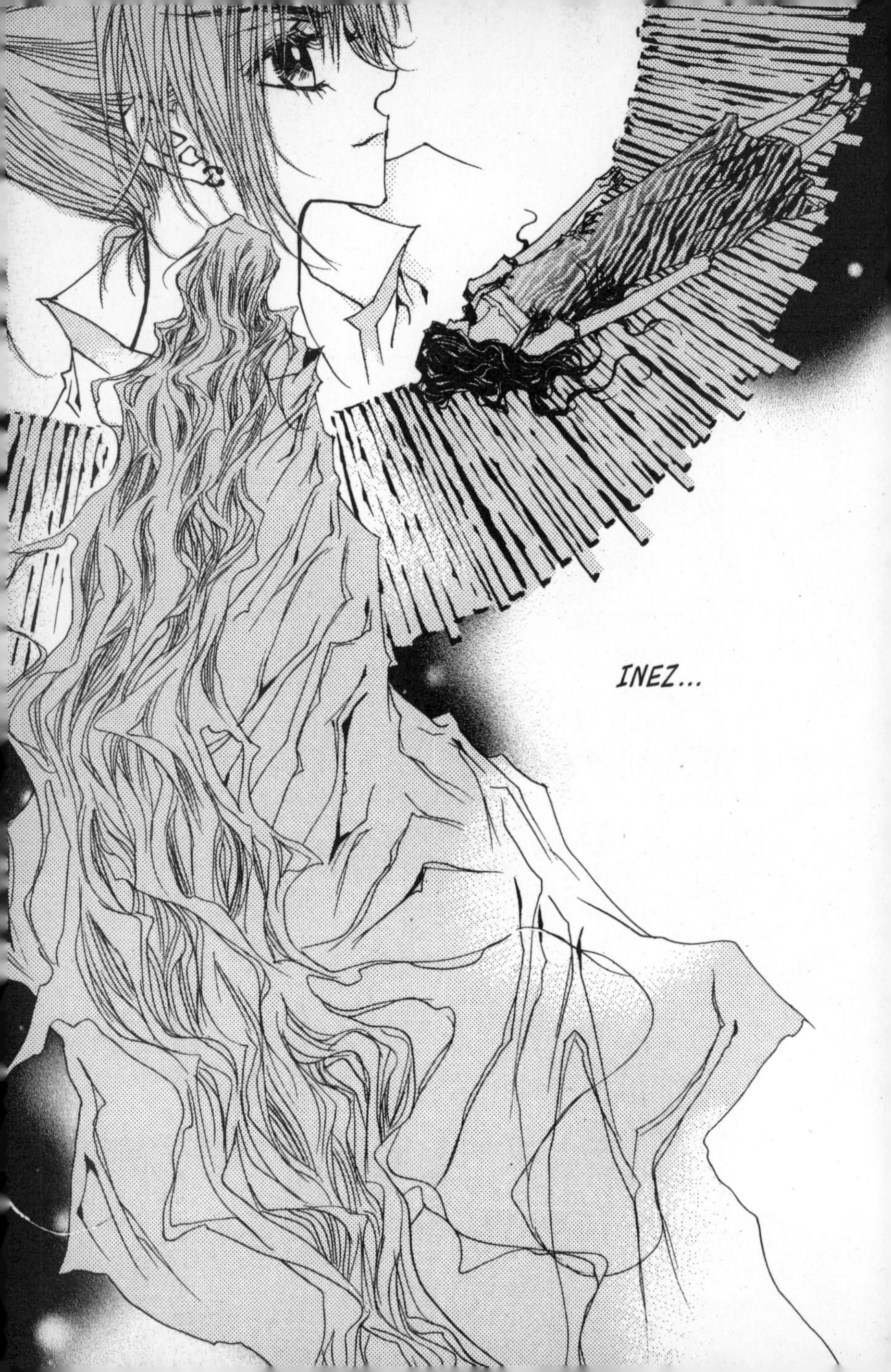
INEZ...

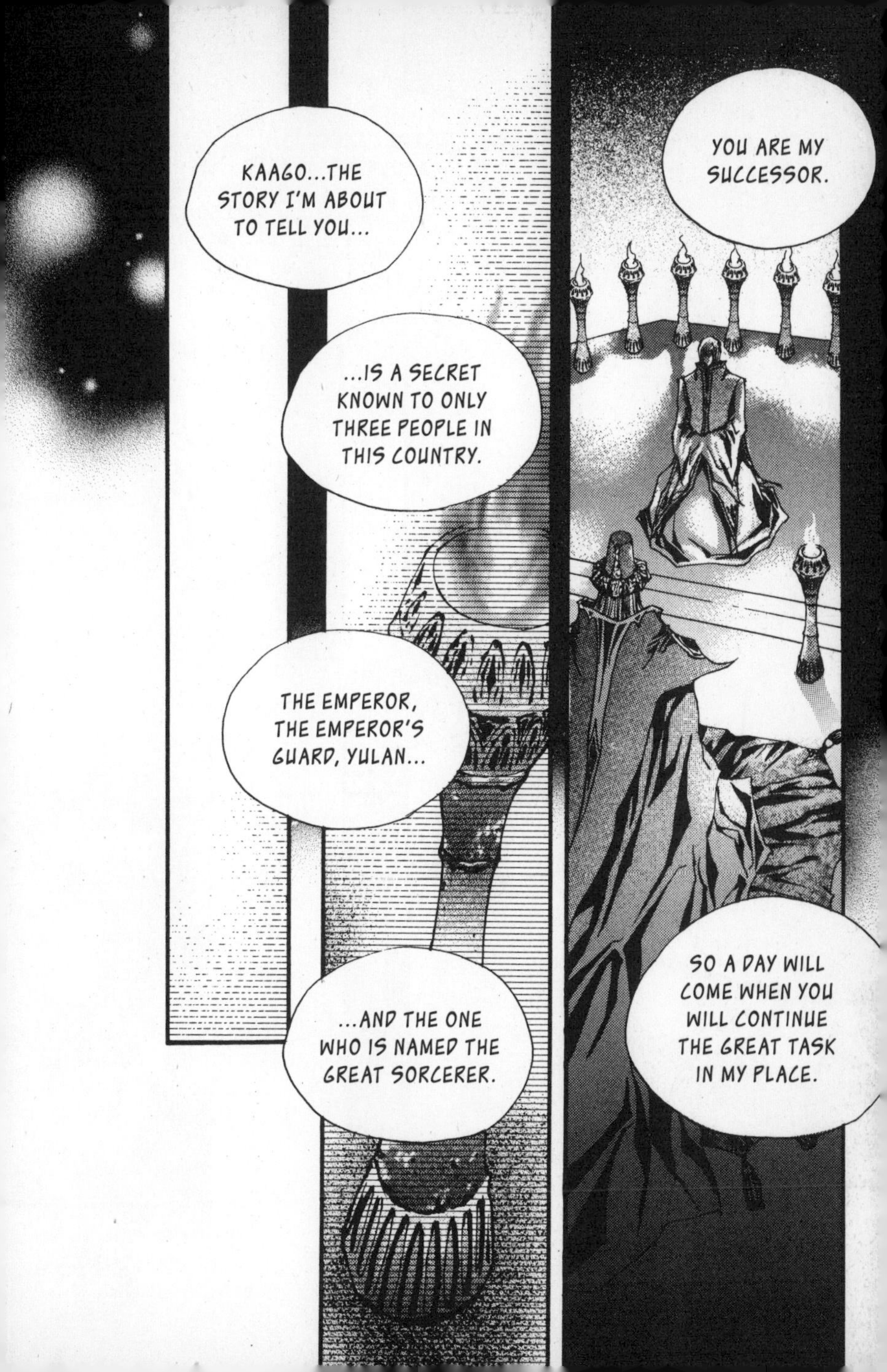
KAAGO...THE STORY I'M ABOUT TO TELL YOU...
...IS A SECRET KNOWN TO ONLY THREE PEOPLE IN THIS COUNTRY.
THE EMPEROR, THE EMPEROR'S GUARD, YULAN...
...AND THE ONE WHO IS NAMED THE GREAT SORCERER.
YOU ARE MY SUCCESSOR.
SO A DAY WILL COME WHEN YOU WILL CONTINUE THE GREAT TASK IN MY PLACE.

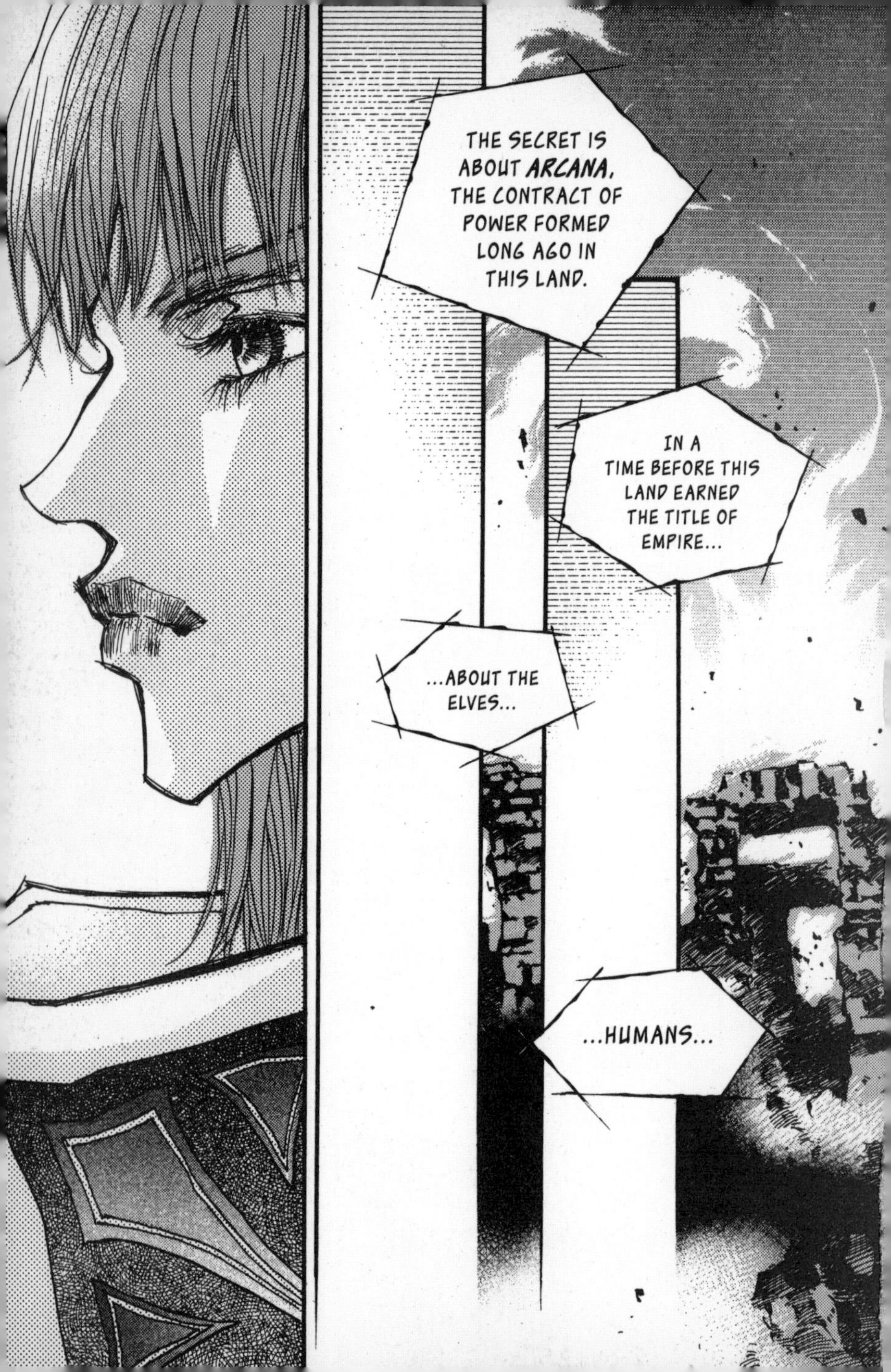
THE SECRET IS ABOUT ARCANA, THE CONTRACT OF POWER FORMED LONG AGO IN THIS LAND.
IN A TIME BEFORE THIS LAND EARNED THE TITLE OF EMPIRE...
...ABOUT THE ELVES...
...HUMANS...

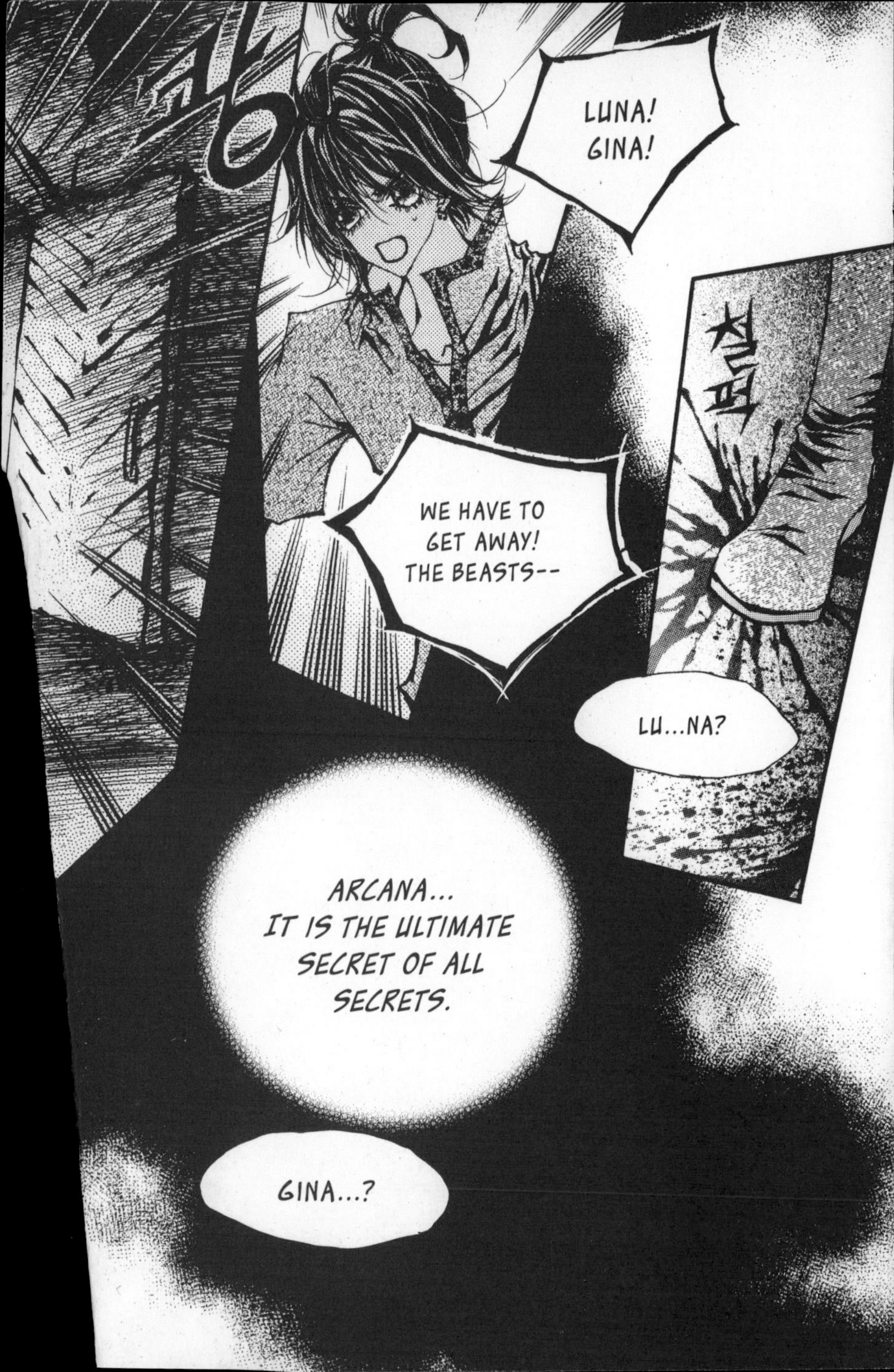
LUNA!
GINA!
WE HAVE TO GET AWAY! THE BEASTS--
LU...NA?
ARCANA... IT IS THE ULTIMATE SECRET OF ALL SECRETS.
GINA...?

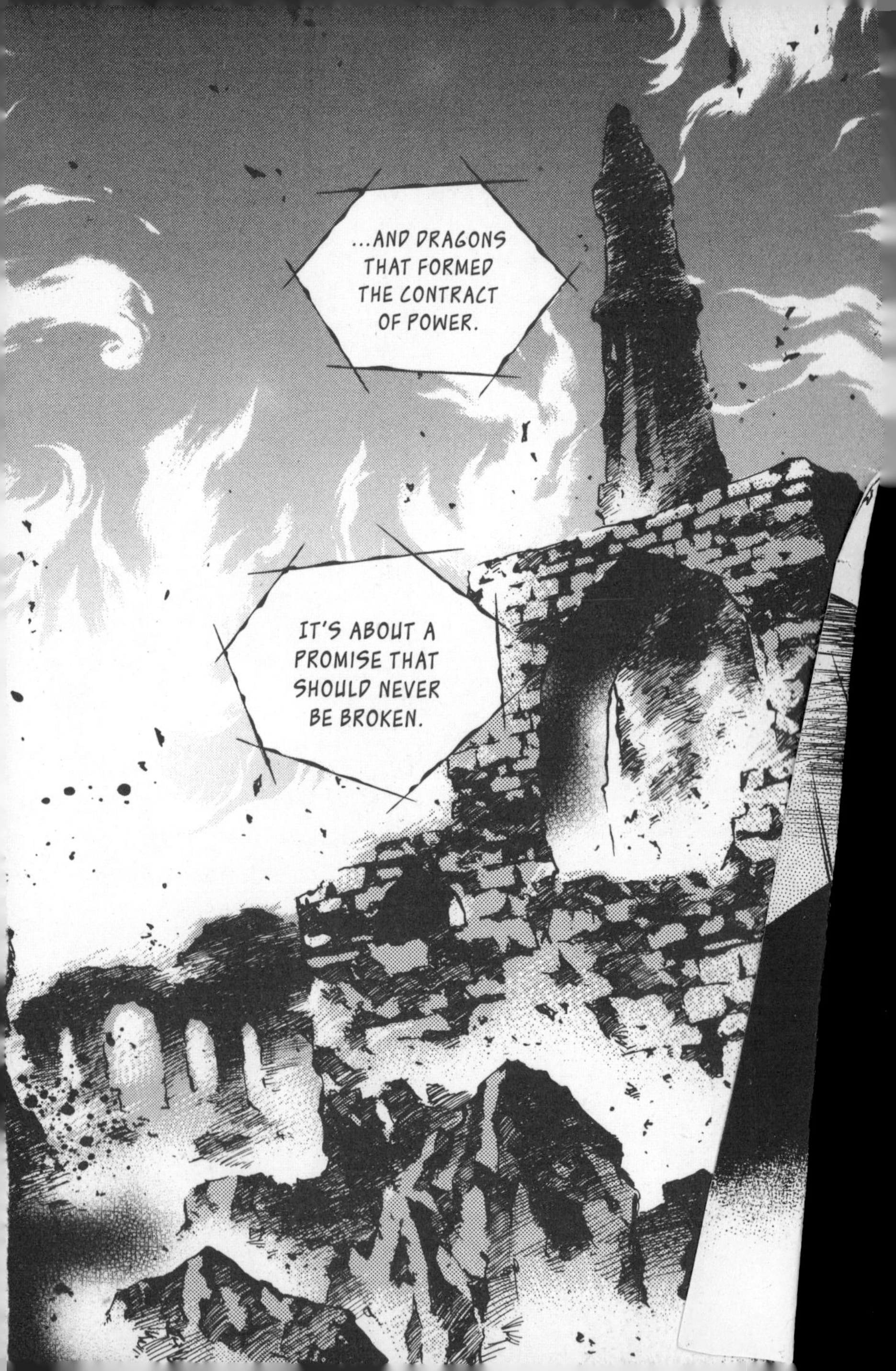
...AND DRAGONS THAT FORMED THE CONTRACT OF POWER.
IT'S ABOUT A PROMISE THAT SHOULD NEVER BE BROKEN.

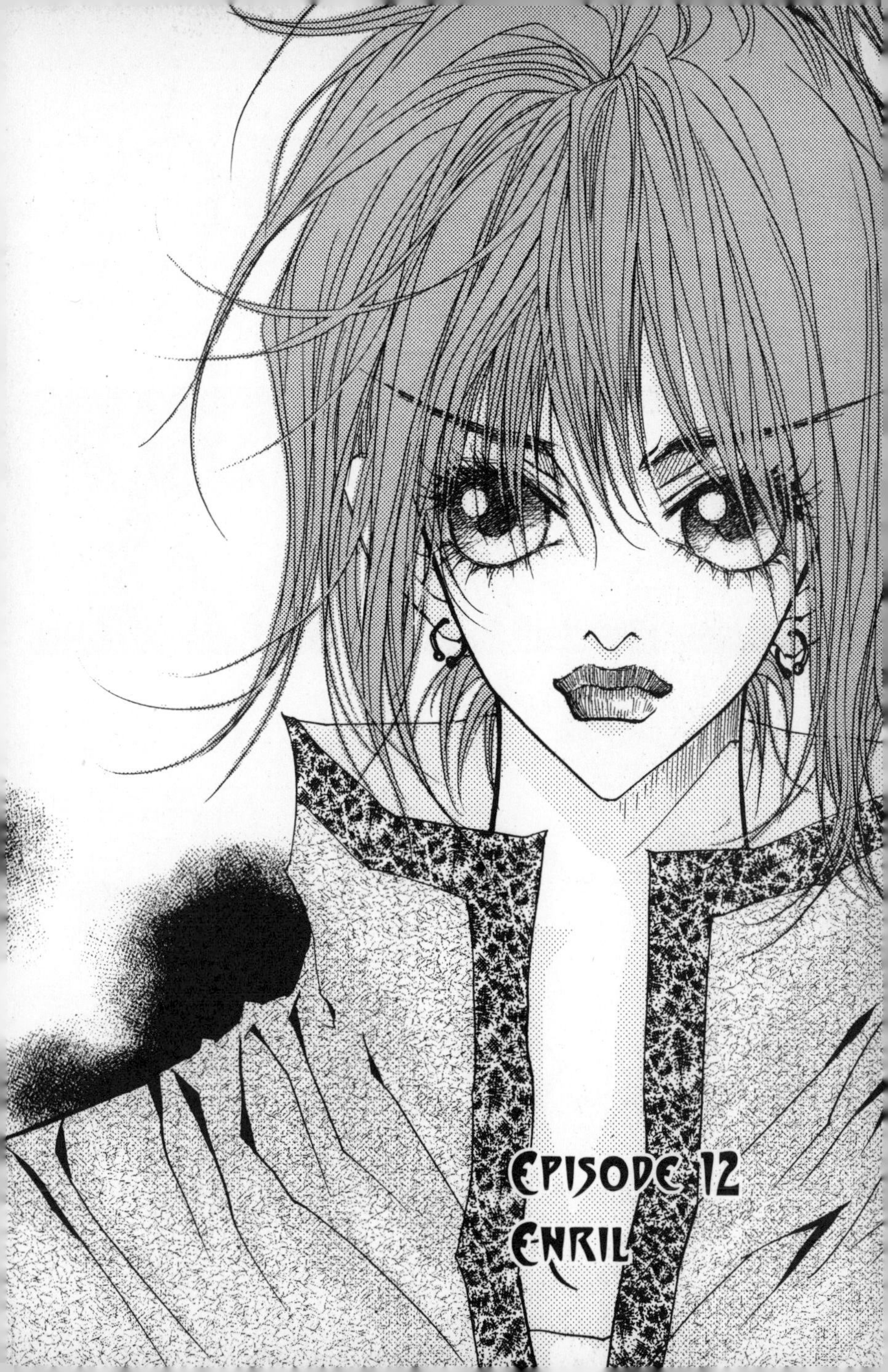
Episode 12
Enril

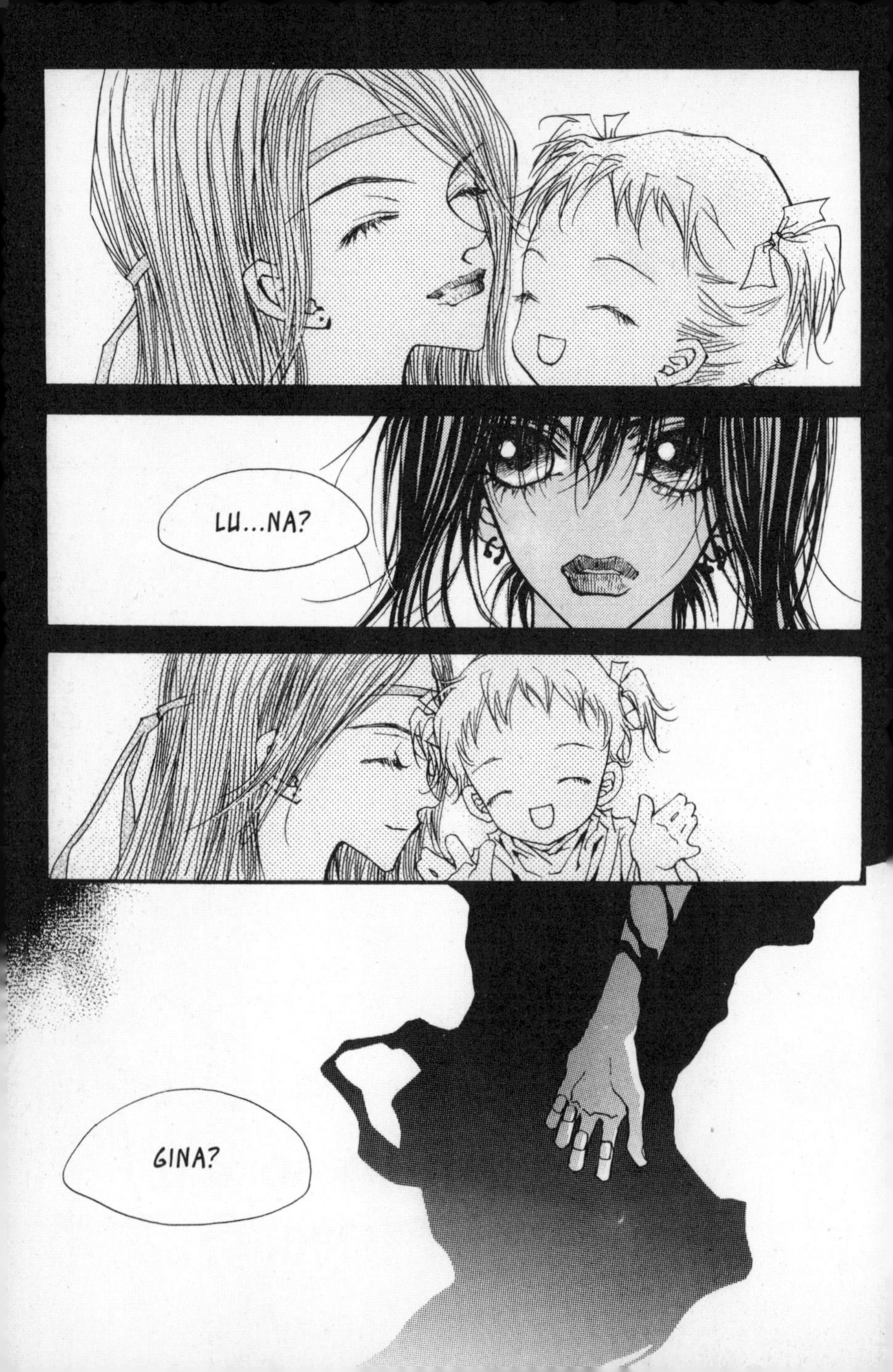
LU...NA?
GINA?

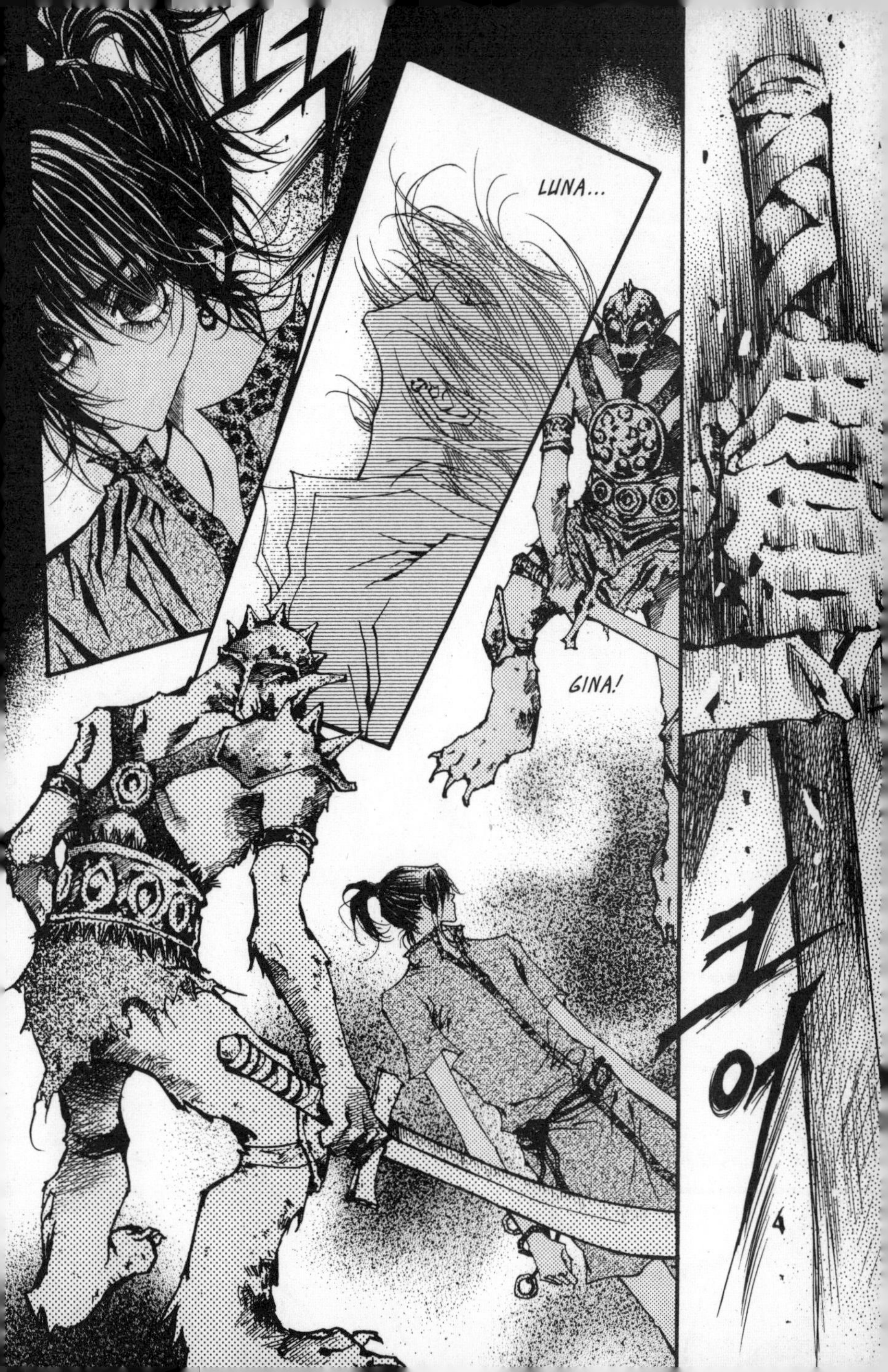
LUNA...
GINA!

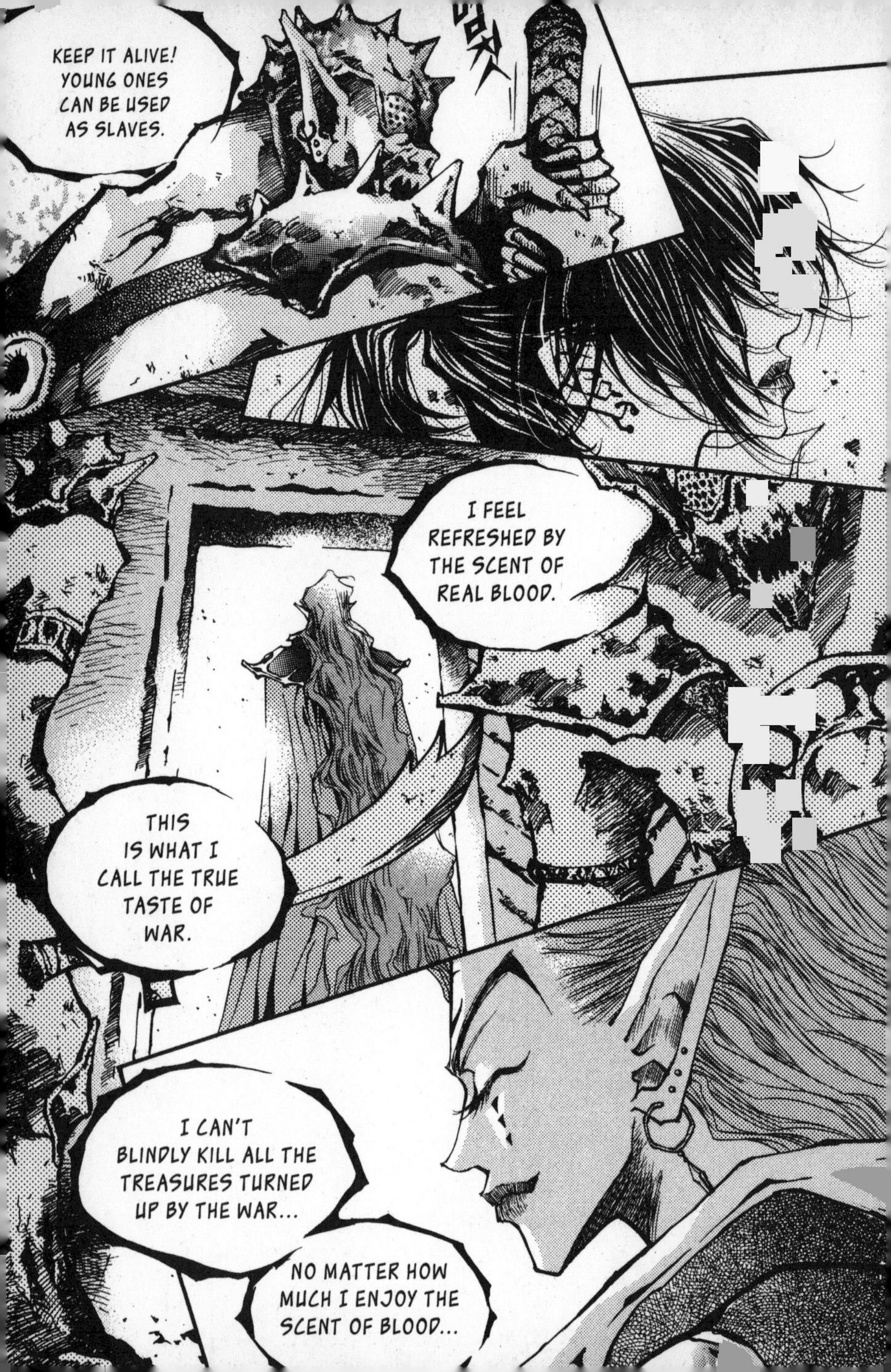
KEEP IT ALIVE! YOUNG ONES CAN BE USED AS SLAVES.
I FEEL REFRESHED BY THE SCENT OF REAL BLOOD.
THIS IS WHAT I CALL THE TRUE TASTE OF WAR.
I CAN'T BLINDLY KILL ALL THE TREASURES TURNED UP BY THE WAR...
NO MATTER HOW MUCH I ENJOY THE SCENT OF BLOOD...

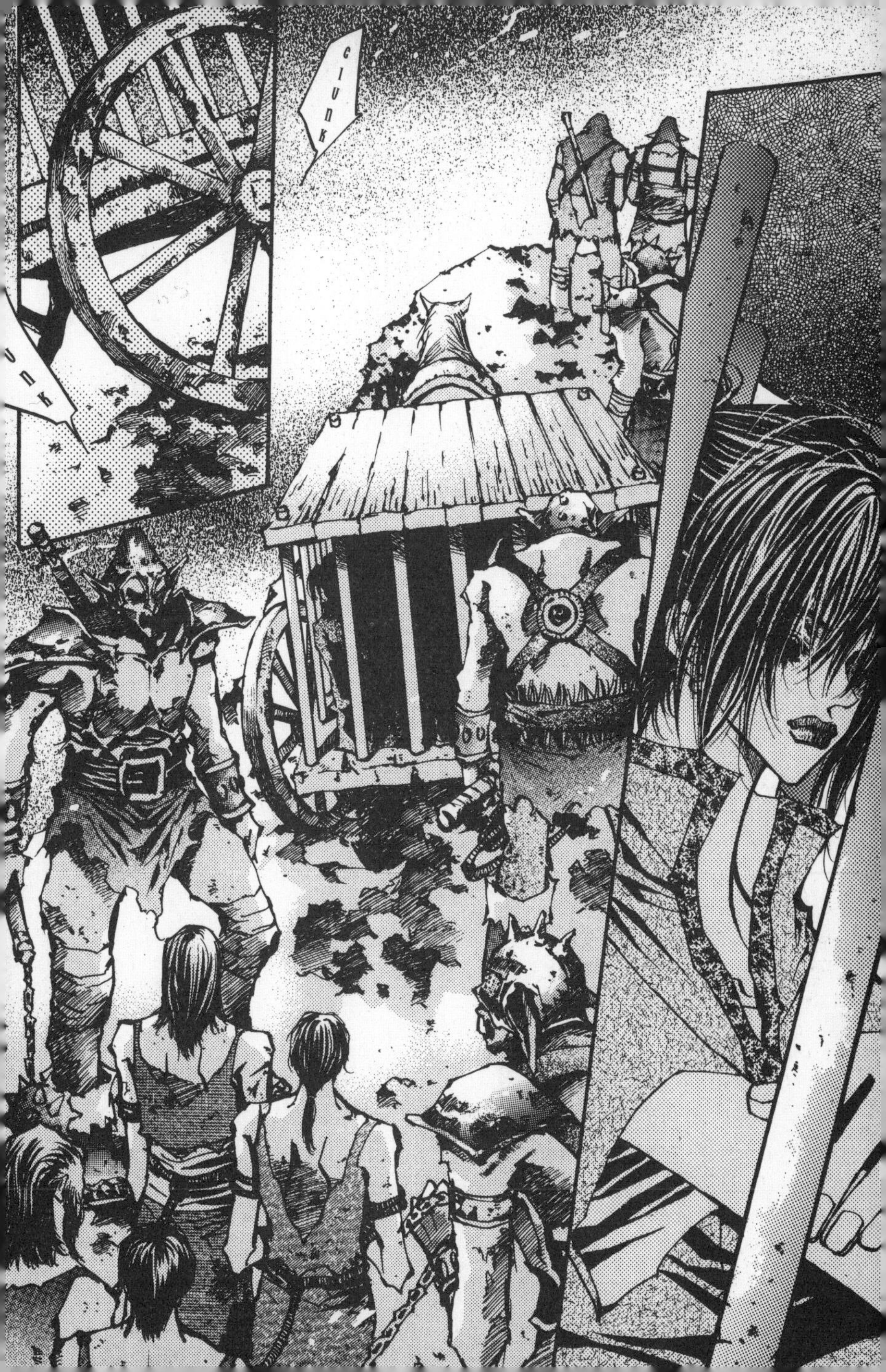
GIUNK
UNK

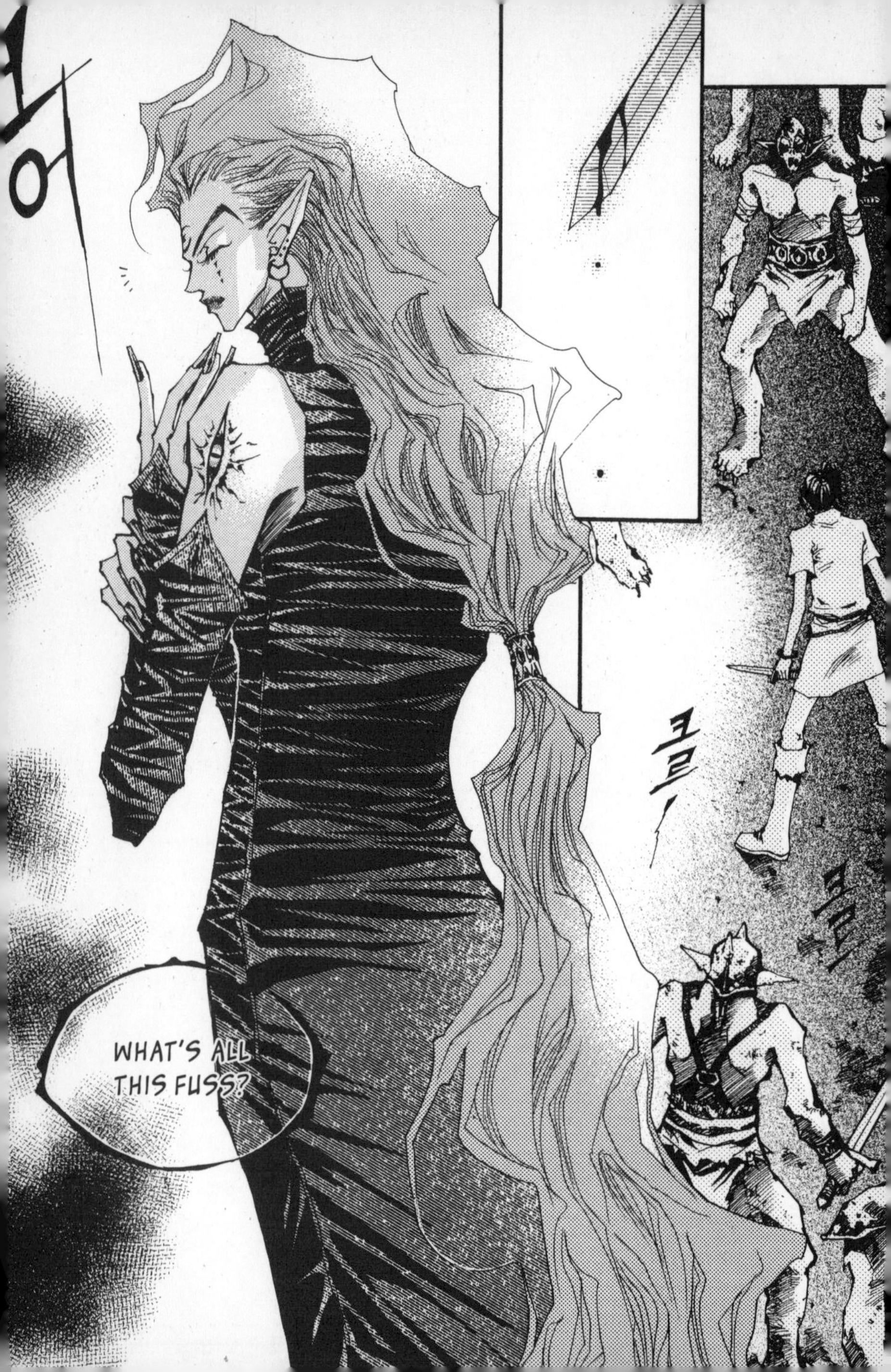
크르
WHAT'S ALL THIS FUSS?

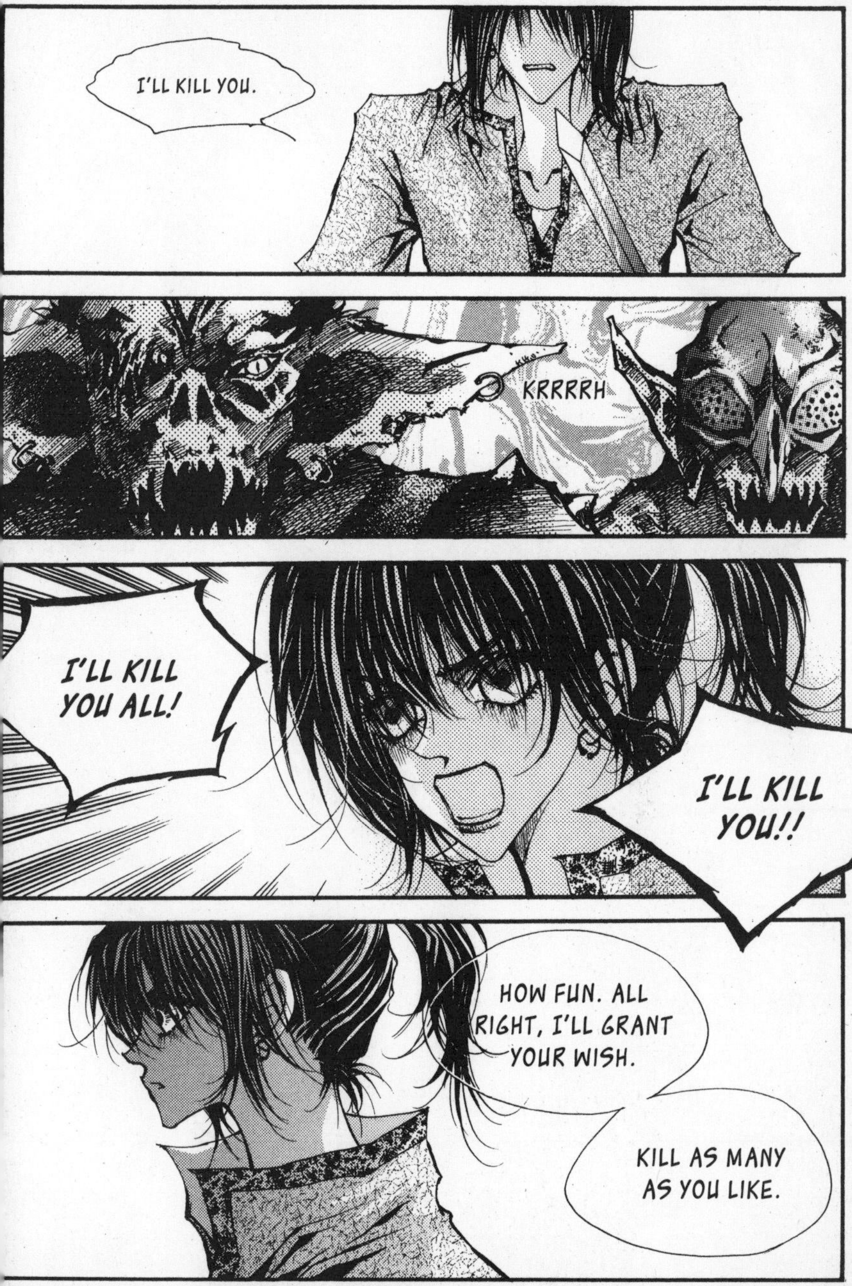
I'LL KILL YOU.
KRRRRH
I'LL KILL YOU!!
I'LL KILL YOU ALL!
HOW FUN. ALL RIGHT, I'LL GRANT YOUR WISH.
KILL AS MANY AS YOU LIKE.

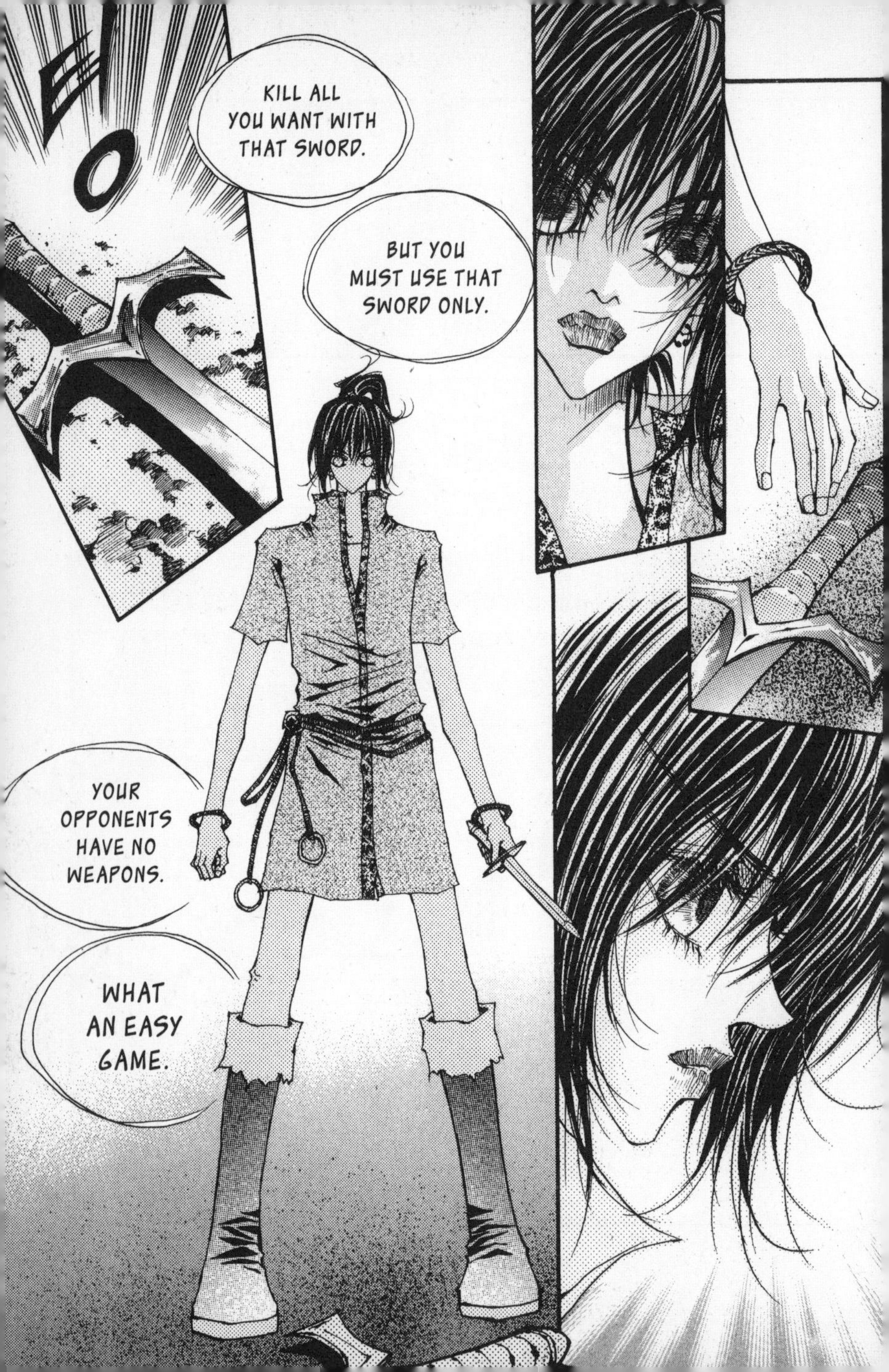
KILL ALL YOU WANT WITH THAT SWORD.
BUT YOU MUST USE THAT SWORD ONLY.
YOUR OPPONENTS HAVE NO WEAPONS.
WHAT AN EASY GAME.

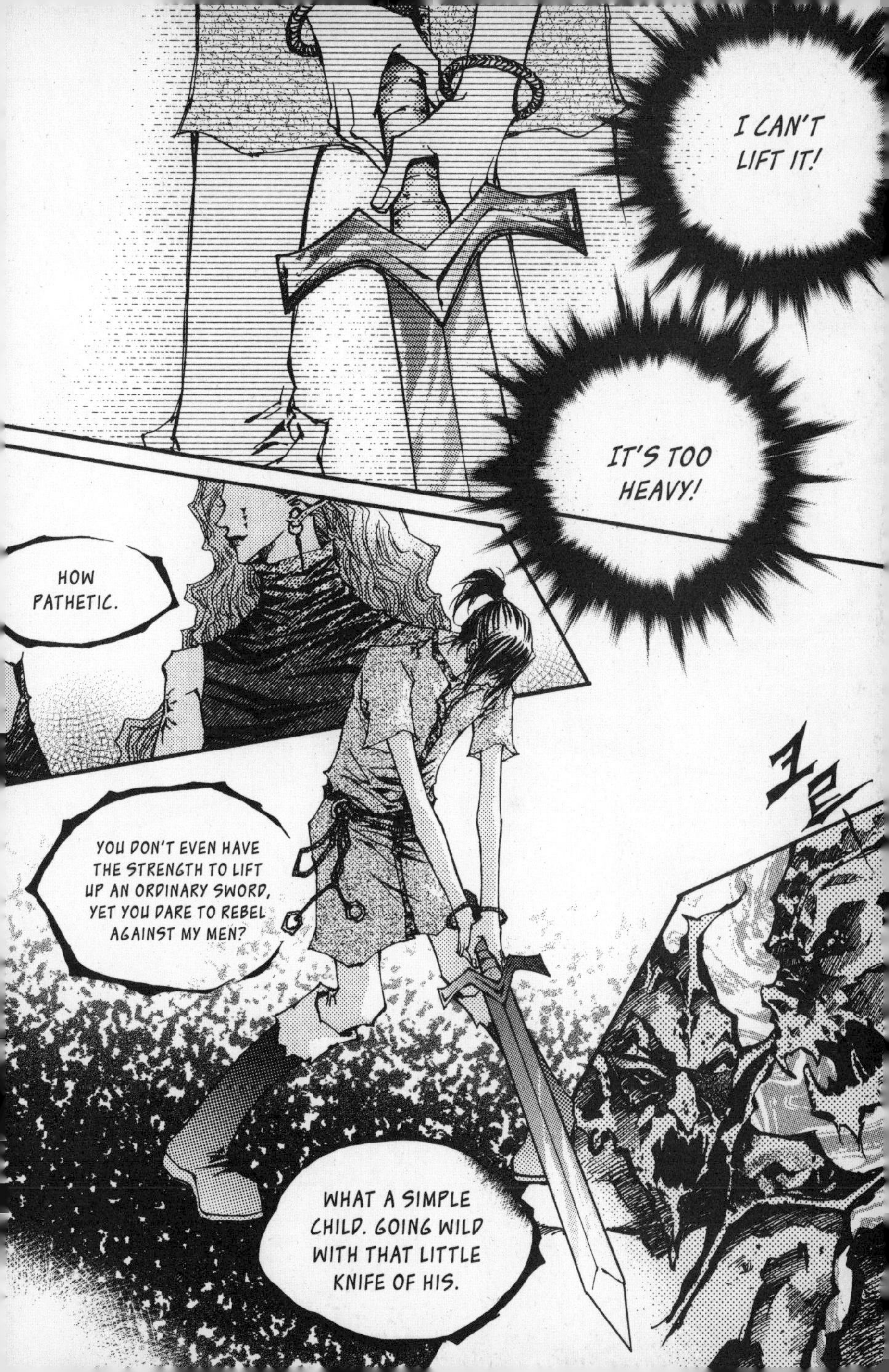
I CAN'T LIFT IT!
IT'S TOO HEAVY!
HOW PATHETIC.
YOU DON'T EVEN HAVE THE STRENGTH TO LIFT UP AN ORDINARY SWORD, YET YOU DARE TO REBEL AGAINST MY MEN?
크르
WHAT A SIMPLE CHILD. GOING WILD WITH THAT LITTLE KNIFE OF HIS.

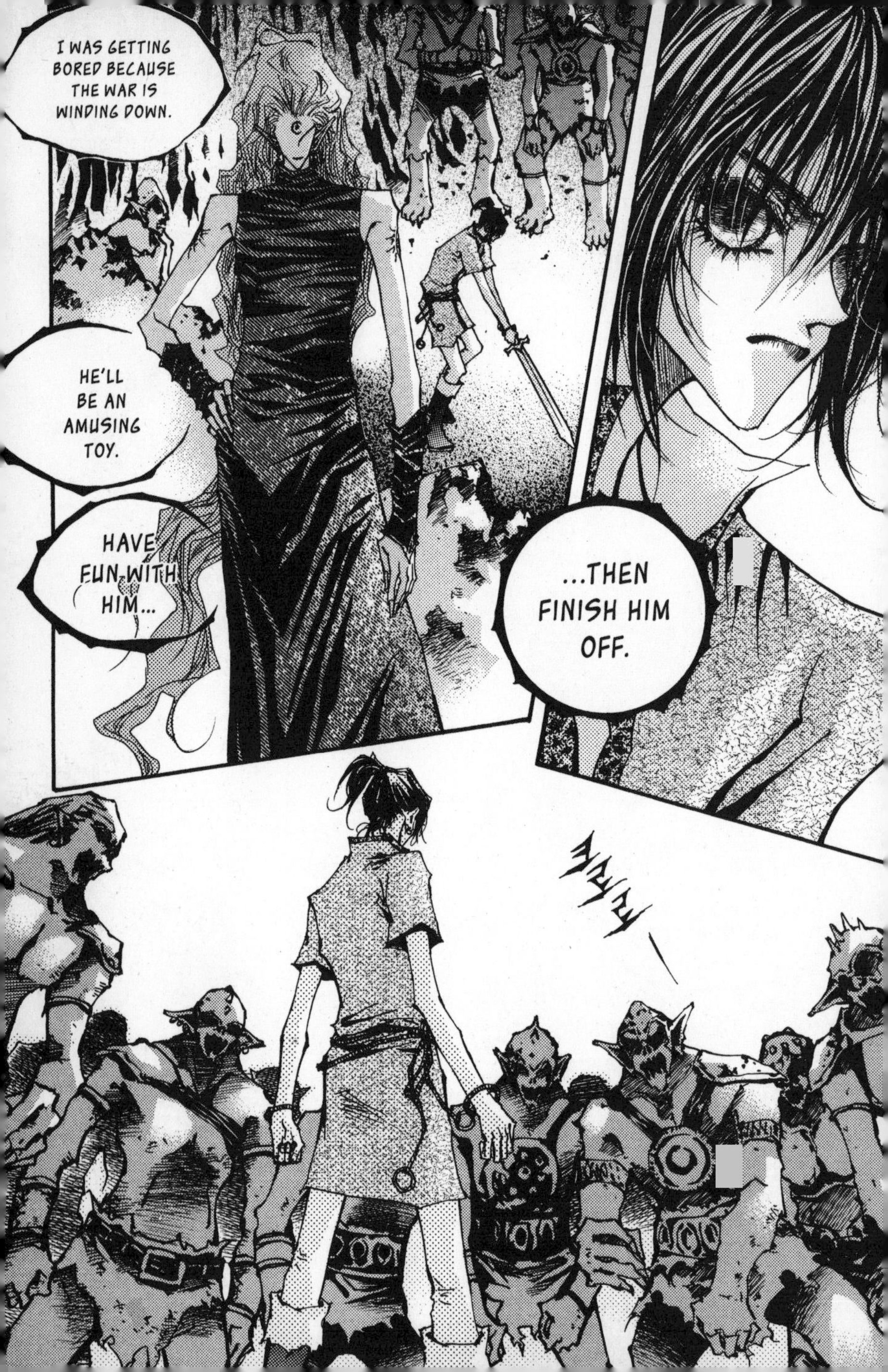
I WAS GETTING BORED BECAUSE THE WAR IS WINDING DOWN.
HE'LL BE AN AMUSING TOY.
HAVE FUN WITH HIM...
...THEN FINISH HIM OFF.

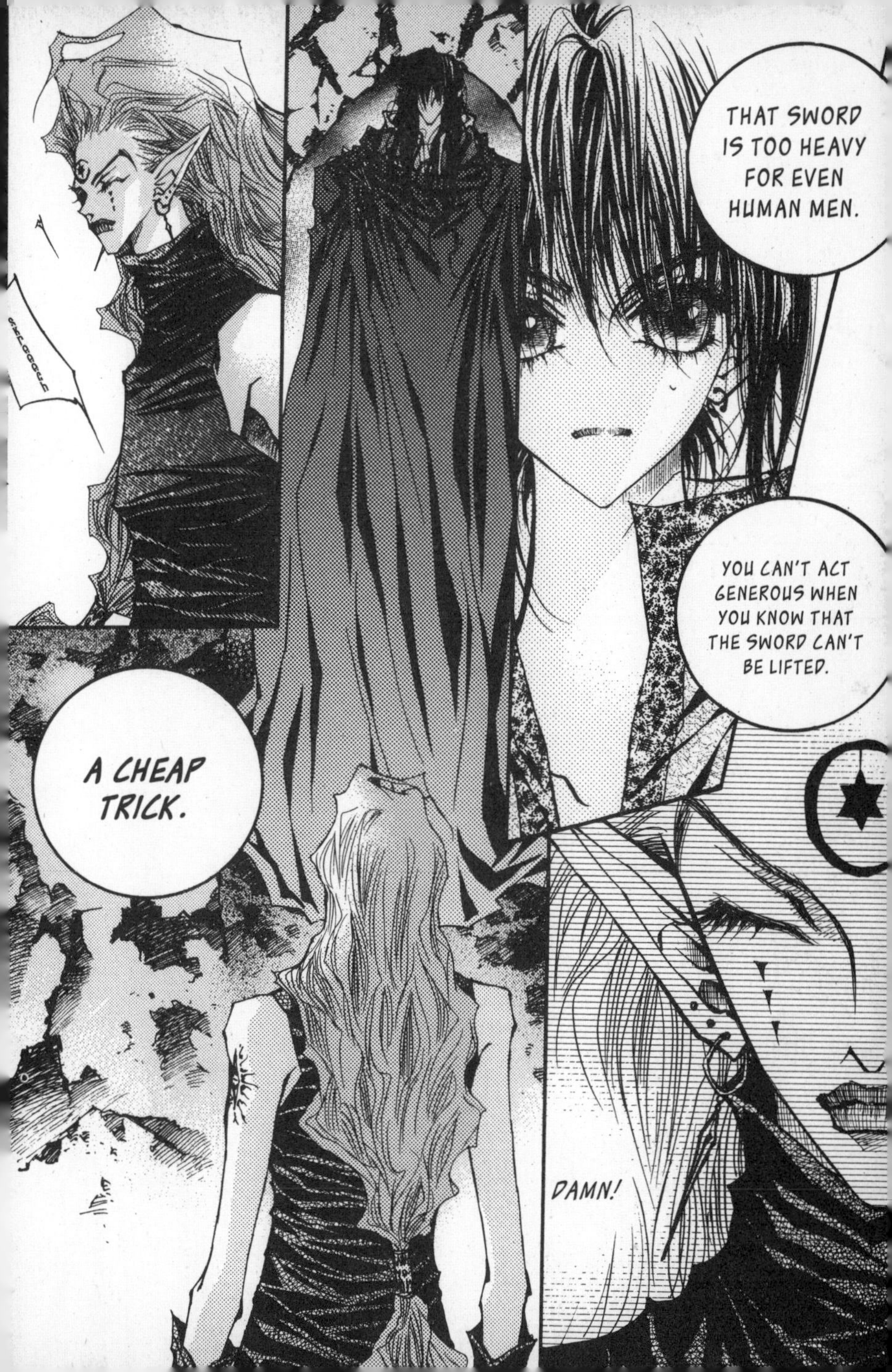
THAT SWORD IS TOO HEAVY FOR EVEN HUMAN MEN.
YOU CAN'T ACT GENEROUS WHEN YOU KNOW THAT THE SWORD CAN'T BE LIFTED.
A CHEAP TRICK.
DAMN!

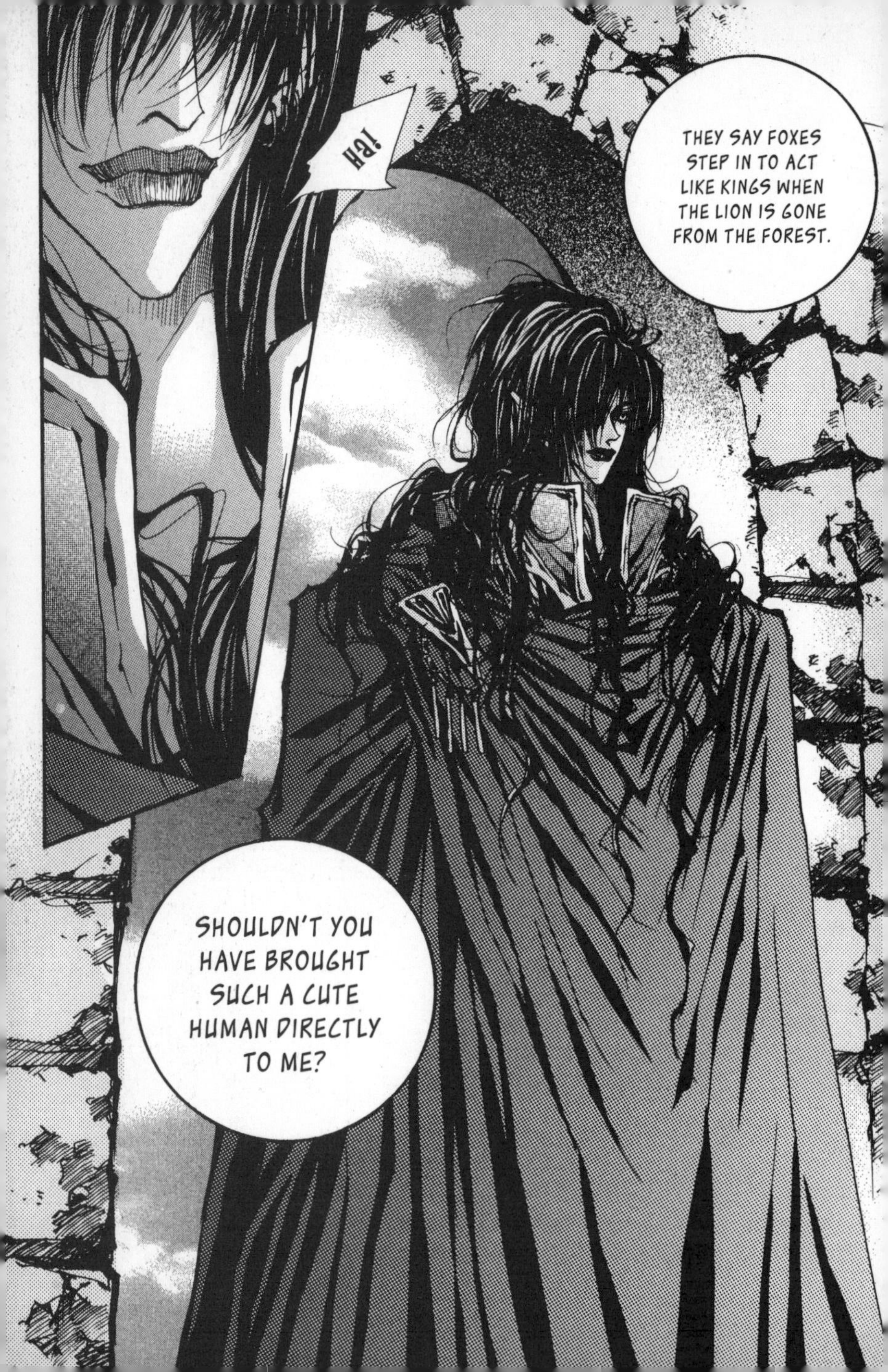
THEY SAY FOXES STEP IN TO ACT LIKE KINGS WHEN THE LION IS GONE FROM THE FOREST.
HA!
SHOULDN'T YOU HAVE BROUGHT SUCH A CUTE HUMAN DIRECTLY TO ME?

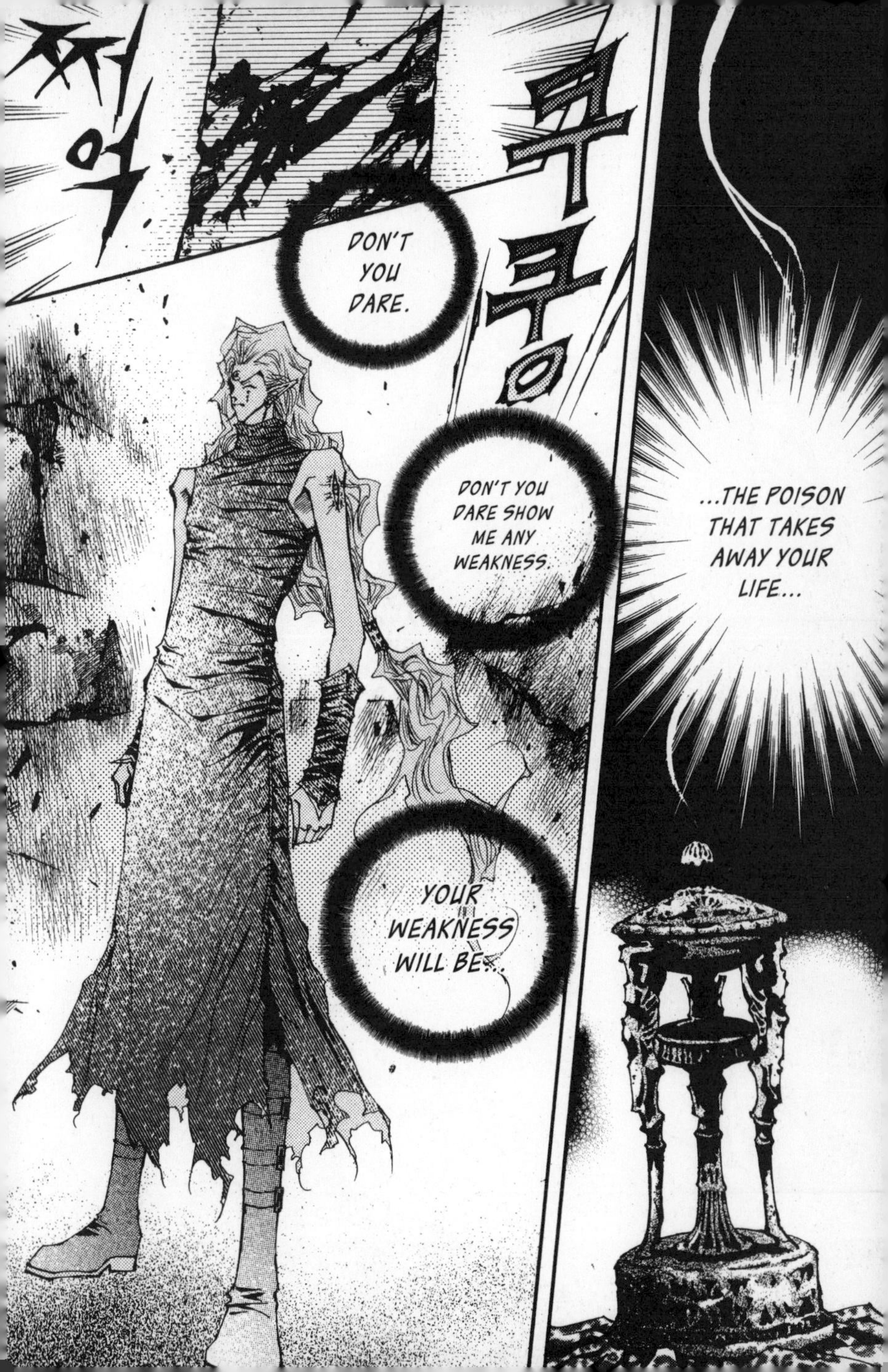
찌억
쿠쿵
DON'T YOU DARE.
DON'T YOU DARE SHOW ME ANY WEAKNESS.
YOUR WEAKNESS WILL BE...
...THE POISON THAT TAKES AWAY YOUR LIFE...

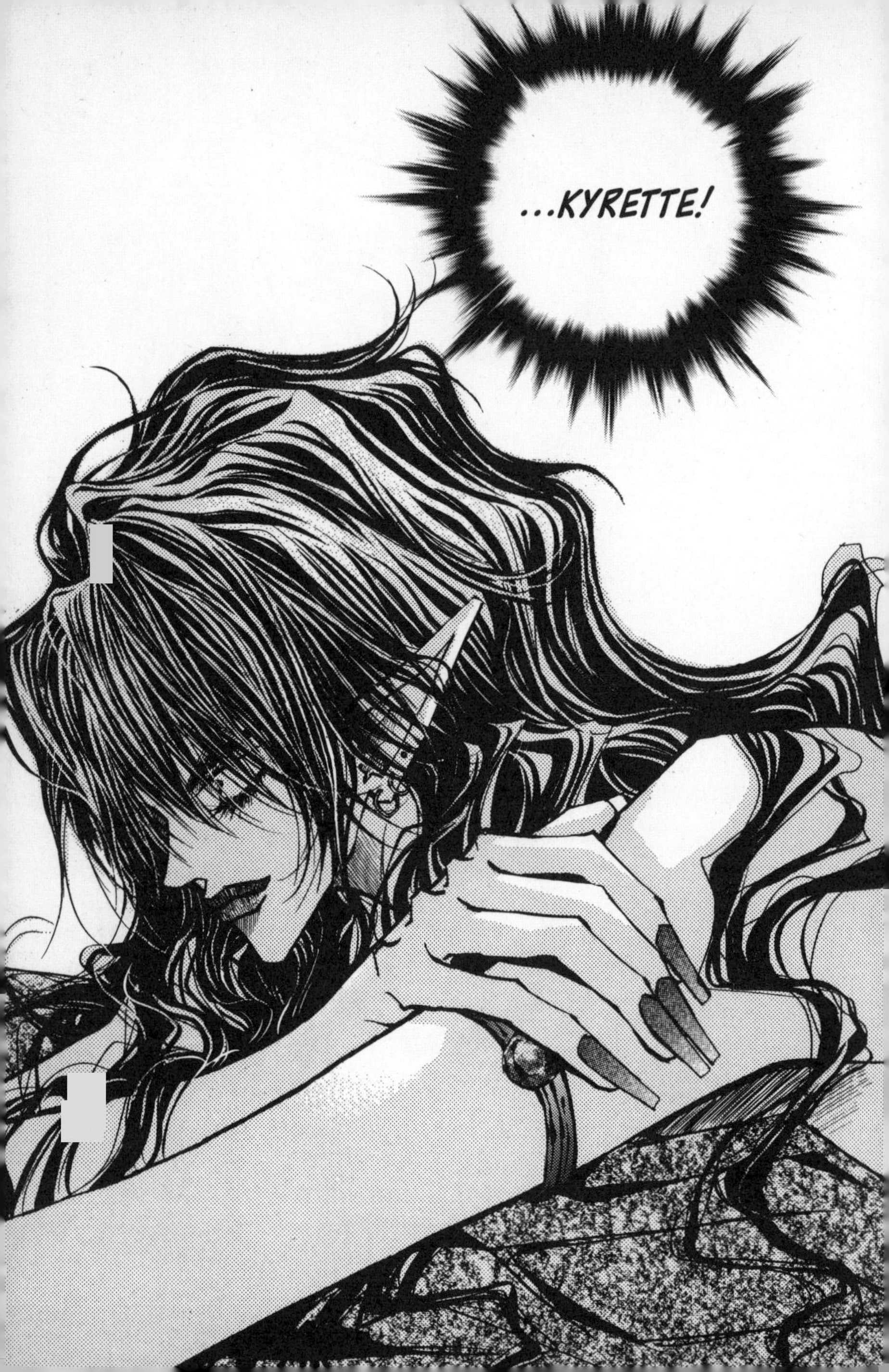
...KYRETTE!

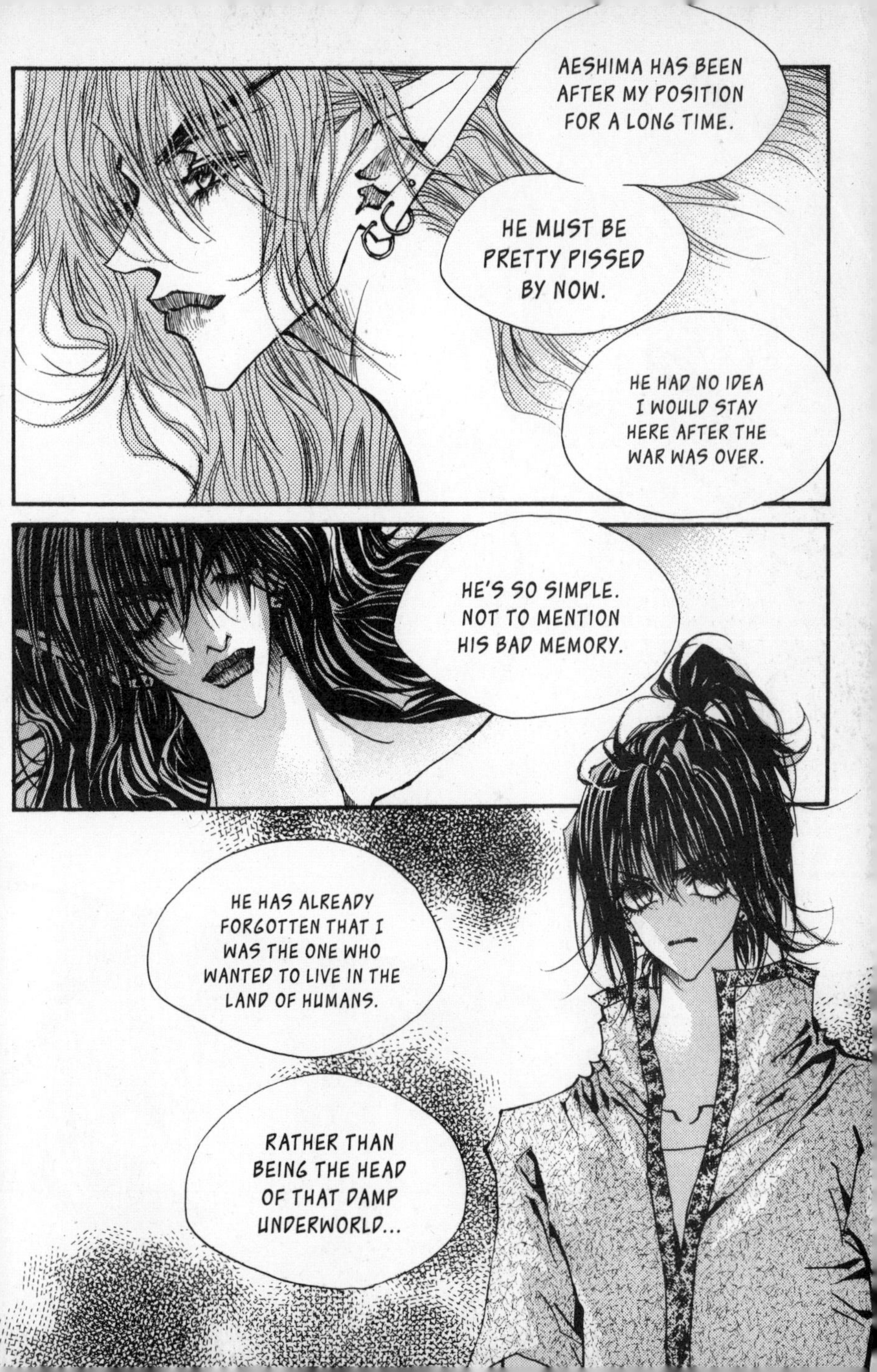
AESHIMA HAS BEEN AFTER MY POSITION FOR A LONG TIME.
HE MUST BE PRETTY PISSED BY NOW.
HE HAD NO IDEA I WOULD STAY HERE AFTER THE WAR WAS OVER.
HE'S SO SIMPLE. NOT TO MENTION HIS BAD MEMORY.
HE HAS ALREADY FORGOTTEN THAT I WAS THE ONE WHO WANTED TO LIVE IN THE LAND OF HUMANS.
RATHER THAN BEING THE HEAD OF THAT DAMP UNDERWORLD...

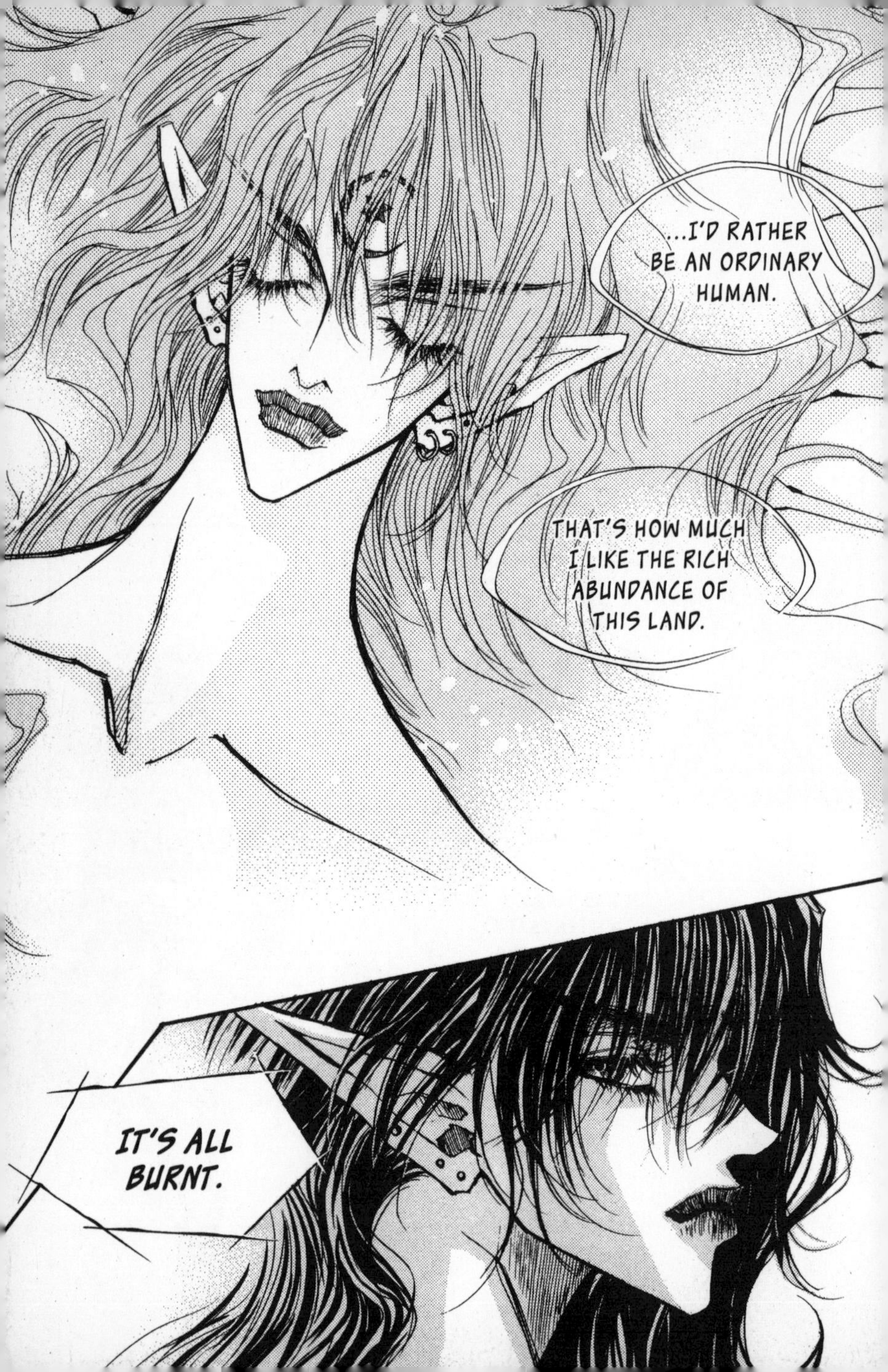
...I'D RATHER BE AN ORDINARY HUMAN.
THAT'S HOW MUCH I LIKE THE RICH ABUNDANCE OF THIS LAND.
IT'S ALL BURNT.

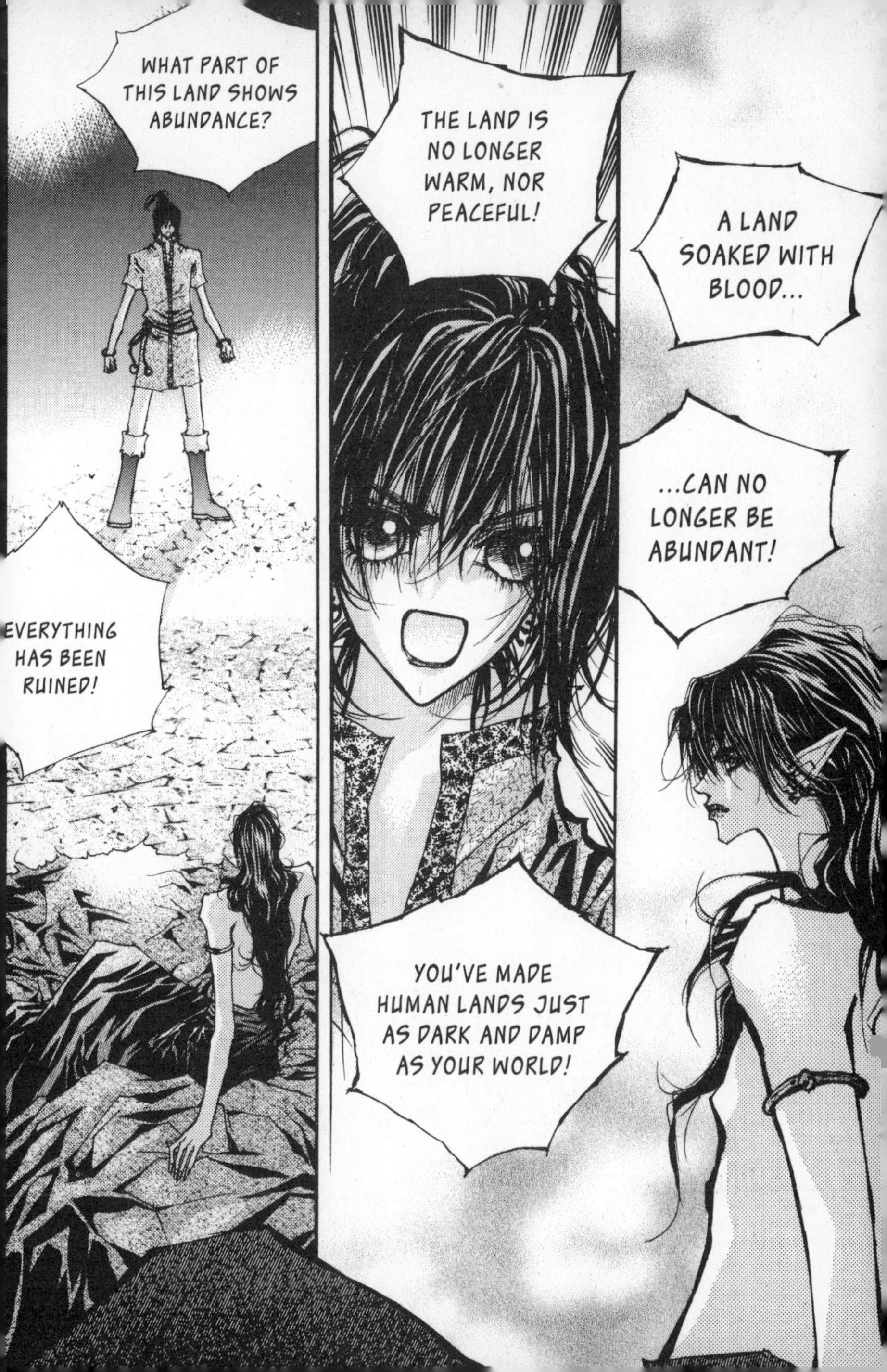

WHAT PART OF THIS LAND SHOWS ABUNDANCE?
EVERYTHING HAS BEEN RUINED!
THE LAND IS NO LONGER WARM, NOR PEACEFUL!
A LAND SOAKED WITH BLOOD...
...CAN NO LONGER BE ABUNDANT!
YOU'VE MADE HUMAN LANDS JUST AS DARK AND DAMP AS YOUR WORLD!

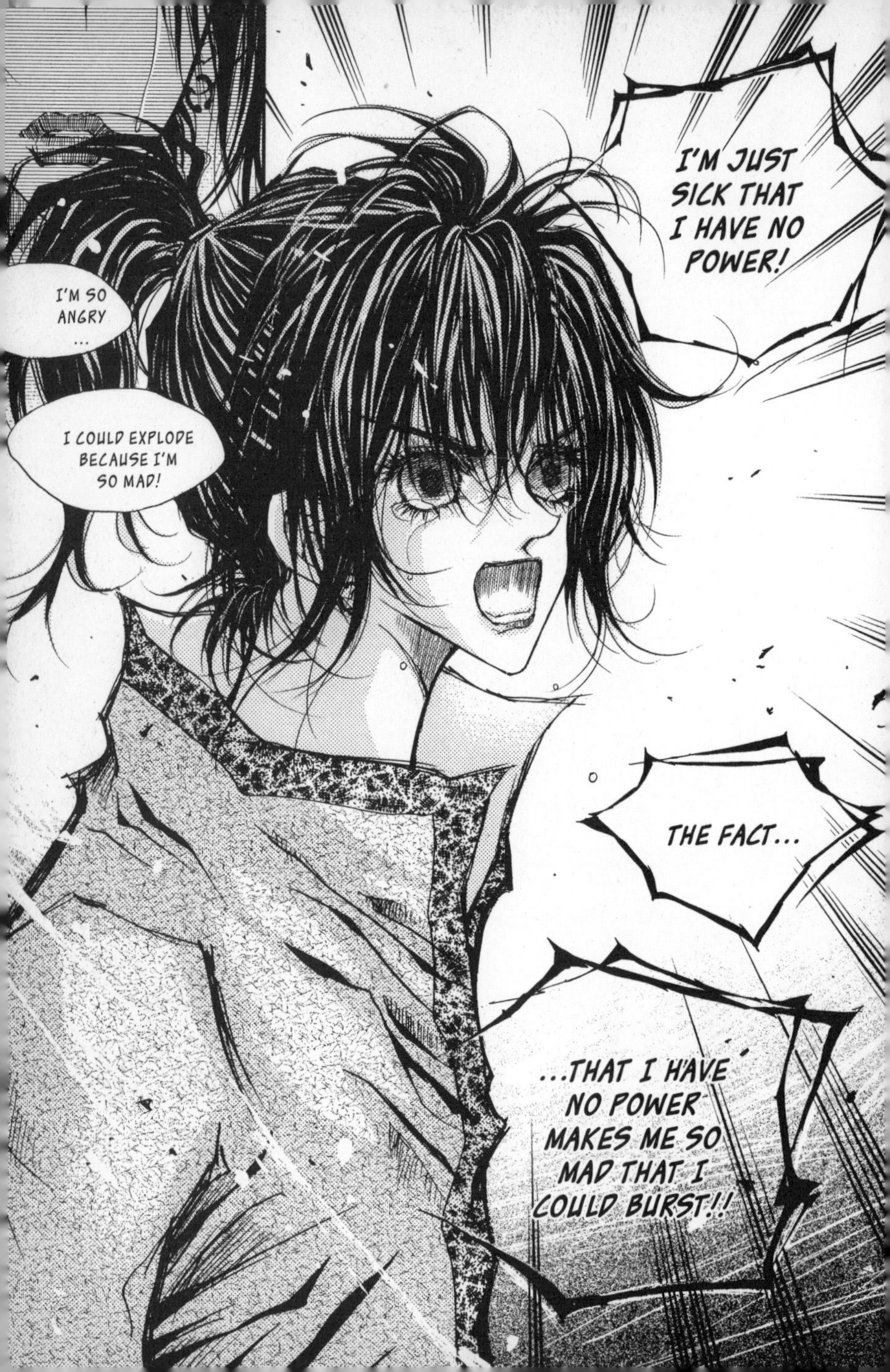
I'M JUST SICK THAT I HAVE NO POWER!
I'M SO ANGRY ...
I COULD EXPLODE BECAUSE I'M SO MAD!
THE FACT...
...THAT I HAVE NO POWER MAKES ME SO MAD THAT I COULD BURST!!

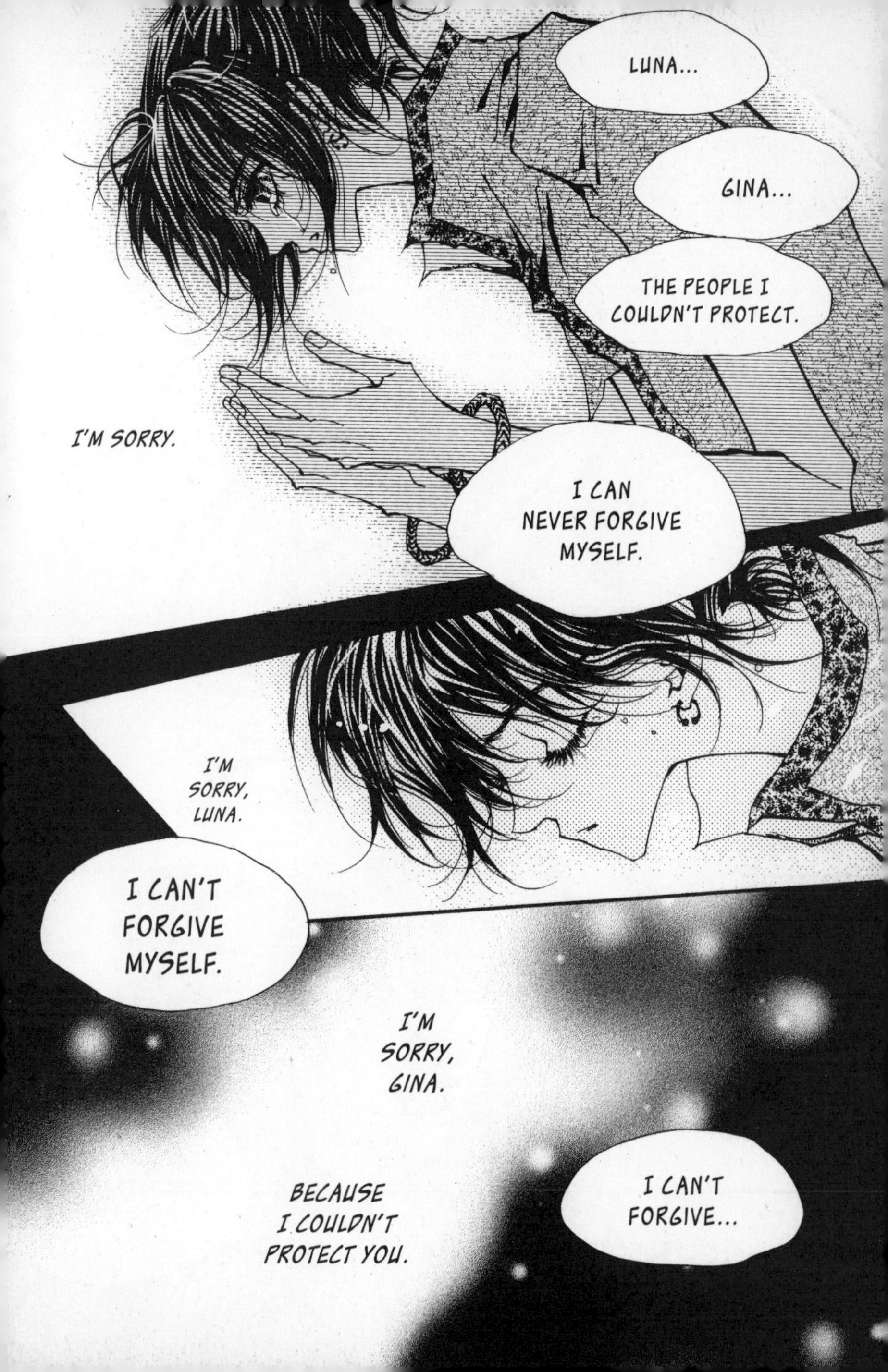
LUNA...
GINA...
THE PEOPLE I COULDN'T PROTECT.
I'M SORRY.
I CAN NEVER FORGIVE MYSELF.
I'M SORRY, LUNA.
I CAN'T FORGIVE MYSELF.
I'M SORRY, GINA.
I CAN'T FORGIVE...
BECAUSE I COULDN'T PROTECT YOU.

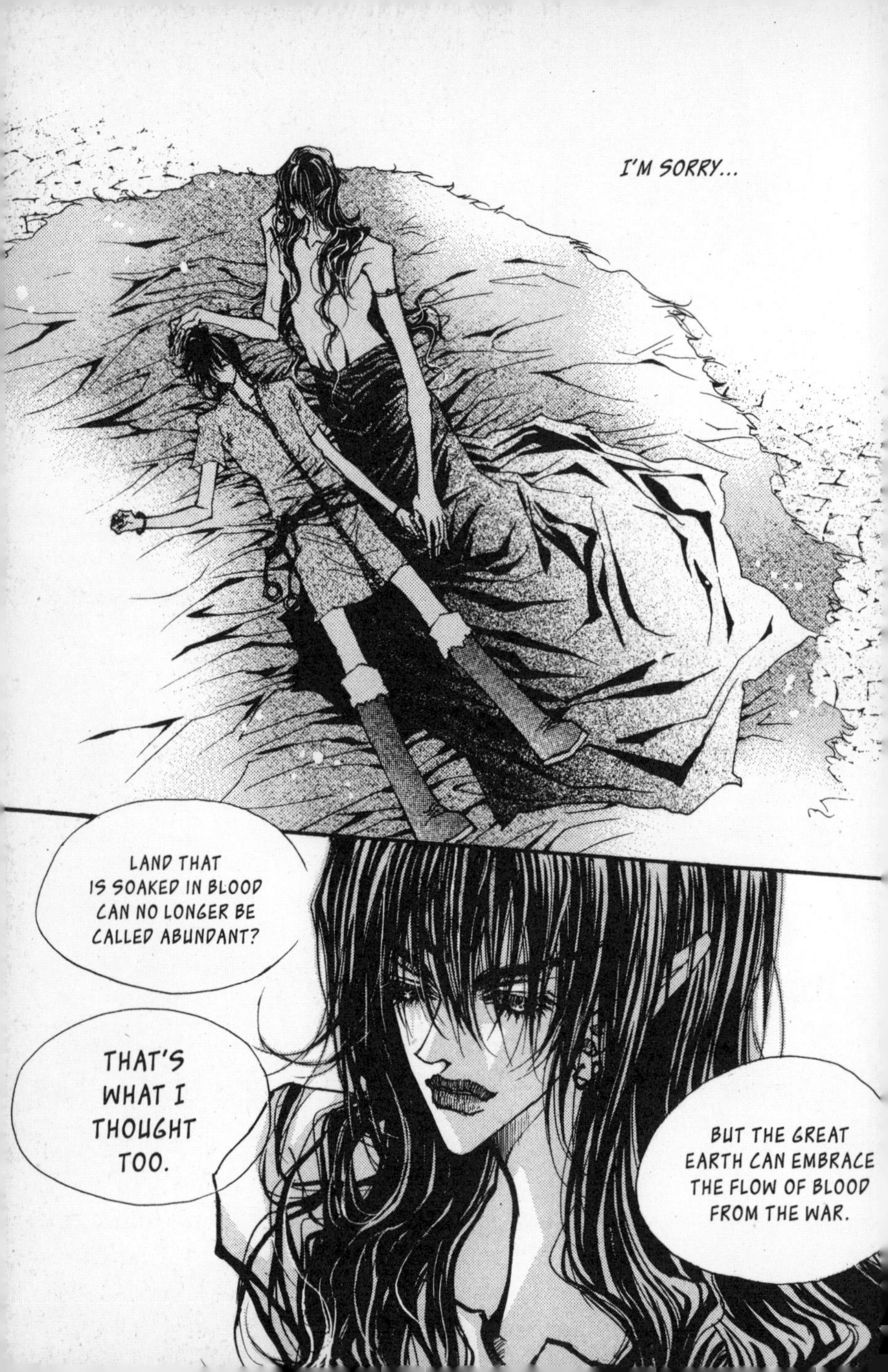
I'M SORRY...
LAND THAT IS SOAKED IN BLOOD CAN NO LONGER BE CALLED ABUNDANT?
THAT'S WHAT I THOUGHT TOO.
BUT THE GREAT EARTH CAN EMBRACE THE FLOW OF BLOOD FROM THE WAR.

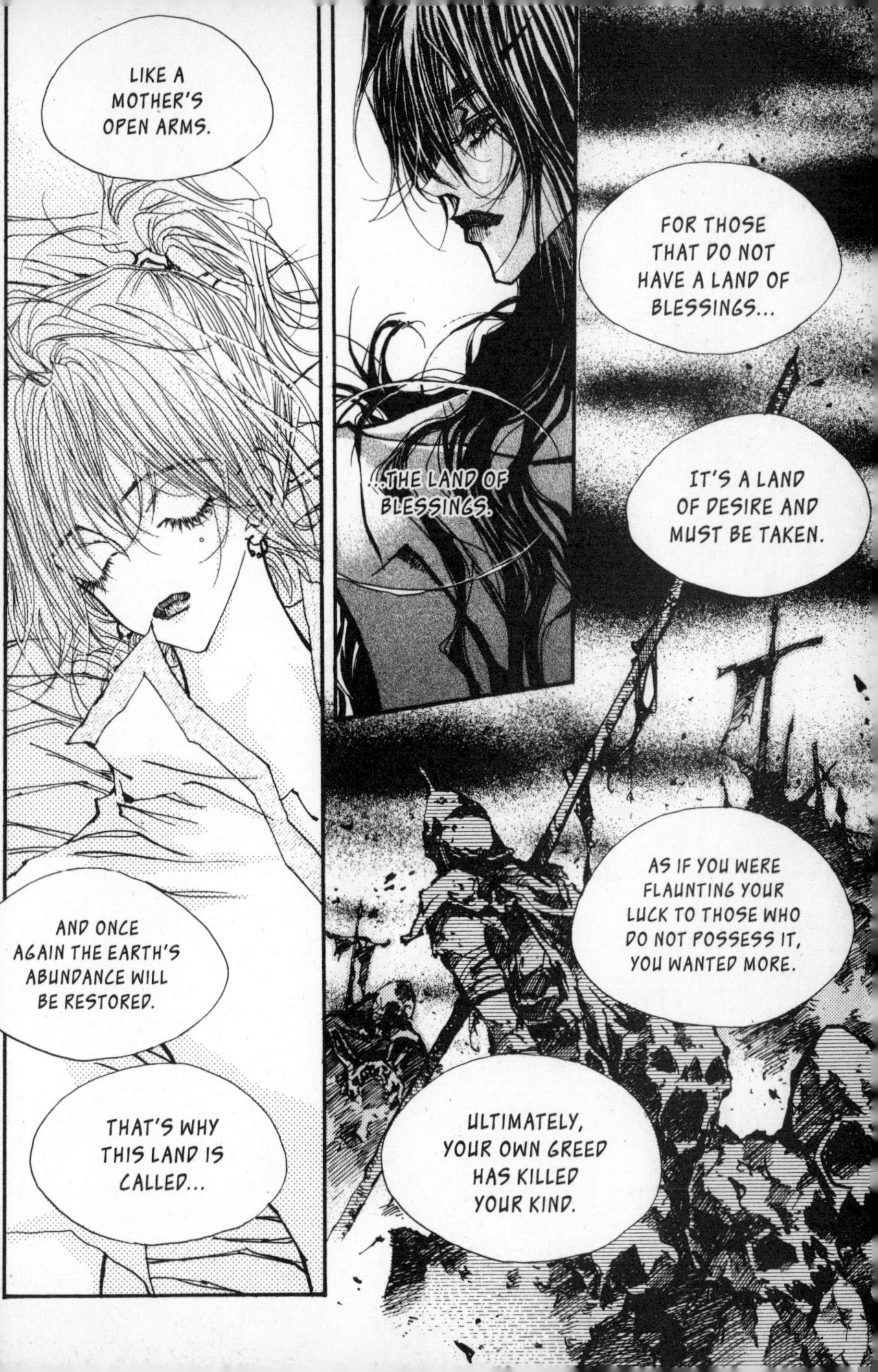
LIKE A MOTHER'S OPEN ARMS.
AND ONCE AGAIN THE EARTH'S ABUNDANCE WILL BE RESTORED.
THAT'S WHY THIS LAND IS CALLED...
...THE LAND OF BLESSINGS.
FOR THOSE THAT DO NOT HAVE A LAND OF BLESSINGS...
IT'S A LAND OF DESIRE AND MUST BE TAKEN.
AS IF YOU WERE FLAUNTING YOUR LUCK TO THOSE WHO DO NOT POSSESS IT, YOU WANTED MORE.
ULTIMATELY, YOUR OWN GREED HAS KILLED YOUR KIND.

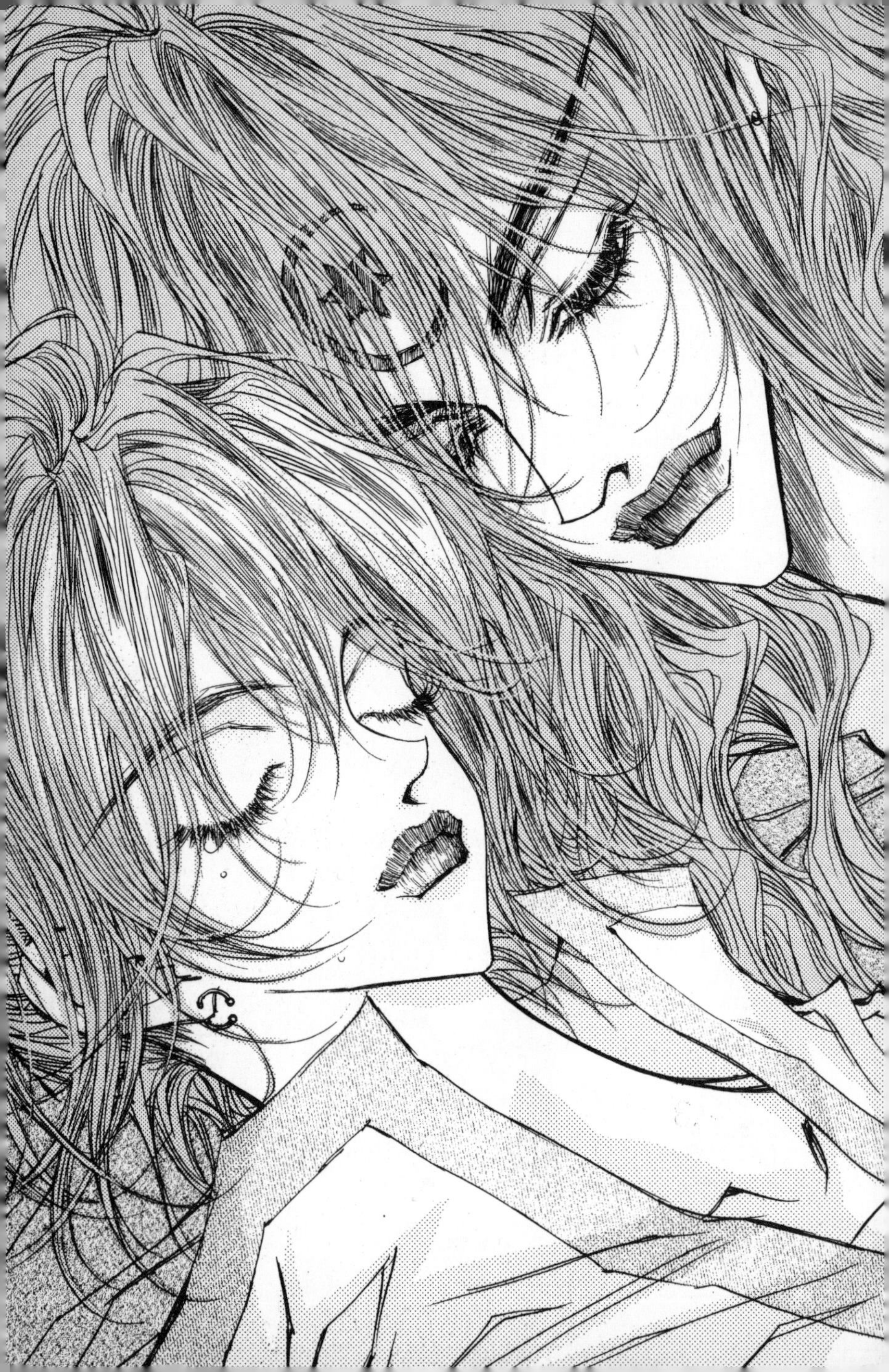

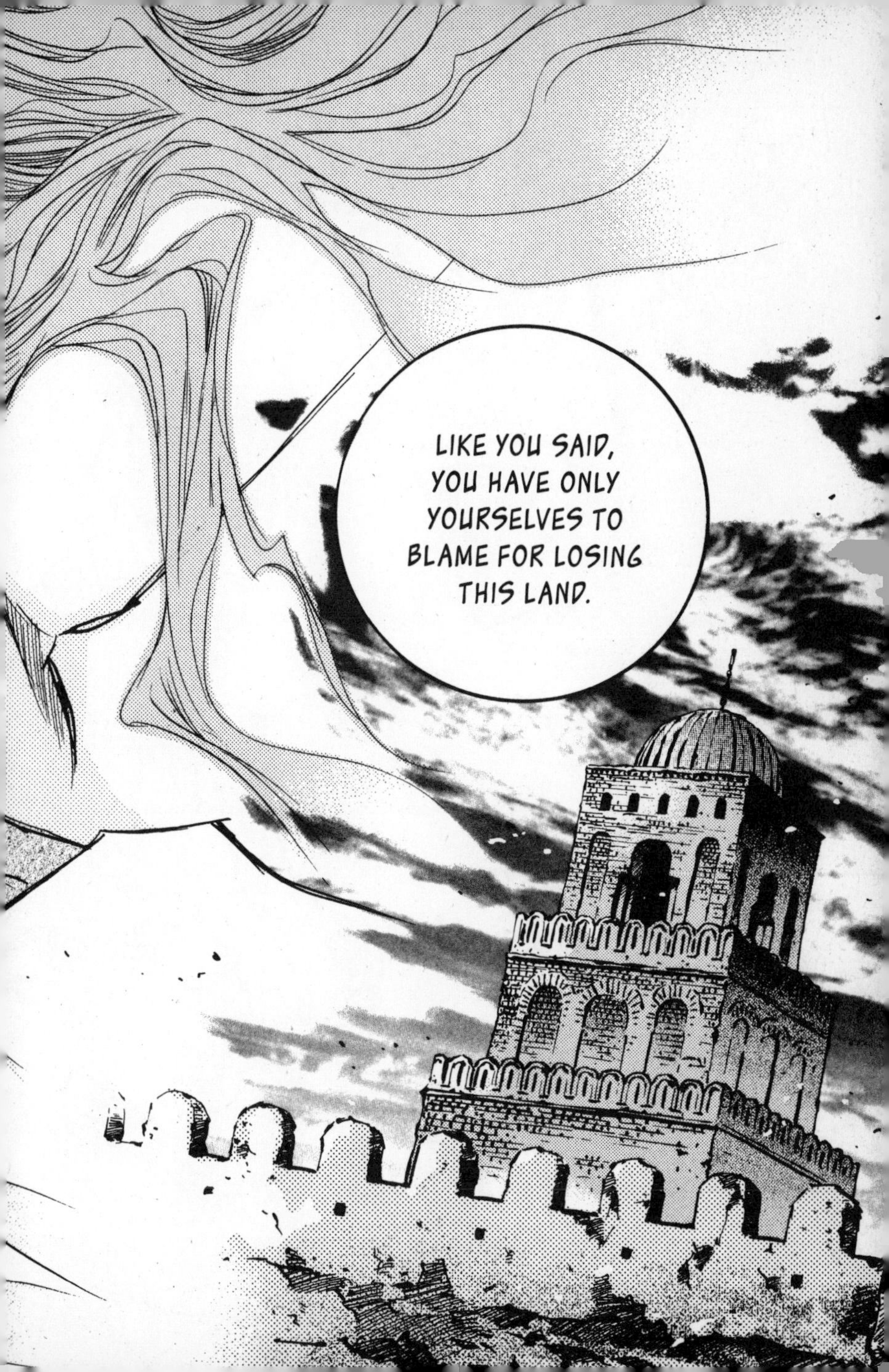
LIKE YOU SAID, YOU HAVE ONLY YOURSELVES TO BLAME FOR LOSING THIS LAND.

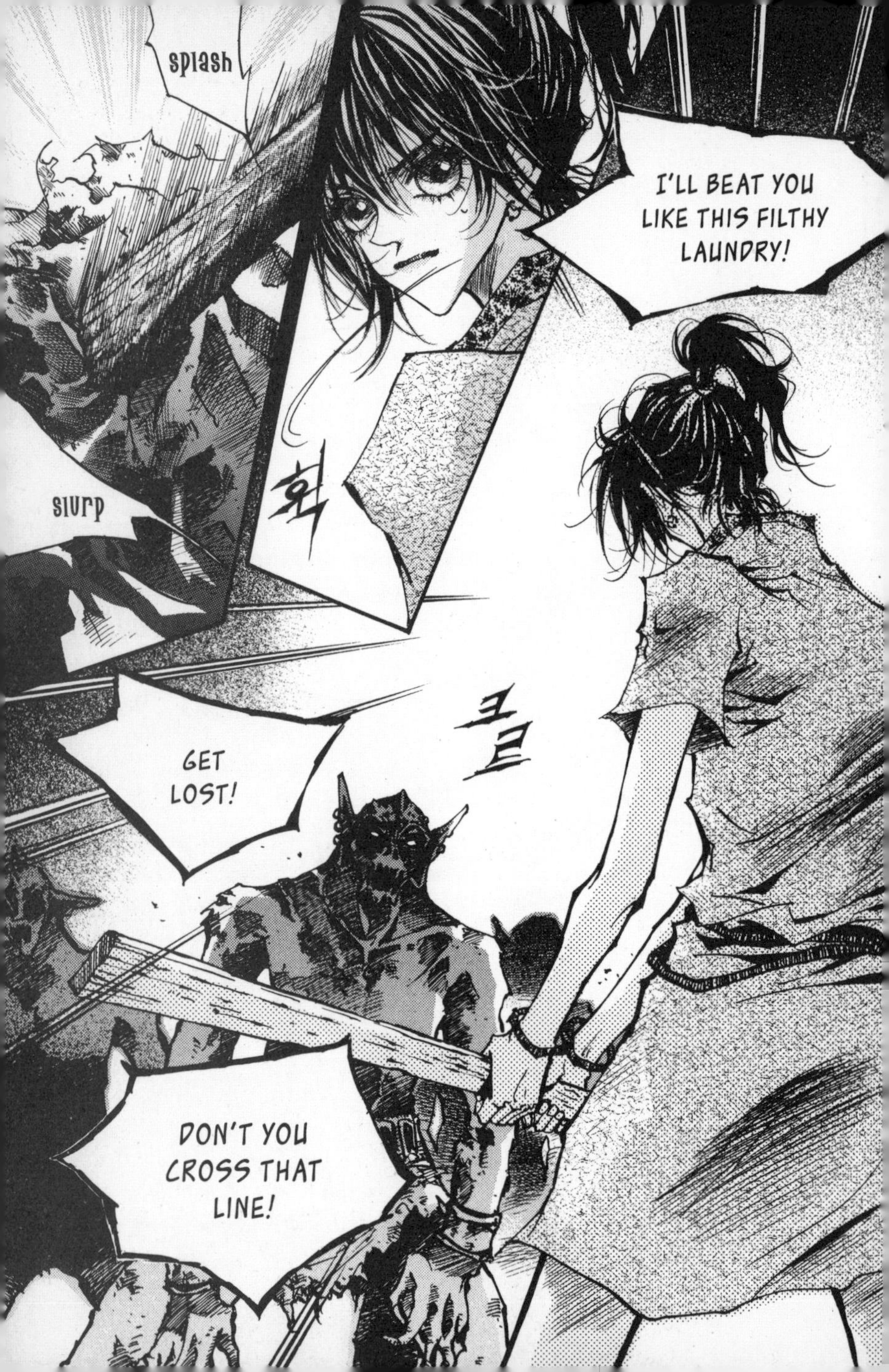
splash
slurp
I'LL BEAT YOU LIKE THIS FILTHY LAUNDRY!
휙
크르
GET LOST!
DON'T YOU CROSS THAT LINE!

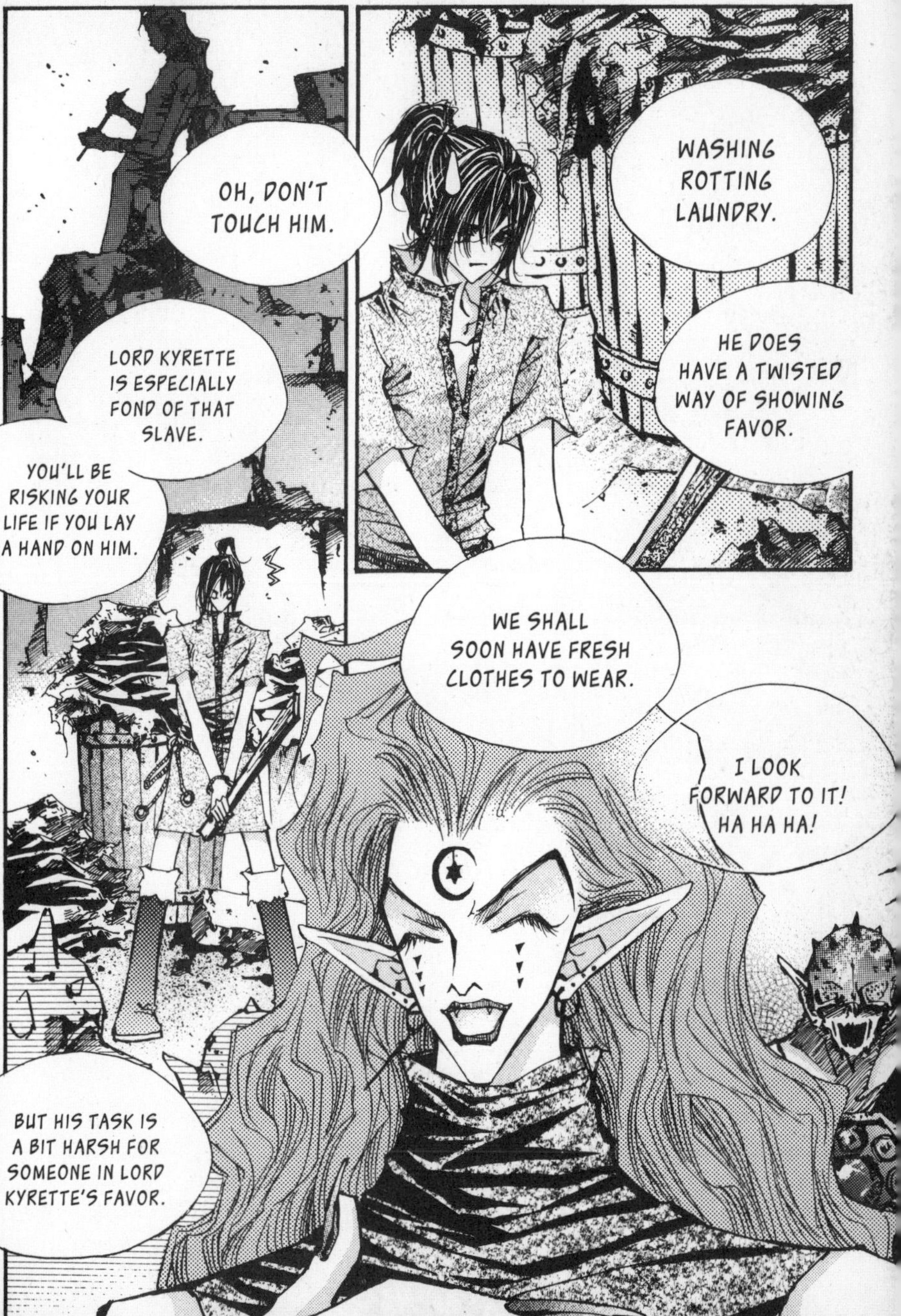
OH, DON'T TOUCH HIM.
LORD KYRETTE IS ESPECIALLY FOND OF THAT SLAVE.
YOU'LL BE RISKING YOUR LIFE IF YOU LAY A HAND ON HIM.
BUT HIS TASK IS A BIT HARSH FOR SOMEONE IN LORD KYRETTE'S FAVOR.
WASHING ROTTING LAUNDRY.
HE DOES HAVE A TWISTED WAY OF SHOWING FAVOR.
WE SHALL SOON HAVE FRESH CLOTHES TO WEAR.
I LOOK FORWARD TO IT! HA HA HA!

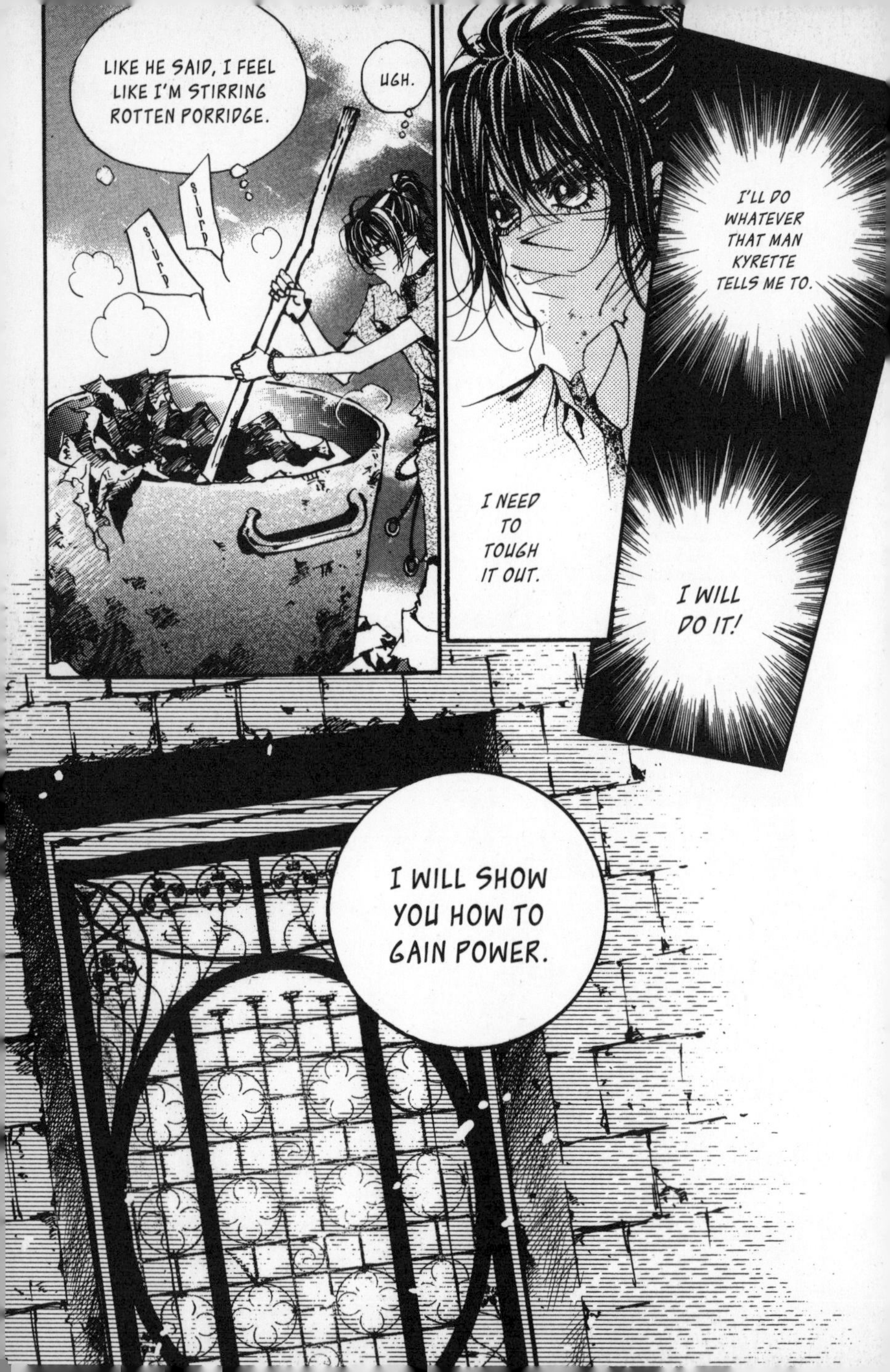
I'LL DO WHATEVER THAT MAN KYRETTE TELLS ME TO.
I NEED TO TOUGH IT OUT.
I WILL DO IT!
UGH.
LIKE HE SAID, I FEEL LIKE I'M STIRRING ROTTEN PORRIDGE.
slurp
slurp
I WILL SHOW YOU HOW TO GAIN POWER.

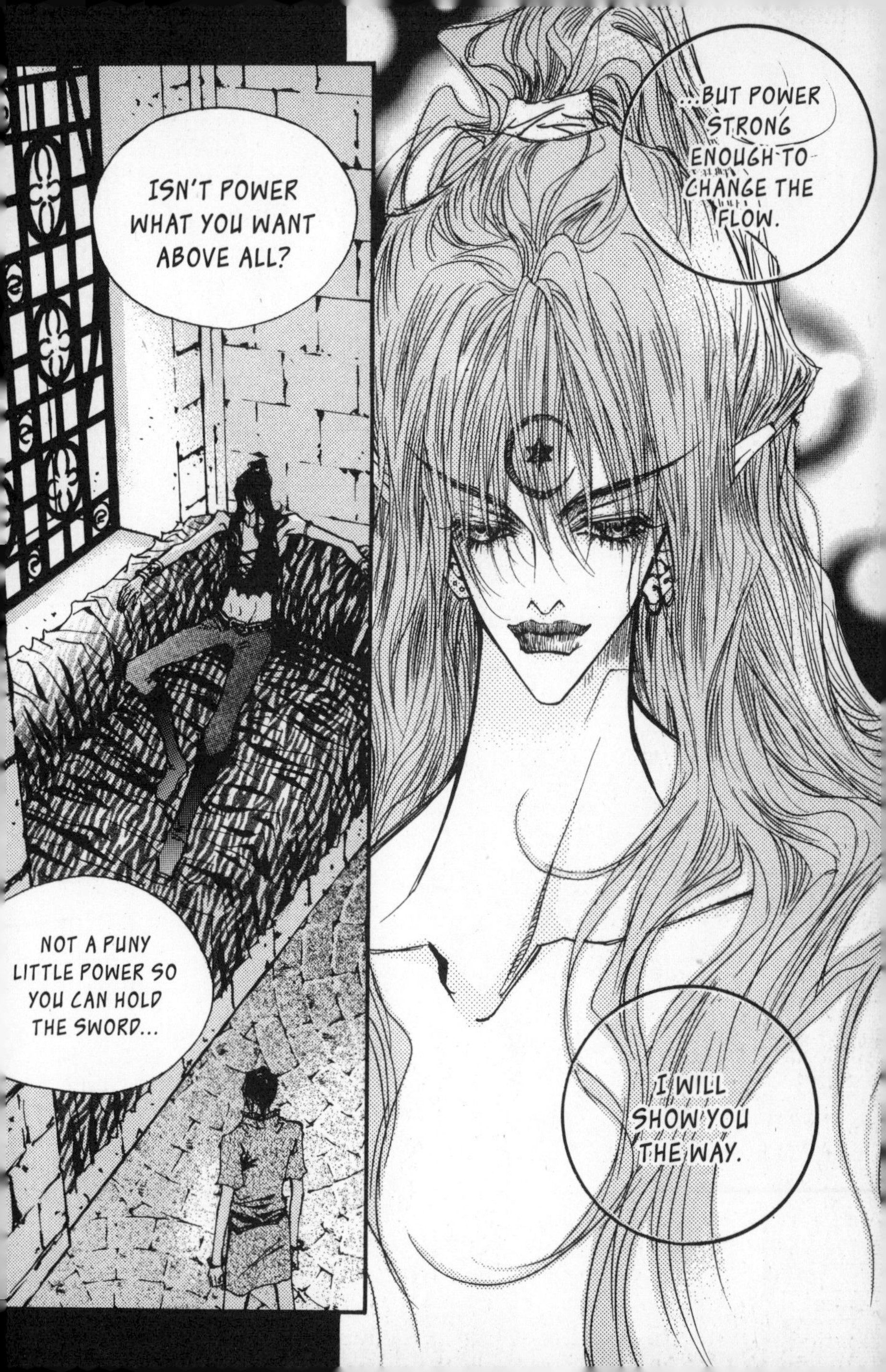
ISN'T POWER WHAT YOU WANT ABOVE ALL?
NOT A PUNY LITTLE POWER SO YOU CAN HOLD THE SWORD...
...BUT POWER STRONG ENOUGH TO CHANGE THE FLOW.
I WILL SHOW YOU THE WAY.

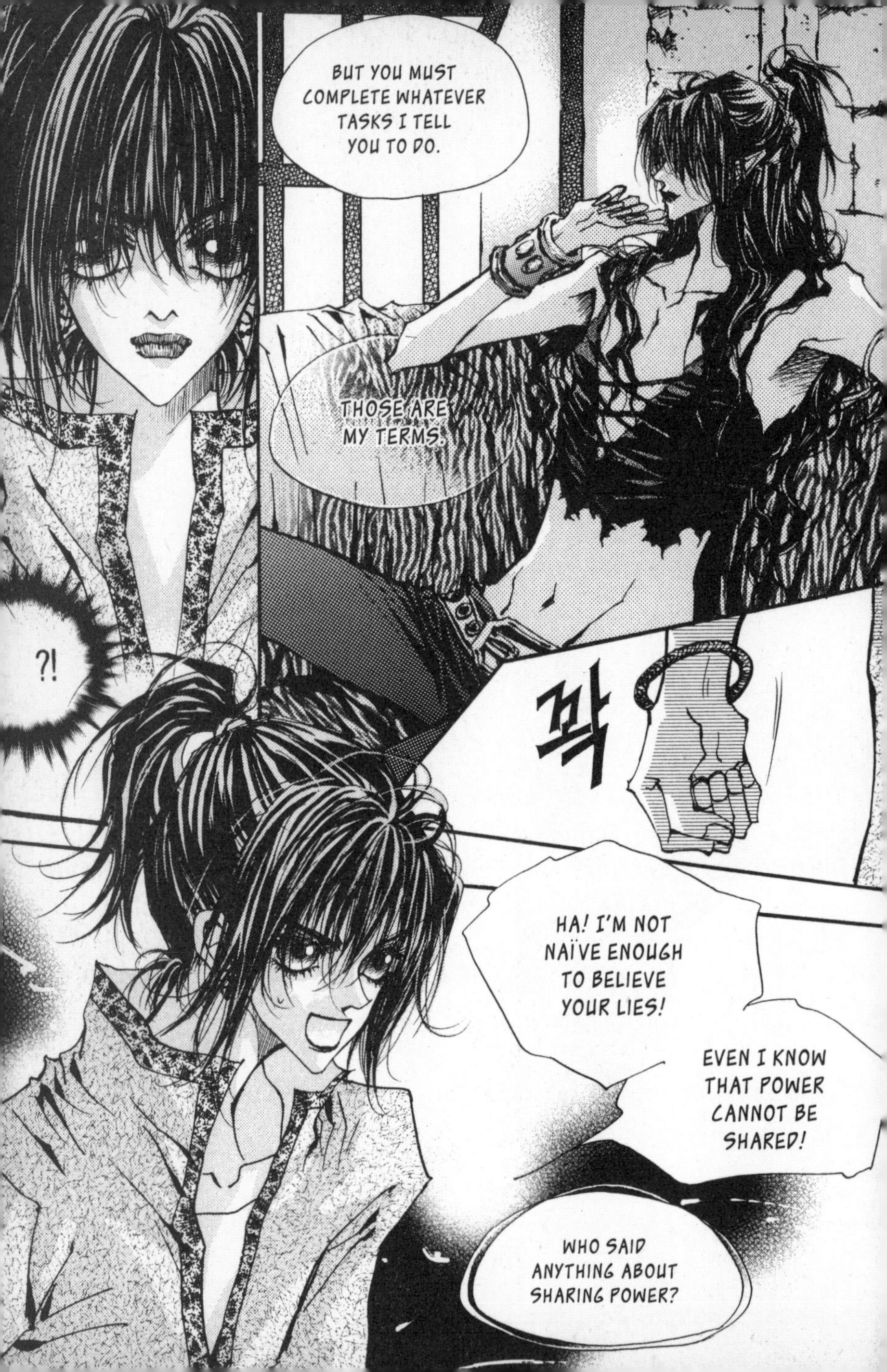
BUT YOU MUST COMPLETE WHATEVER TASKS I TELL YOU TO DO.
THOSE ARE MY TERMS.
?!
꽉
HA! I'M NOT NAÏVE ENOUGH TO BELIEVE YOUR LIES!
EVEN I KNOW THAT POWER CANNOT BE SHARED!
WHO SAID ANYTHING ABOUT SHARING POWER?

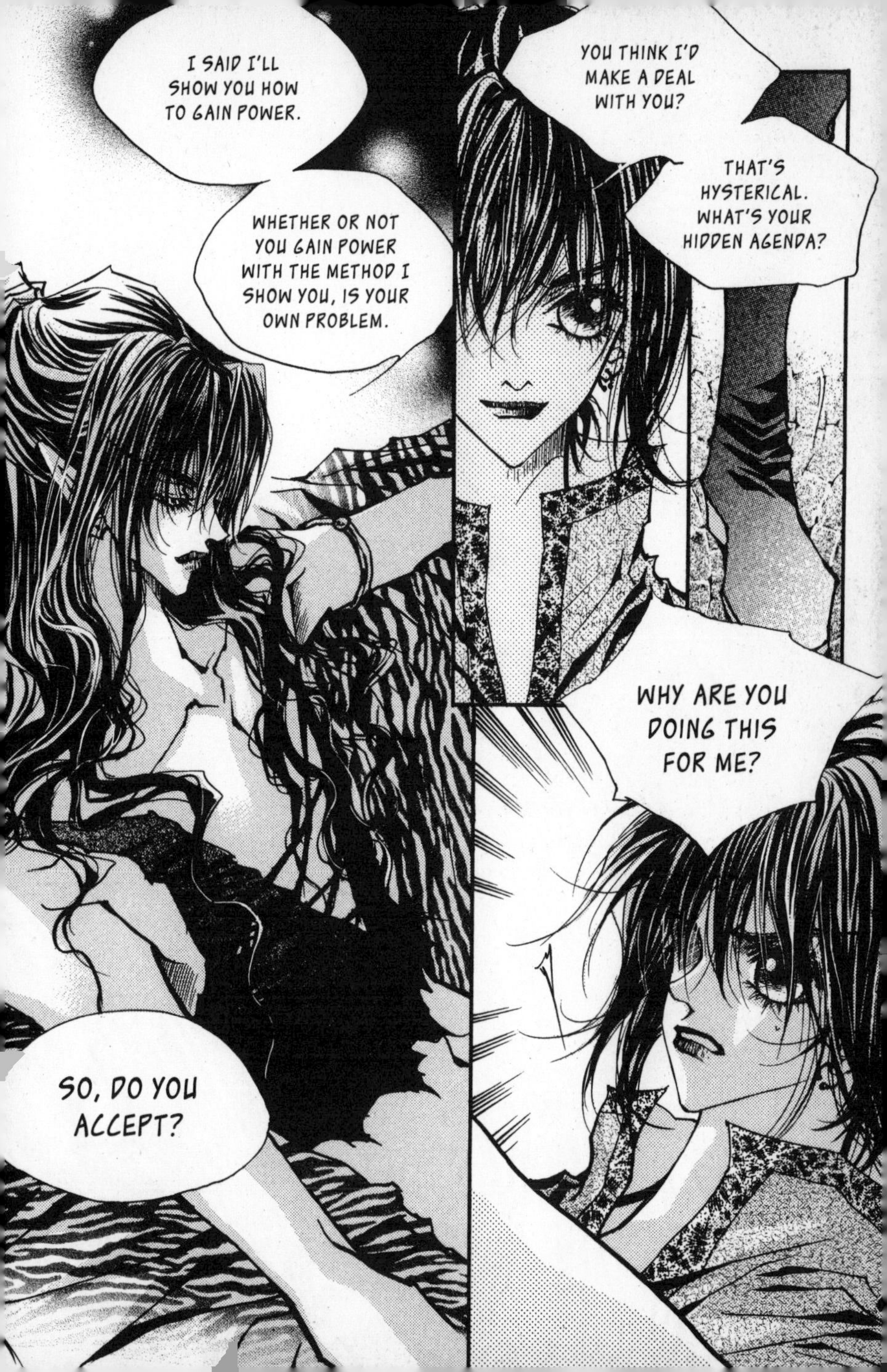
YOU THINK I'D MAKE A DEAL WITH YOU?
THAT'S HYSTERICAL. WHAT'S YOUR HIDDEN AGENDA?
WHY ARE YOU DOING THIS FOR ME?
I SAID I'LL SHOW YOU HOW TO GAIN POWER.
WHETHER OR NOT YOU GAIN POWER WITH THE METHOD I SHOW YOU, IS YOUR OWN PROBLEM.
SO, DO YOU ACCEPT?

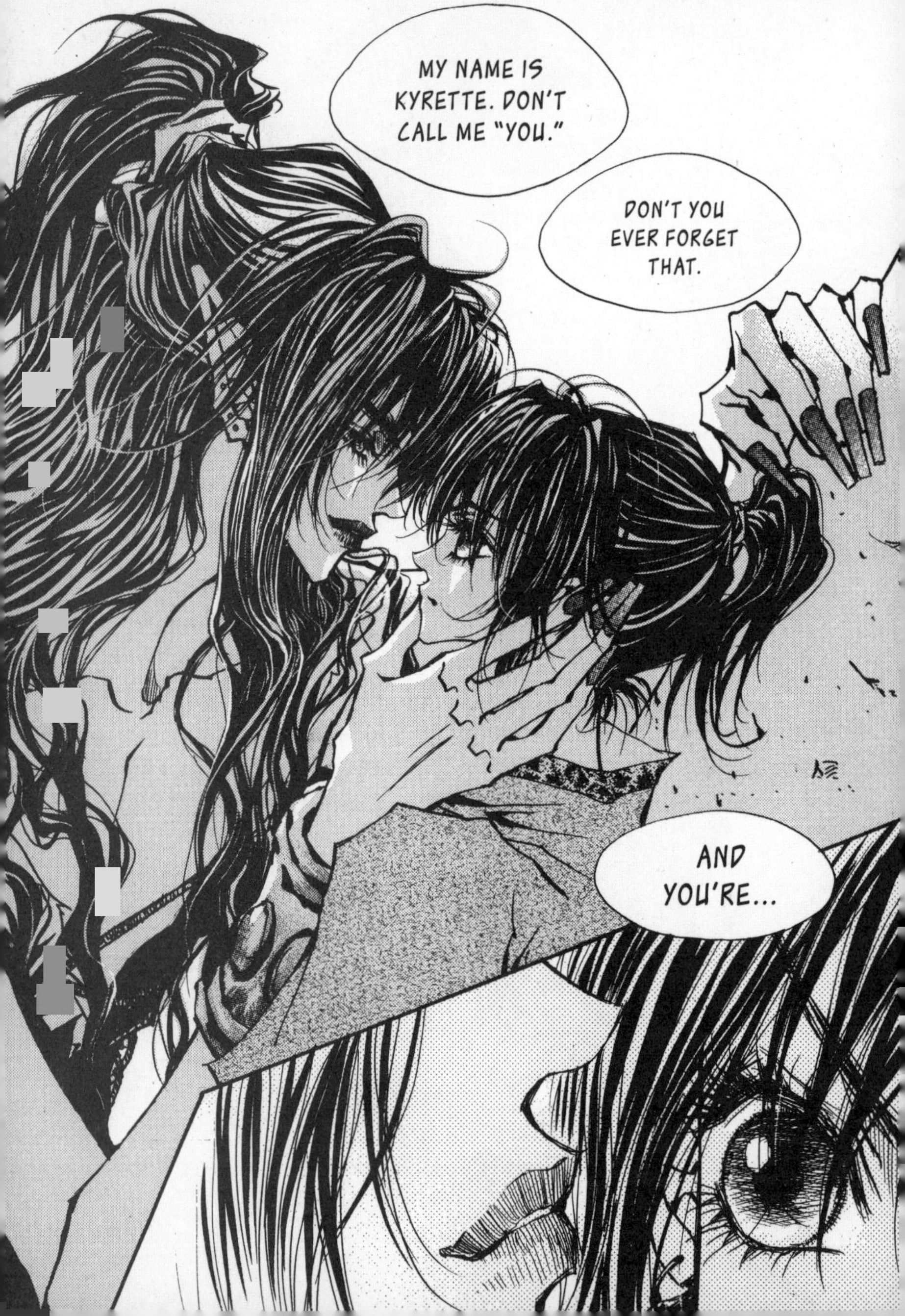
MY NAME IS KYRETTE. DON'T CALL ME "YOU."
DON'T YOU EVER FORGET THAT.
AND YOU'RE...

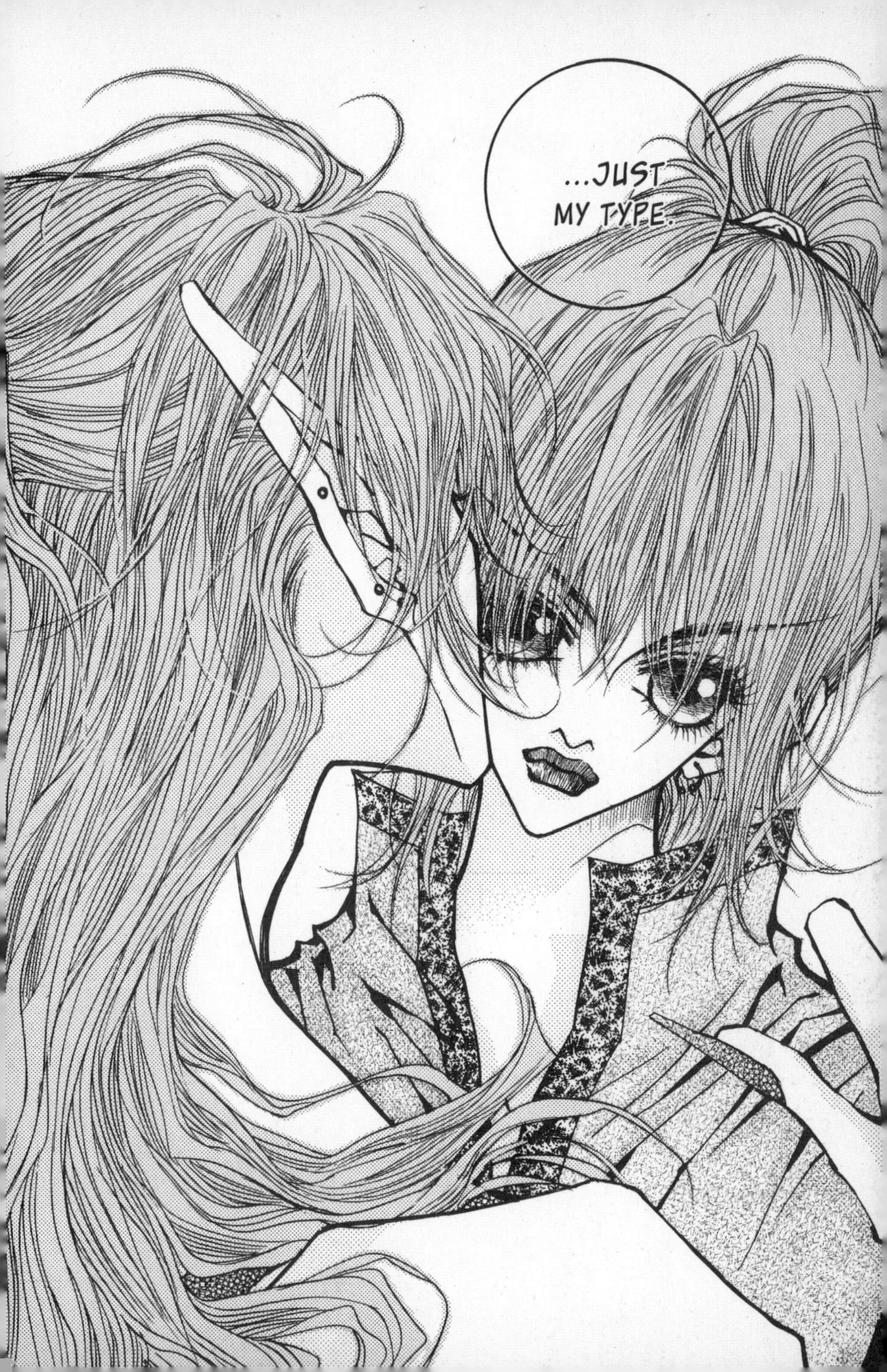
...JUST MY TYPE.

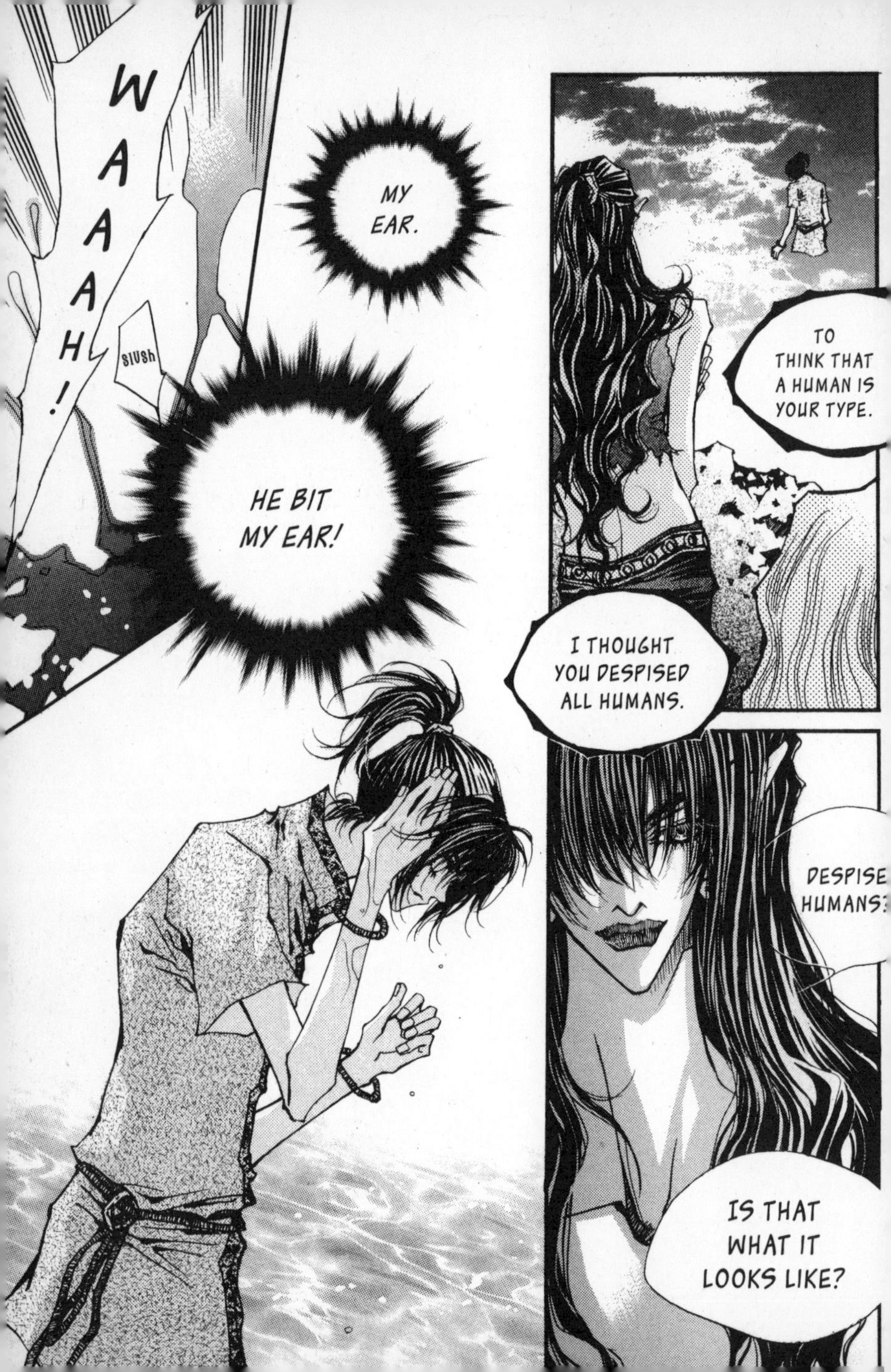
TO THINK THAT A HUMAN IS YOUR TYPE.
I THOUGHT YOU DESPISED ALL HUMANS.
DESPISE HUMANS?
IS THAT WHAT IT LOOKS LIKE?
WAAAH!
SLUSH
MY EAR.
HE BIT MY EAR!

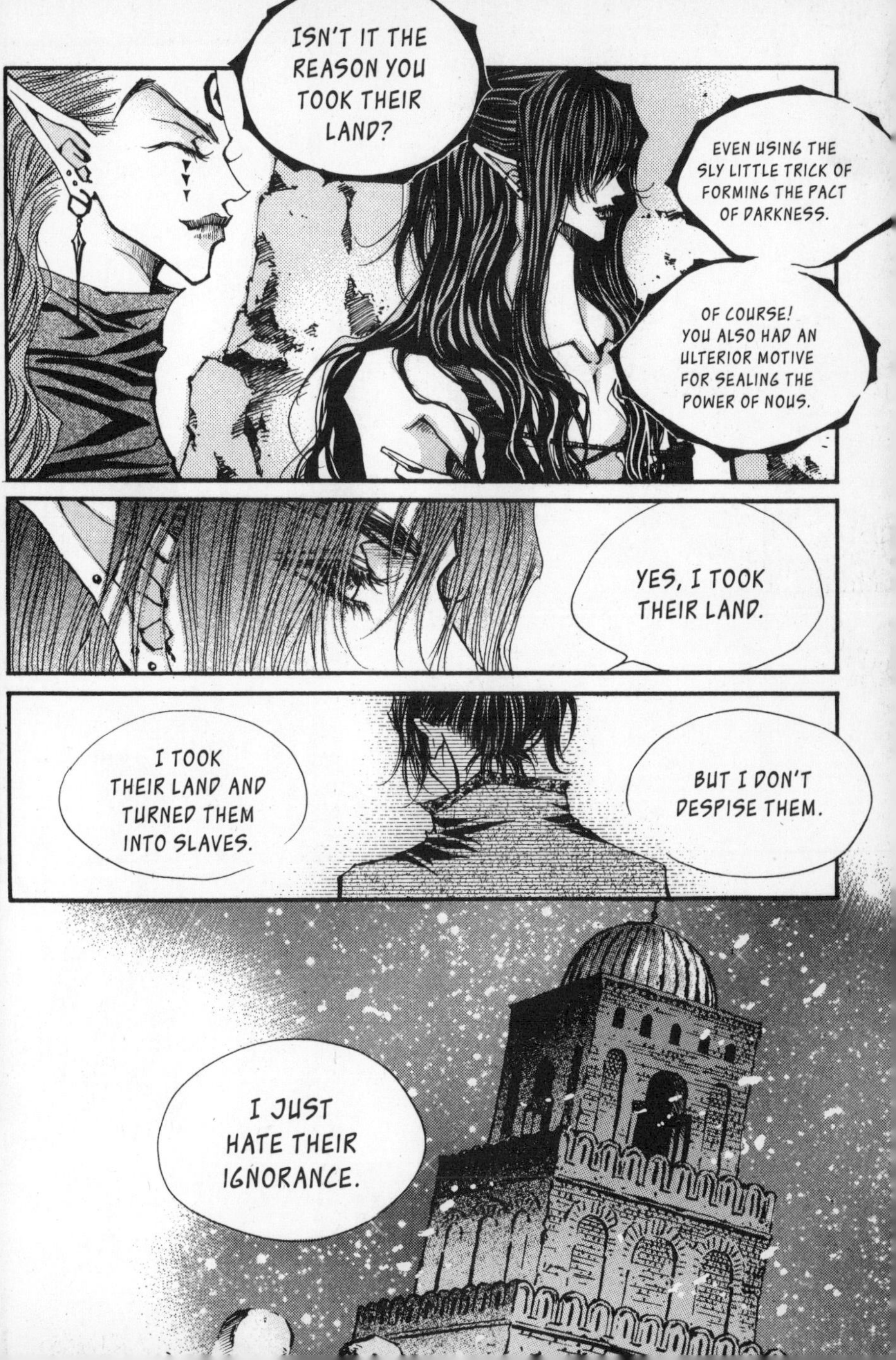
ISN'T IT THE REASON YOU TOOK THEIR LAND?
EVEN USING THE SLY LITTLE TRICK OF FORMING THE PACT OF DARKNESS.
OF COURSE! YOU ALSO HAD AN ULTERIOR MOTIVE FOR SEALING THE POWER OF NOUS.
YES, I TOOK THEIR LAND.
I TOOK THEIR LAND AND TURNED THEM INTO SLAVES.
BUT I DON'T DESPISE THEM.
I JUST HATE THEIR IGNORANCE.

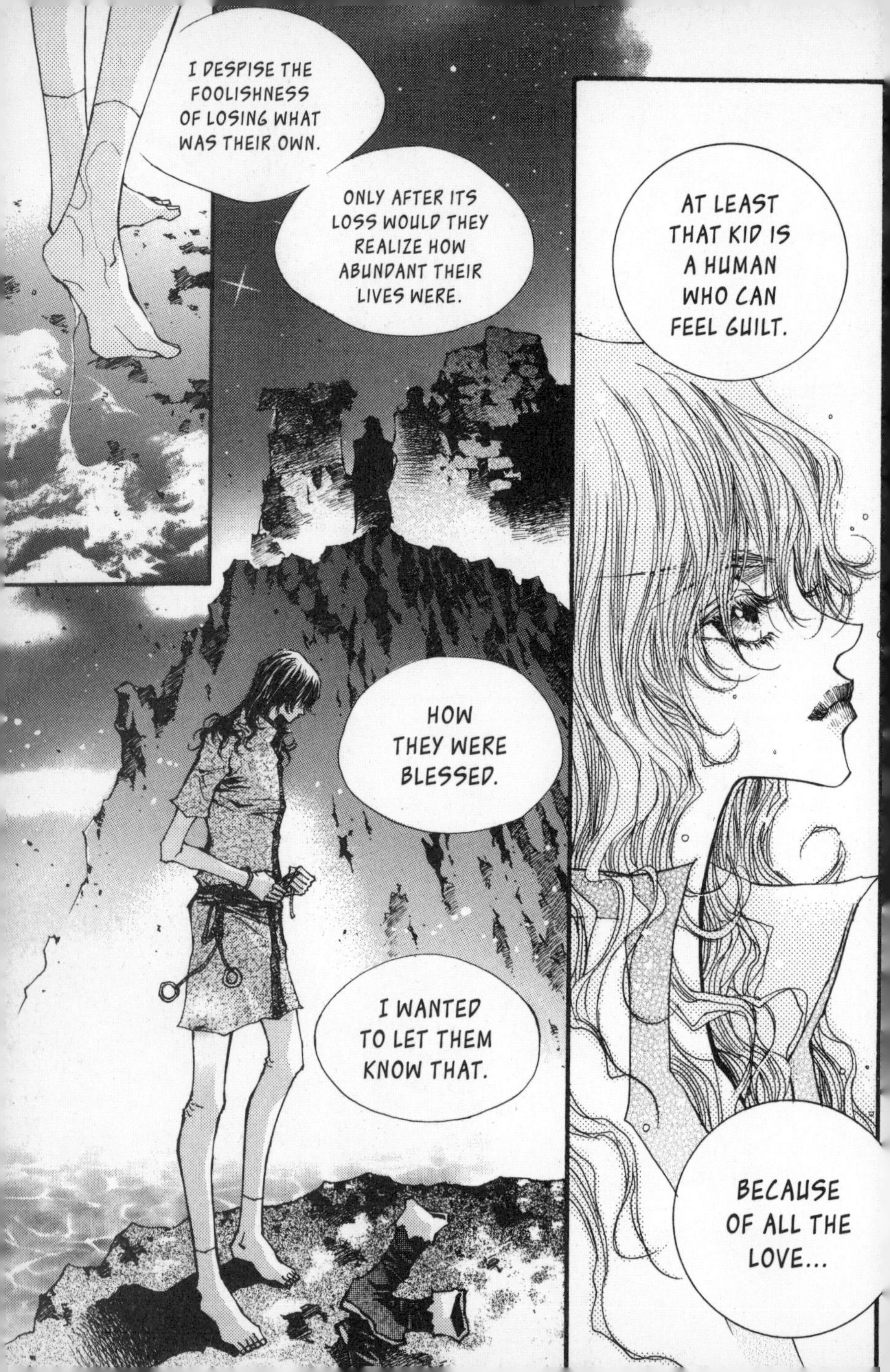
I DESPISE THE FOOLISHNESS OF LOSING WHAT WAS THEIR OWN.
ONLY AFTER ITS LOSS WOULD THEY REALIZE HOW ABUNDANT THEIR LIVES WERE.
AT LEAST THAT KID IS A HUMAN WHO CAN FEEL GUILT.
HOW THEY WERE BLESSED.
I WANTED TO LET THEM KNOW THAT.
BECAUSE OF ALL THE LOVE...

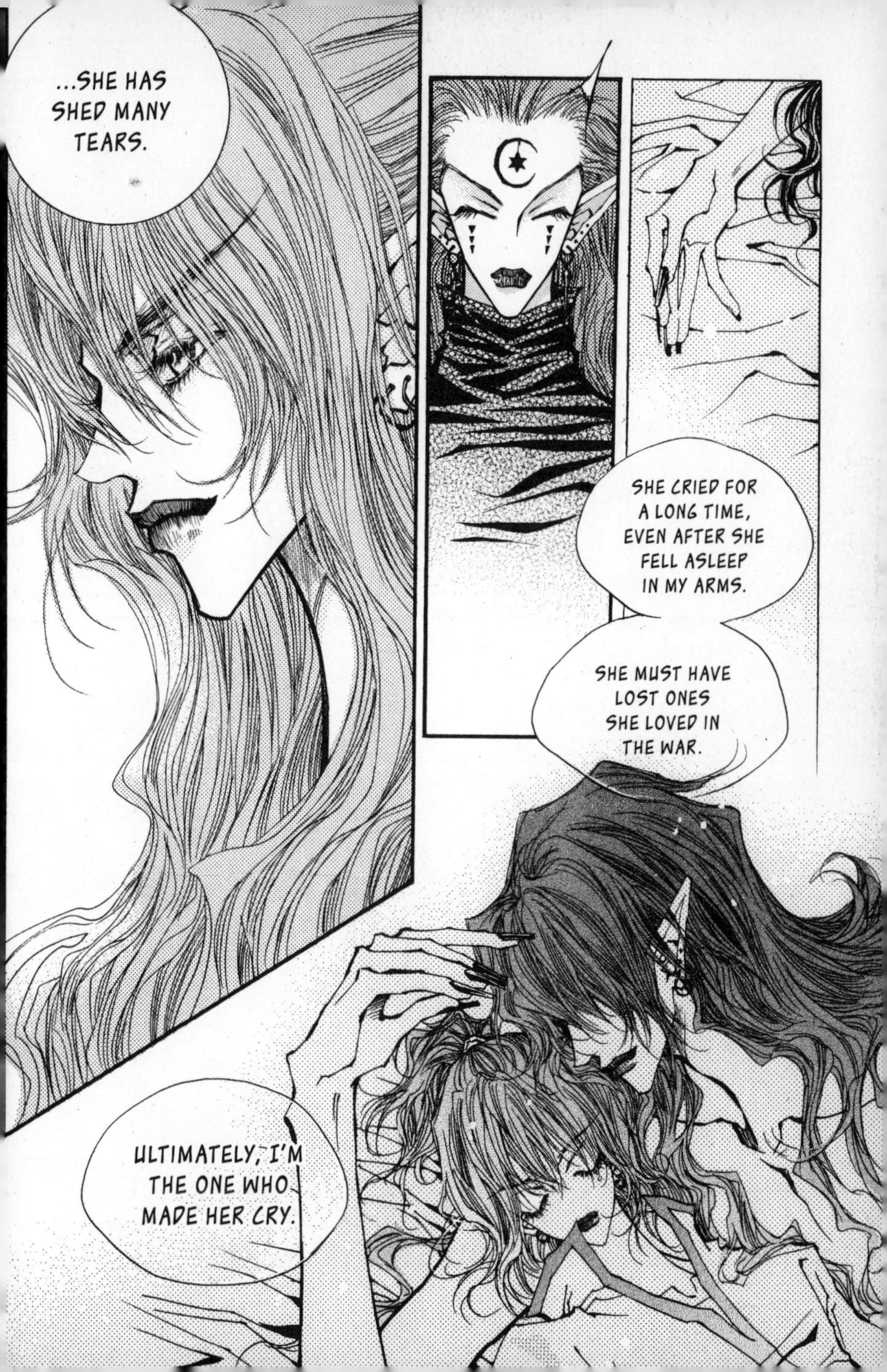
...SHE HAS SHED MANY TEARS.
SHE CRIED FOR A LONG TIME, EVEN AFTER SHE FELL ASLEEP IN MY ARMS.
SHE MUST HAVE LOST ONES SHE LOVED IN THE WAR.
ULTIMATELY, I'M THE ONE WHO MADE HER CRY.

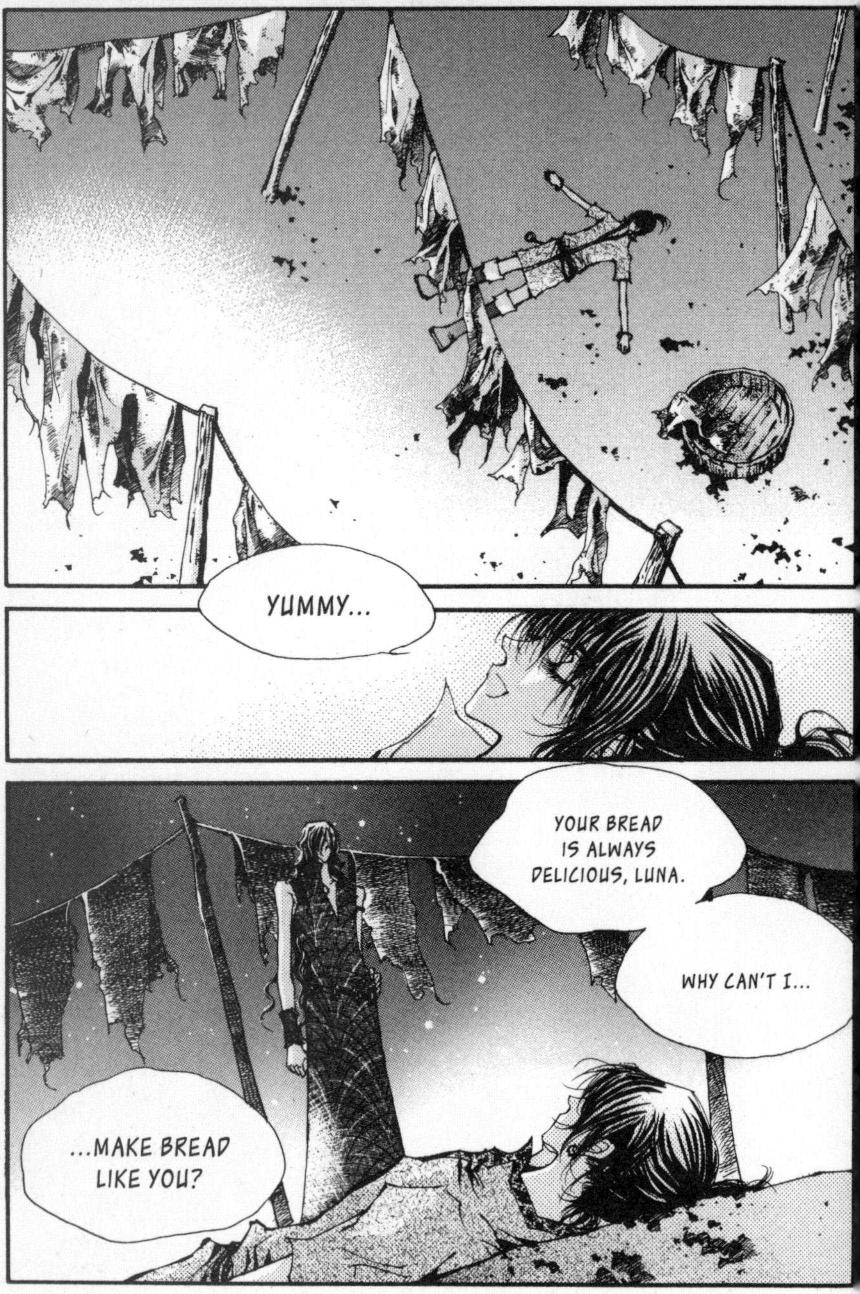
YUMMY...
YOUR BREAD IS ALWAYS DELICIOUS, LUNA.
WHY CAN'T I...
...MAKE BREAD LIKE YOU?

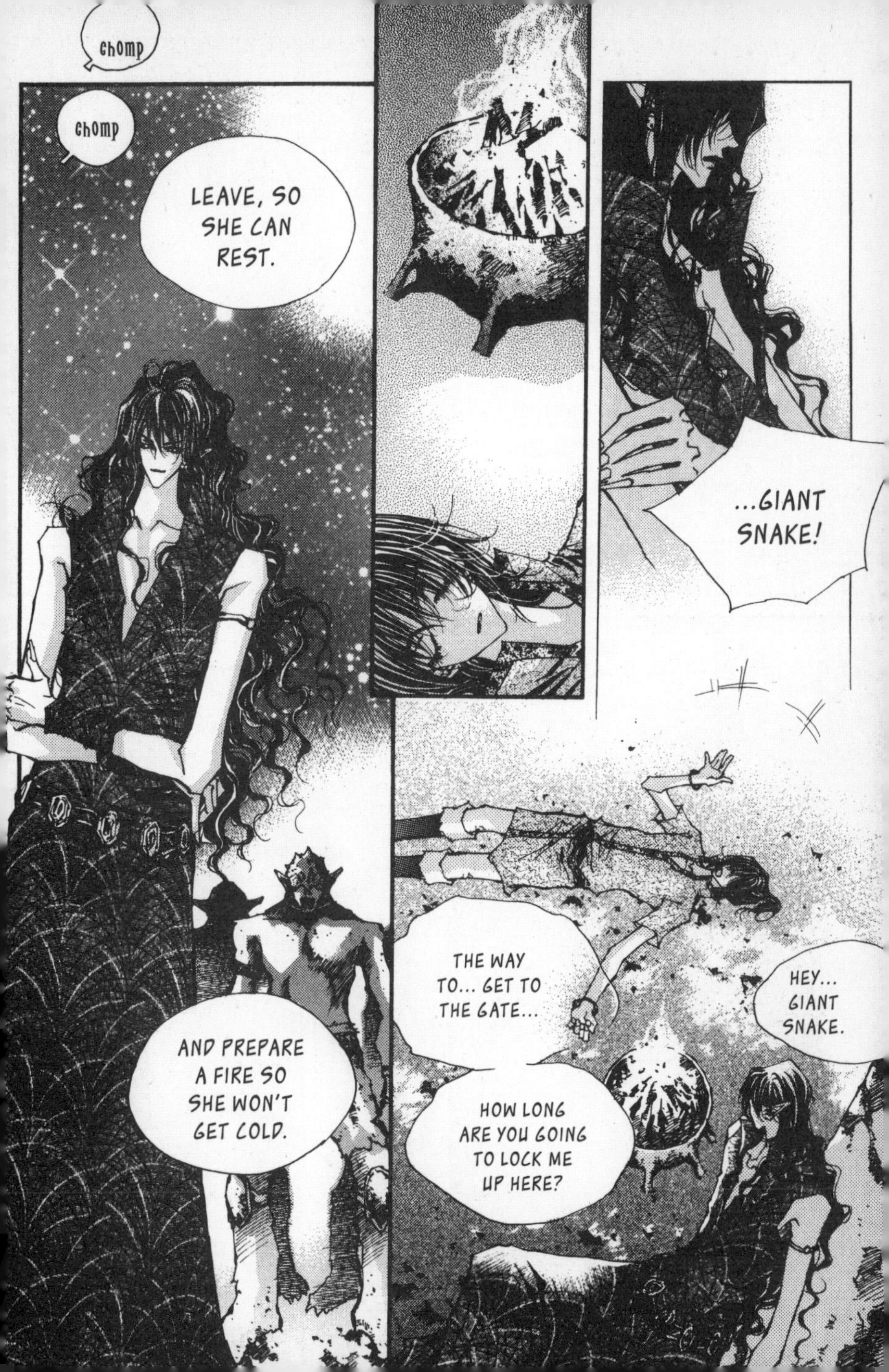
CHOMP
CHOMP
LEAVE, SO SHE CAN REST.
AND PREPARE A FIRE SO SHE WON'T GET COLD.
...GIANT SNAKE!
THE WAY TO... GET TO THE GATE...
HEY... GIANT SNAKE.
HOW LONG ARE YOU GOING TO LOCK ME UP HERE?

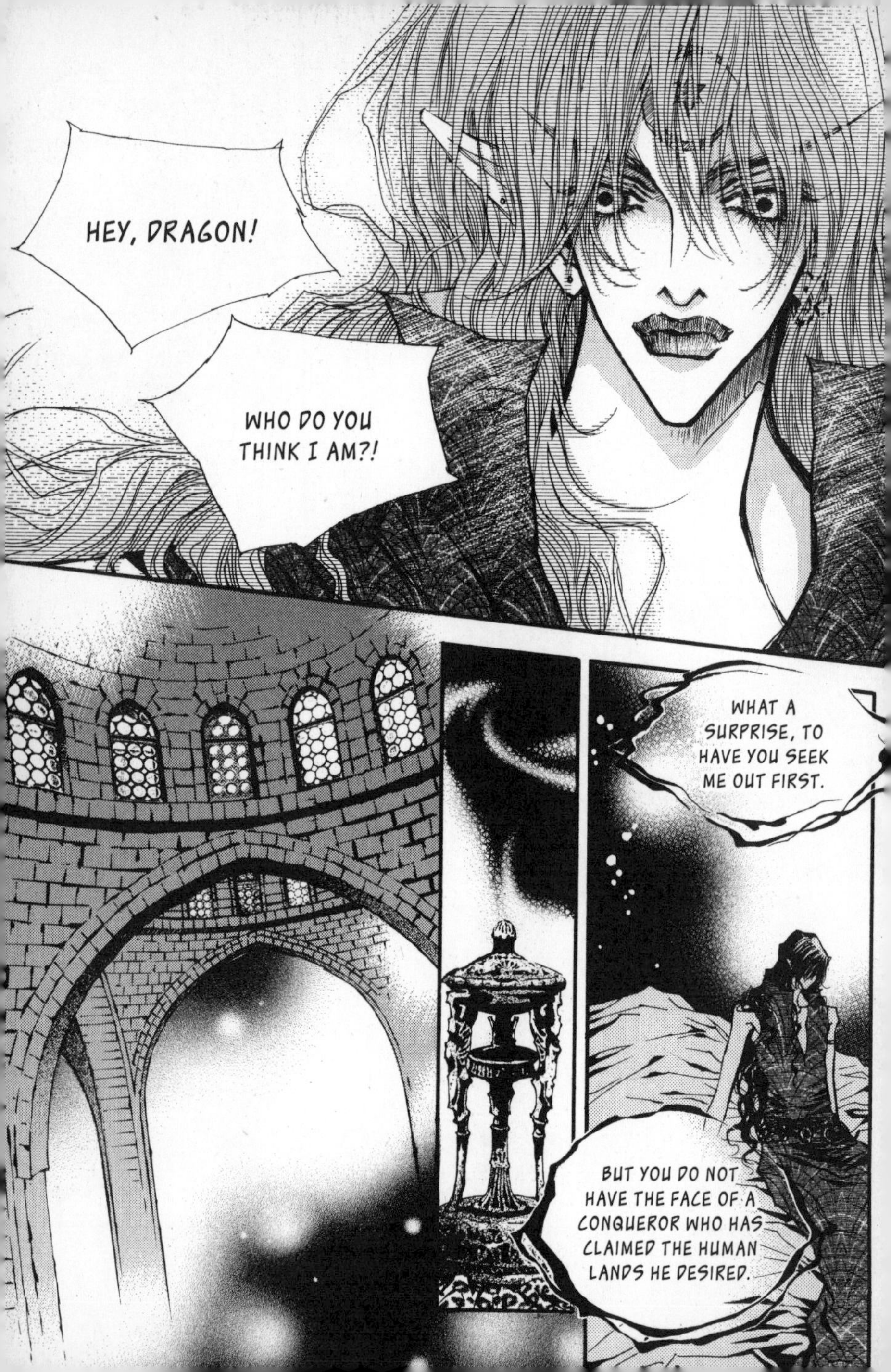
HEY, DRAGON!
WHO DO YOU THINK I AM?!
WHAT A SURPRISE, TO HAVE YOU SEEK ME OUT FIRST.
BUT YOU DO NOT HAVE THE FACE OF A CONQUEROR WHO HAS CLAIMED THE HUMAN LANDS HE DESIRED.

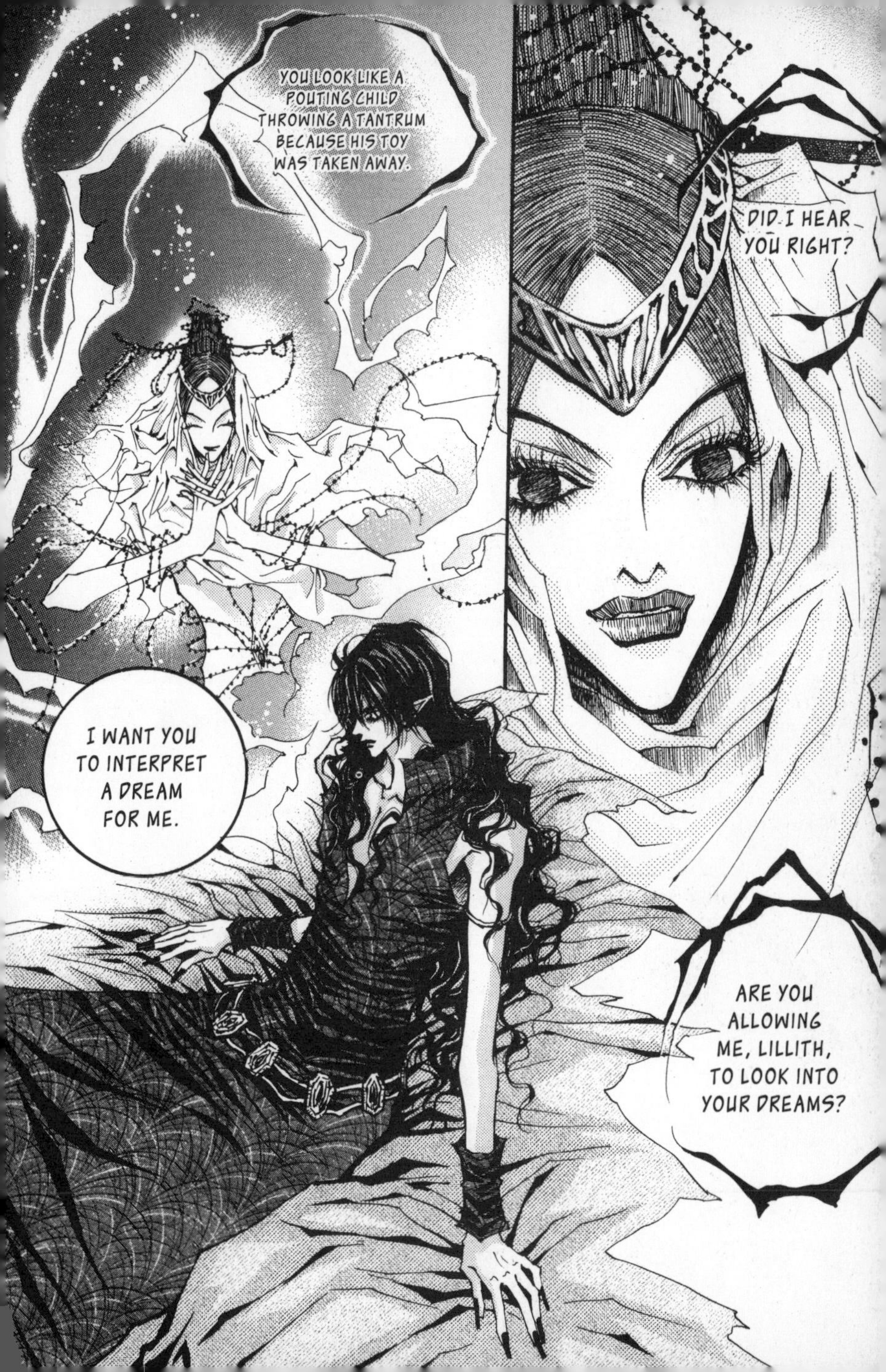
YOU LOOK LIKE A POUTING CHILD THROWING A TANTRUM BECAUSE HIS TOY WAS TAKEN AWAY.
I WANT YOU TO INTERPRET A DREAM FOR ME.
DID I HEAR YOU RIGHT?
ARE YOU ALLOWING ME, LILLITH, TO LOOK INTO YOUR DREAMS?

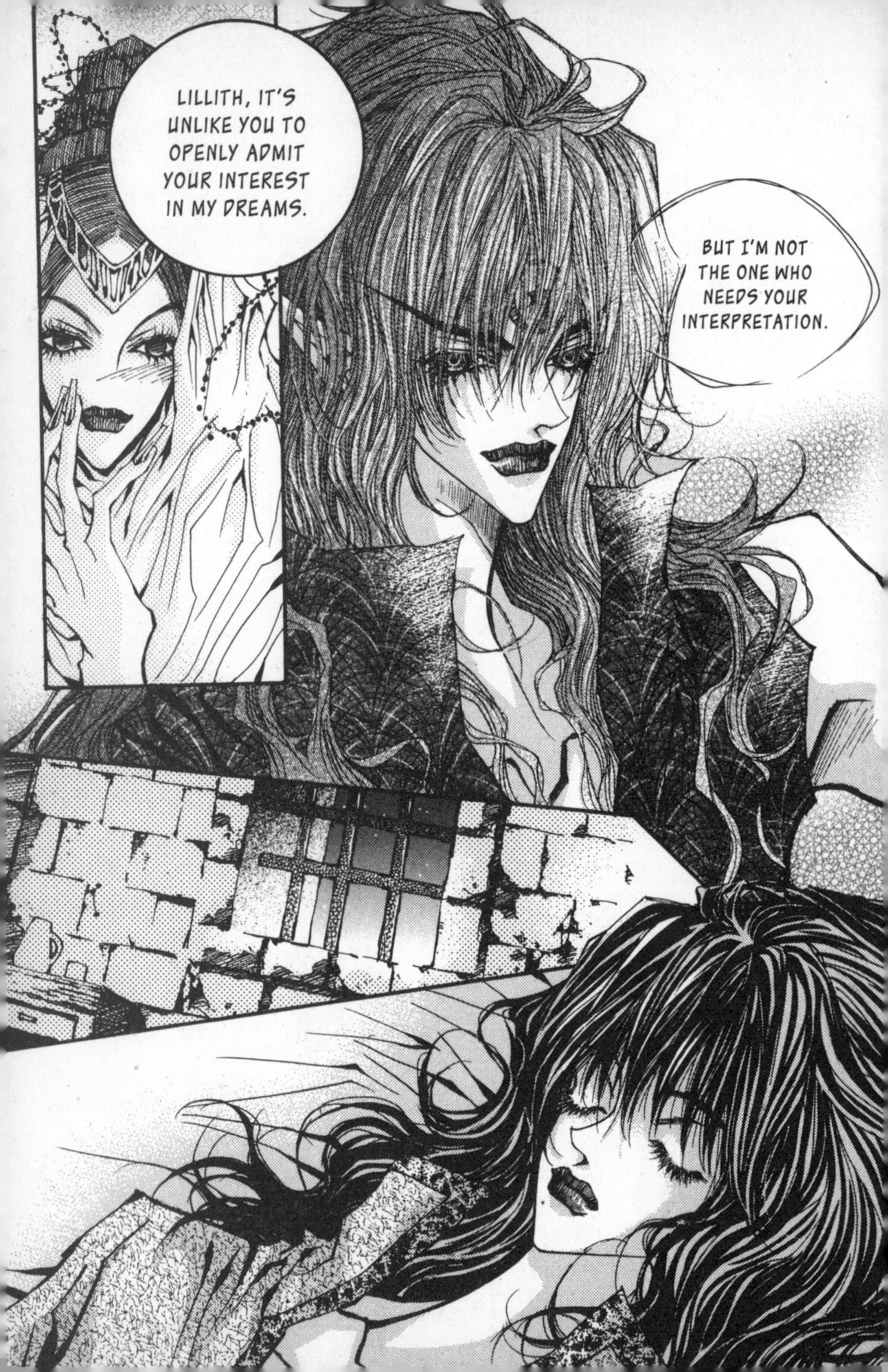
LILLITH, IT'S UNLIKE YOU TO OPENLY ADMIT YOUR INTEREST IN MY DREAMS.
BUT I'M NOT THE ONE WHO NEEDS YOUR INTERPRETATION.

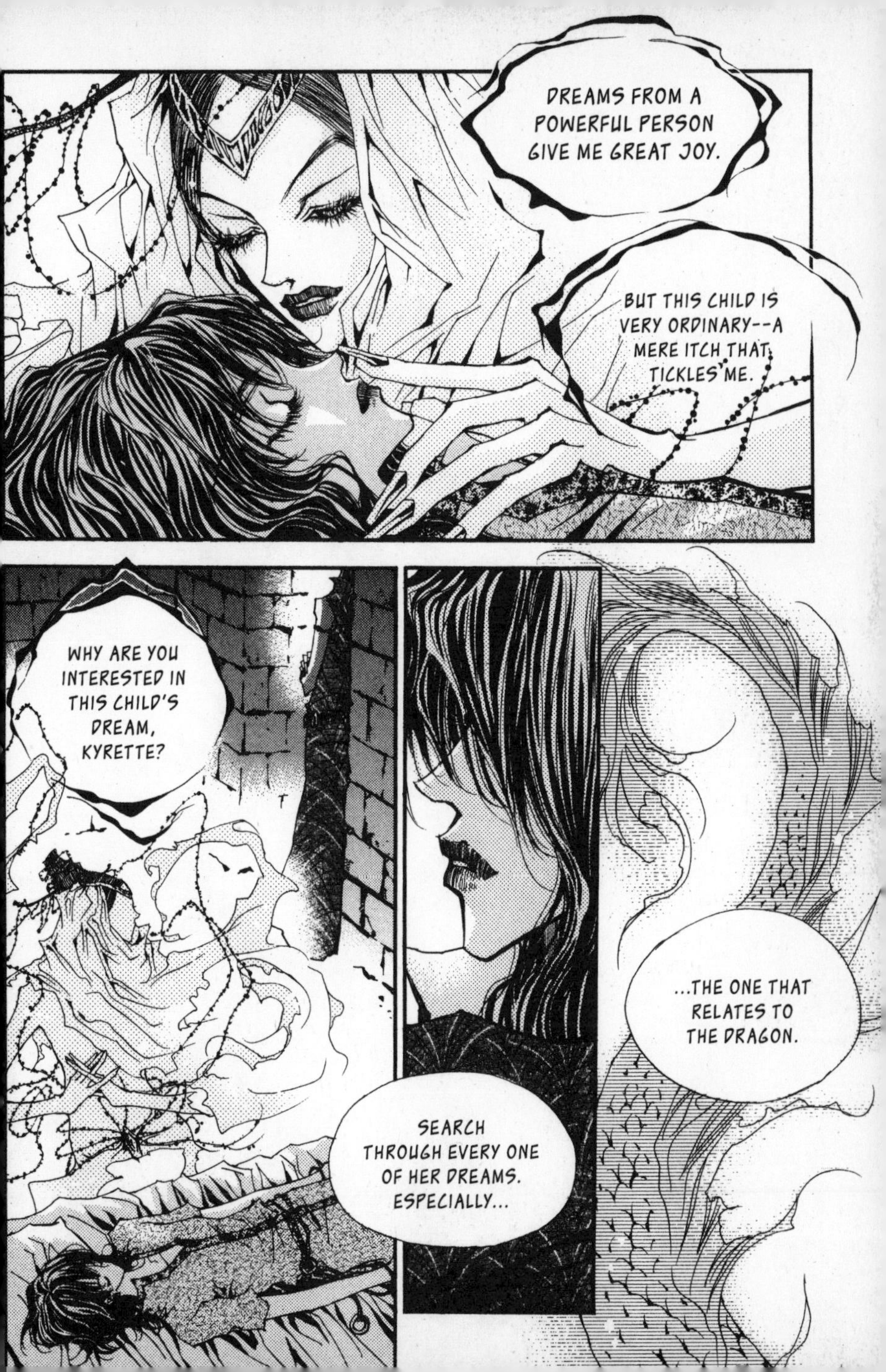
DREAMS FROM A POWERFUL PERSON GIVE ME GREAT JOY.
BUT THIS CHILD IS VERY ORDINARY--A MERE ITCH THAT TICKLES ME.
WHY ARE YOU INTERESTED IN THIS CHILD'S DREAM, KYRETTE?
SEARCH THROUGH EVERY ONE OF HER DREAMS. ESPECIALLY...
...THE ONE THAT RELATES TO THE DRAGON.

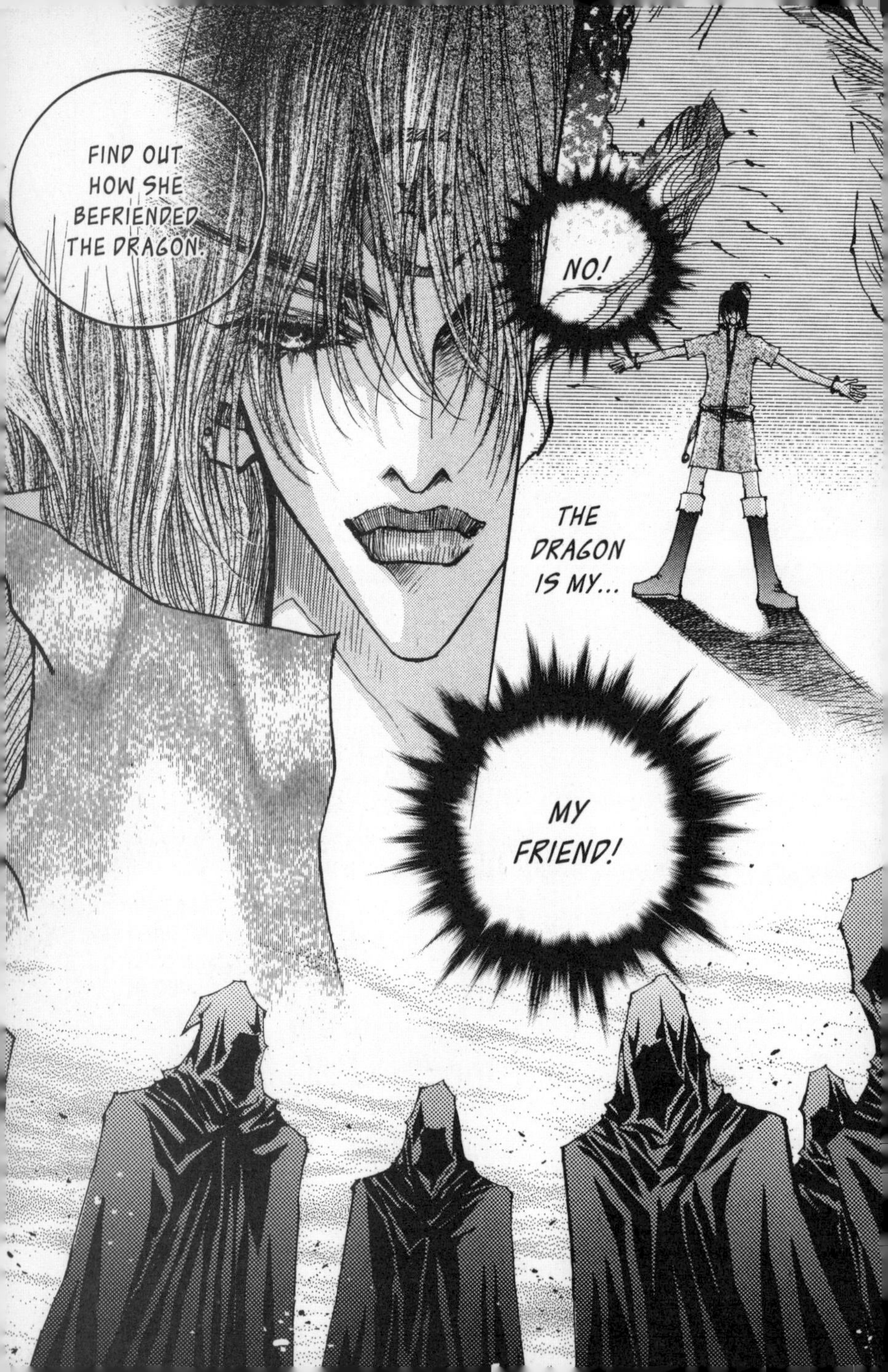
NO!
THE DRAGON IS MY...
MY FRIEND!
FIND OUT HOW SHE BEFRIENDED THE DRAGON.

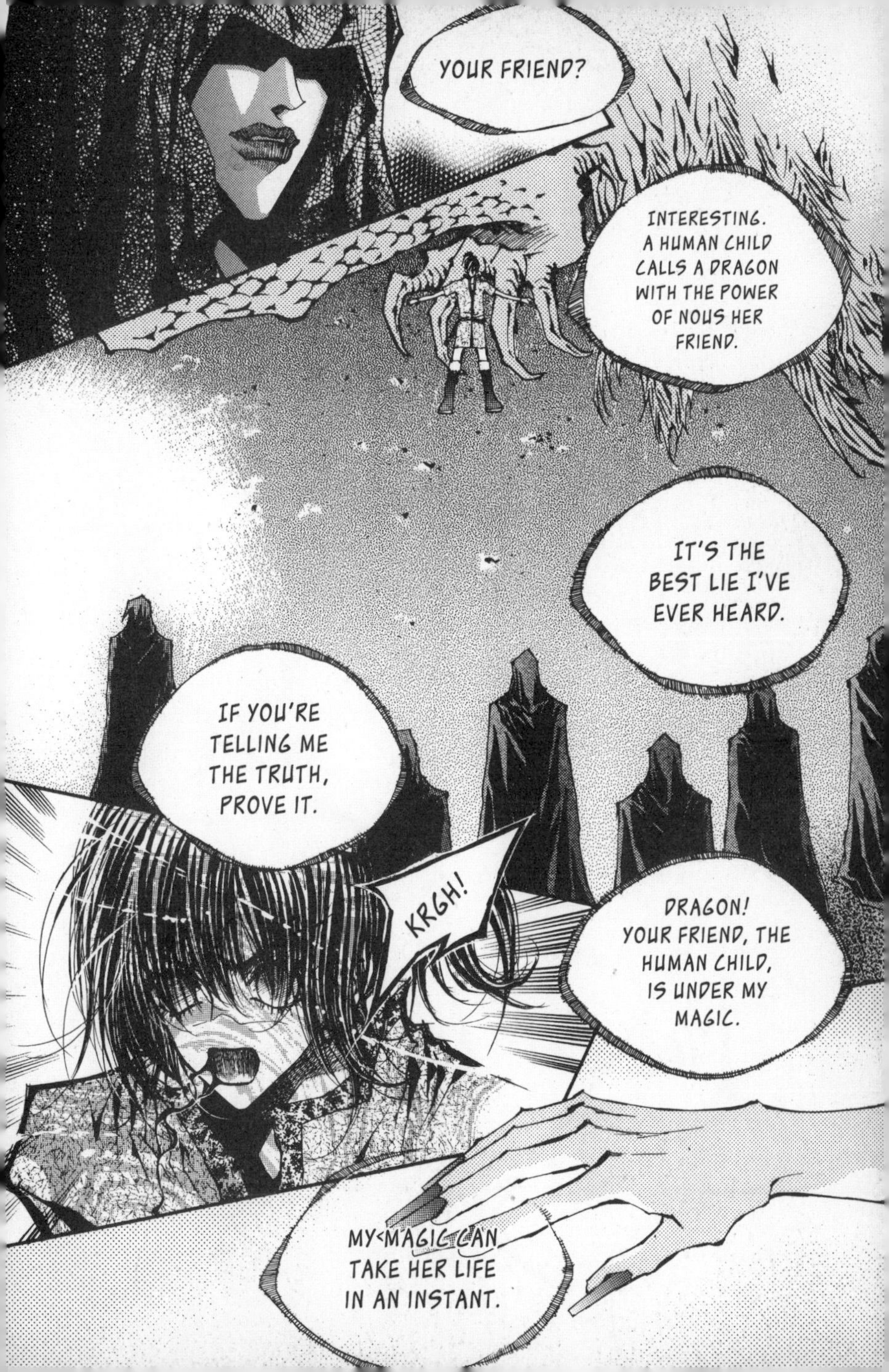
YOUR FRIEND?
INTERESTING. A HUMAN CHILD CALLS A DRAGON WITH THE POWER OF NOUS HER FRIEND.
IT'S THE BEST LIE I'VE EVER HEARD.
IF YOU'RE TELLING ME THE TRUTH, PROVE IT.
KRGH!
DRAGON! YOUR FRIEND, THE HUMAN CHILD, IS UNDER MY MAGIC.
MY MAGIC CAN TAKE HER LIFE IN AN INSTANT.

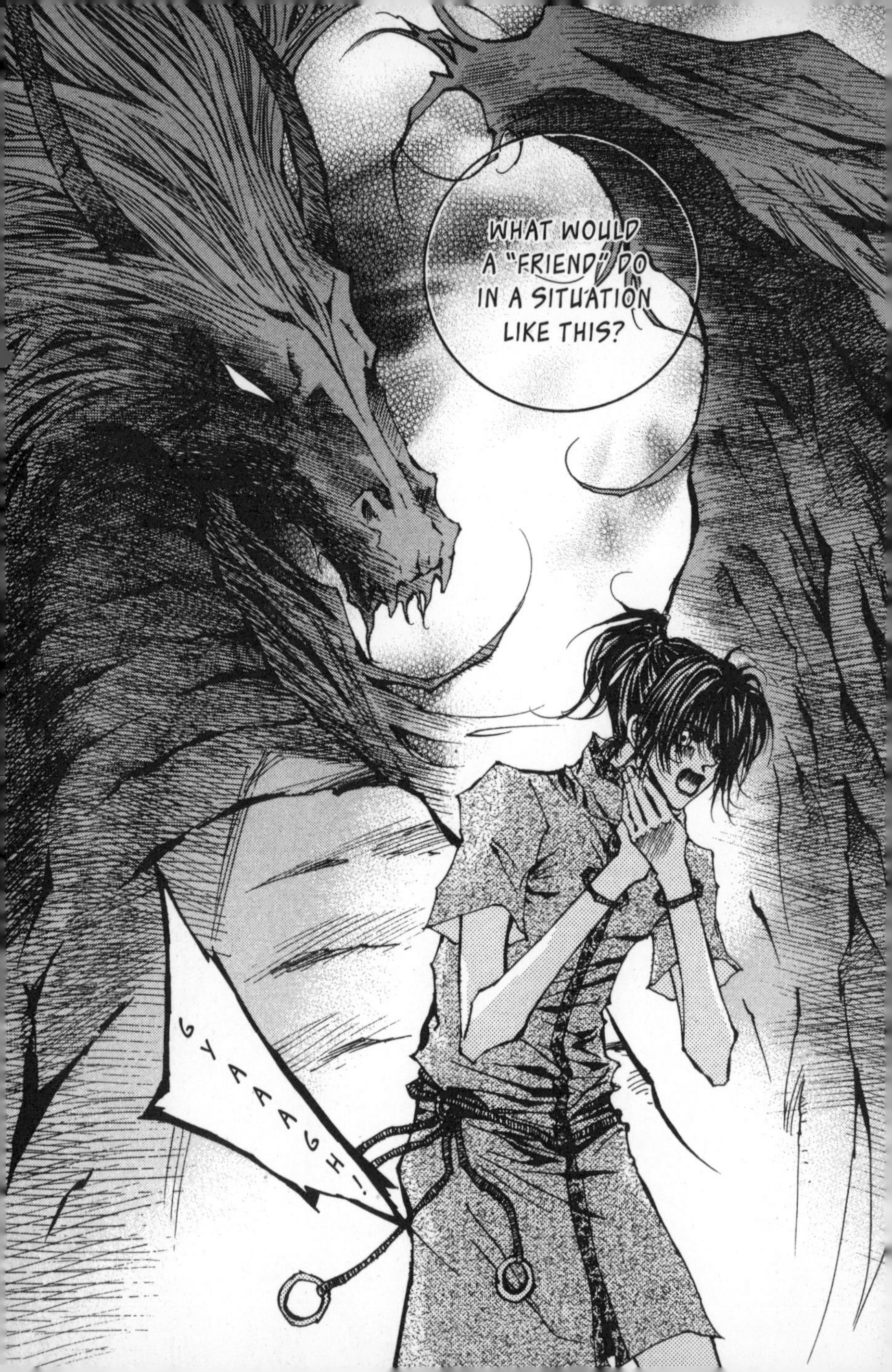
WHAT WOULD A "FRIEND" DO IN A SITUATION LIKE THIS?
GYAAAGH!!

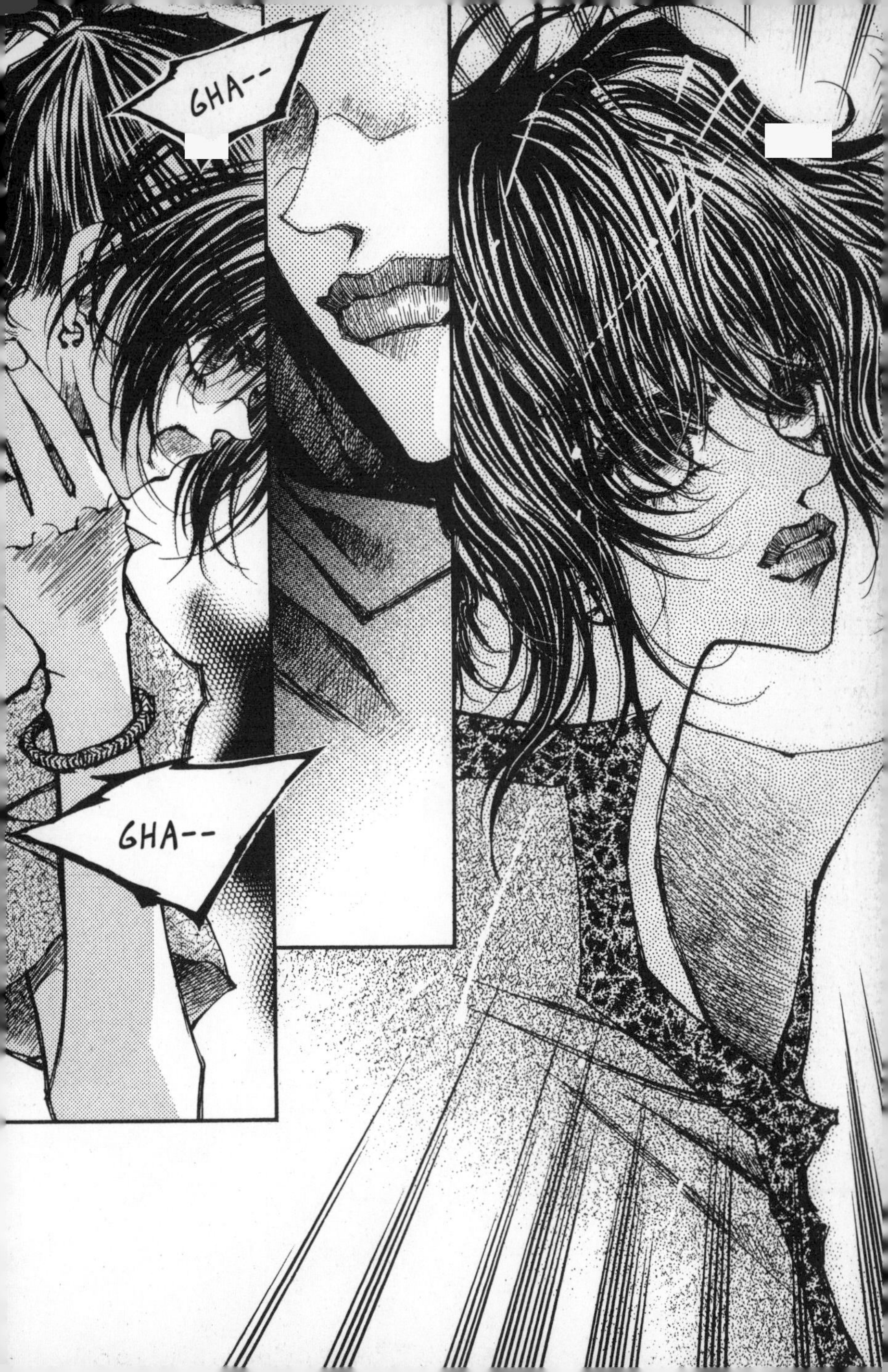
GHA--
GHA--

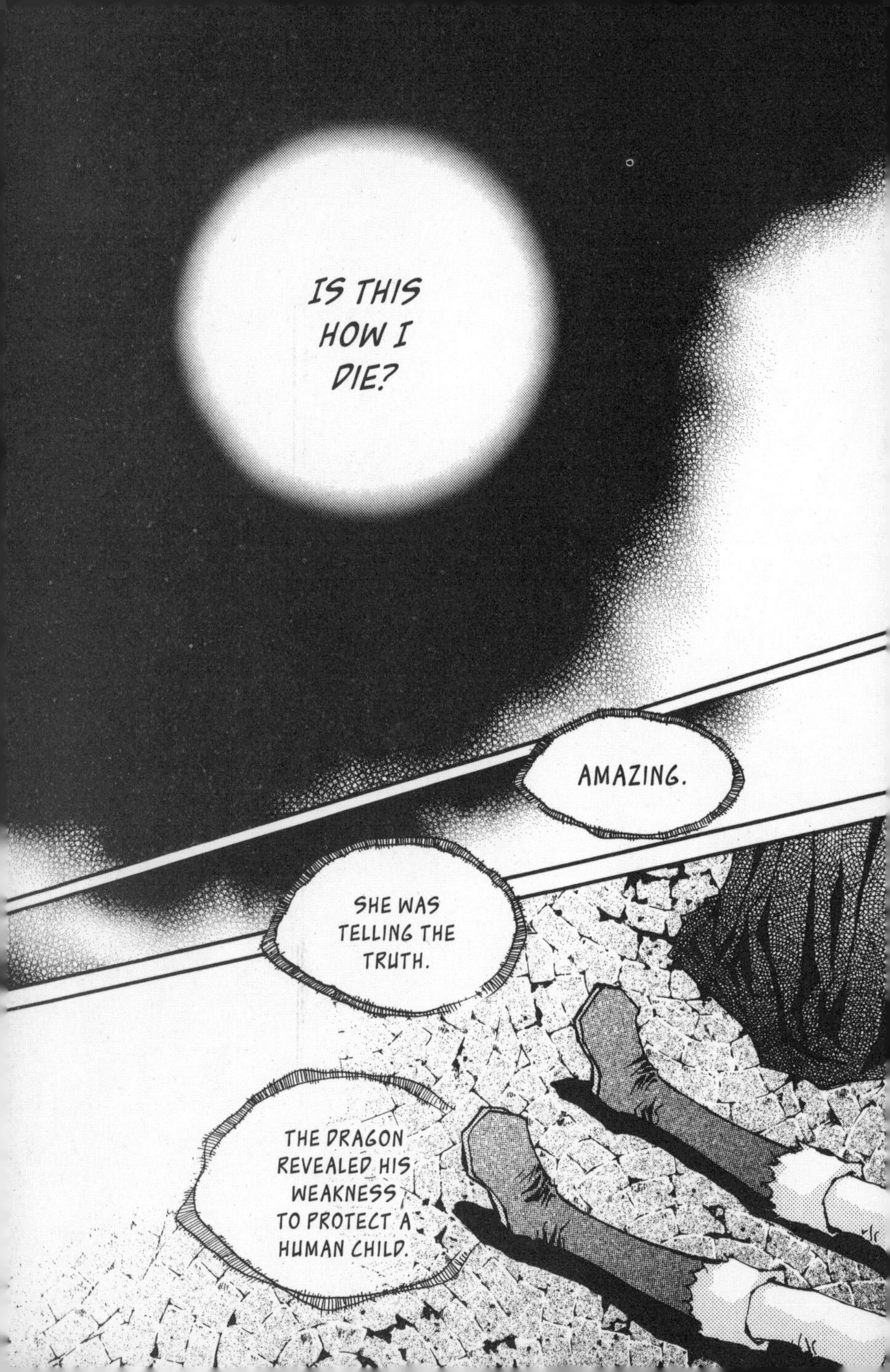
IS THIS HOW I DIE?
AMAZING.
SHE WAS TELLING THE TRUTH.
THE DRAGON REVEALED HIS WEAKNESS TO PROTECT A HUMAN CHILD.

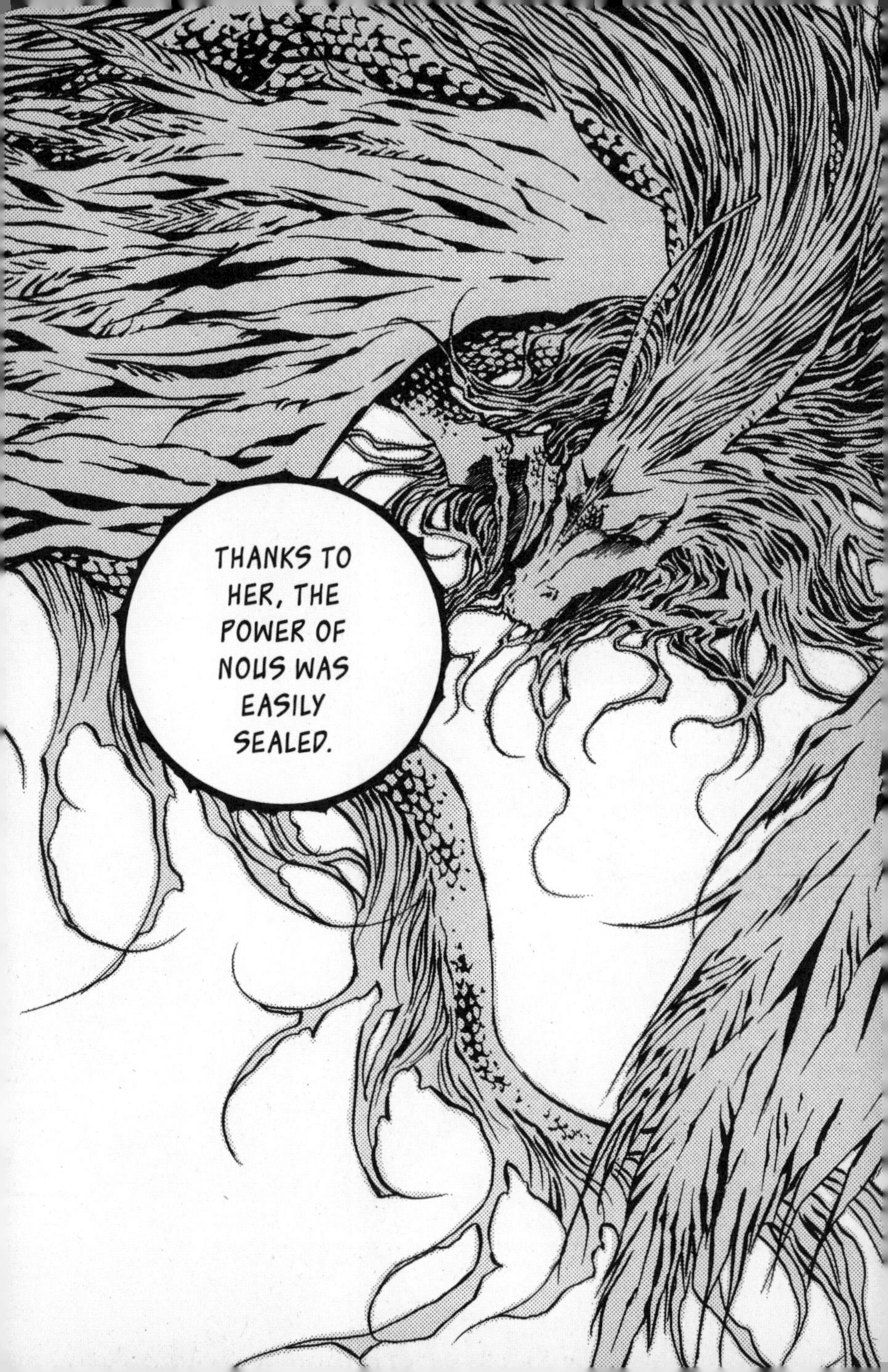
THANKS TO HER, THE POWER OF NOUS WAS EASILY SEALED.

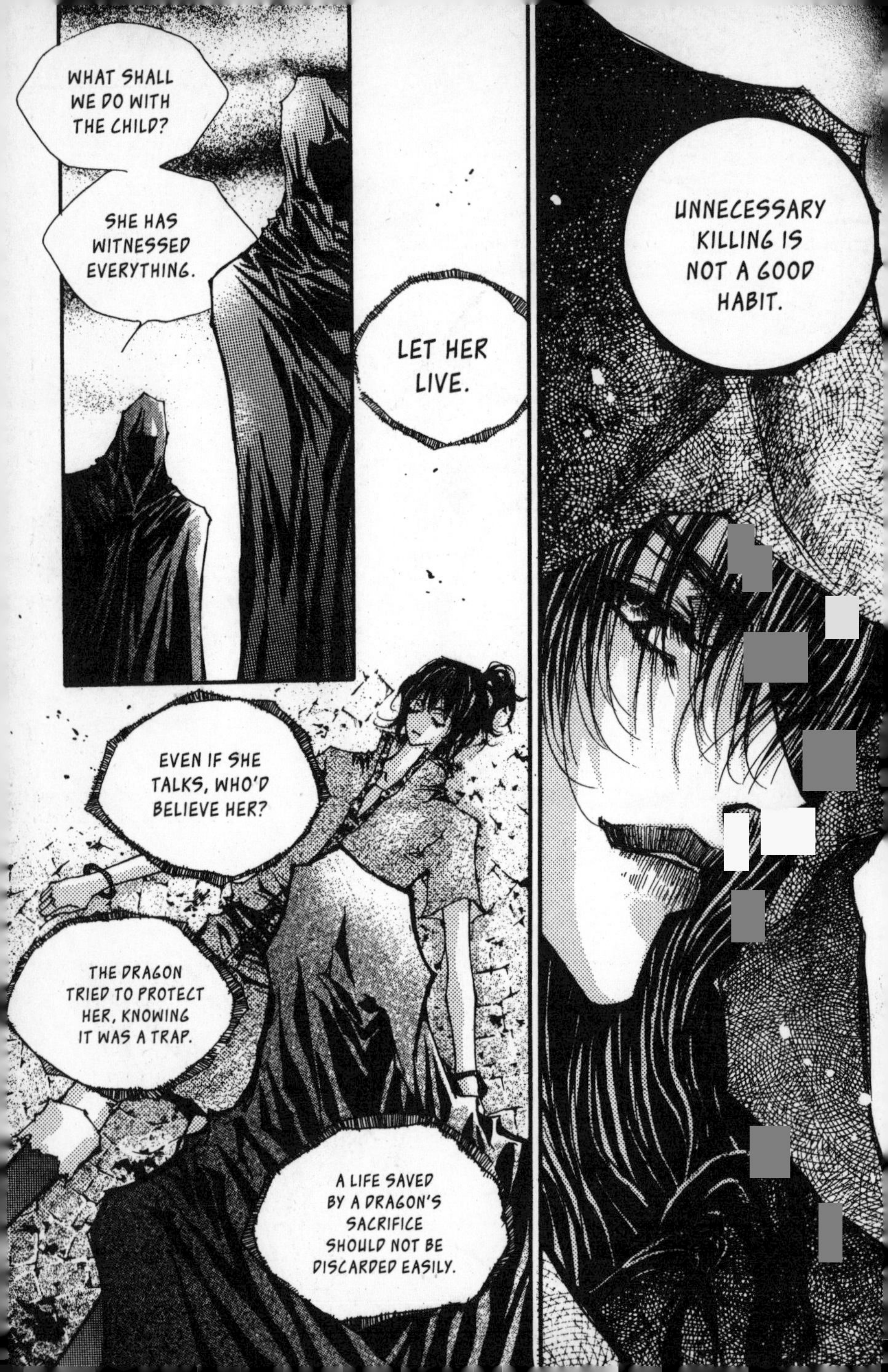
WHAT SHALL WE DO WITH THE CHILD?
SHE HAS WITNESSED EVERYTHING.
LET HER LIVE.
UNNECESSARY KILLING IS NOT A GOOD HABIT.
EVEN IF SHE TALKS, WHO'D BELIEVE HER?
THE DRAGON TRIED TO PROTECT HER, KNOWING IT WAS A TRAP.
A LIFE SAVED BY A DRAGON'S SACRIFICE SHOULD NOT BE DISCARDED EASILY.

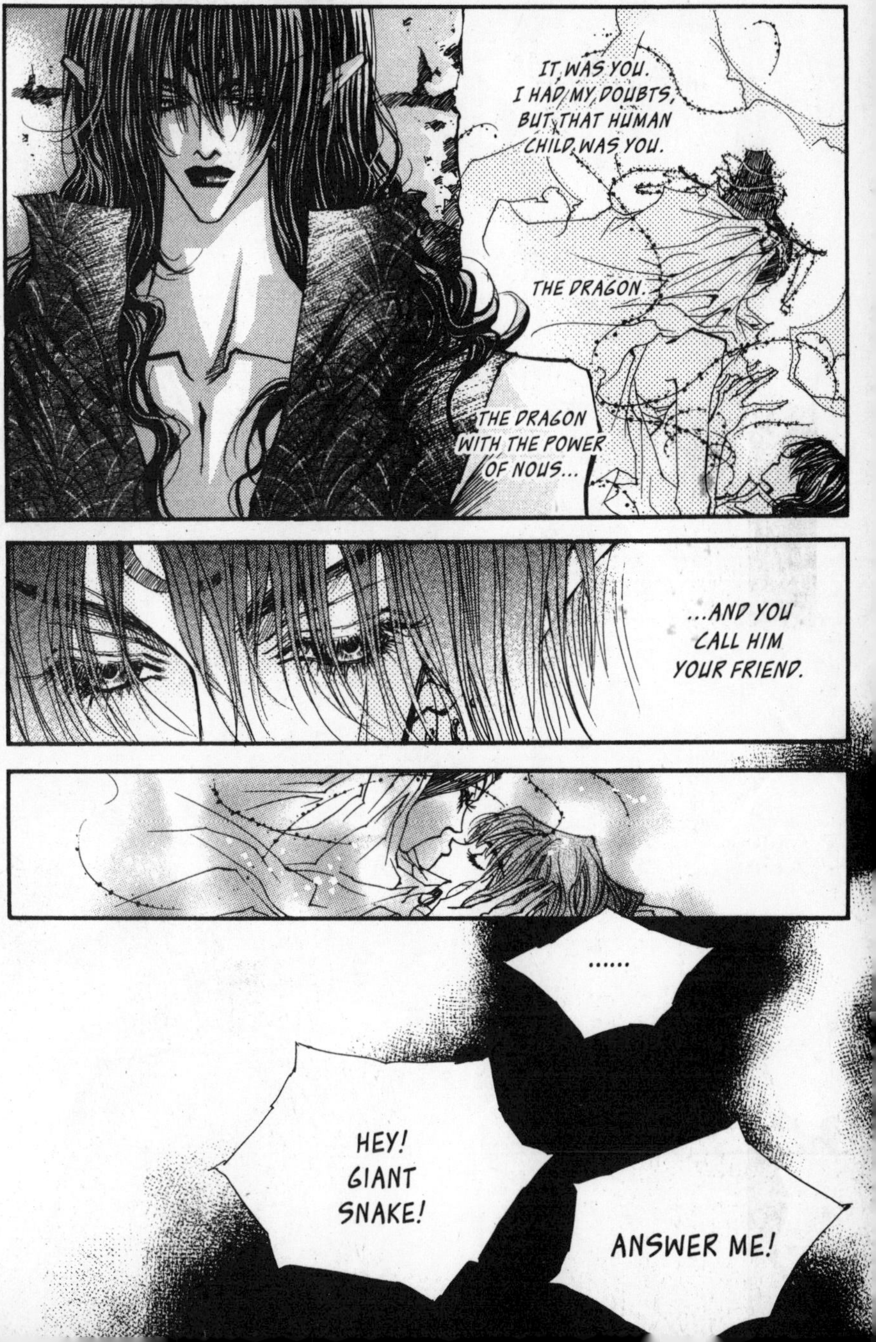
IT WAS YOU. I HAD MY DOUBTS, BUT THAT HUMAN CHILD WAS YOU.
THE DRAGON.
THE DRAGON WITH THE POWER OF NOUS...
...AND YOU CALL HIM YOUR FRIEND.
......
ANSWER ME!
HEY! GIANT SNAKE!

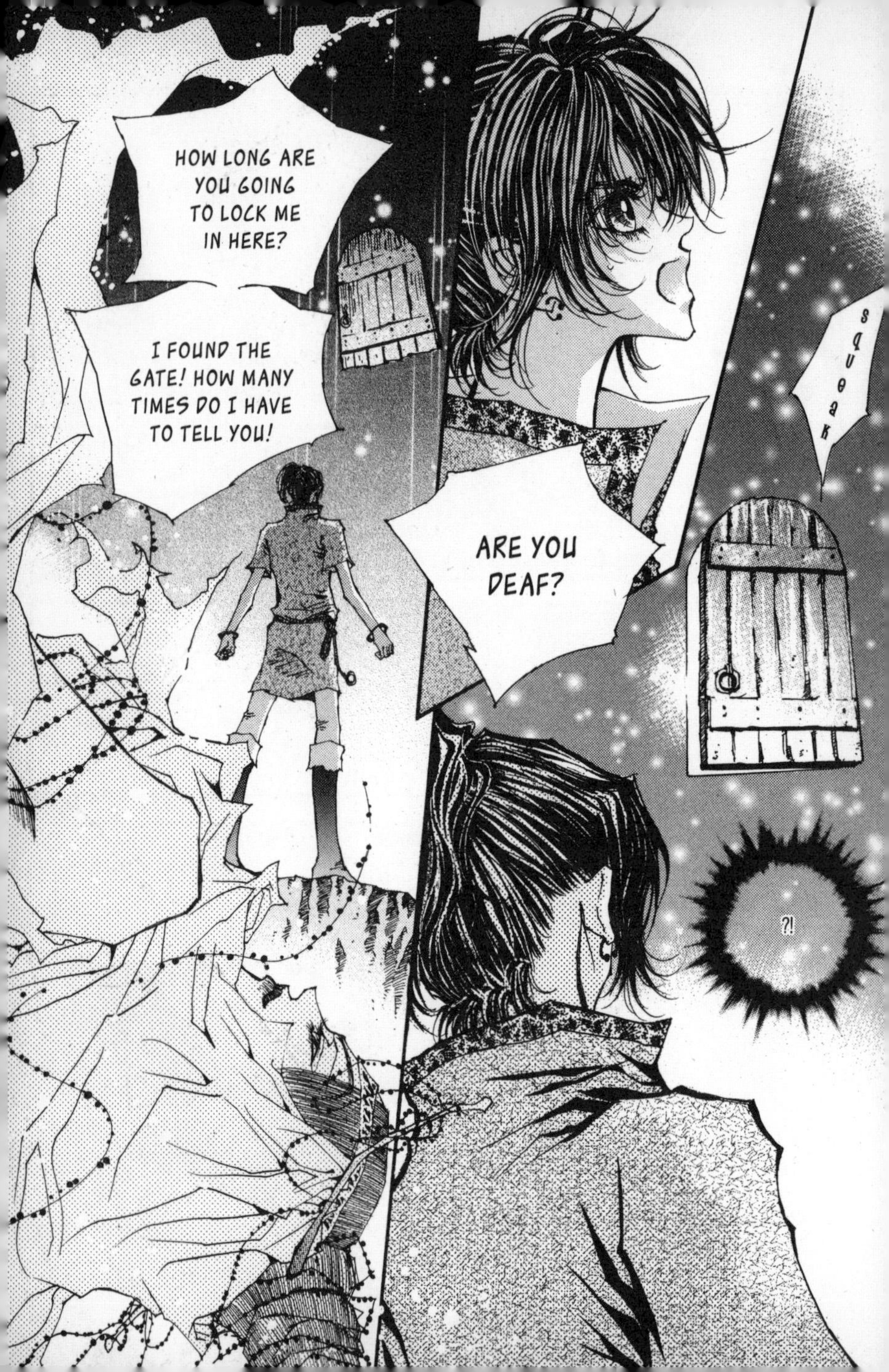

HOW LONG ARE YOU GOING TO LOCK ME IN HERE?
I FOUND THE GATE! HOW MANY TIMES DO I HAVE TO TELL YOU!
ARE YOU DEAF?
squeak
?!

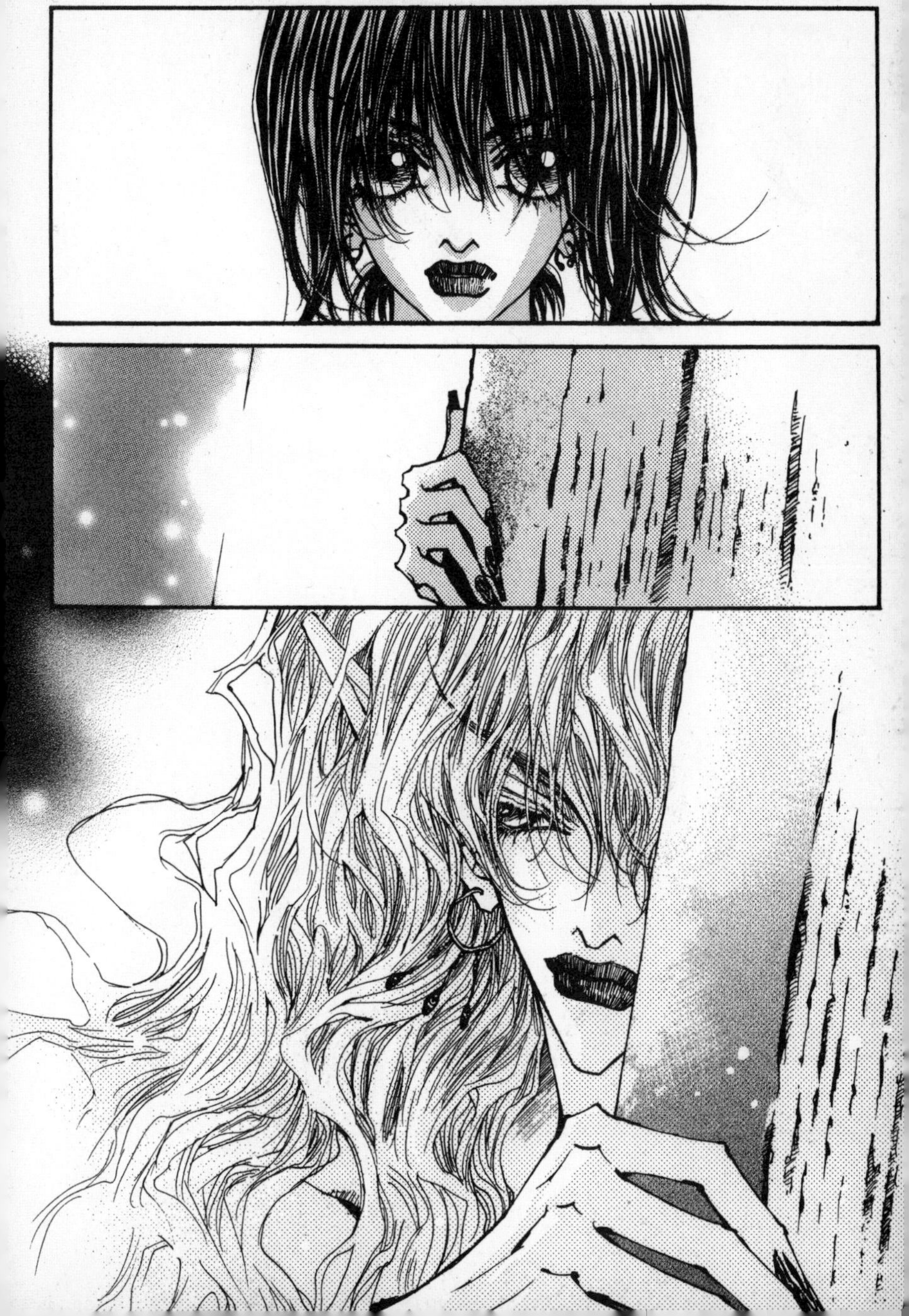

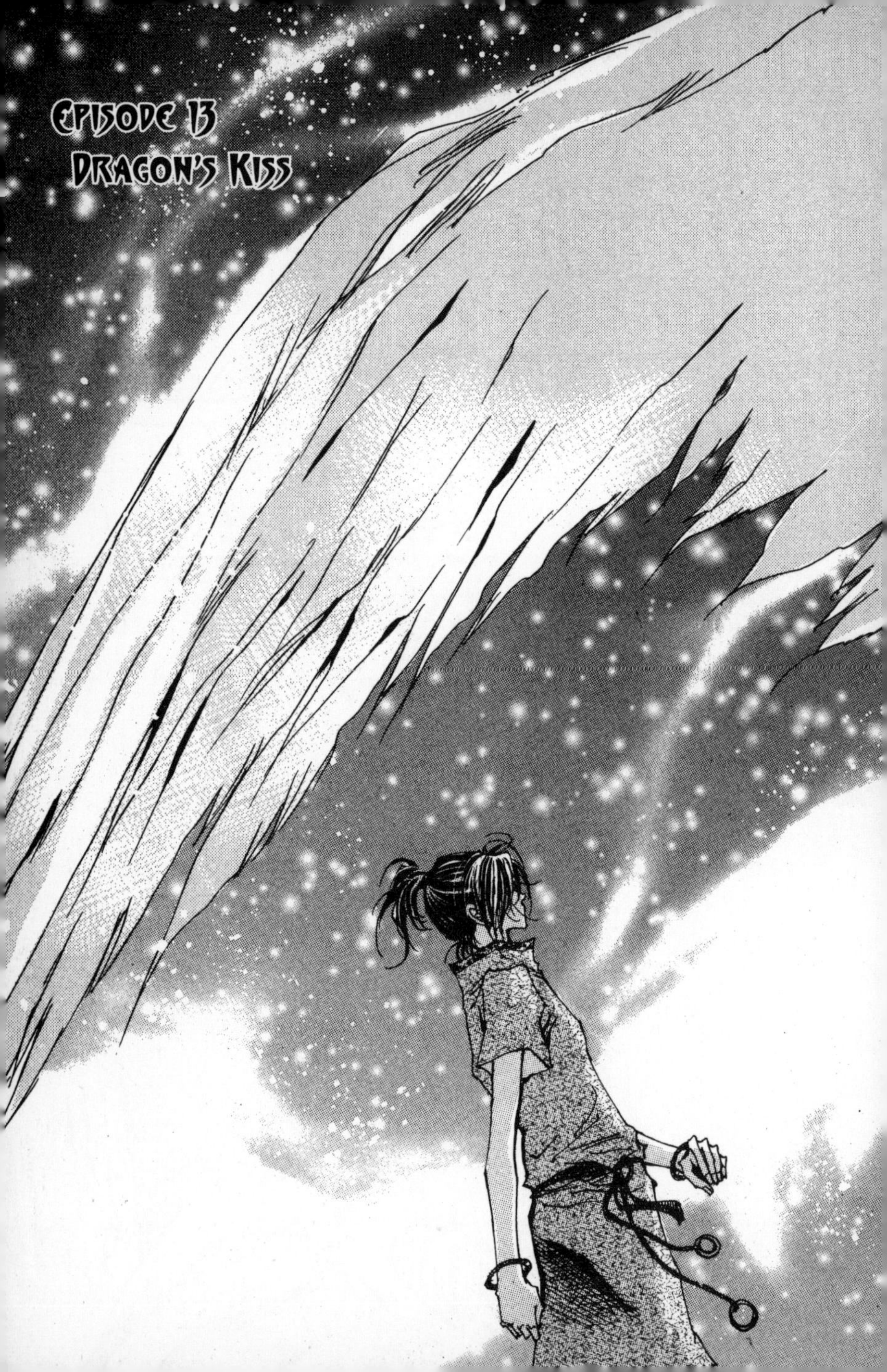
Episode 13
Dragon's Kiss

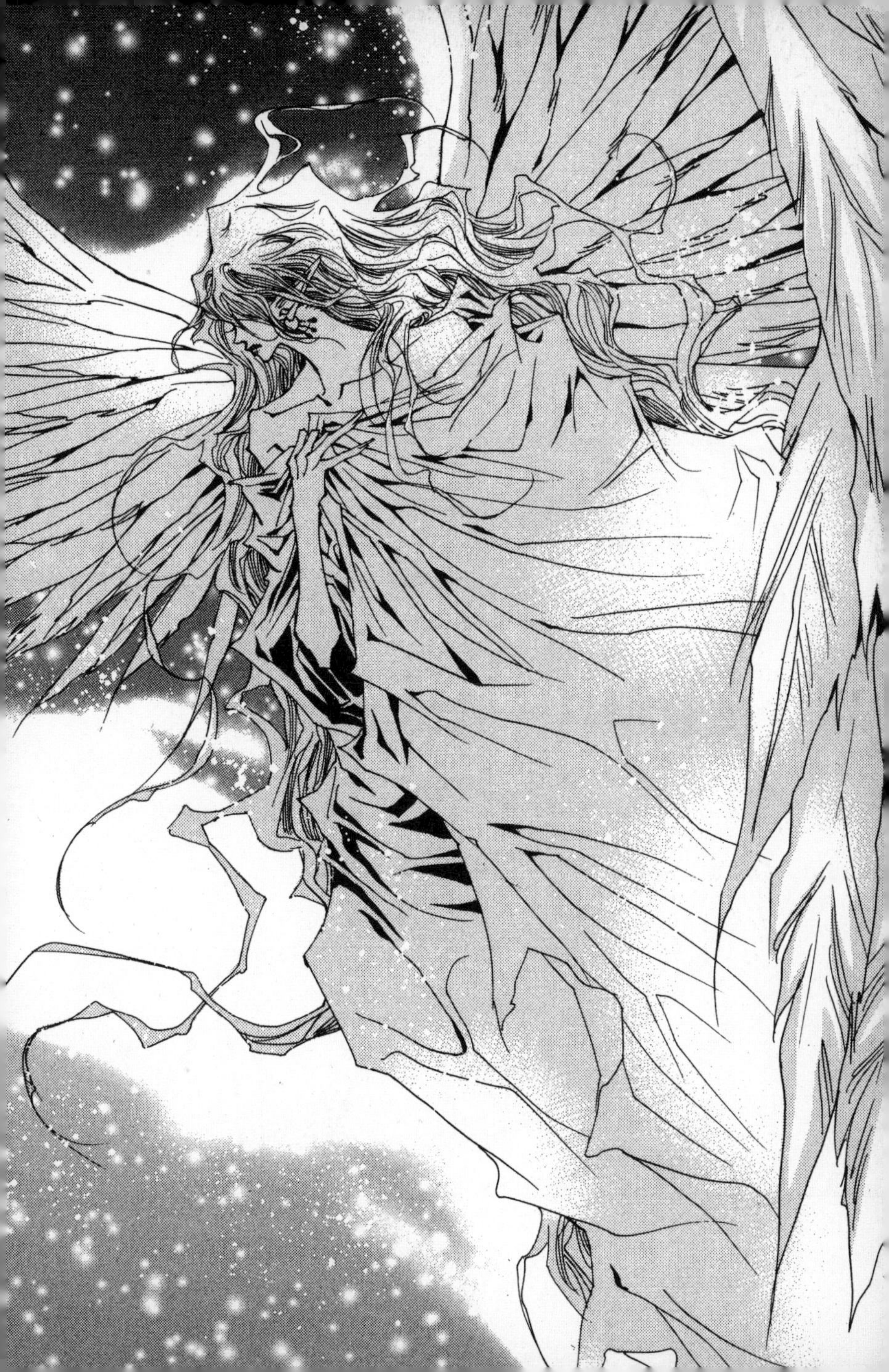

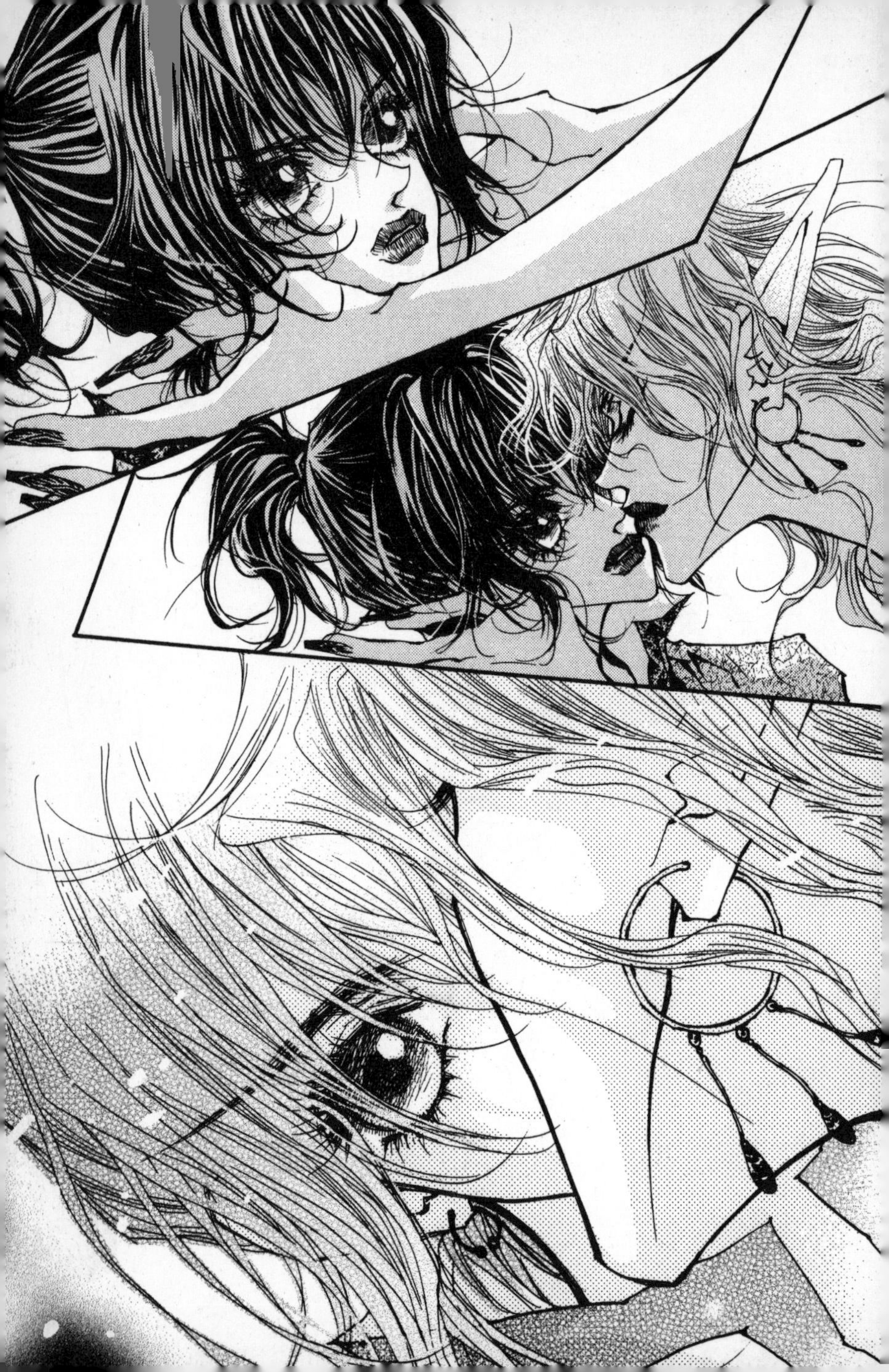

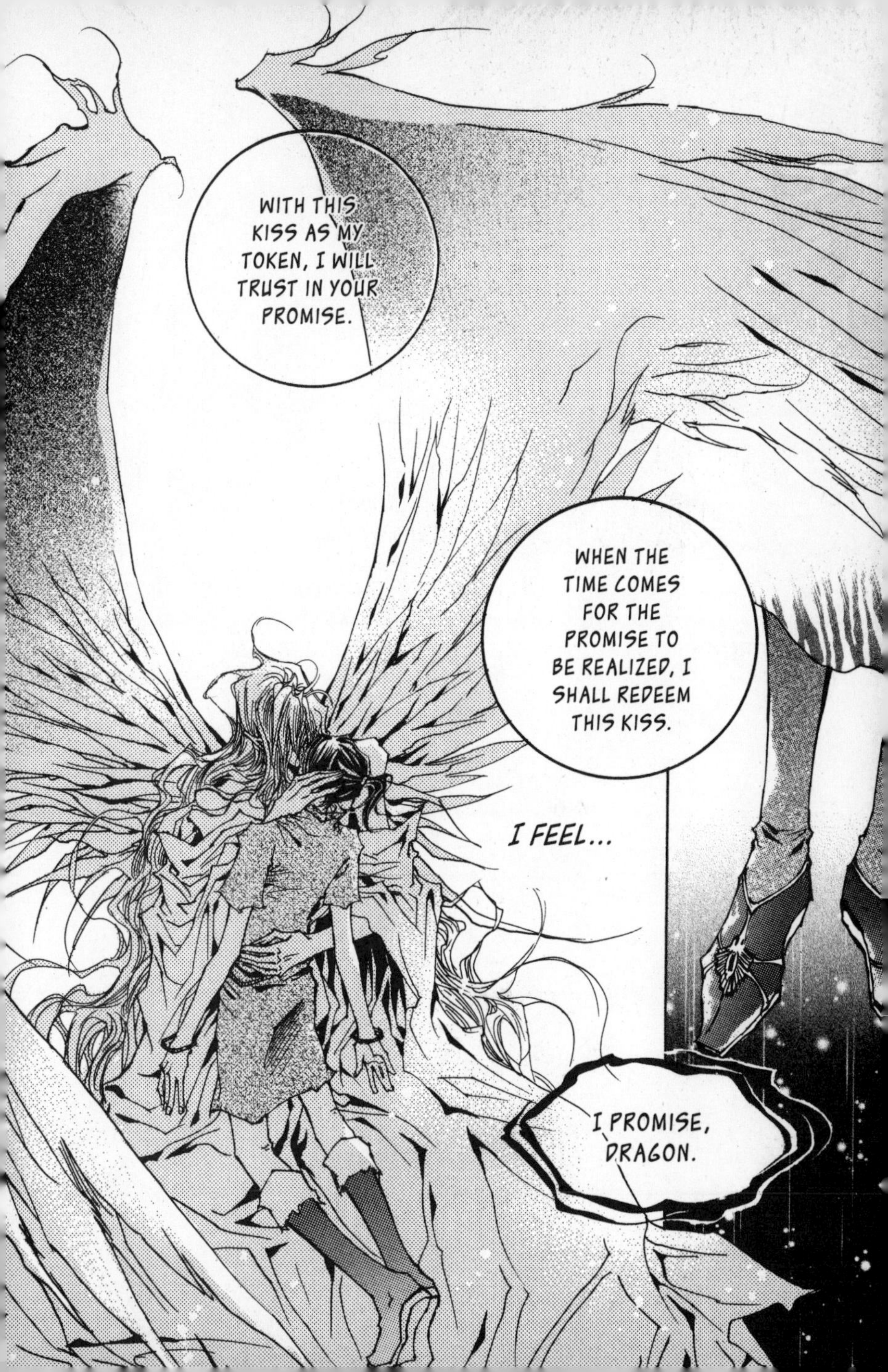
WITH THIS KISS AS MY TOKEN, I WILL TRUST IN YOUR PROMISE.
WHEN THE TIME COMES FOR THE PROMISE TO BE REALIZED, I SHALL REDEEM THIS KISS.
I FEEL...
I PROMISE, DRAGON.

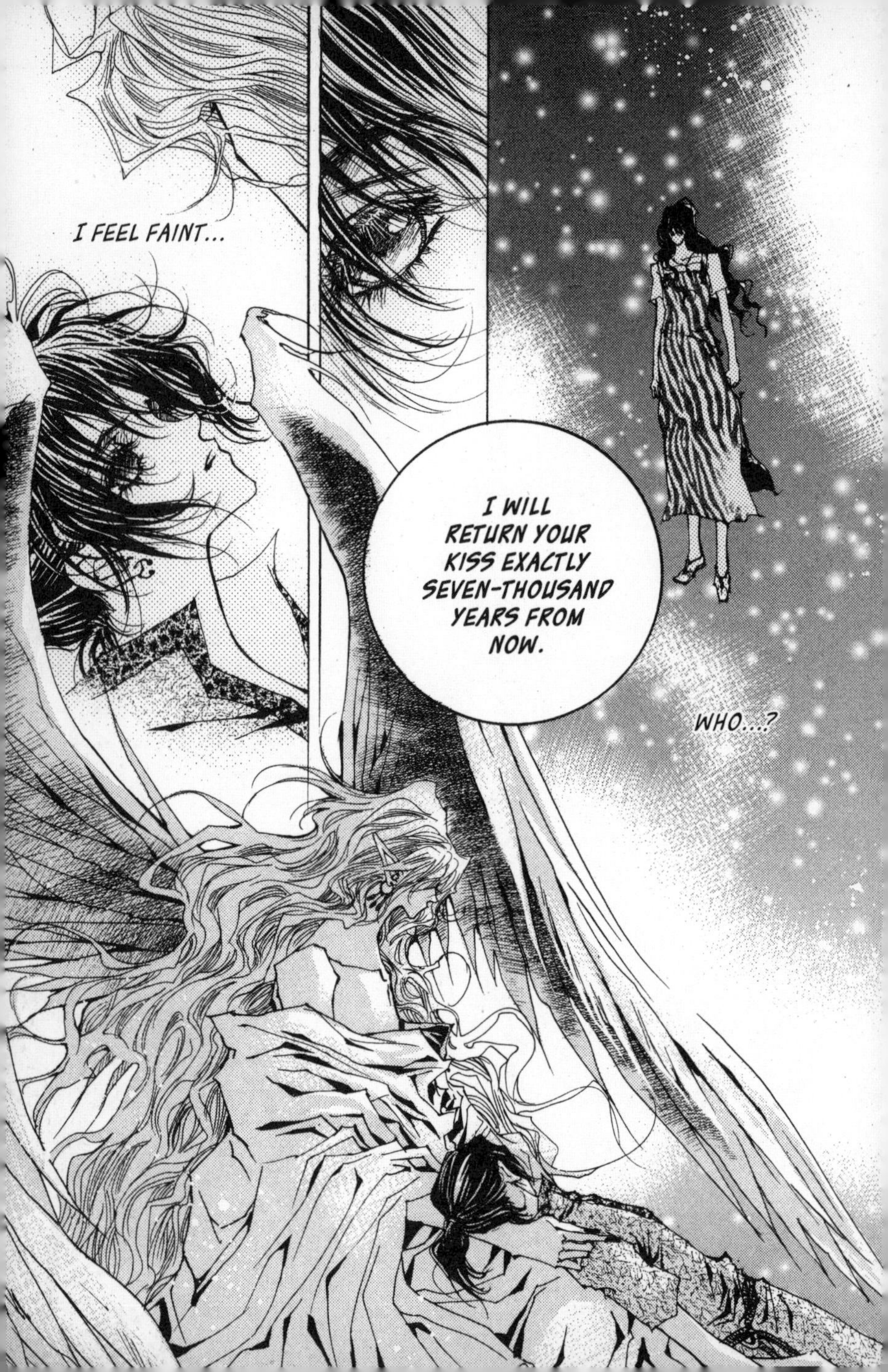
I WILL RETURN YOUR KISS EXACTLY SEVEN-THOUSAND YEARS FROM NOW.
WHO...?
I FEEL FAINT...

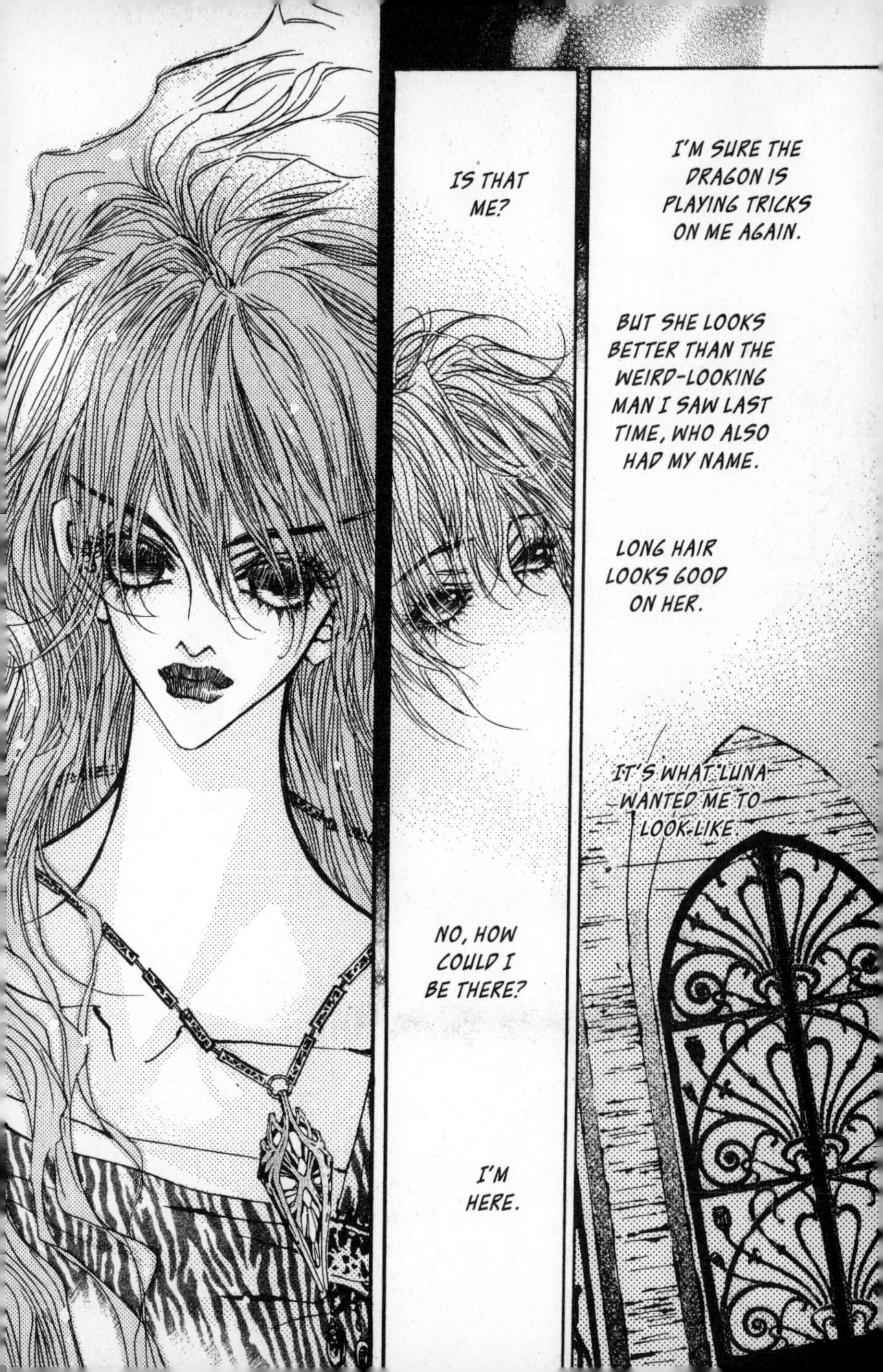
I'M SURE THE DRAGON IS PLAYING TRICKS ON ME AGAIN.
BUT SHE LOOKS BETTER THAN THE WEIRD-LOOKING MAN I SAW LAST TIME, WHO ALSO HAD MY NAME.
LONG HAIR LOOKS GOOD ON HER.
IT'S WHAT LUNA WANTED ME TO LOOK LIKE.
IS THAT ME?
NO, HOW COULD I BE THERE?
I'M HERE.

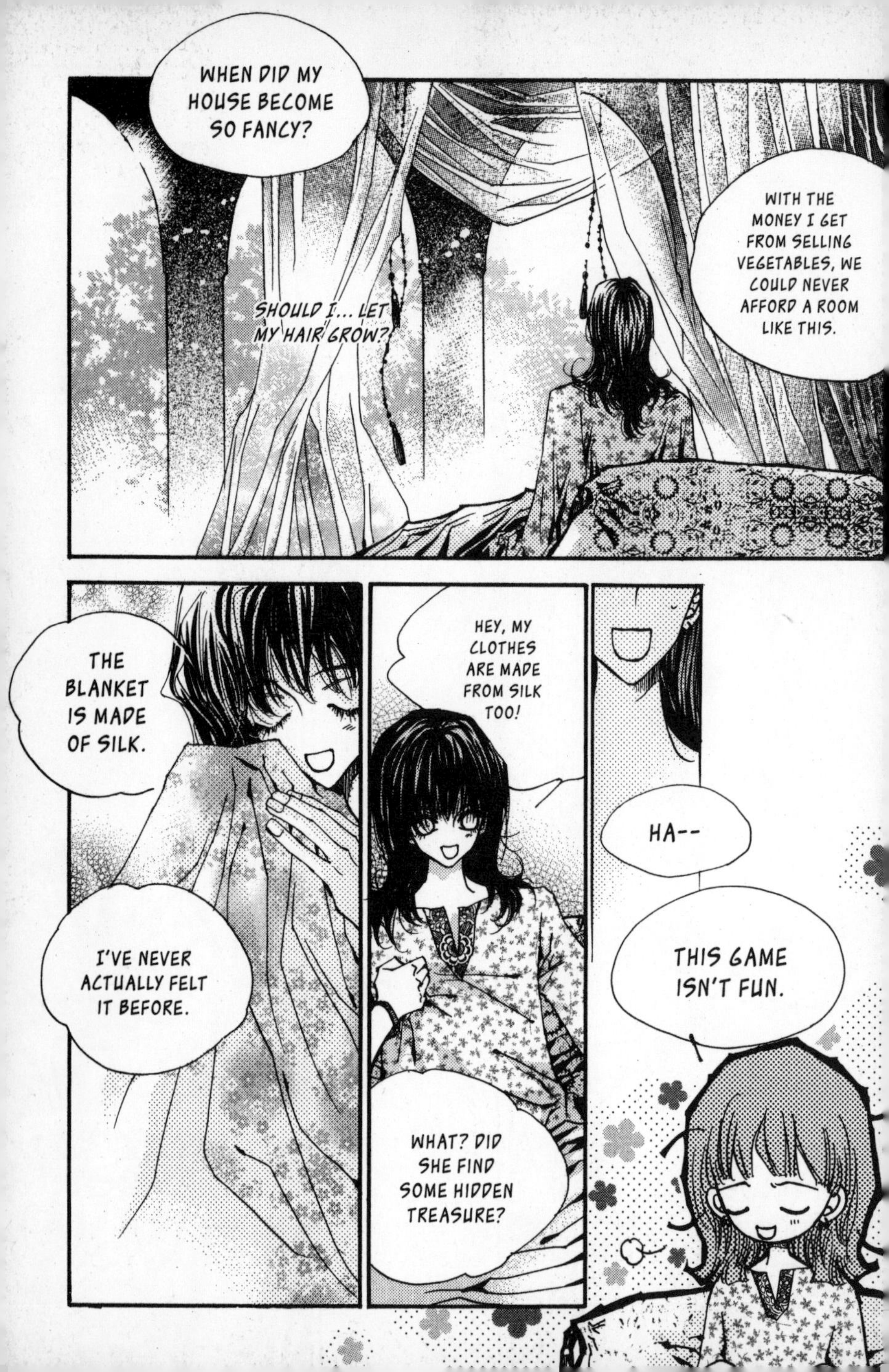
WHEN DID MY HOUSE BECOME SO FANCY?
SHOULD I... LET MY HAIR GROW?
WITH THE MONEY I GET FROM SELLING VEGETABLES, WE COULD NEVER AFFORD A ROOM LIKE THIS.
THE BLANKET IS MADE OF SILK.
I'VE NEVER ACTUALLY FELT IT BEFORE.
HEY, MY CLOTHES ARE MADE FROM SILK TOO!
WHAT? DID SHE FIND SOME HIDDEN TREASURE?
HA--
THIS GAME ISN'T FUN.

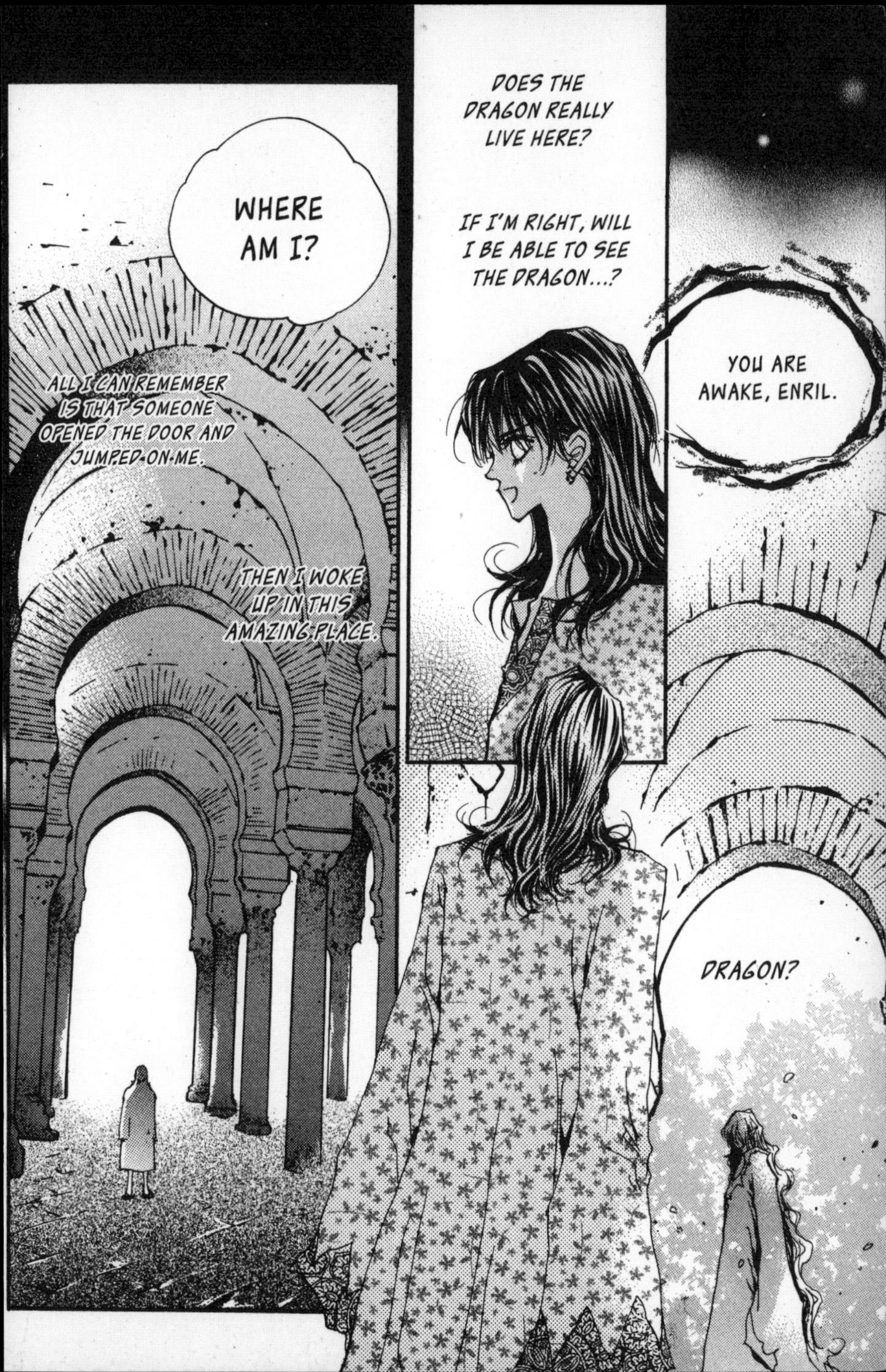
WHERE AM I?
ALL I CAN REMEMBER IS THAT SOMEONE OPENED THE DOOR AND JUMPED ON ME.
THEN I WOKE UP IN THIS AMAZING PLACE.
DOES THE DRAGON REALLY LIVE HERE?
IF I'M RIGHT, WILL I BE ABLE TO SEE THE DRAGON...?
YOU ARE AWAKE, ENRIL.
DRAGON?

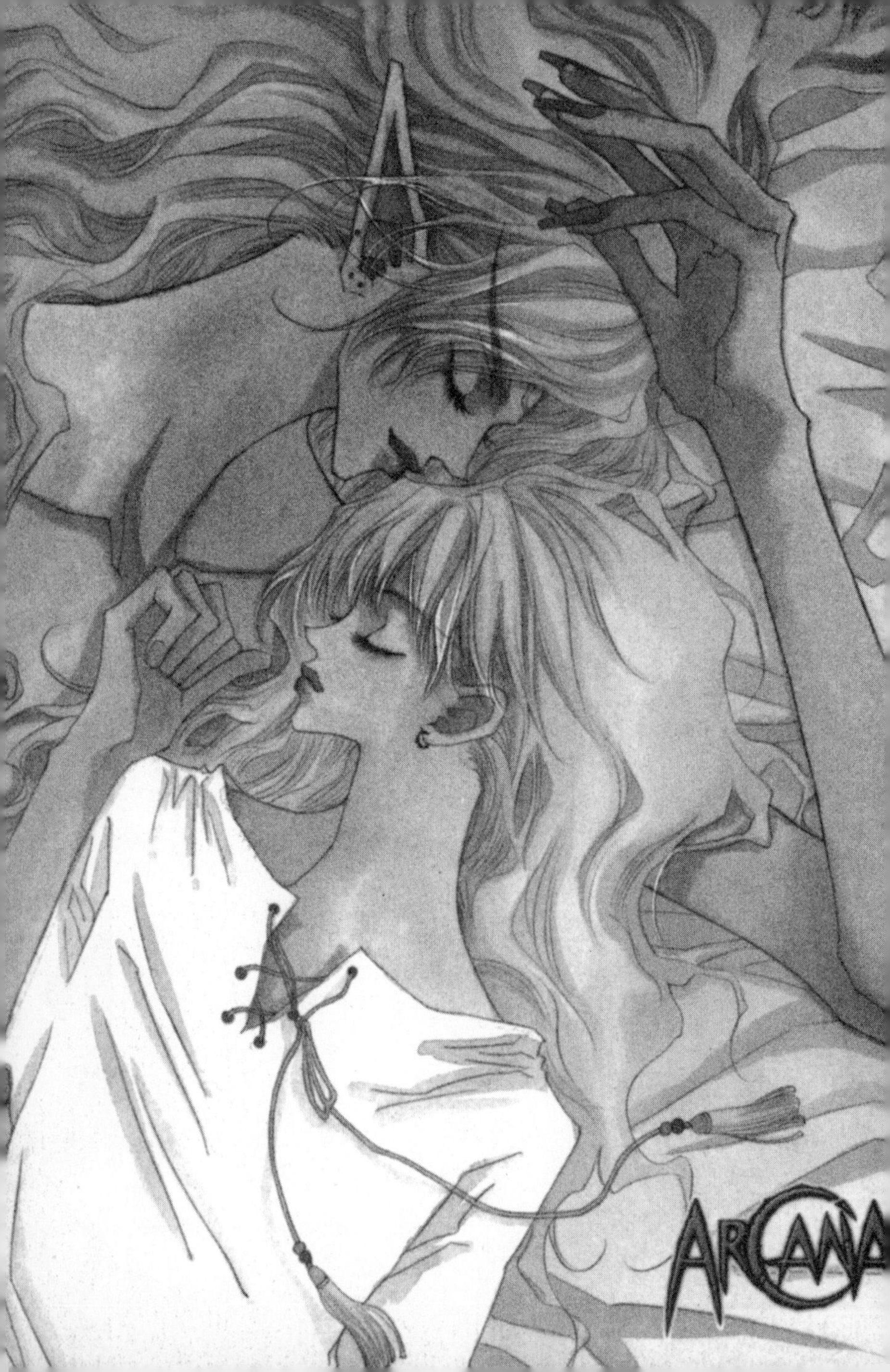
ArCana

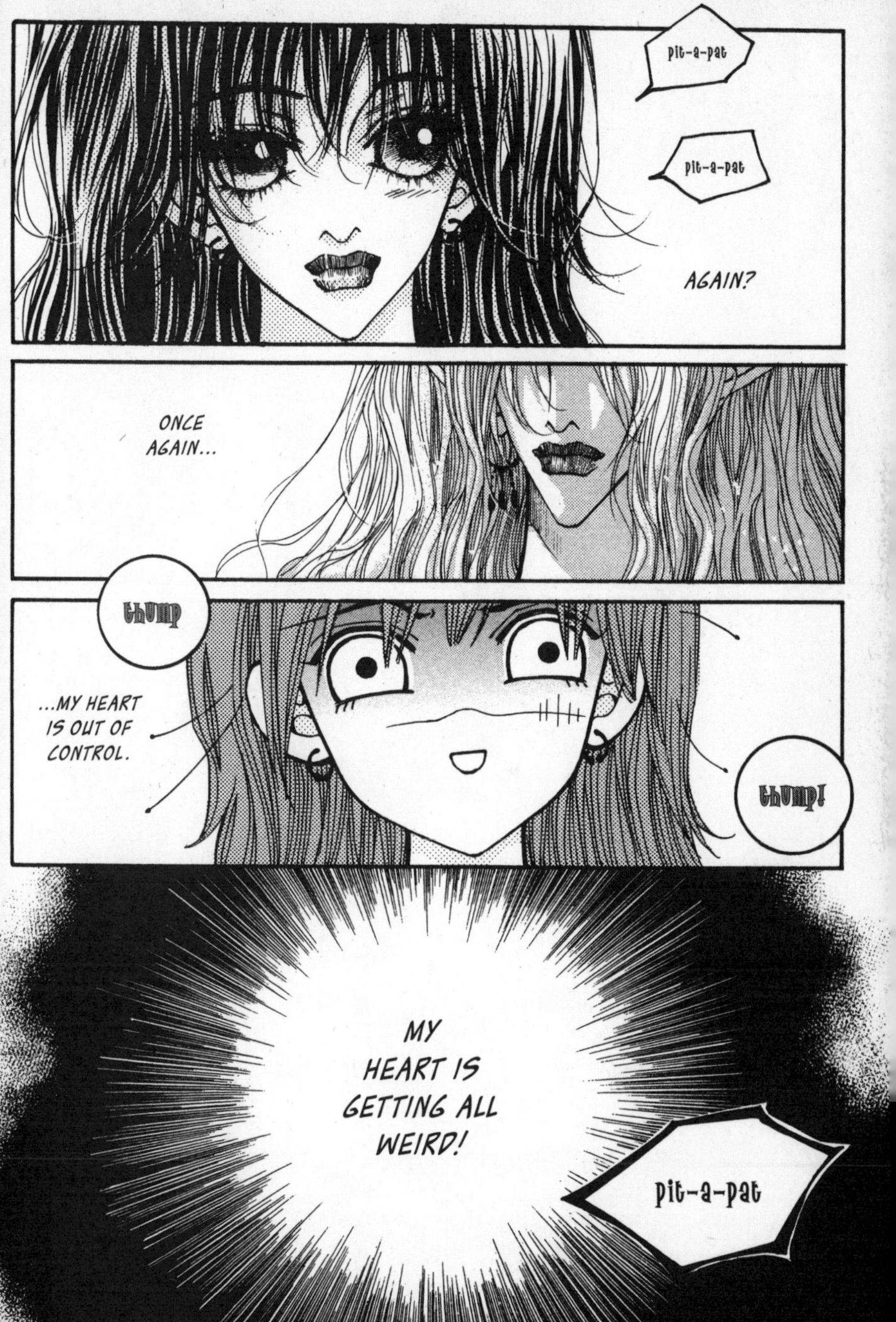
pit-a-pat
pit-a-pat
AGAIN?
ONCE AGAIN...
thump
...MY HEART IS OUT OF CONTROL.
thump!
MY HEART IS GETTING ALL WEIRD!
pit-a-pat

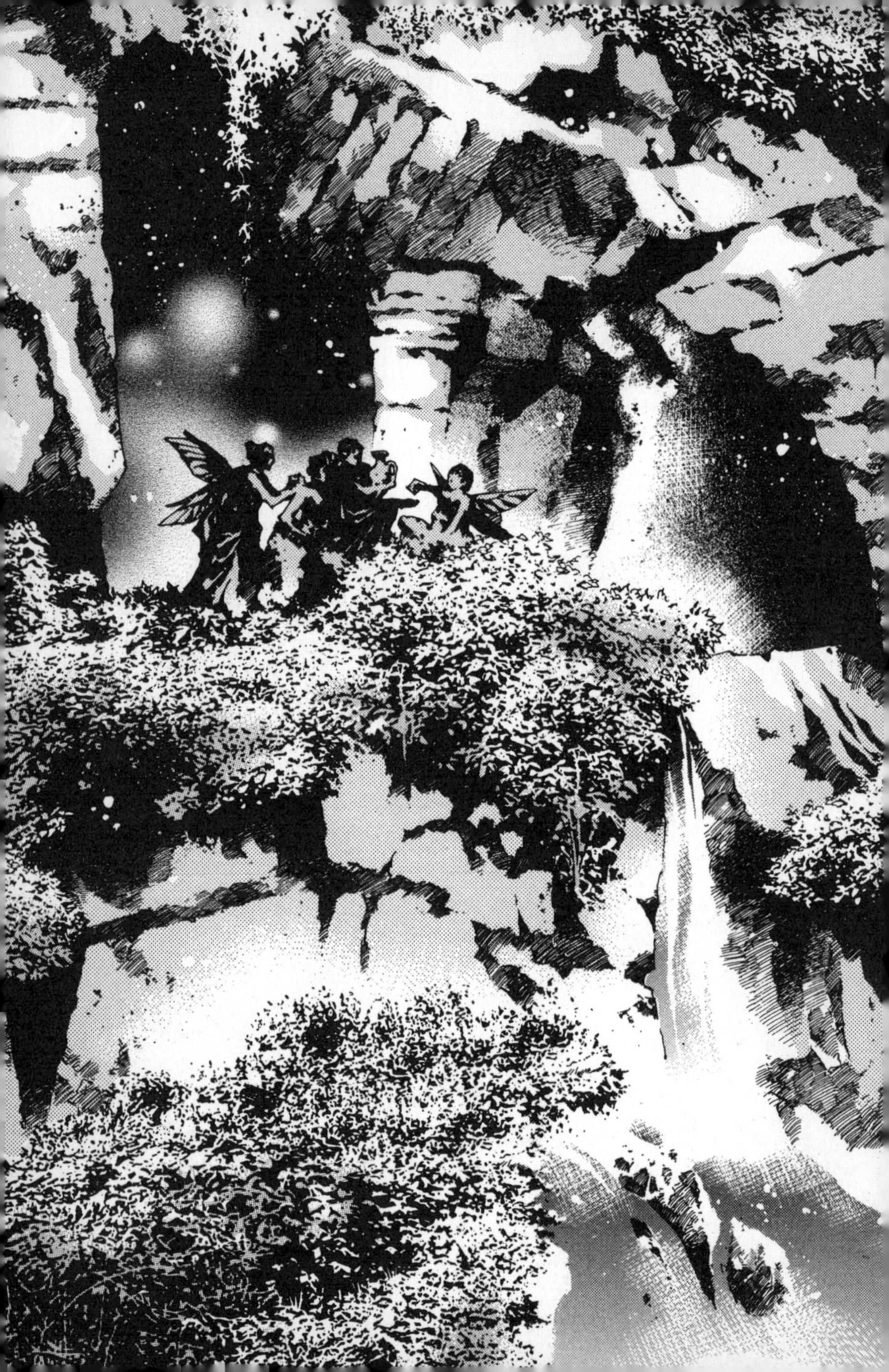

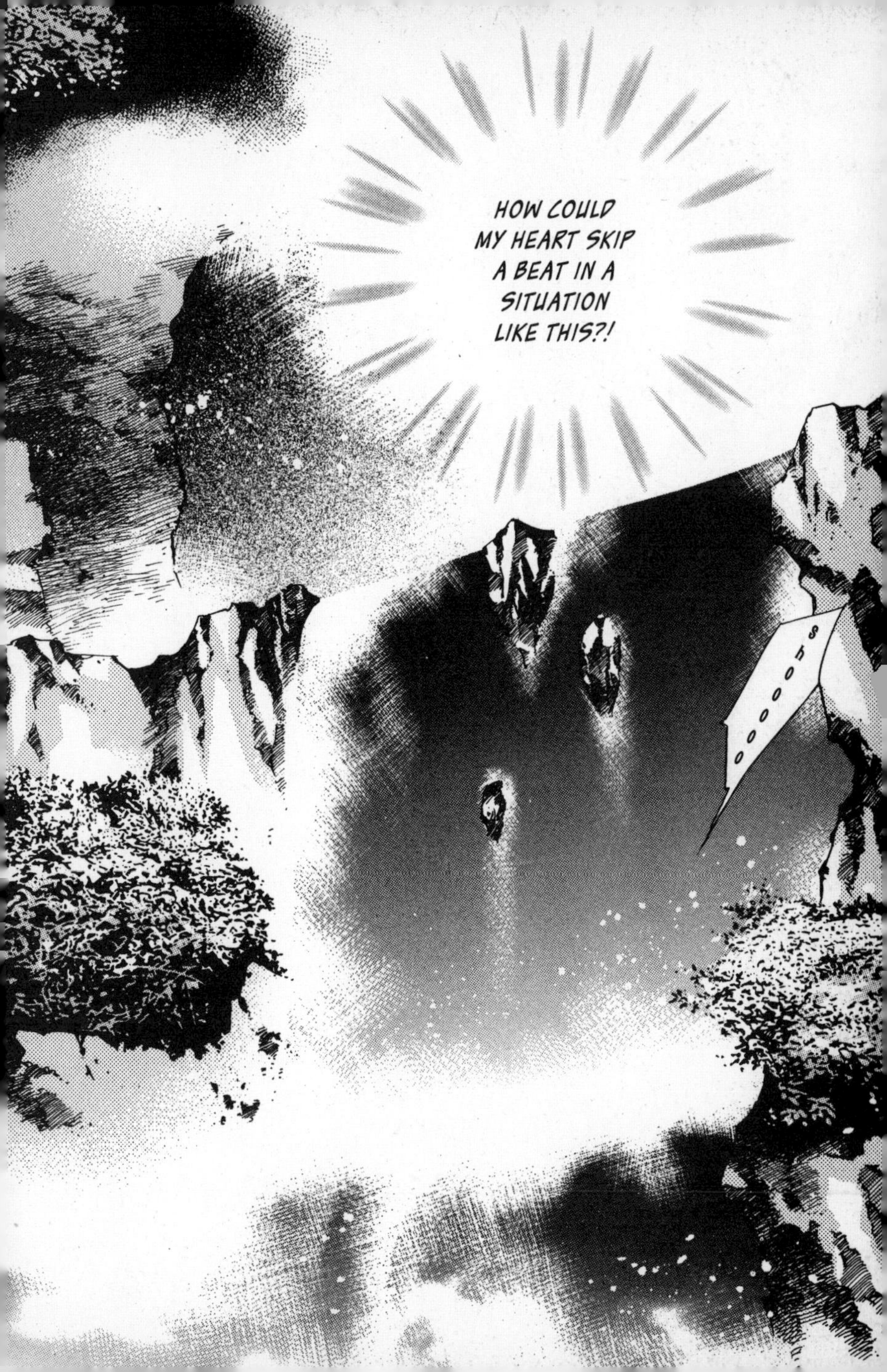
HOW COULD MY HEART SKIP A BEAT IN A SITUATION LIKE THIS?!
shooooooo

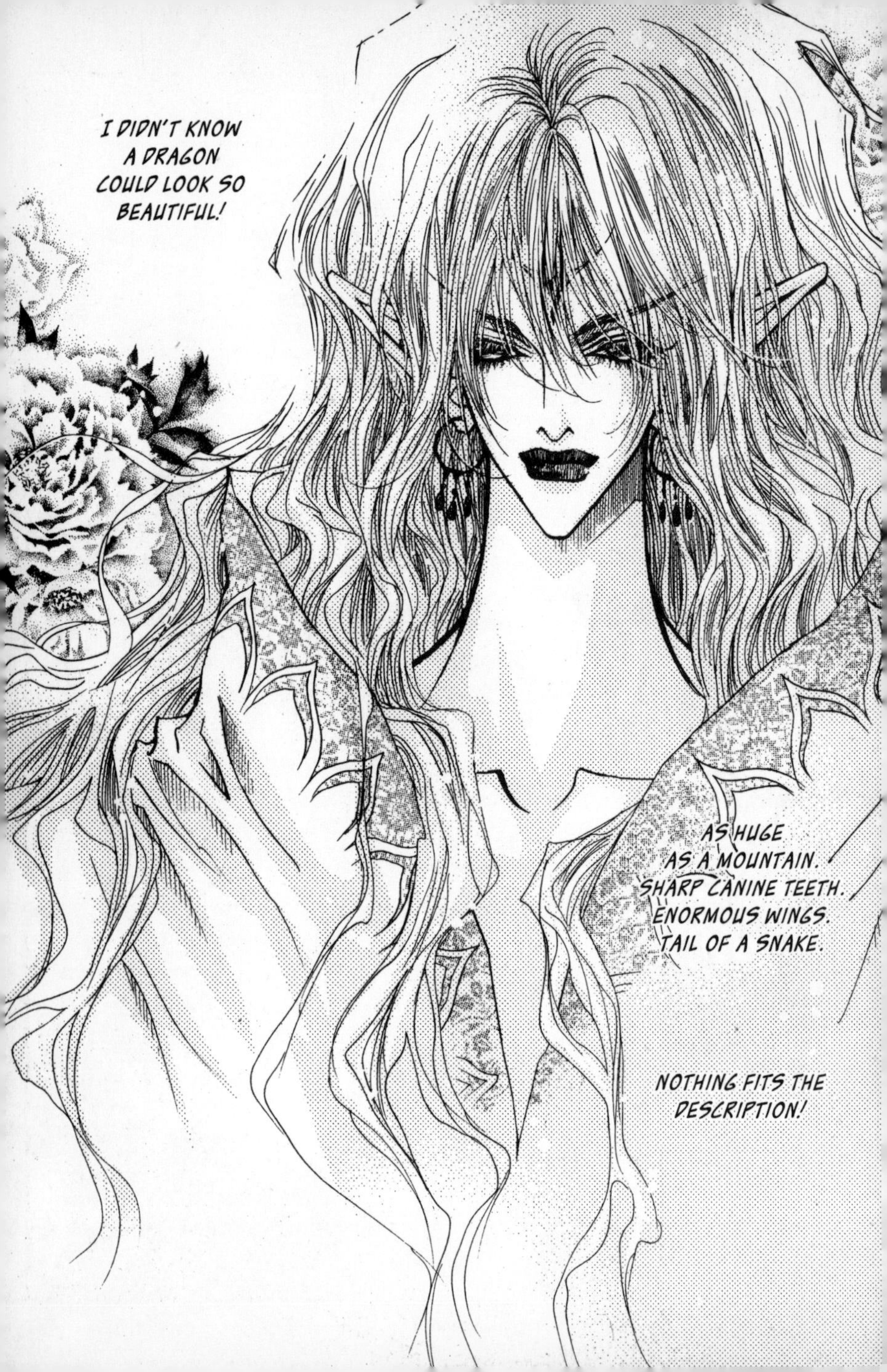
I DIDN'T KNOW A DRAGON COULD LOOK SO BEAUTIFUL!
AS HUGE AS A MOUNTAIN. SHARP CANINE TEETH. ENORMOUS WINGS. TAIL OF A SNAKE.
NOTHING FITS THE DESCRIPTION!

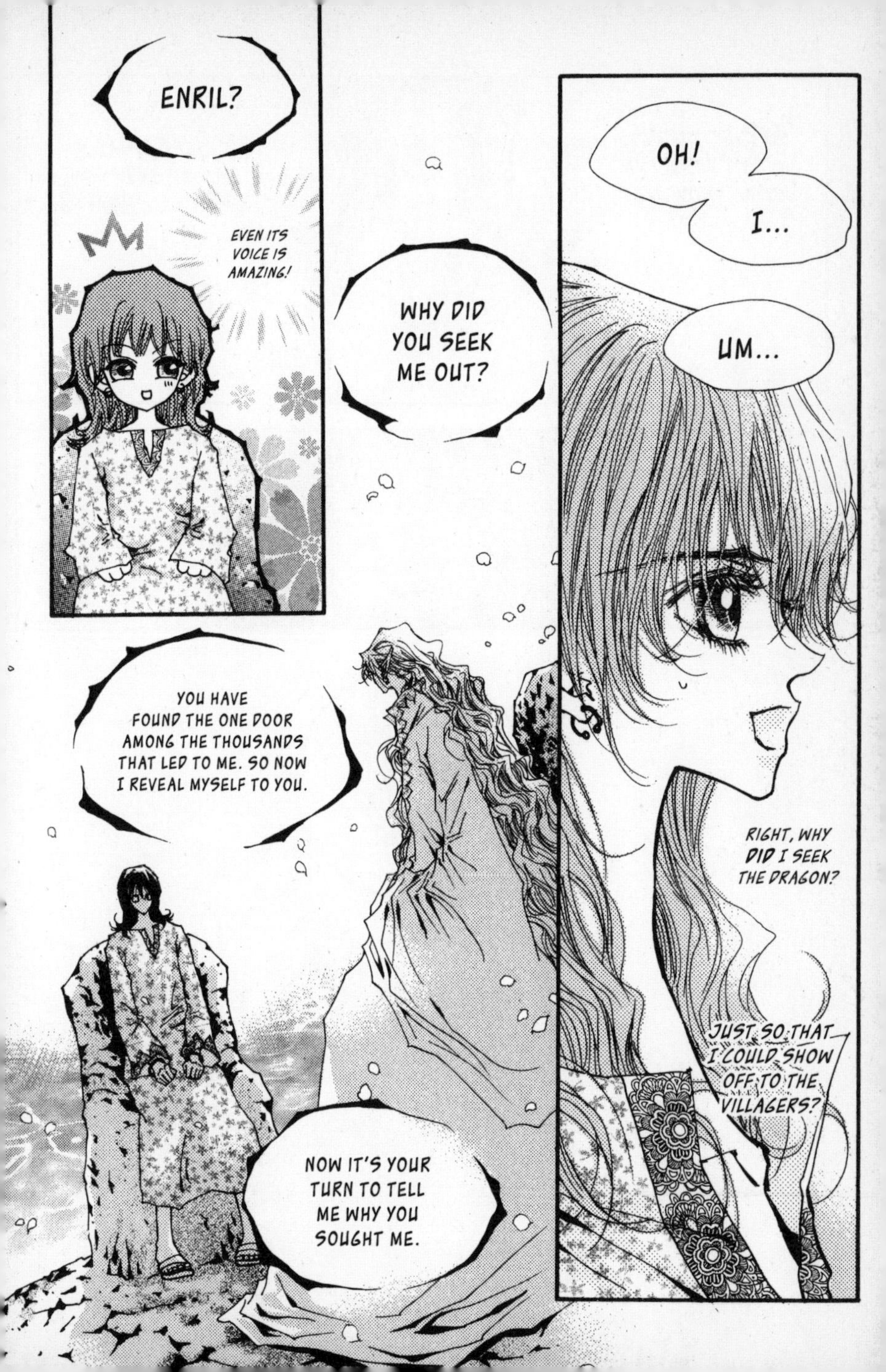
ENRIL?
EVEN ITS VOICE IS AMAZING!
WHY DID YOU SEEK ME OUT?
YOU HAVE FOUND THE ONE DOOR AMONG THE THOUSANDS THAT LED TO ME. SO NOW I REVEAL MYSELF TO YOU.
NOW IT'S YOUR TURN TO TELL ME WHY YOU SOUGHT ME.
OH!
I...
UM...
RIGHT, WHY DID I SEEK THE DRAGON?
JUST SO THAT I COULD SHOW OFF TO THE VILLAGERS?

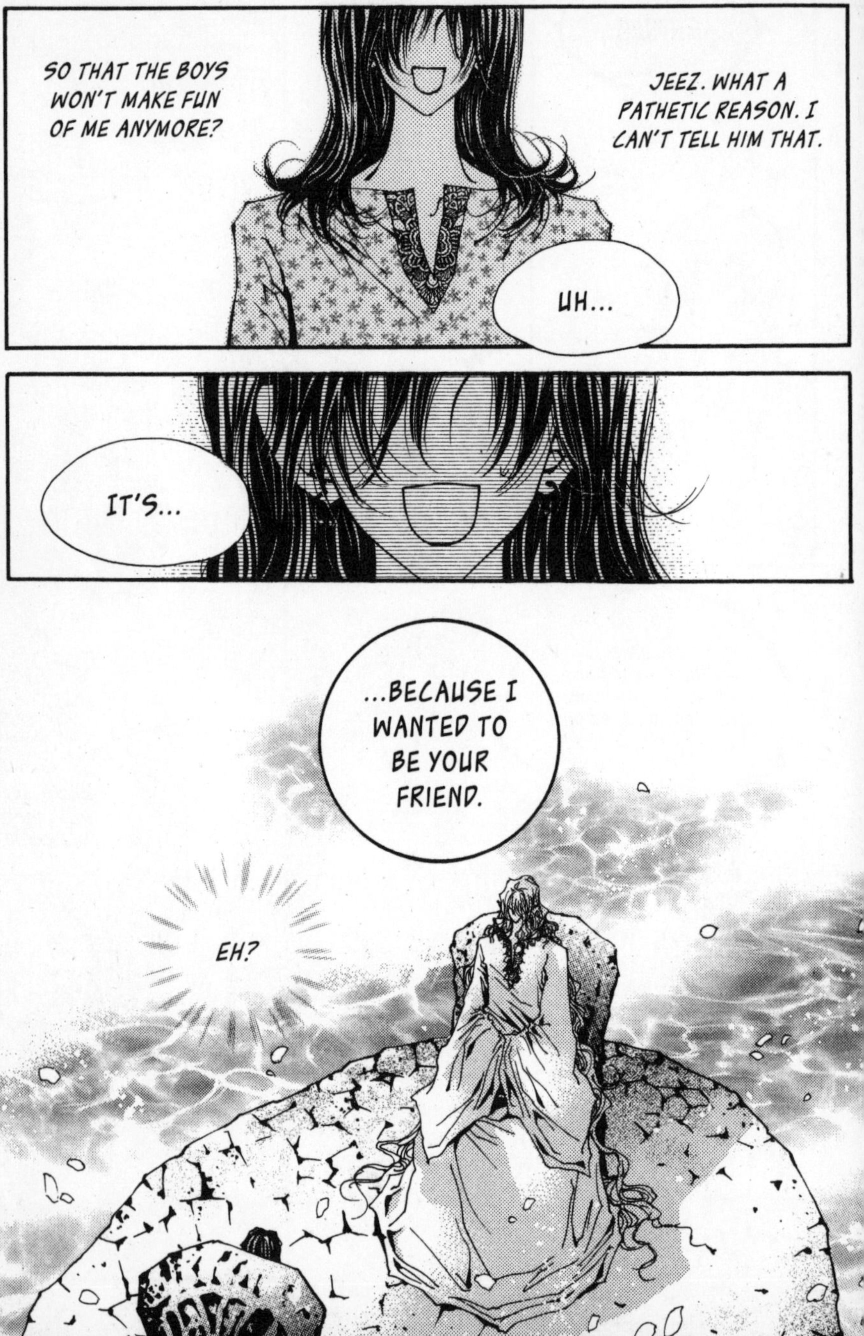
SO THAT THE BOYS WON'T MAKE FUN OF ME ANYMORE?
JEEZ. WHAT A PATHETIC REASON. I CAN'T TELL HIM THAT.
UH...
IT'S...
...BECAUSE I WANTED TO BE YOUR FRIEND.
EH?

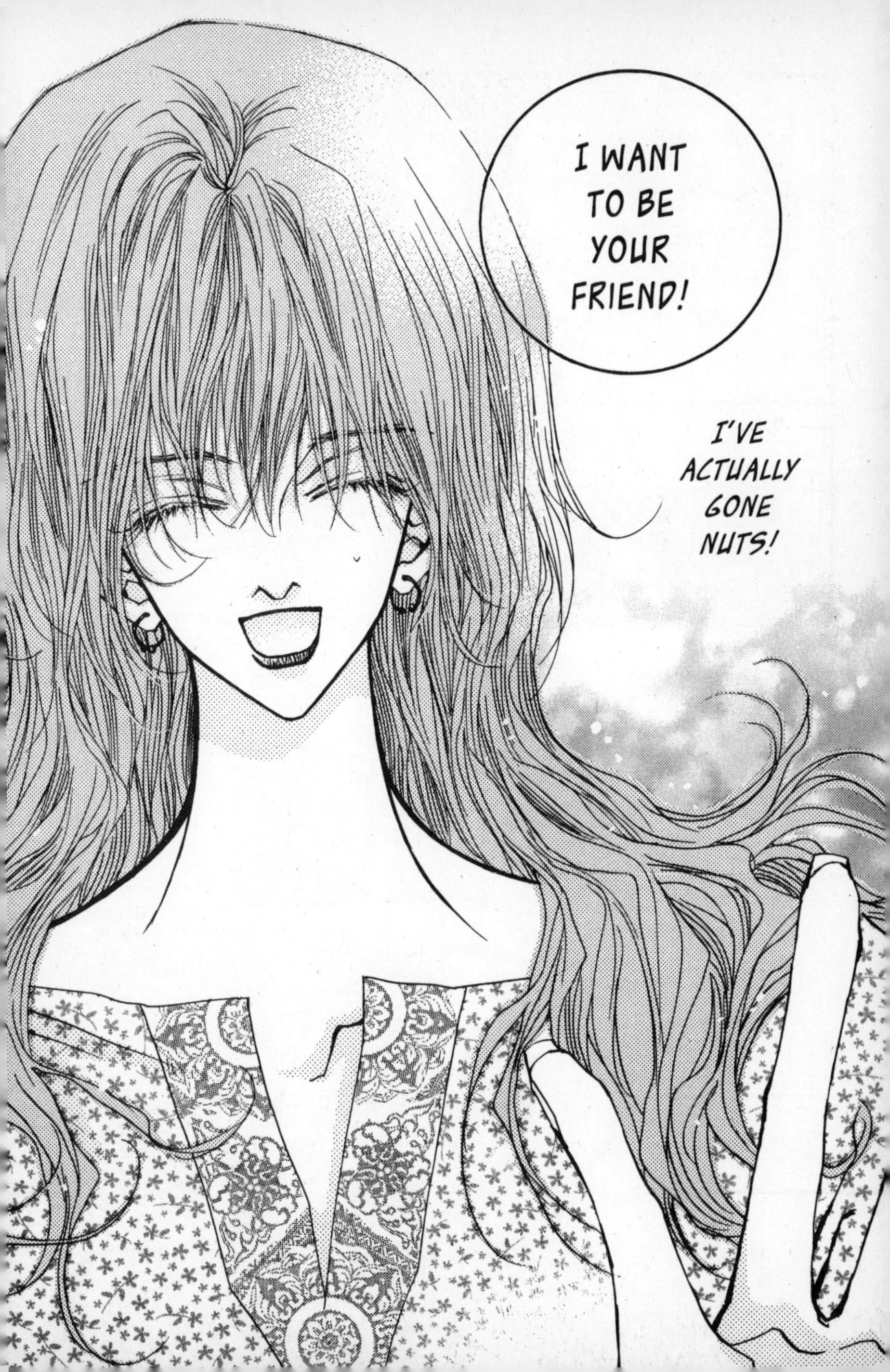
I WANT TO BE YOUR FRIEND!
I'VE ACTUALLY GONE NUTS!

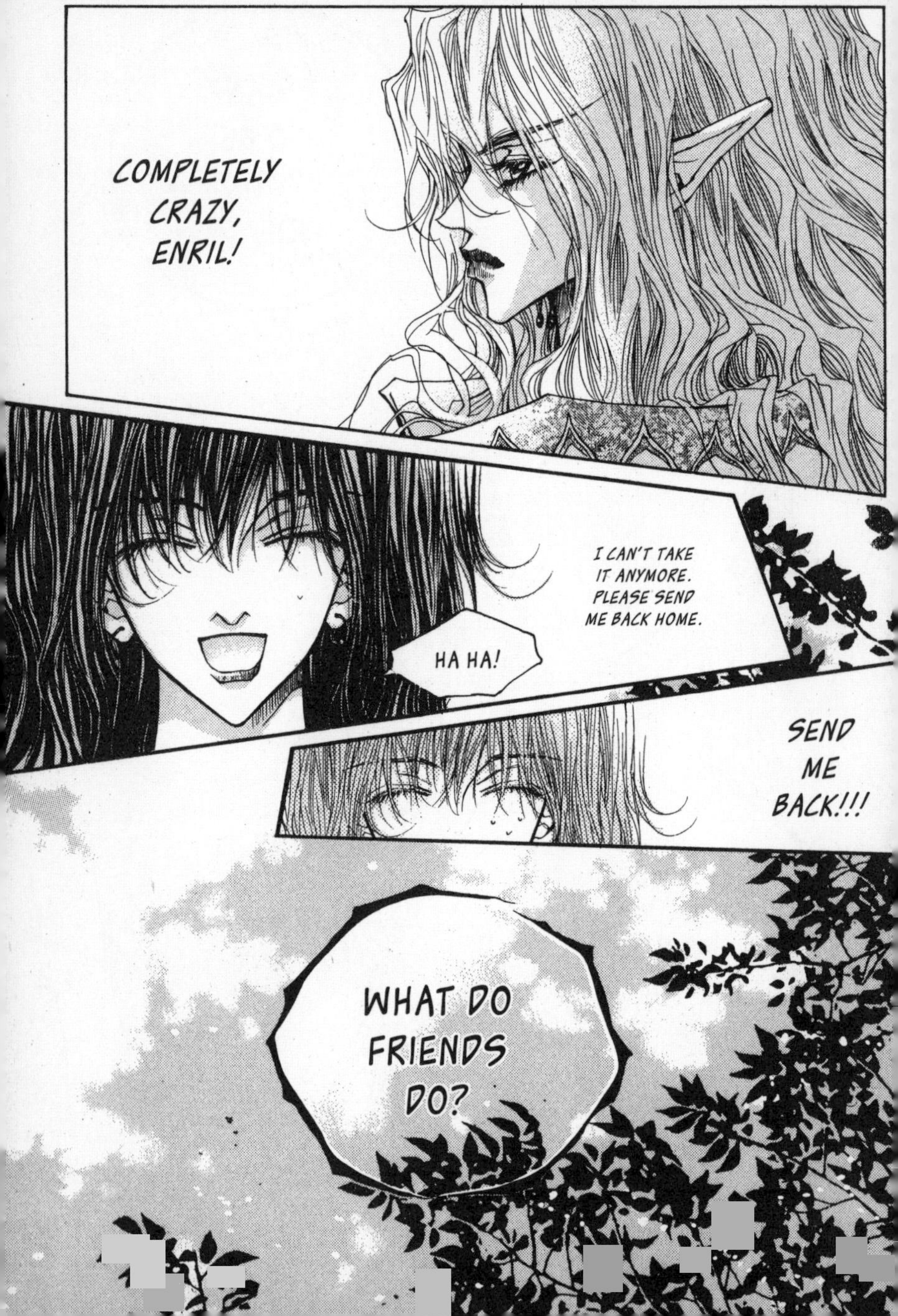
COMPLETELY CRAZY, ENRIL!
I CAN'T TAKE IT ANYMORE. PLEASE SEND ME BACK HOME.
HA HA!
SEND ME BACK!!!
WHAT DO FRIENDS DO?

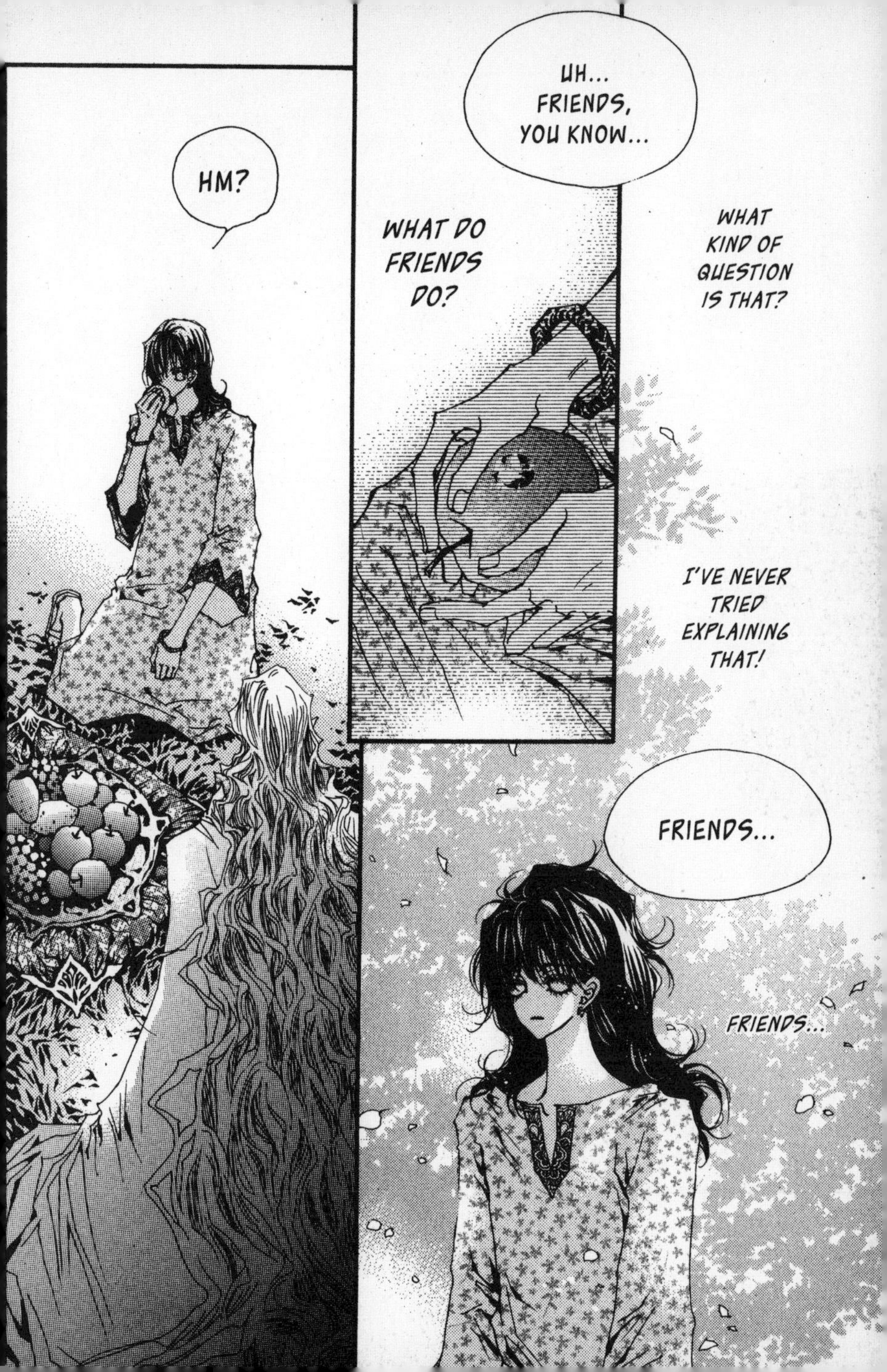

UH... FRIENDS, YOU KNOW...
WHAT DO FRIENDS DO?
WHAT KIND OF QUESTION IS THAT?
I'VE NEVER TRIED EXPLAINING THAT!
FRIENDS...
FRIENDS...
HM?

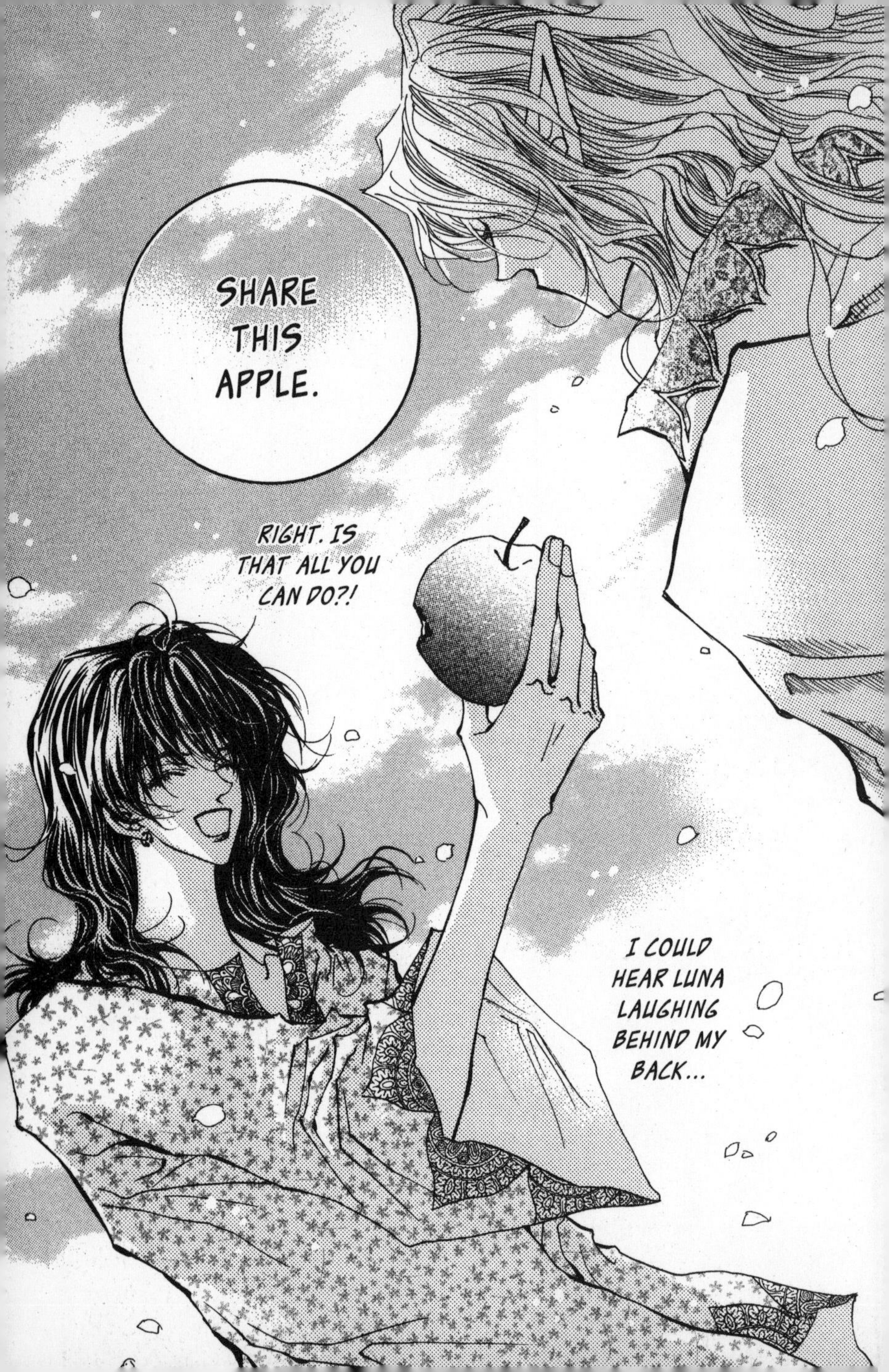
SHARE THIS APPLE.
RIGHT. IS THAT ALL YOU CAN DO?!
I COULD HEAR LUNA LAUGHING BEHIND MY BACK...

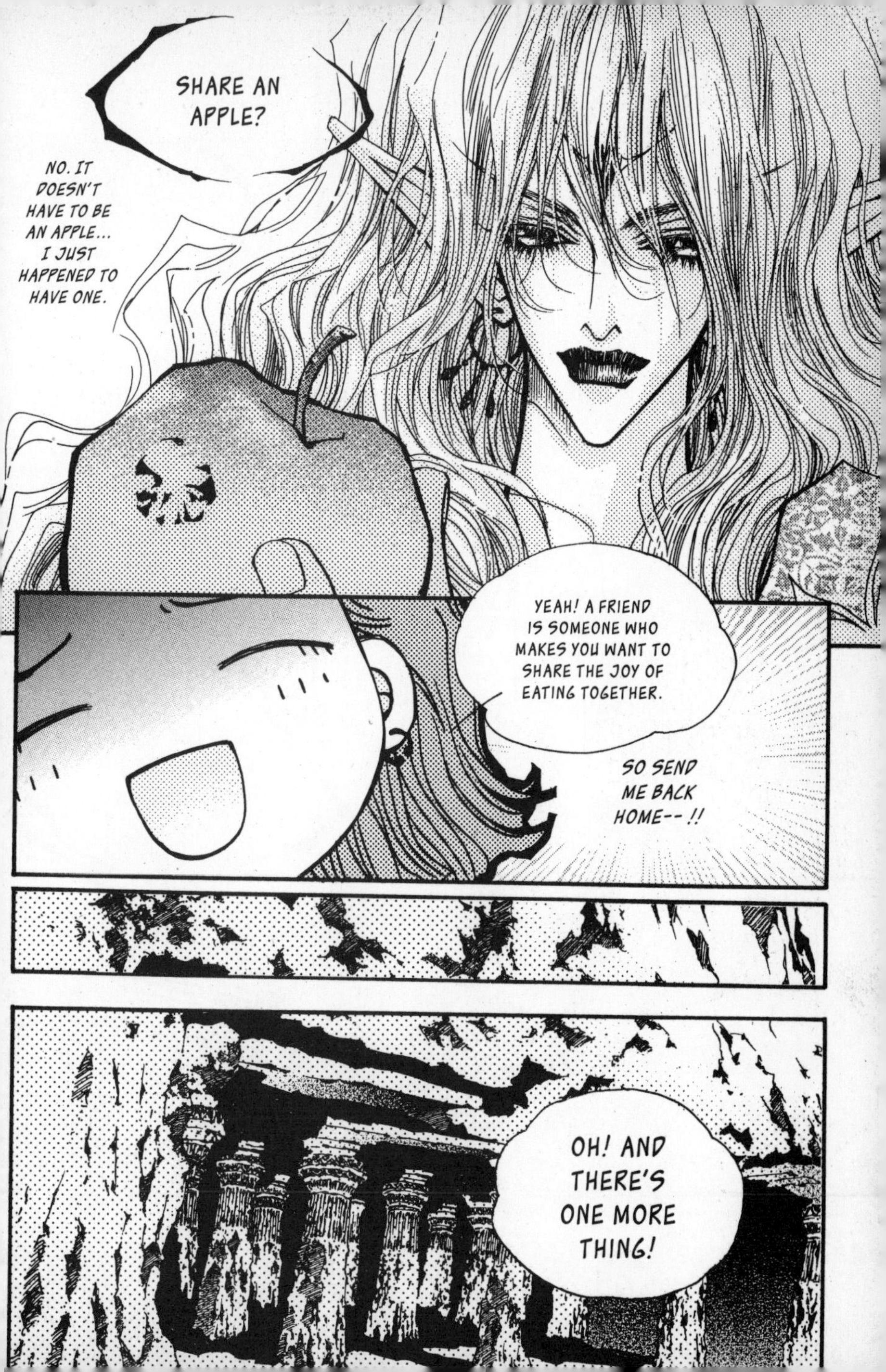
SHARE AN APPLE?
NO. IT DOESN'T HAVE TO BE AN APPLE... I JUST HAPPENED TO HAVE ONE.
YEAH! A FRIEND IS SOMEONE WHO MAKES YOU WANT TO SHARE THE JOY OF EATING TOGETHER.
SO SEND ME BACK HOME-- !!
OH! AND THERE'S ONE MORE THING!

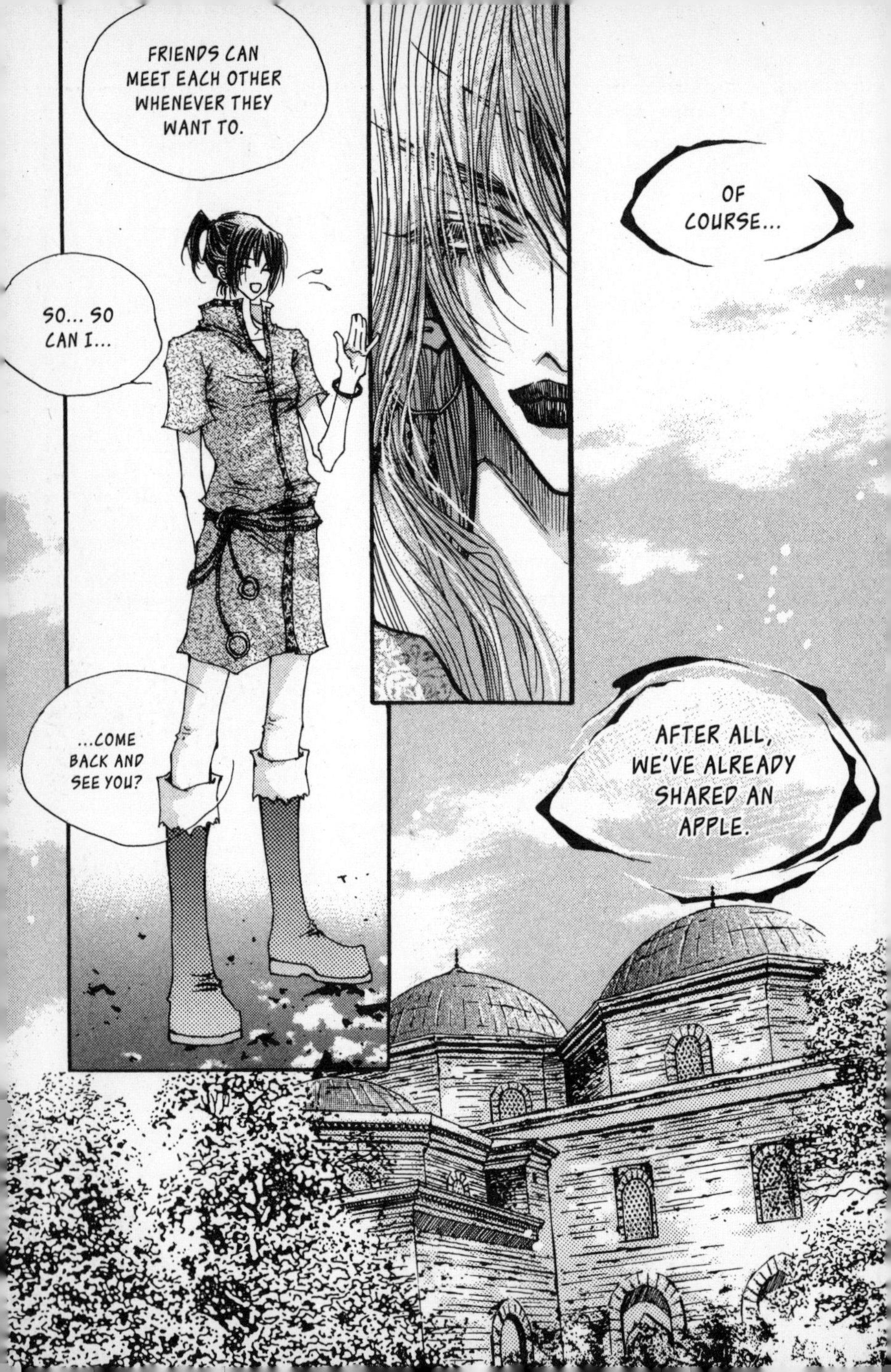
FRIENDS CAN MEET EACH OTHER WHENEVER THEY WANT TO.
SO... SO CAN I...
...COME BACK AND SEE YOU?
OF COURSE...
AFTER ALL, WE'VE ALREADY SHARED AN APPLE.

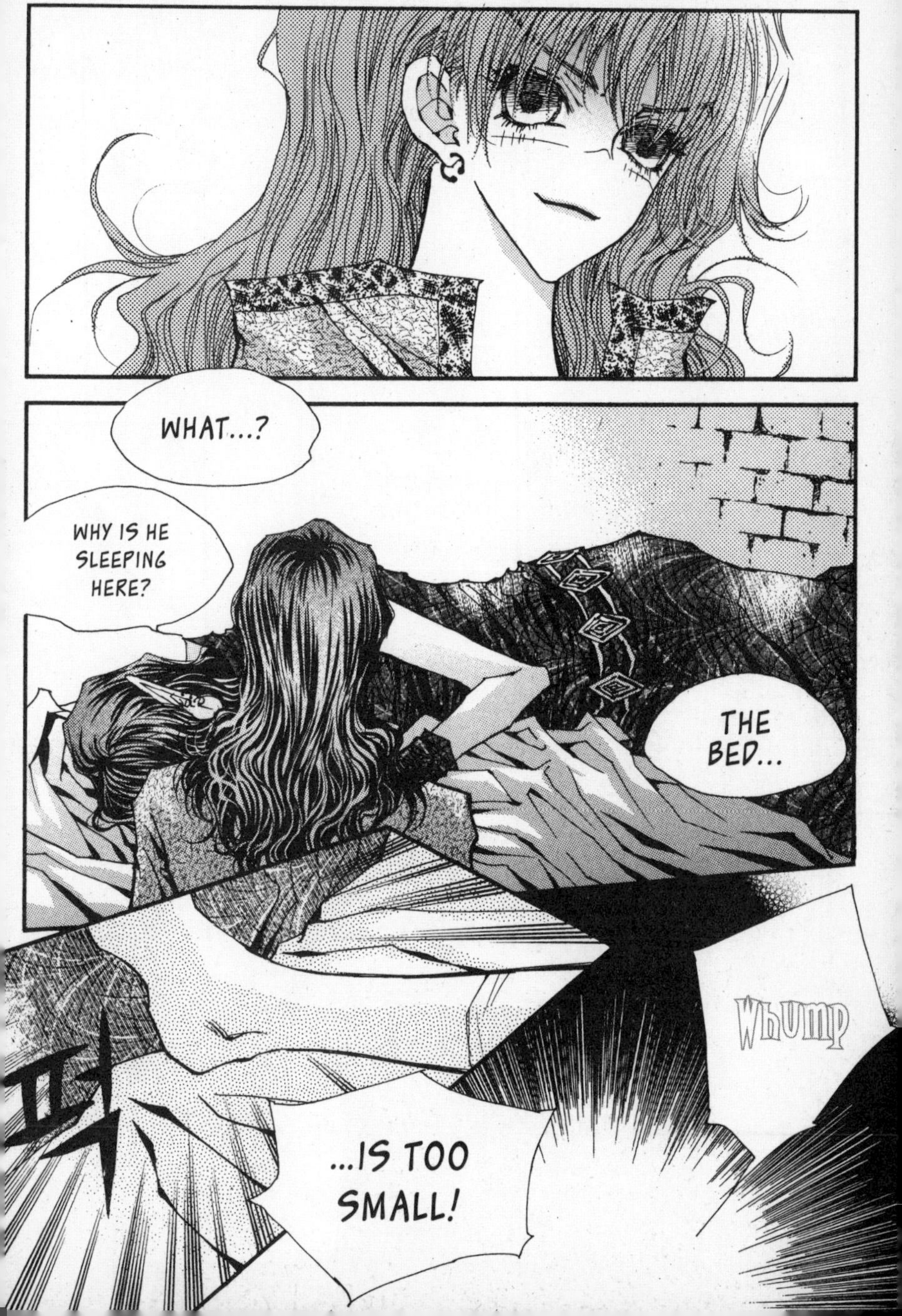
WHAT...?
WHY IS HE SLEEPING HERE?
THE BED...
WHUMP
...IS TOO SMALL!

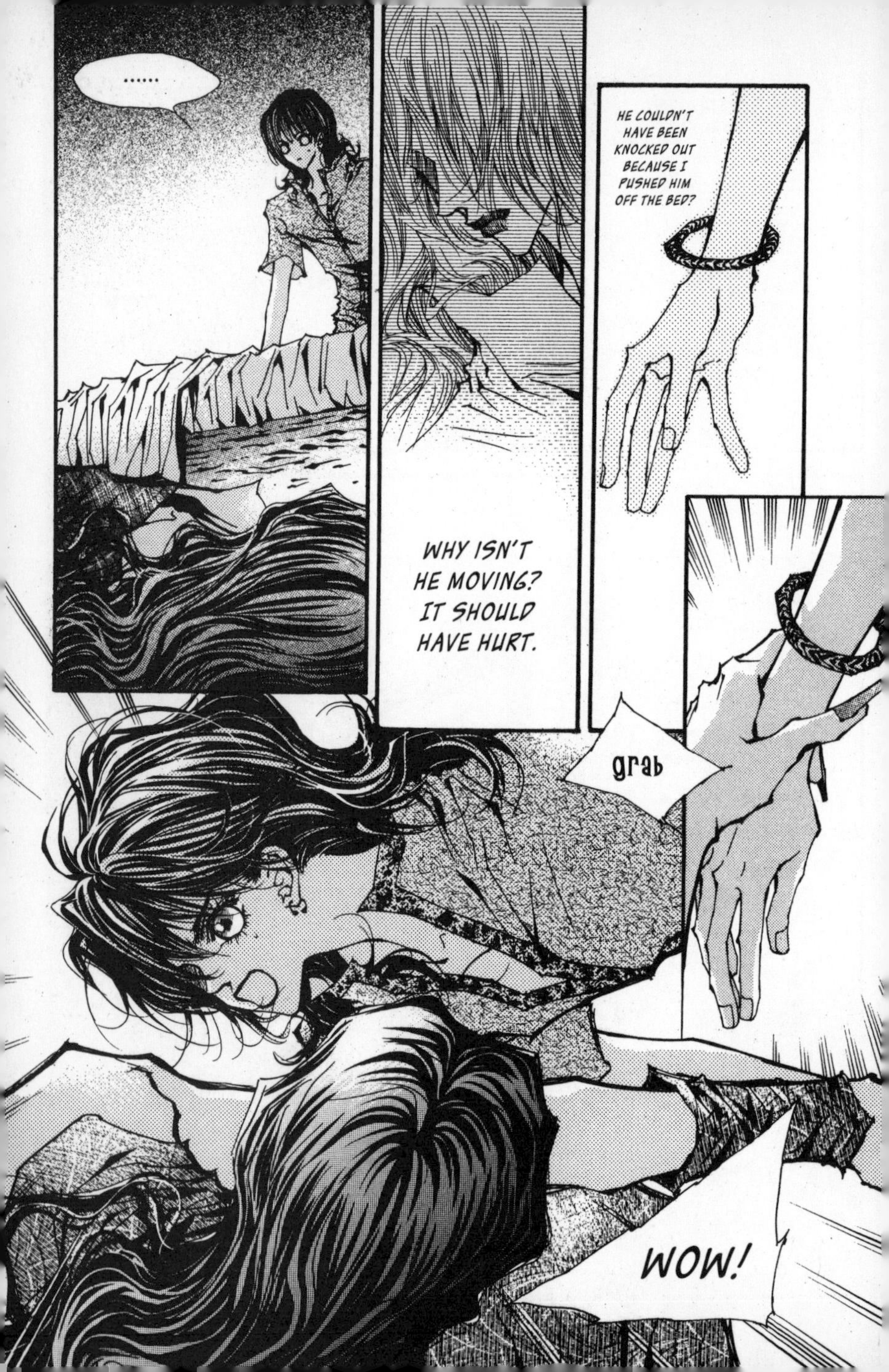
HE COULDN'T HAVE BEEN KNOCKED OUT BECAUSE I PUSHED HIM OFF THE BED?
WHY ISN'T HE MOVING? IT SHOULD HAVE HURT.
......
grab
WOW!

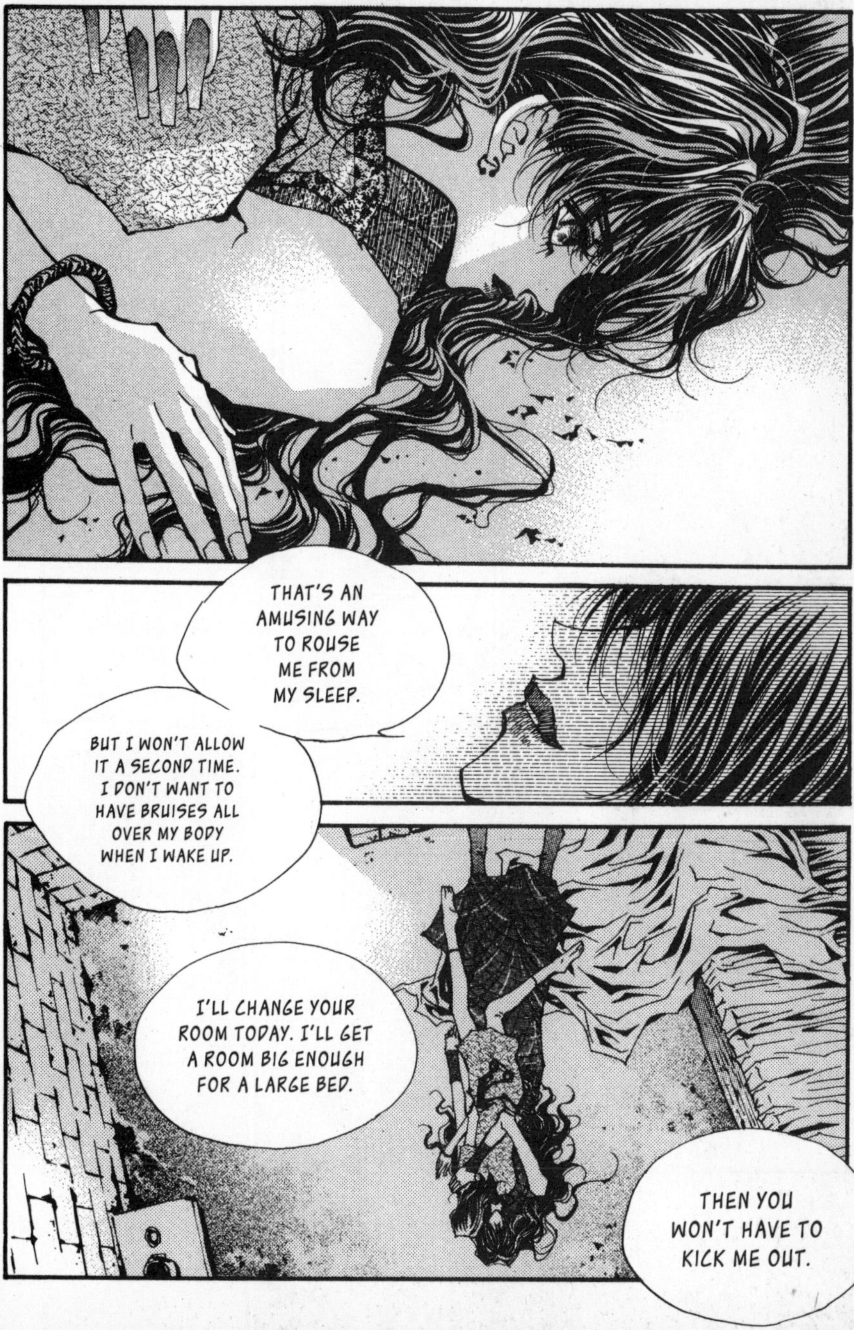
THAT'S AN AMUSING WAY TO ROUSE ME FROM MY SLEEP.
BUT I WON'T ALLOW IT A SECOND TIME. I DON'T WANT TO HAVE BRUISES ALL OVER MY BODY WHEN I WAKE UP.
I'LL CHANGE YOUR ROOM TODAY. I'LL GET A ROOM BIG ENOUGH FOR A LARGE BED.
THEN YOU WON'T HAVE TO KICK ME OUT.

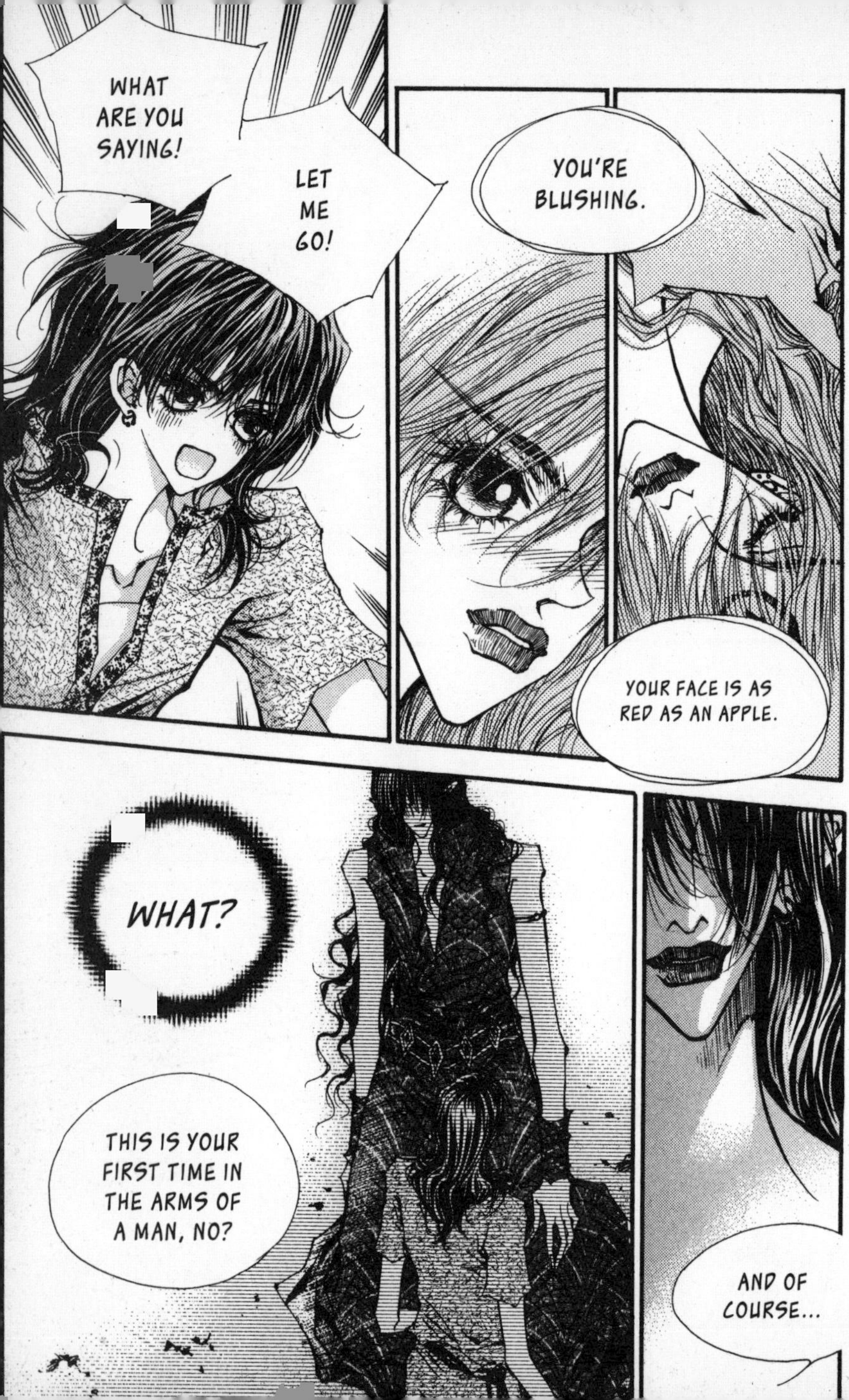
YOU'RE BLUSHING.
YOUR FACE IS AS RED AS AN APPLE.
WHAT ARE YOU SAYING!
LET ME GO!
AND OF COURSE...
WHAT?
THIS IS YOUR FIRST TIME IN THE ARMS OF A MAN, NO?

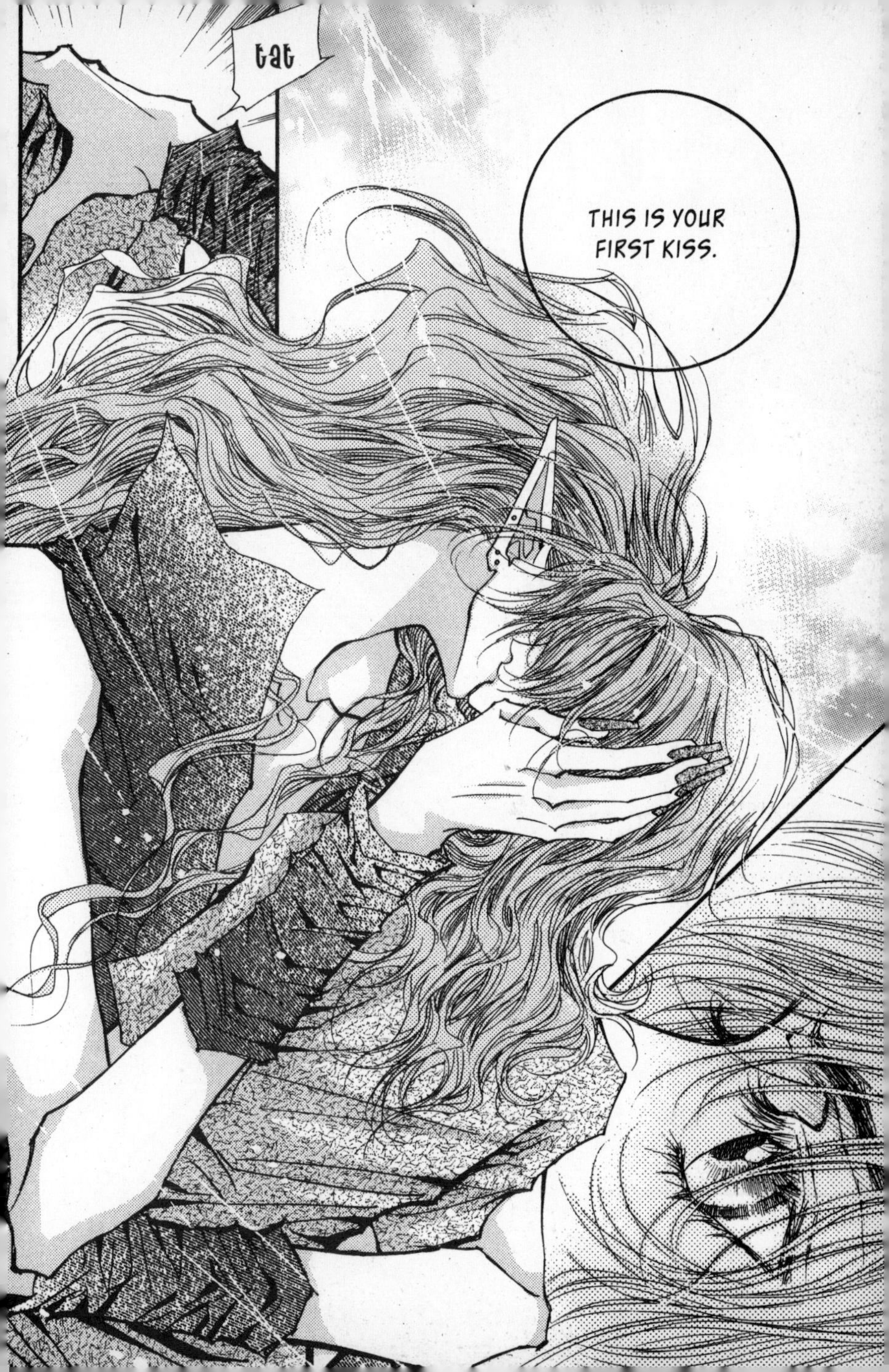
THIS IS YOUR FIRST KISS.
tat

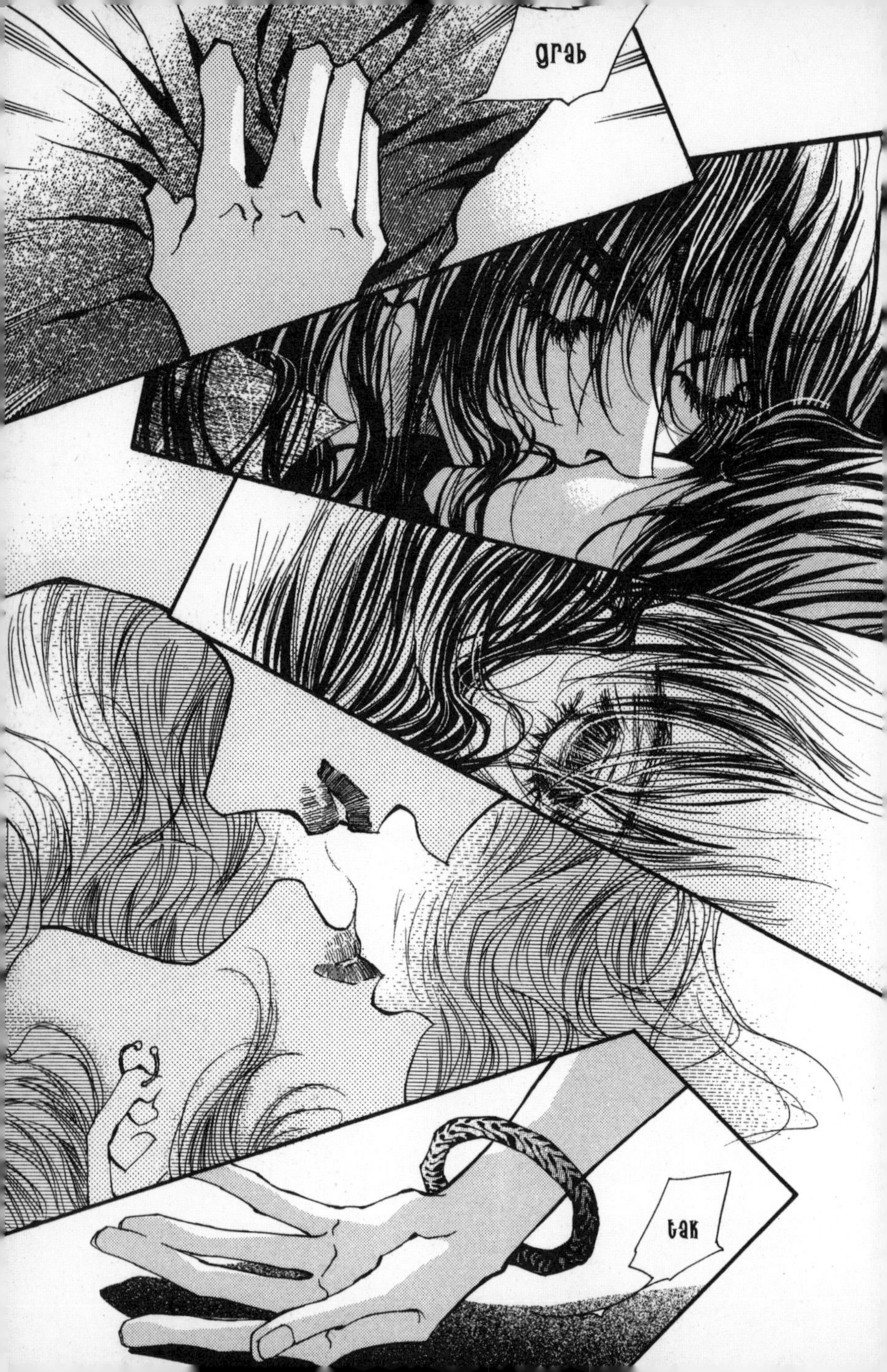
grab
tak

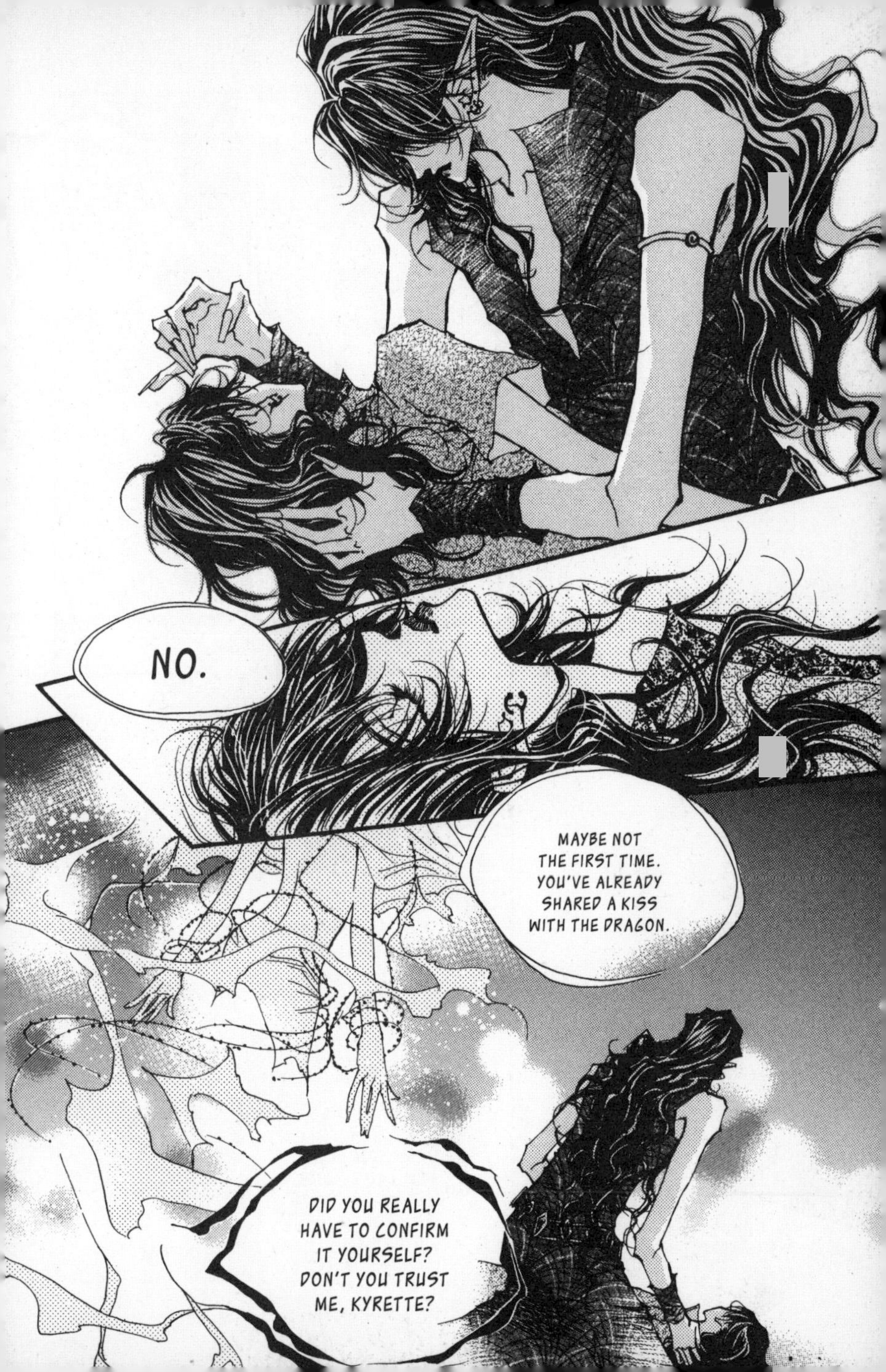
NO.
MAYBE NOT THE FIRST TIME. YOU'VE ALREADY SHARED A KISS WITH THE DRAGON.
DID YOU REALLY HAVE TO CONFIRM IT YOURSELF? DON'T YOU TRUST ME, KYRETTE?

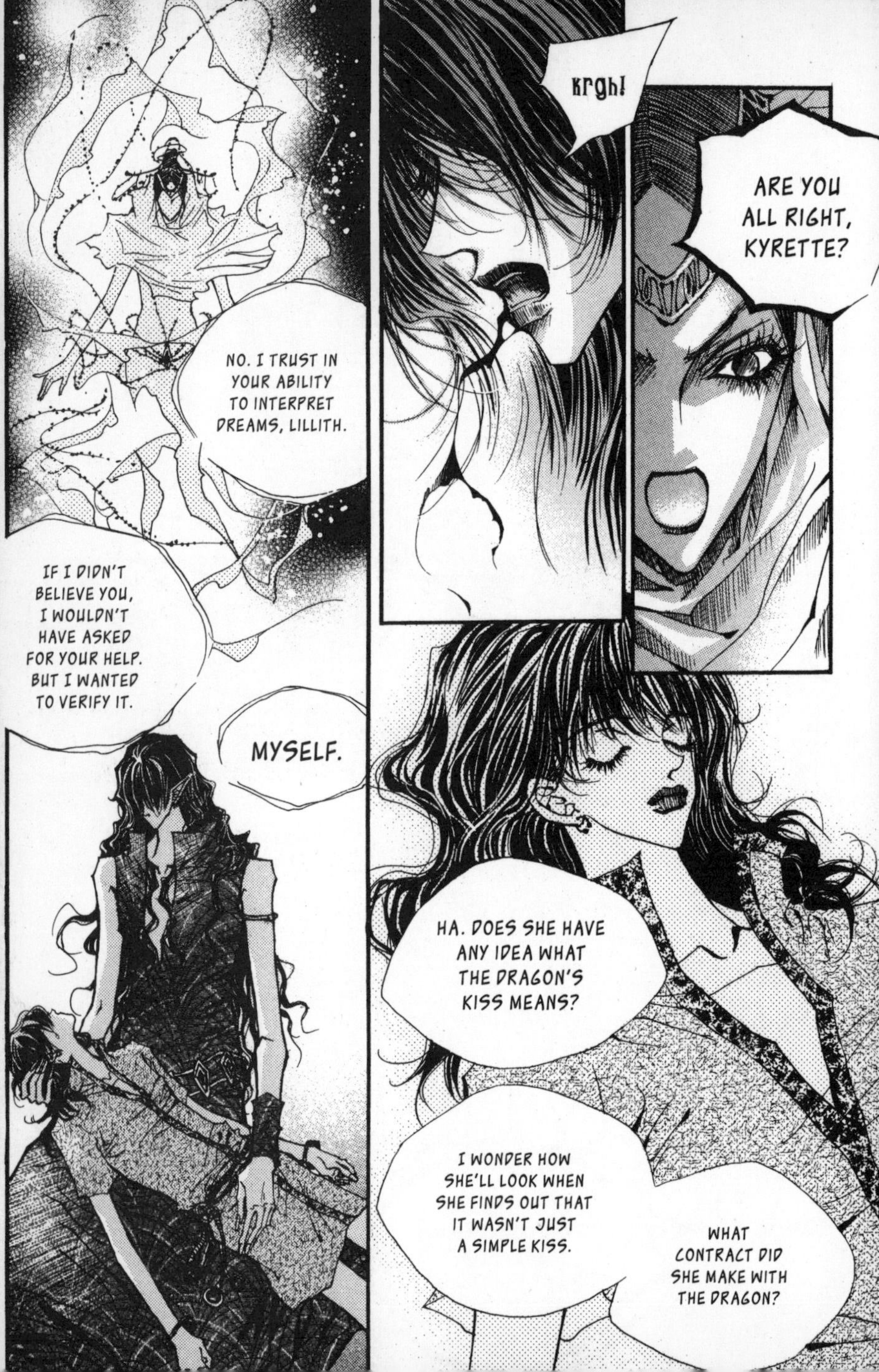

NO. I TRUST IN YOUR ABILITY TO INTERPRET DREAMS, LILLITH.
IF I DIDN'T BELIEVE YOU, I WOULDN'T HAVE ASKED FOR YOUR HELP. BUT I WANTED TO VERIFY IT.
MYSELF.
KRGH!
ARE YOU ALL RIGHT, KYRETTE?
HA. DOES SHE HAVE ANY IDEA WHAT THE DRAGON'S KISS MEANS?
I WONDER HOW SHE'LL LOOK WHEN SHE FINDS OUT THAT IT WASN'T JUST A SIMPLE KISS.
WHAT CONTRACT DID SHE MAKE WITH THE DRAGON?

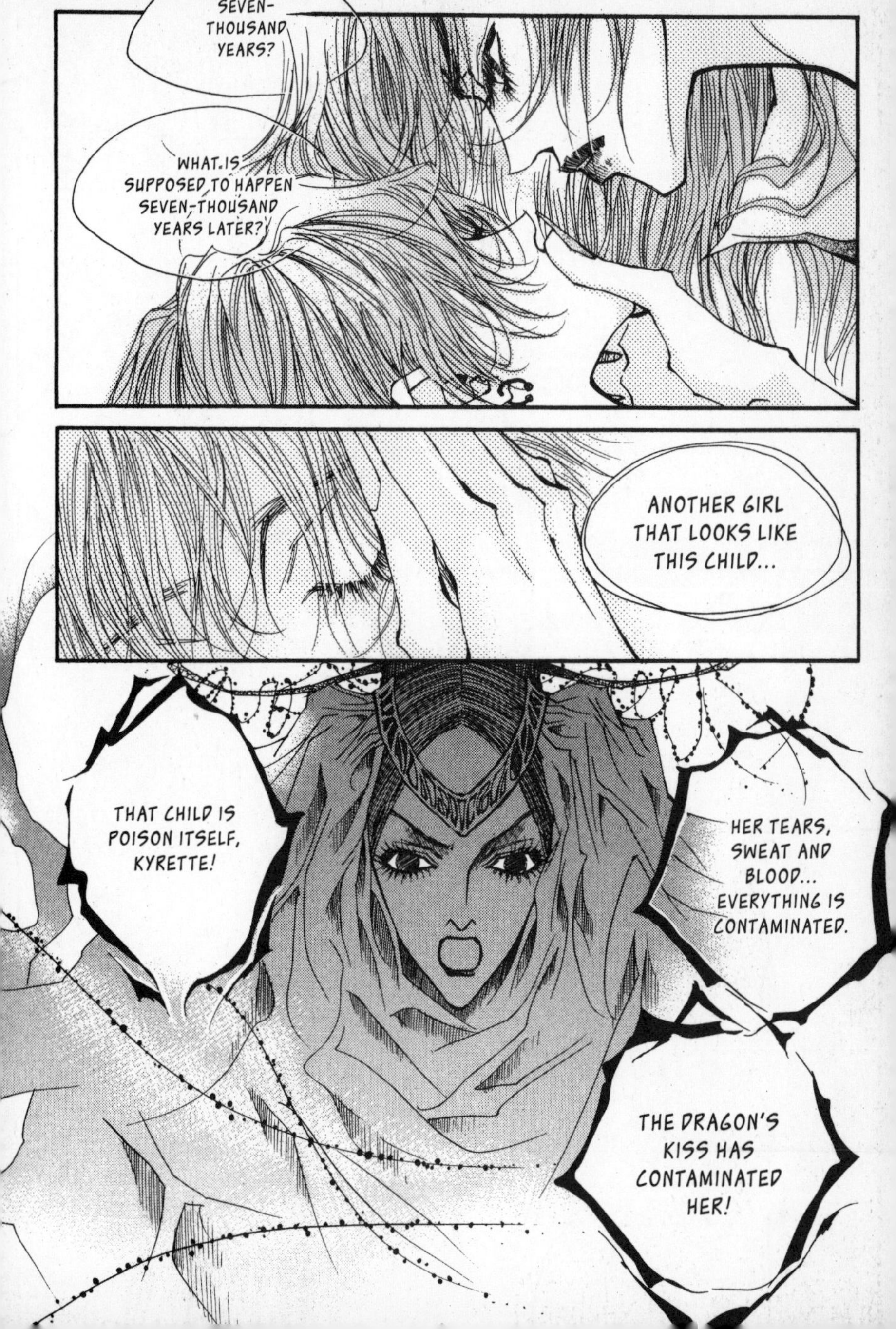
SEVEN-THOUSAND YEARS?
WHAT IS SUPPOSED TO HAPPEN SEVEN-THOUSAND YEARS LATER?
ANOTHER GIRL THAT LOOKS LIKE THIS CHILD...
HER TEARS, SWEAT AND BLOOD... EVERYTHING IS CONTAMINATED.
THAT CHILD IS POISON ITSELF, KYRETTE!
THE DRAGON'S KISS HAS CONTAMINATED HER!

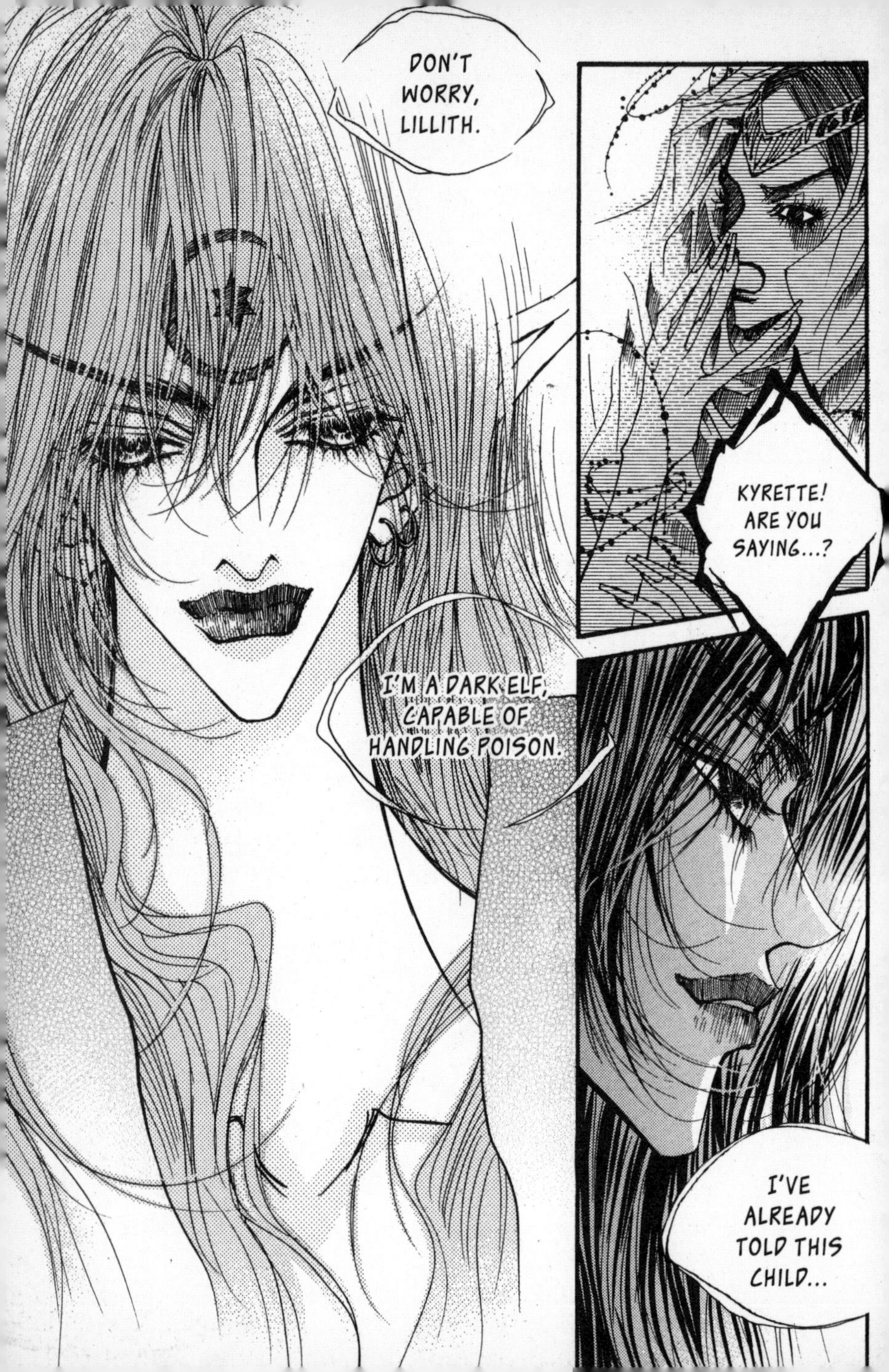
DON'T WORRY, LILLITH.
KYRETTE! ARE YOU SAYING...?
I'M A DARK ELF, CAPABLE OF HANDLING POISON.
I'VE ALREADY TOLD THIS CHILD...

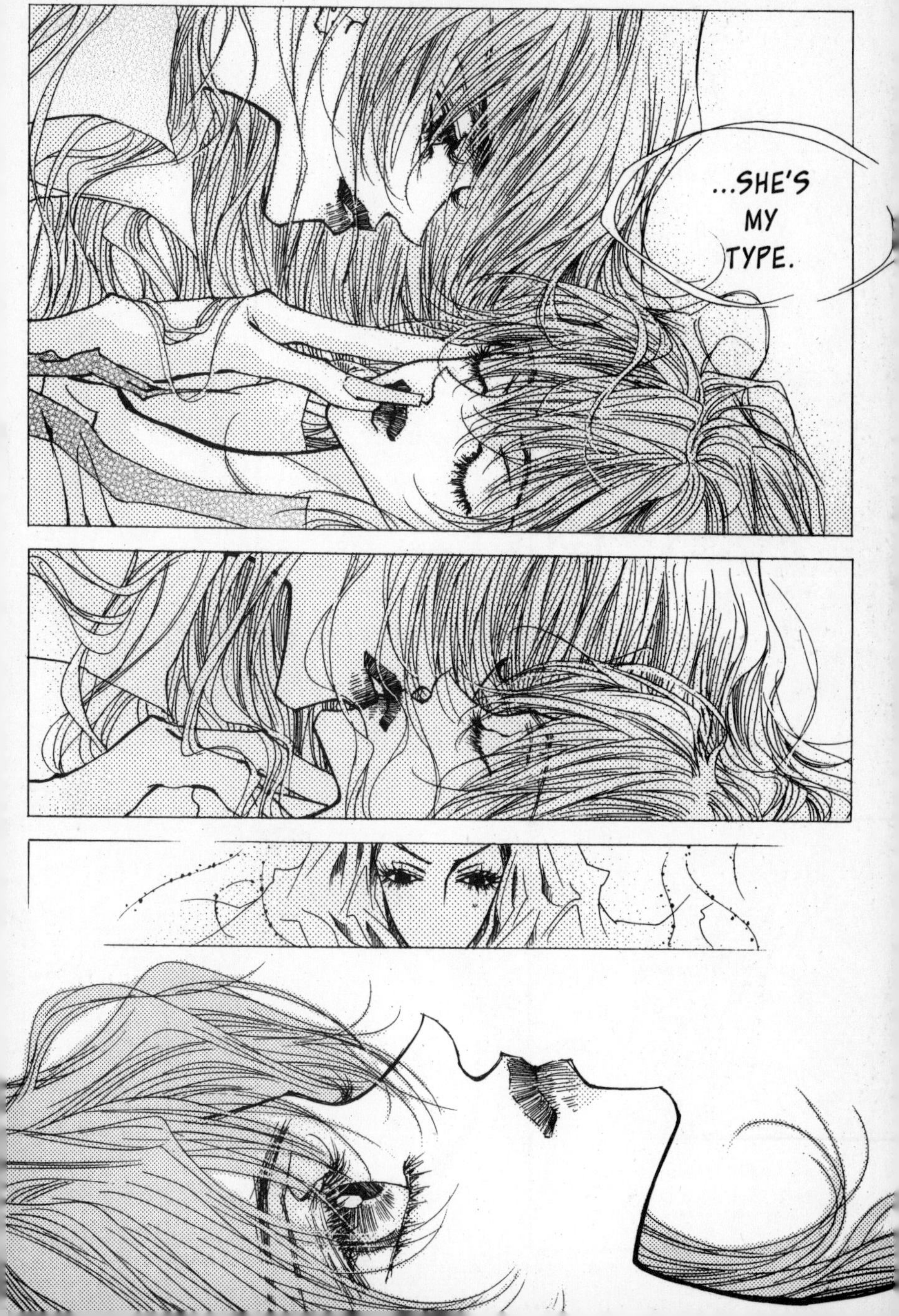
...SHE'S MY TYPE.

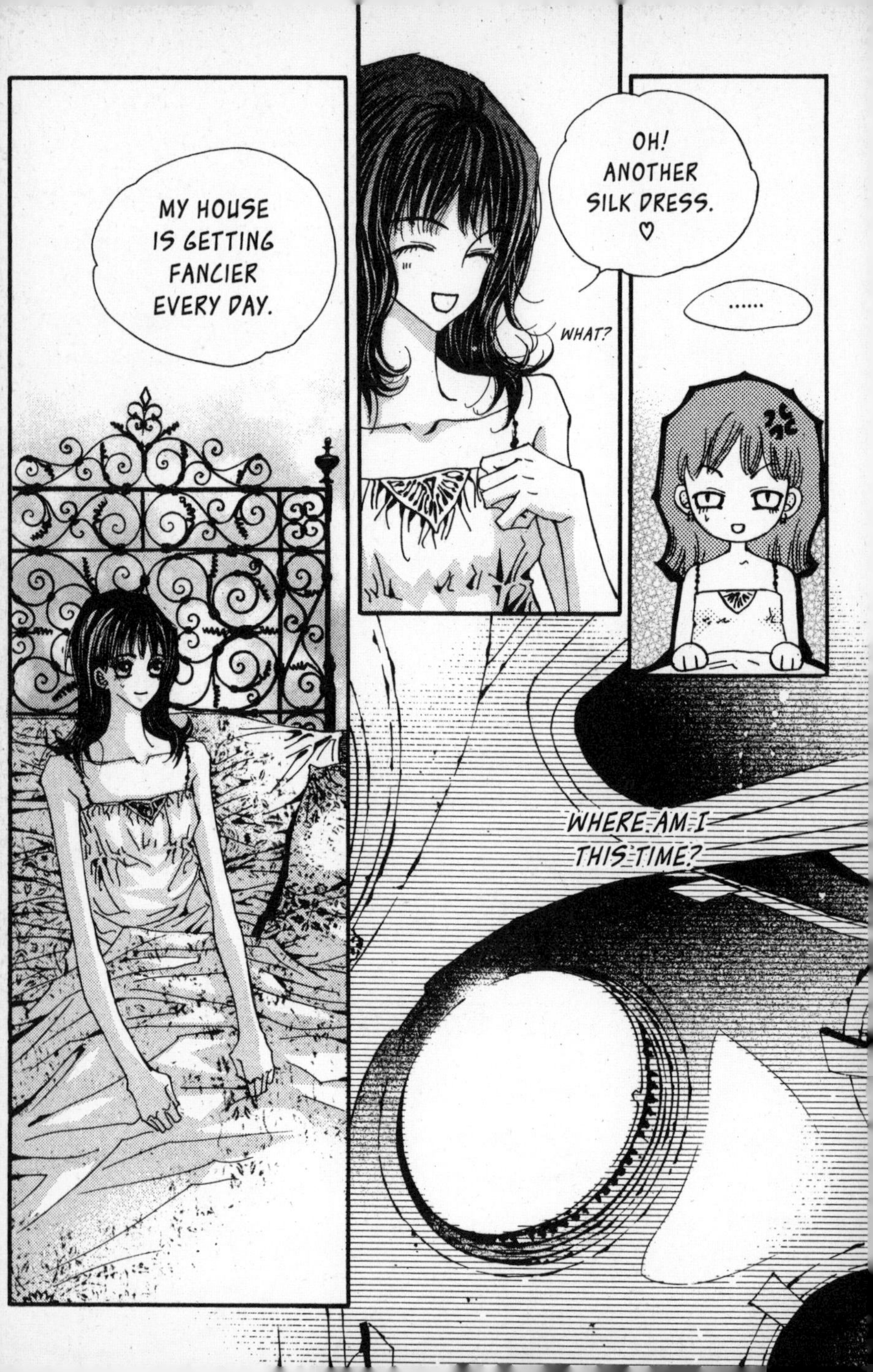
MY HOUSE IS GETTING FANCIER EVERY DAY.
OH! ANOTHER SILK DRESS. ♡
WHAT?
......
WHERE AM I THIS TIME?

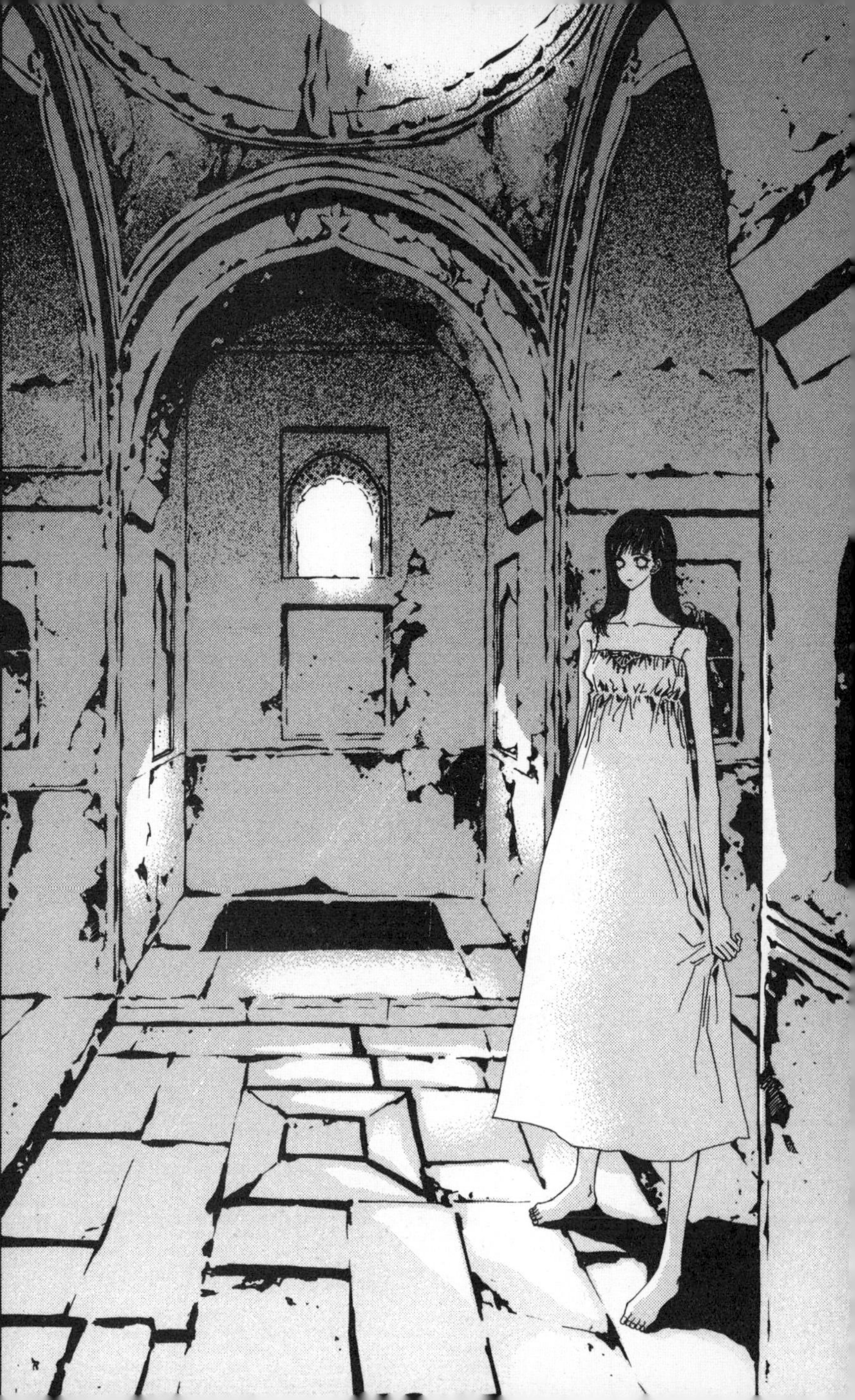

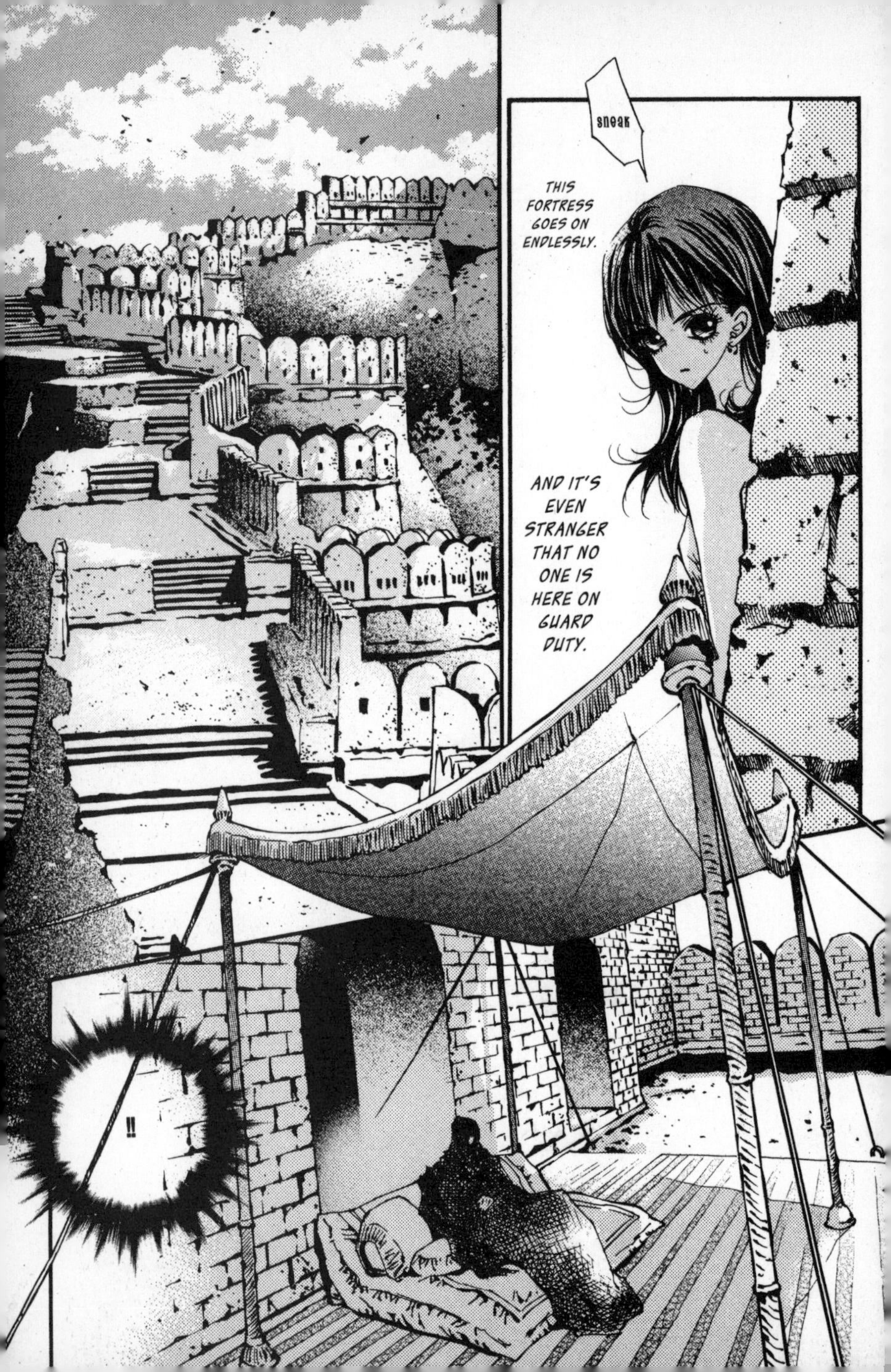
sneak
THIS FORTRESS GOES ON ENDLESSLY.
AND IT'S EVEN STRANGER THAT NO ONE IS HERE ON GUARD DUTY.
!!

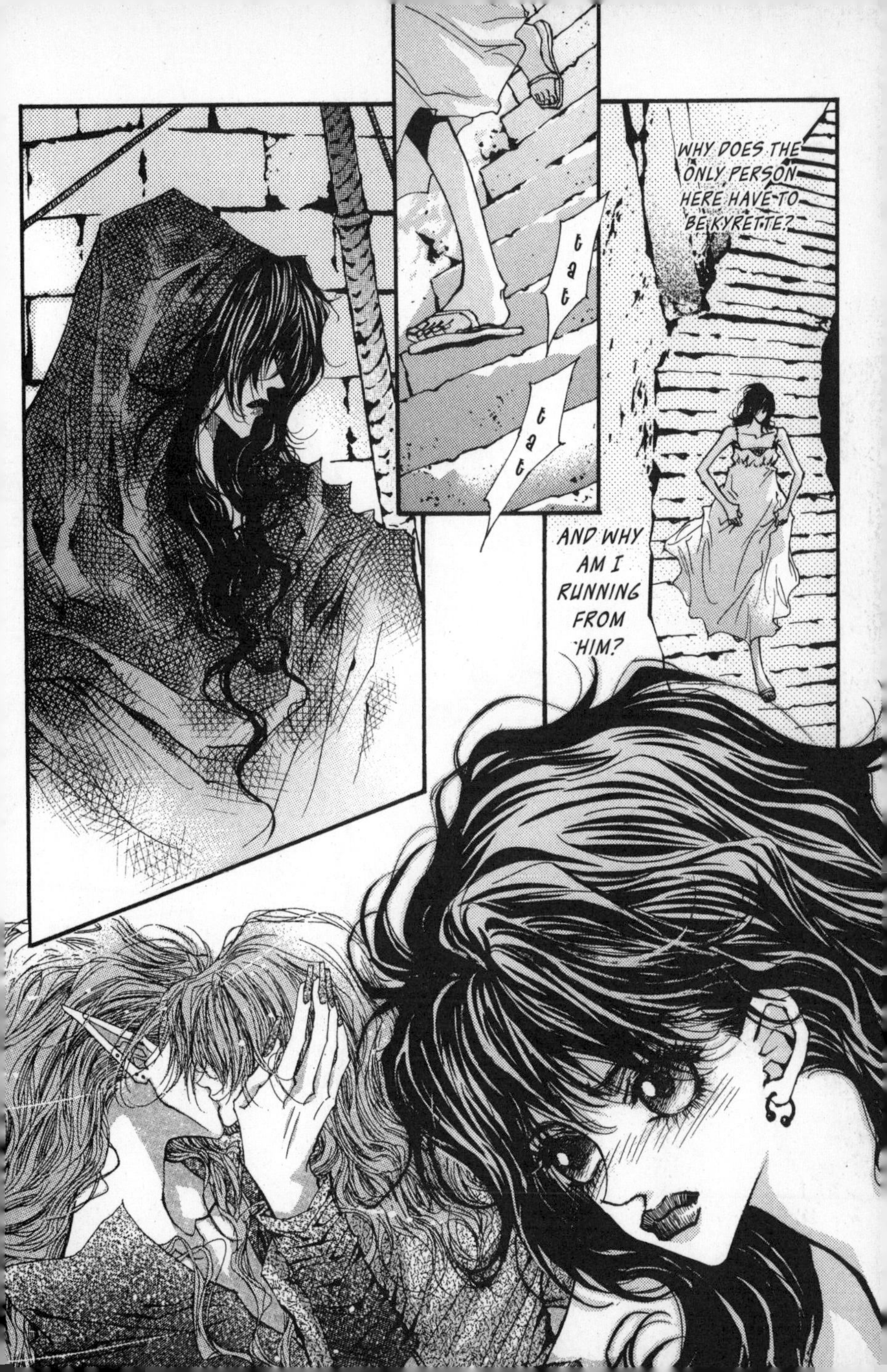
WHY DOES THE ONLY PERSON HERE HAVE TO BE KYRETTE?
tat
tat
AND WHY AM I RUNNING FROM HIM?

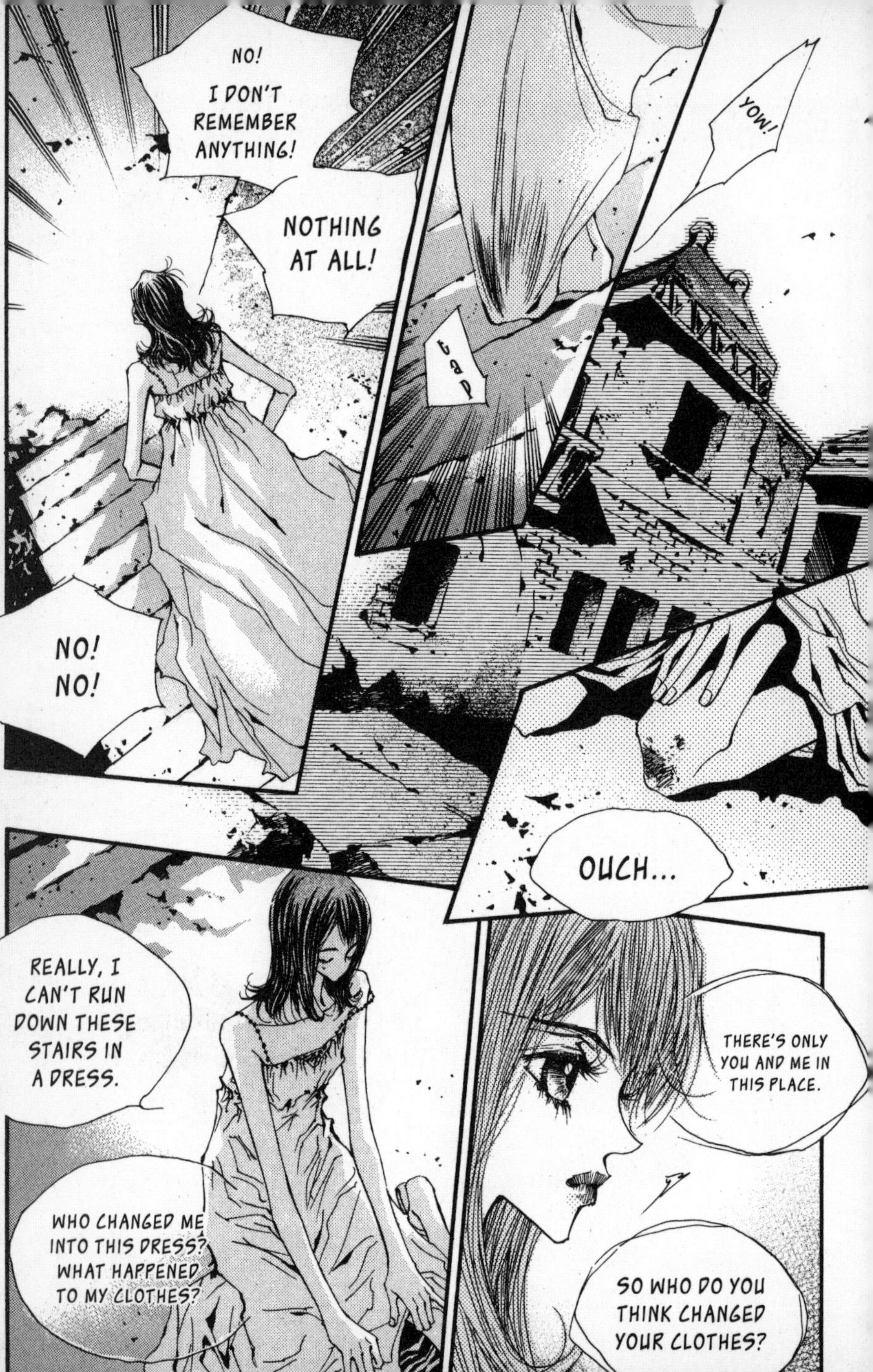
NO!
I DON'T REMEMBER ANYTHING!
NOTHING AT ALL!
NO! NO!
tap
YOW!
OUCH...
REALLY, I CAN'T RUN DOWN THESE STAIRS IN A DRESS.
WHO CHANGED ME INTO THIS DRESS? WHAT HAPPENED TO MY CLOTHES?
THERE'S ONLY YOU AND ME IN THIS PLACE.
SO WHO DO YOU THINK CHANGED YOUR CLOTHES?

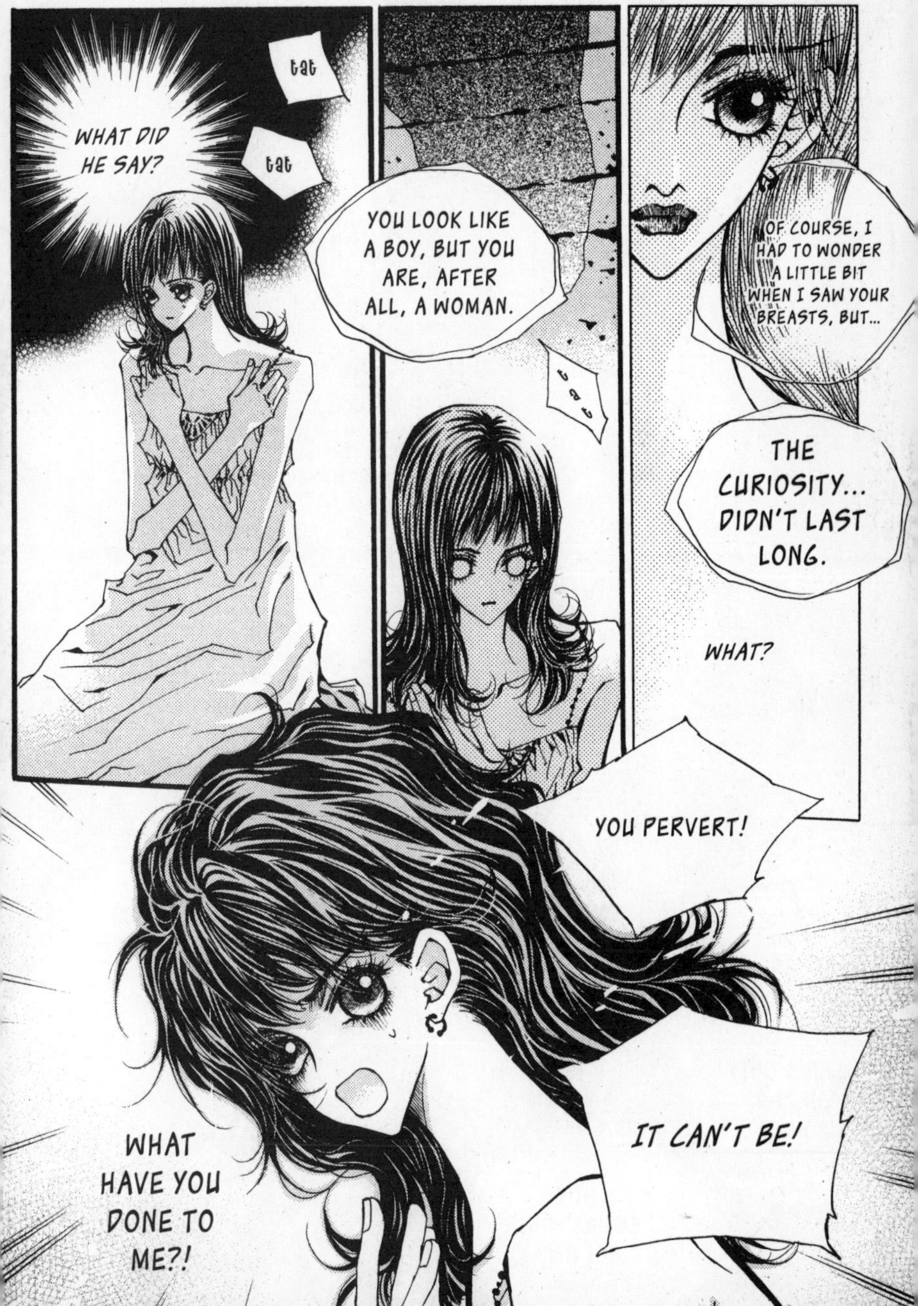
OF COURSE, I HAD TO WONDER A LITTLE BIT WHEN I SAW YOUR BREASTS, BUT...
THE CURIOSITY... DIDN'T LAST LONG.
WHAT?
YOU LOOK LIKE A BOY, BUT YOU ARE, AFTER ALL, A WOMAN.
tat
tat
tat
WHAT DID HE SAY?
YOU PERVERT!
IT CAN'T BE!
WHAT HAVE YOU DONE TO ME?!

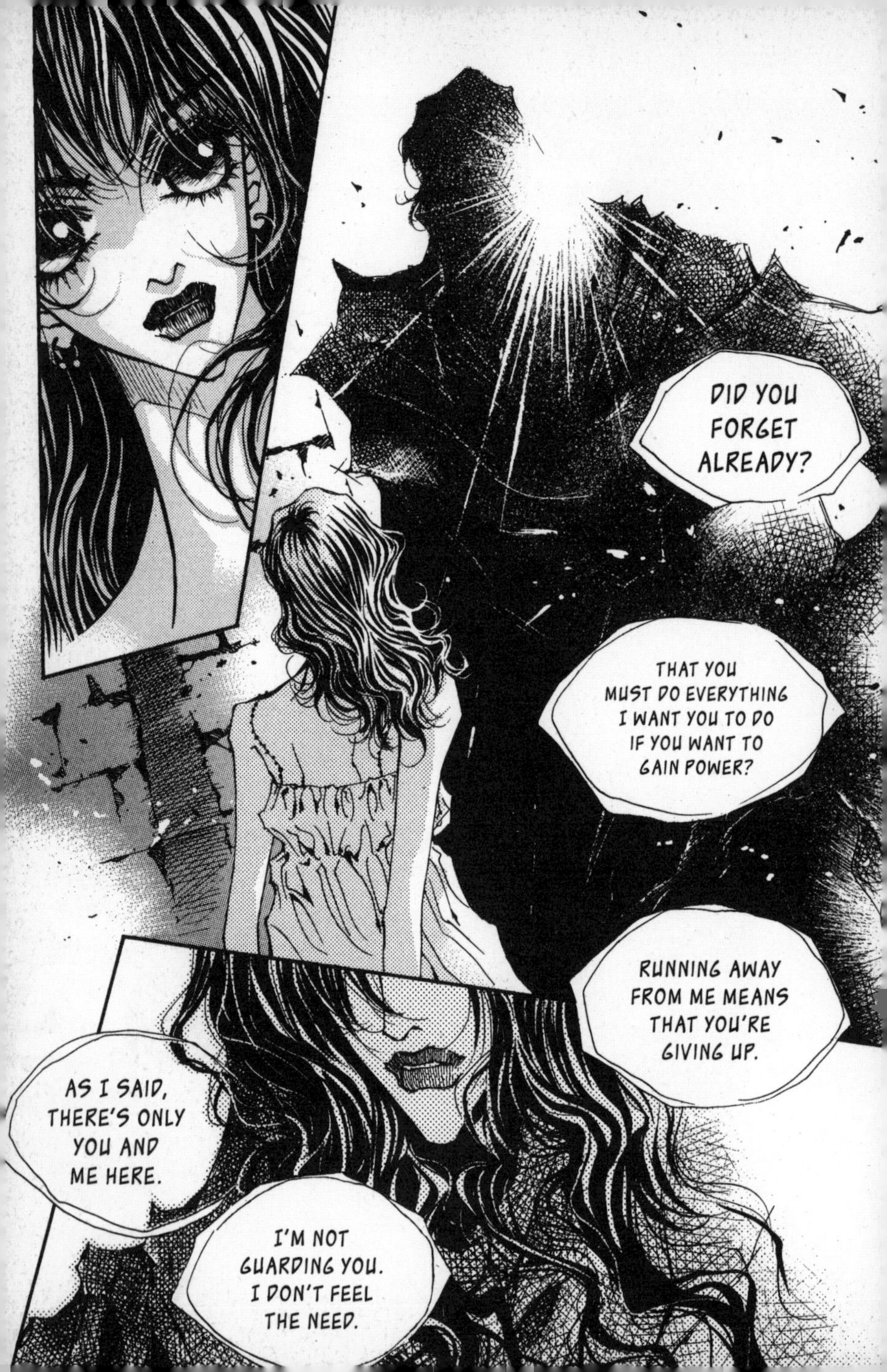
DID YOU FORGET ALREADY?
THAT YOU MUST DO EVERYTHING I WANT YOU TO DO IF YOU WANT TO GAIN POWER?
RUNNING AWAY FROM ME MEANS THAT YOU'RE GIVING UP.
AS I SAID, THERE'S ONLY YOU AND ME HERE.
I'M NOT GUARDING YOU. I DON'T FEEL THE NEED.

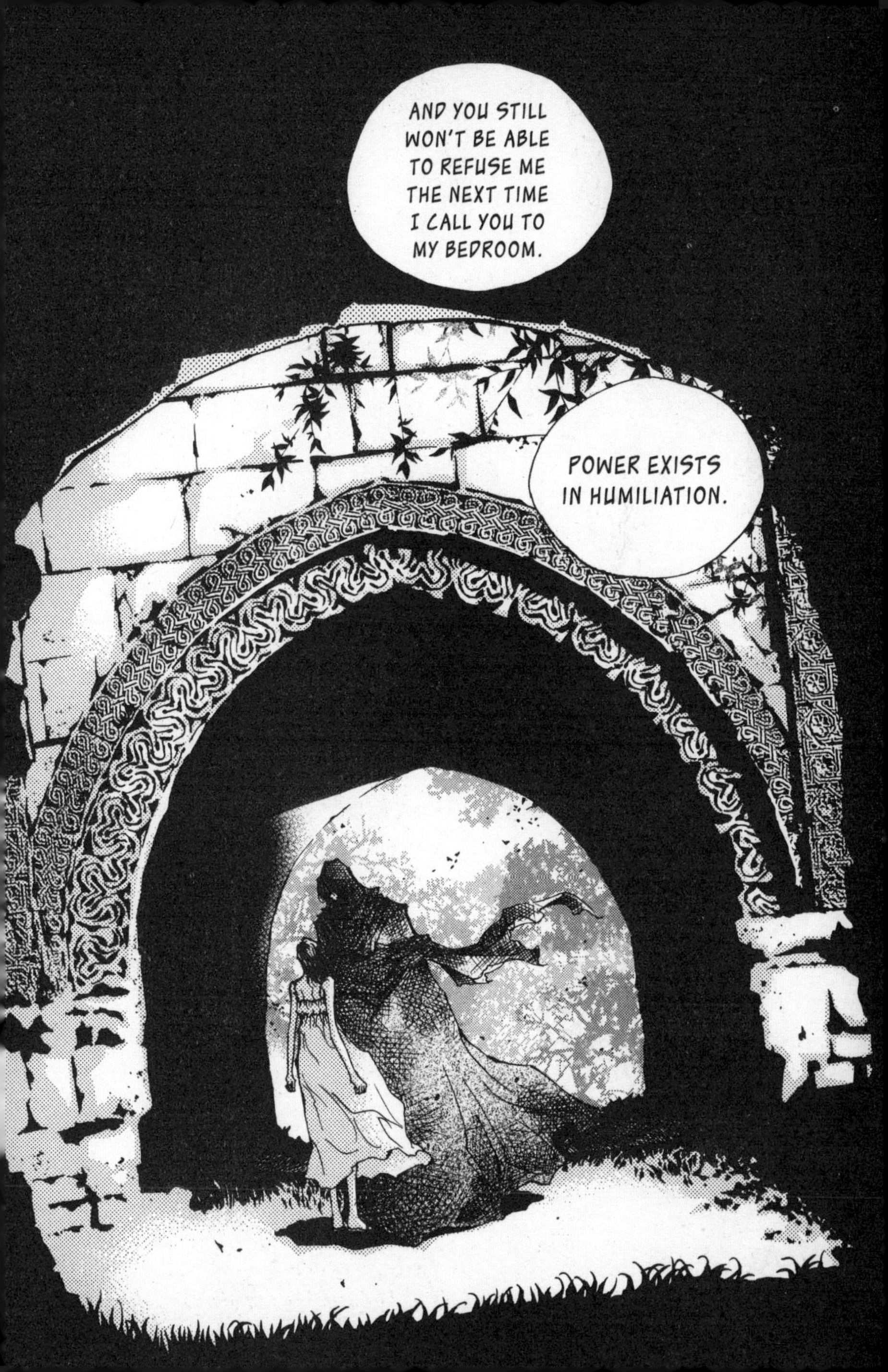
AND YOU STILL WON'T BE ABLE TO REFUSE ME THE NEXT TIME I CALL YOU TO MY BEDROOM.
POWER EXISTS IN HUMILIATION.

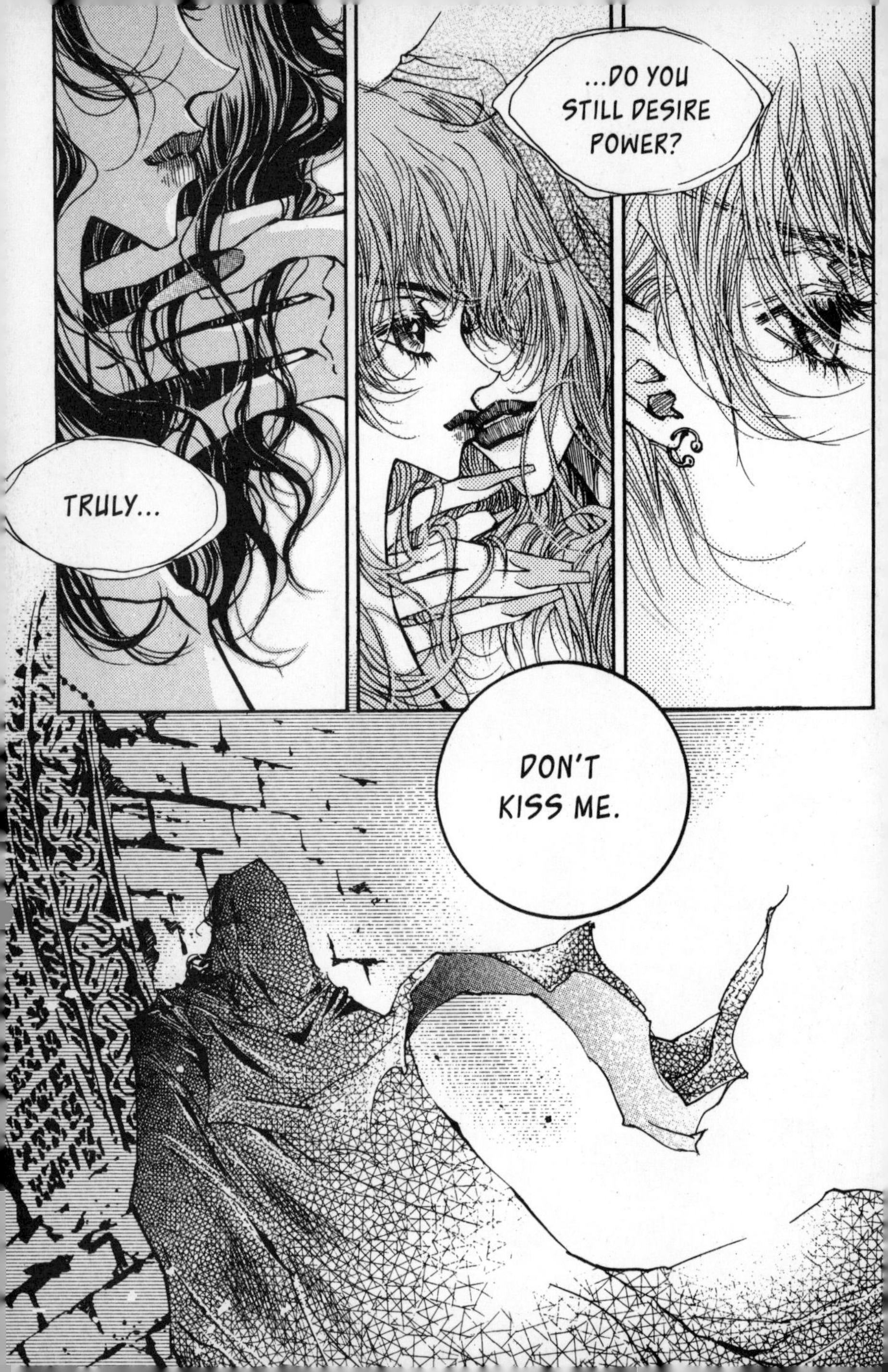
TRULY...
...DO YOU STILL DESIRE POWER?
DON'T KISS ME.

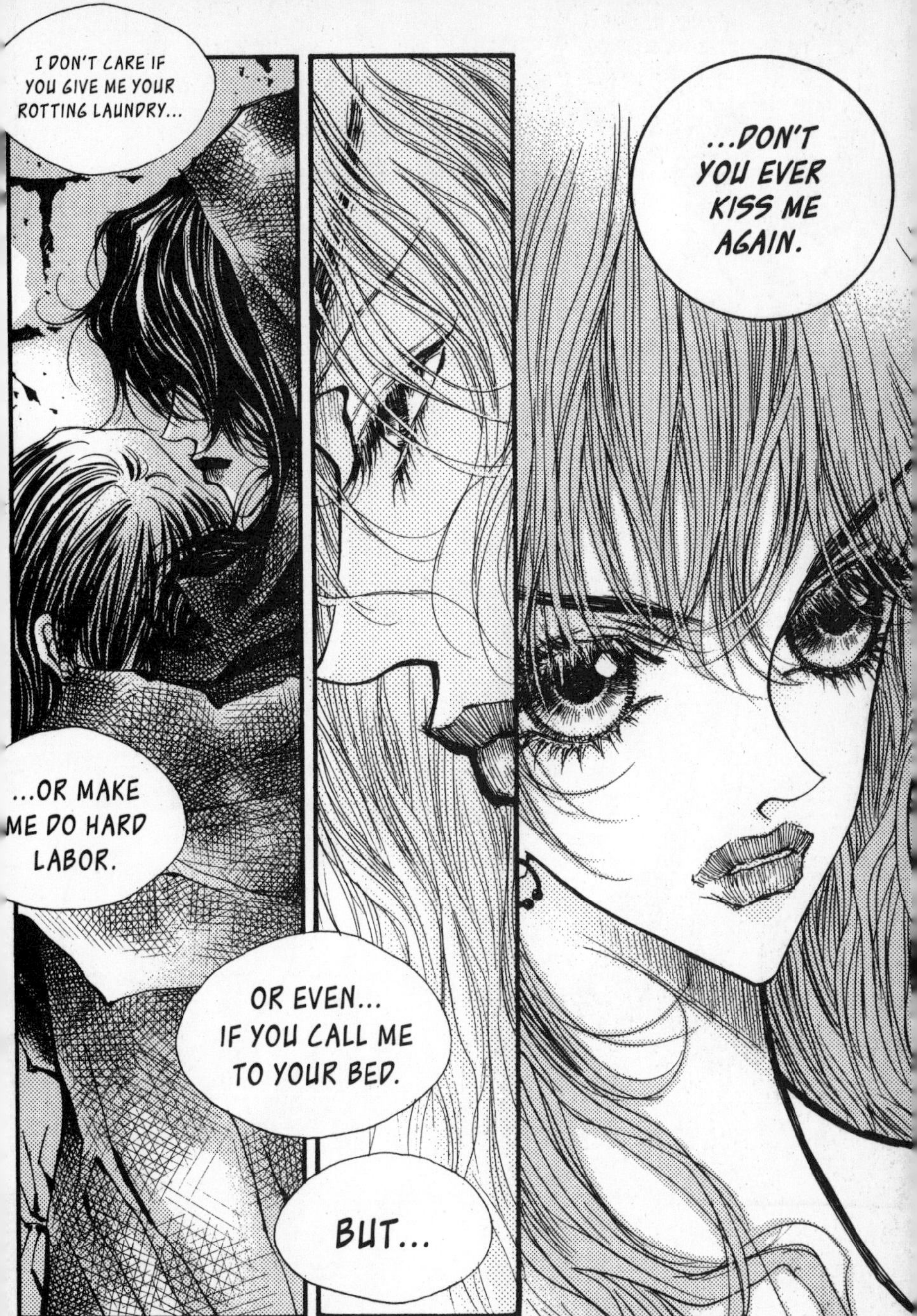
I DON'T CARE IF YOU GIVE ME YOUR ROTTING LAUNDRY...
...OR MAKE ME DO HARD LABOR.
OR EVEN... IF YOU CALL ME TO YOUR BED.
BUT...
...DON'T YOU EVER KISS ME AGAIN.

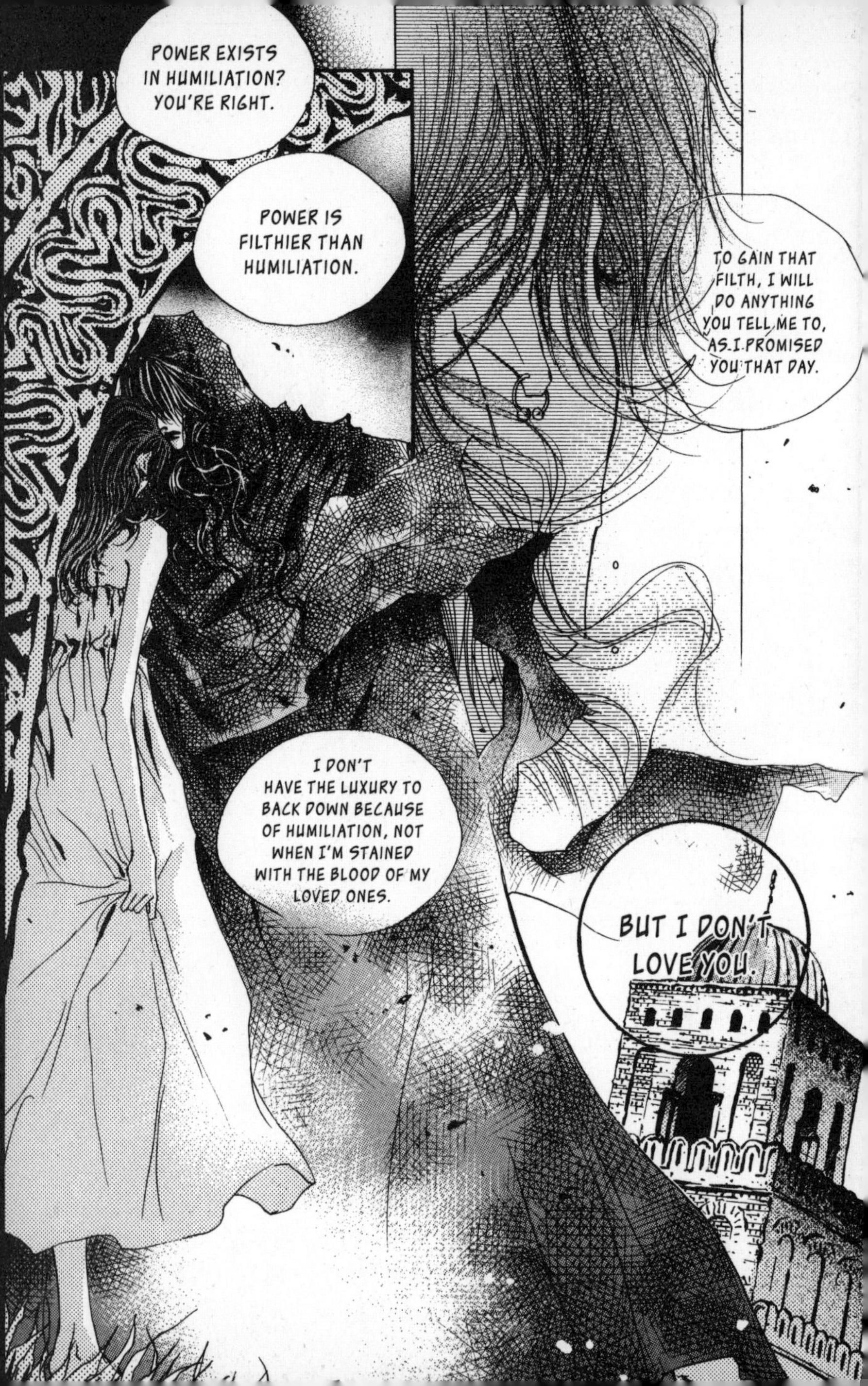
POWER EXISTS IN HUMILIATION? YOU'RE RIGHT.
POWER IS FILTHIER THAN HUMILIATION.
TO GAIN THAT FILTH, I WILL DO ANYTHING YOU TELL ME TO, AS I PROMISED YOU THAT DAY.
I DON'T HAVE THE LUXURY TO BACK DOWN BECAUSE OF HUMILIATION, NOT WHEN I'M STAINED WITH THE BLOOD OF MY LOVED ONES.
BUT I DON'T LOVE YOU.

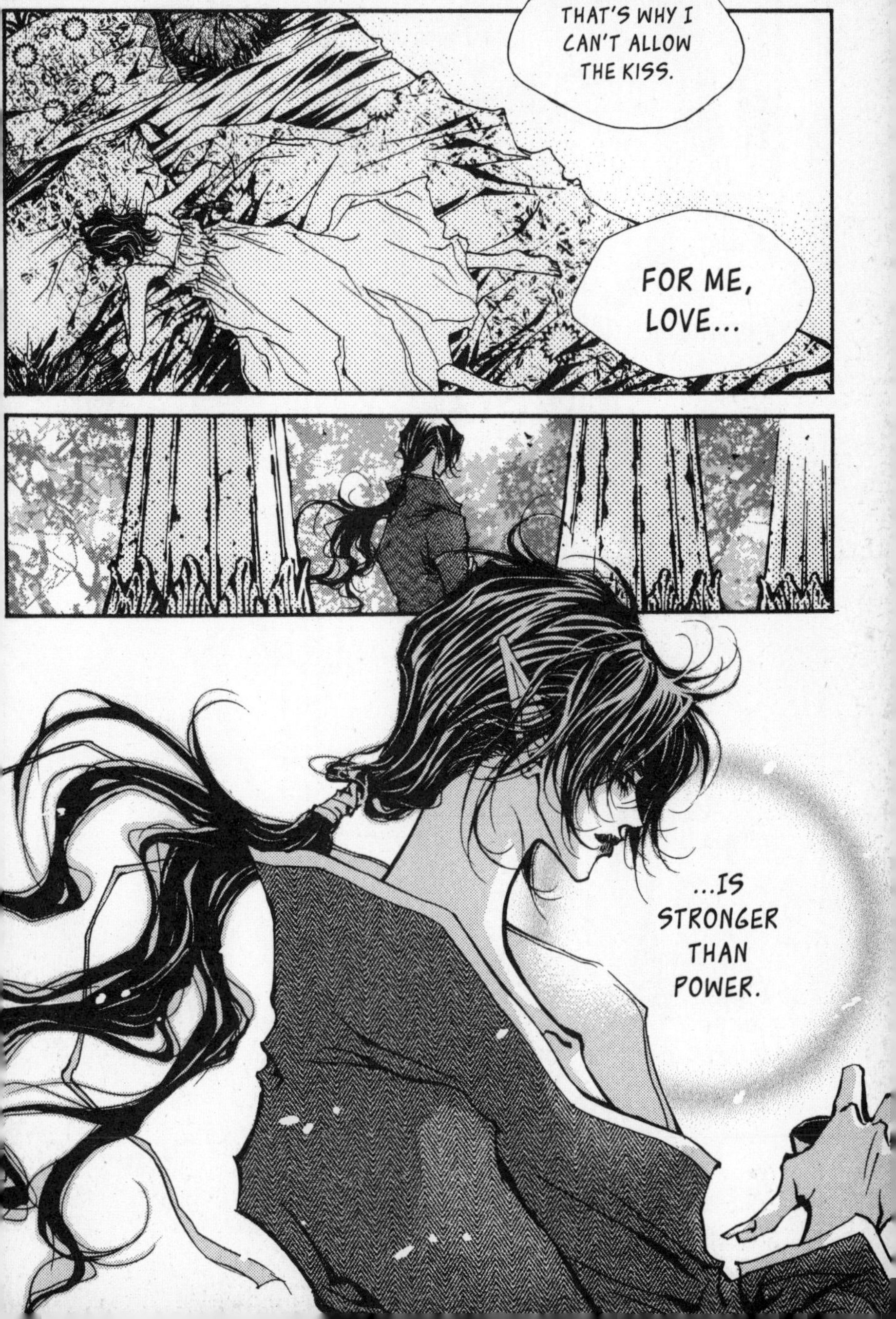
THAT'S WHY I CAN'T ALLOW THE KISS.
FOR ME, LOVE...
...IS STRONGER THAN POWER.

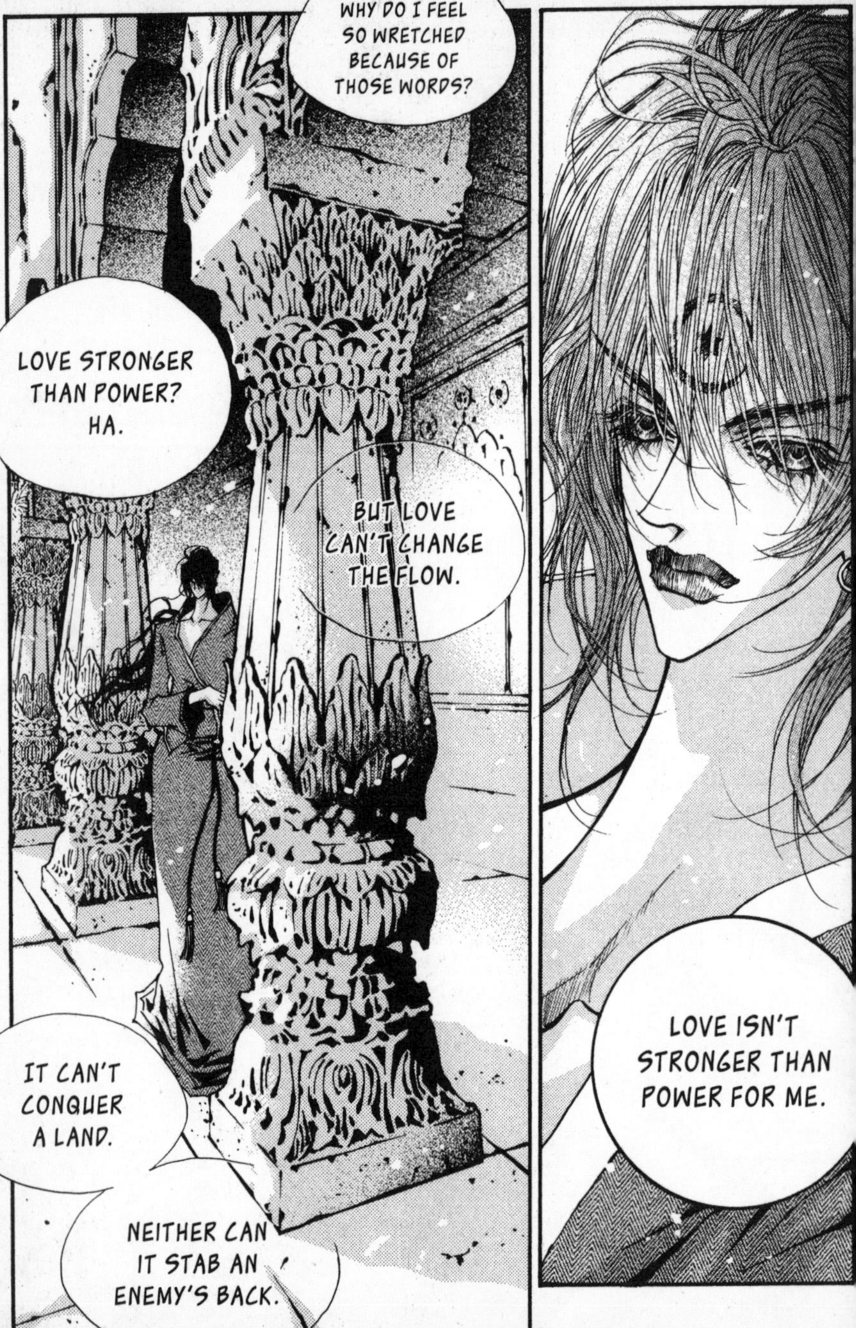
WHY DO I FEEL SO WRETCHED BECAUSE OF THOSE WORDS?
LOVE STRONGER THAN POWER? HA.
BUT LOVE CAN'T CHANGE THE FLOW.
IT CAN'T CONQUER A LAND.
NEITHER CAN IT STAB AN ENEMY'S BACK.
LOVE ISN'T STRONGER THAN POWER FOR ME.

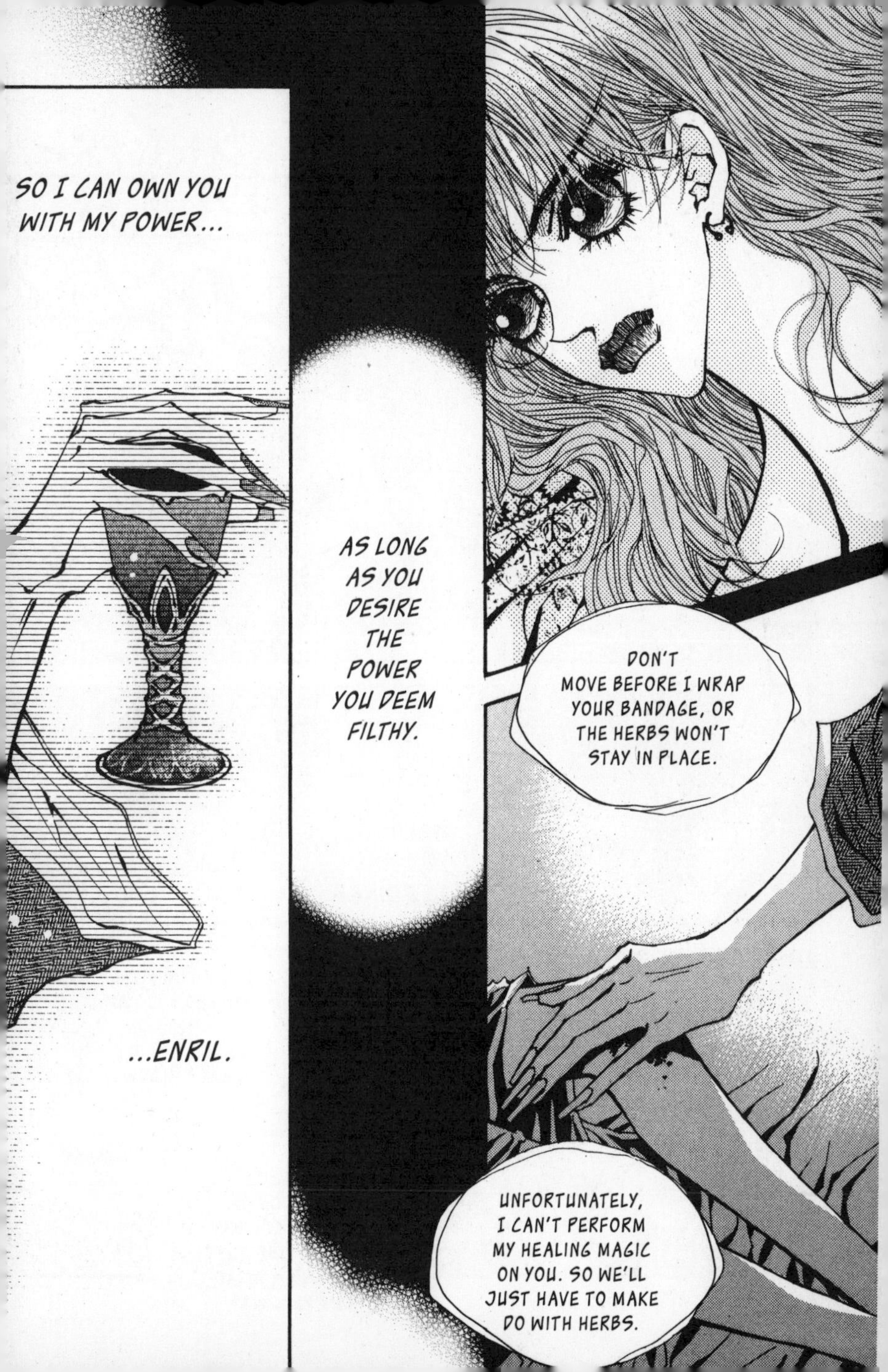
SO I CAN OWN YOU WITH MY POWER...
...ENRIL.
AS LONG AS YOU DESIRE THE POWER YOU DEEM FILTHY.
DON'T MOVE BEFORE I WRAP YOUR BANDAGE, OR THE HERBS WON'T STAY IN PLACE.
UNFORTUNATELY, I CAN'T PERFORM MY HEALING MAGIC ON YOU. SO WE'LL JUST HAVE TO MAKE DO WITH HERBS.

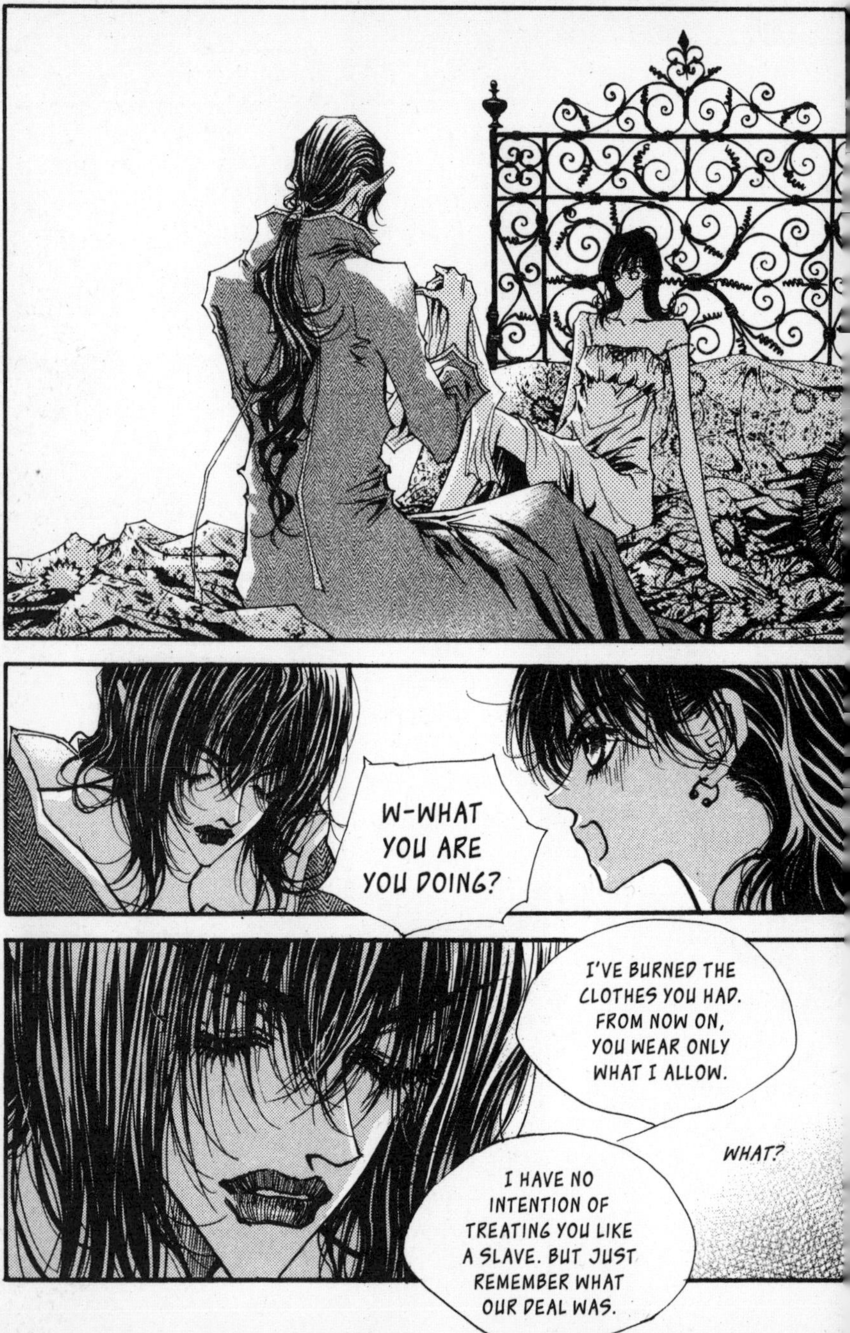
W-WHAT YOU ARE YOU DOING?
I'VE BURNED THE CLOTHES YOU HAD. FROM NOW ON, YOU WEAR ONLY WHAT I ALLOW.
WHAT?
I HAVE NO INTENTION OF TREATING YOU LIKE A SLAVE. BUT JUST REMEMBER WHAT OUR DEAL WAS.

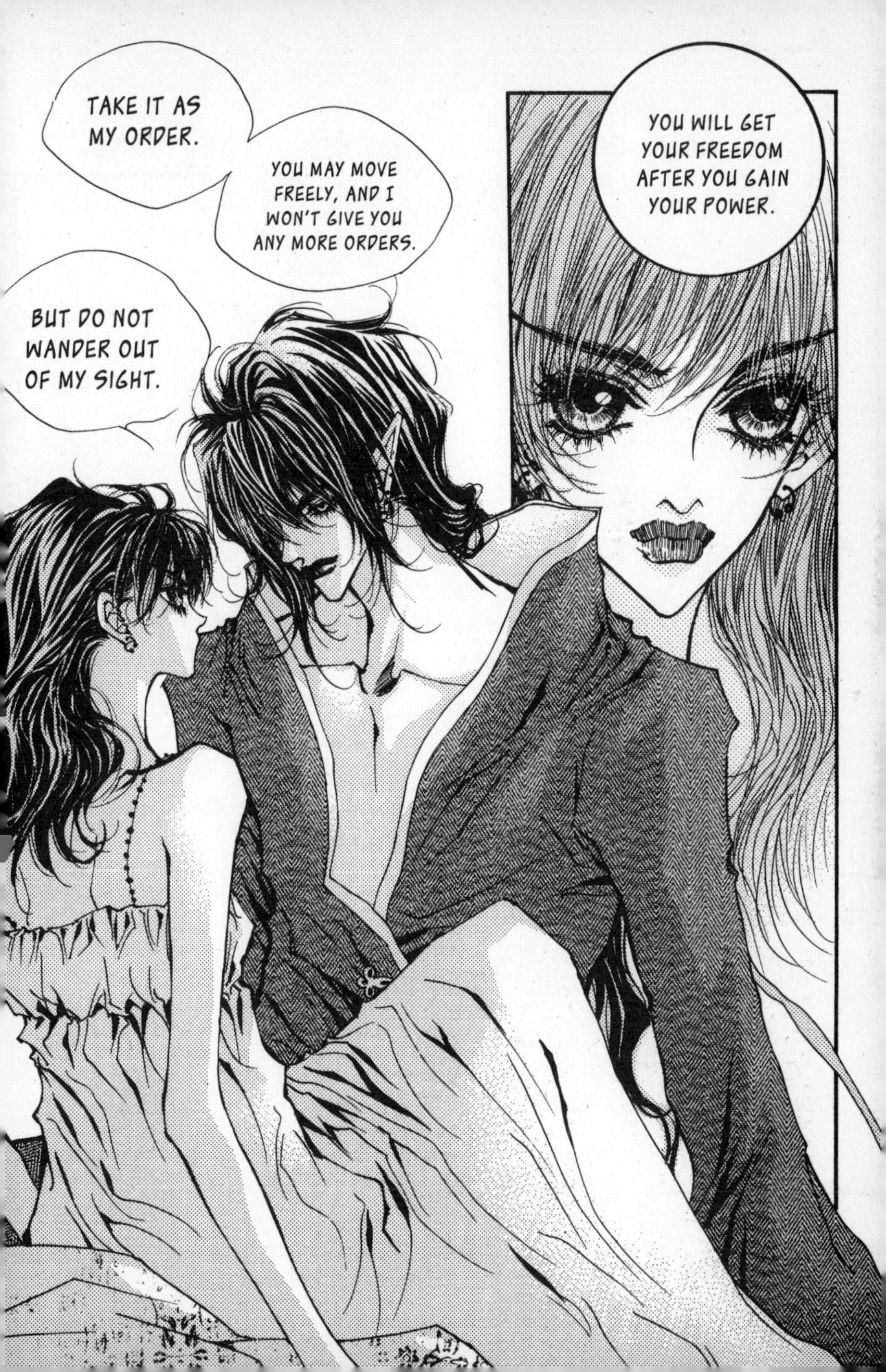
TAKE IT AS MY ORDER.
YOU MAY MOVE FREELY, AND I WON'T GIVE YOU ANY MORE ORDERS.
BUT DO NOT WANDER OUT OF MY SIGHT.
YOU WILL GET YOUR FREEDOM AFTER YOU GAIN YOUR POWER.

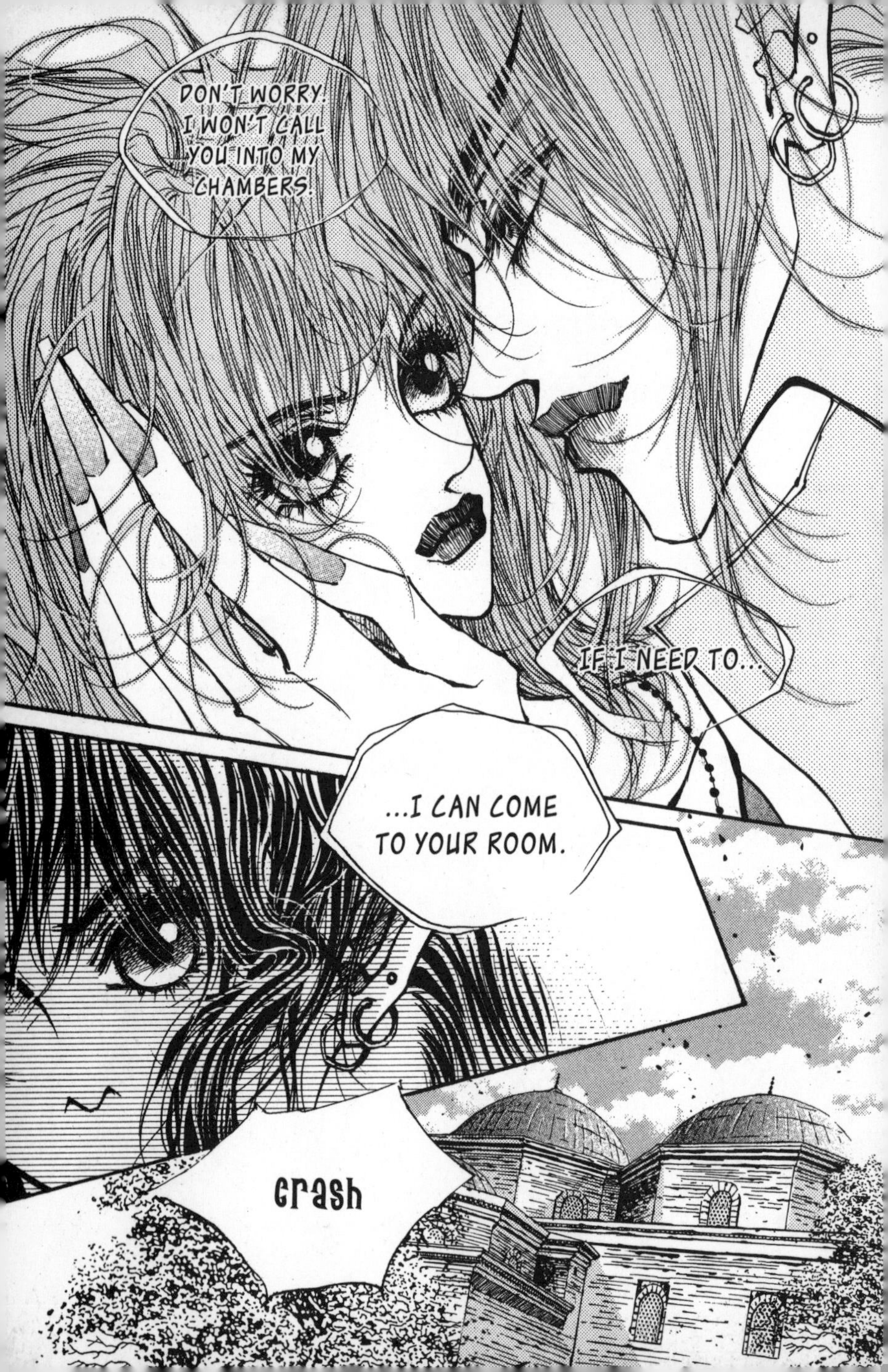
DON'T WORRY. I WON'T CALL YOU INTO MY CHAMBERS.
IF I NEED TO...
...I CAN COME TO YOUR ROOM.
CRASH

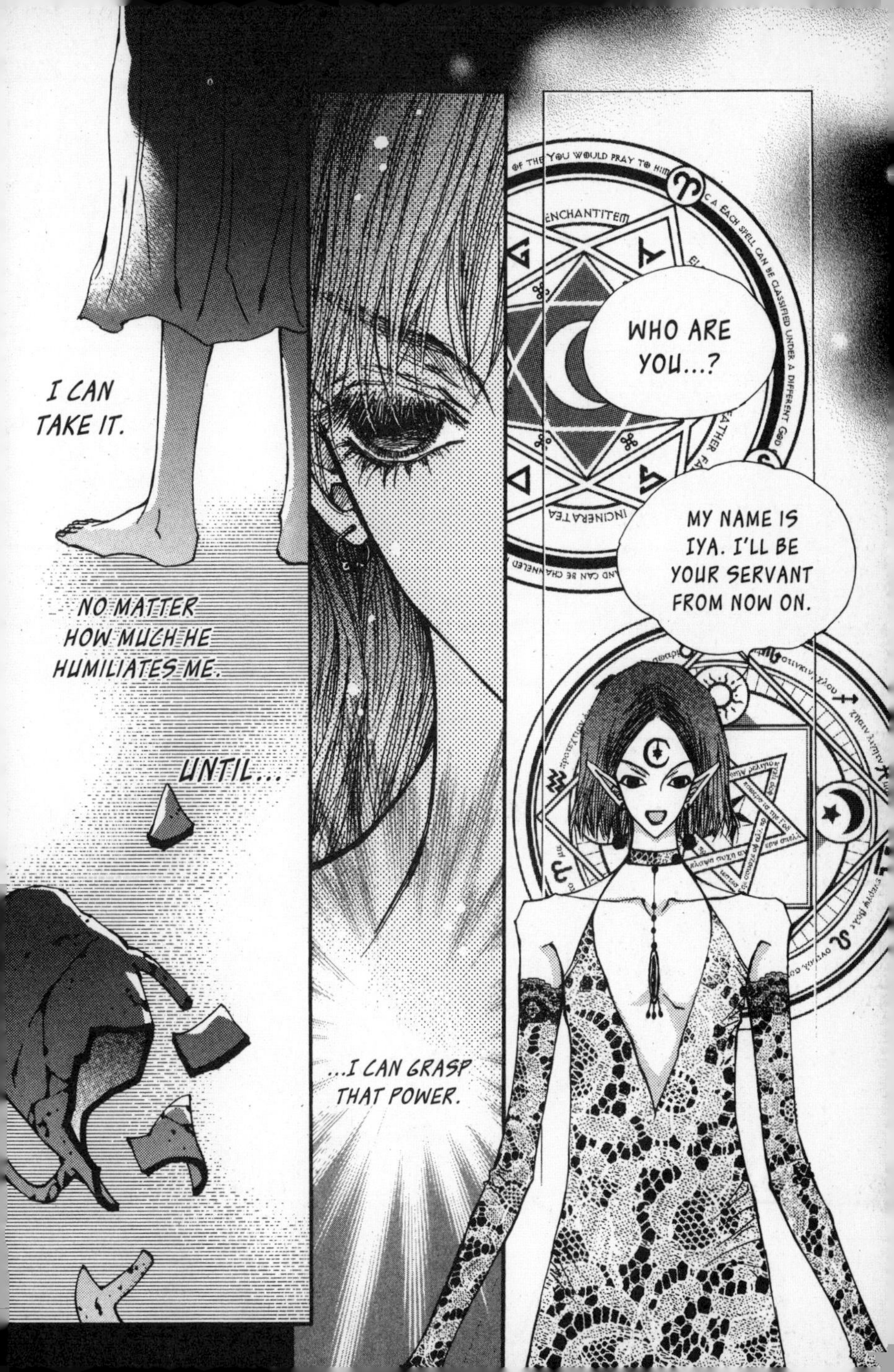
I CAN TAKE IT.
NO MATTER HOW MUCH HE HUMILIATES ME.
UNTIL...
...I CAN GRASP THAT POWER.
WHO ARE YOU...?
MY NAME IS IYA. I'LL BE YOUR SERVANT FROM NOW ON.

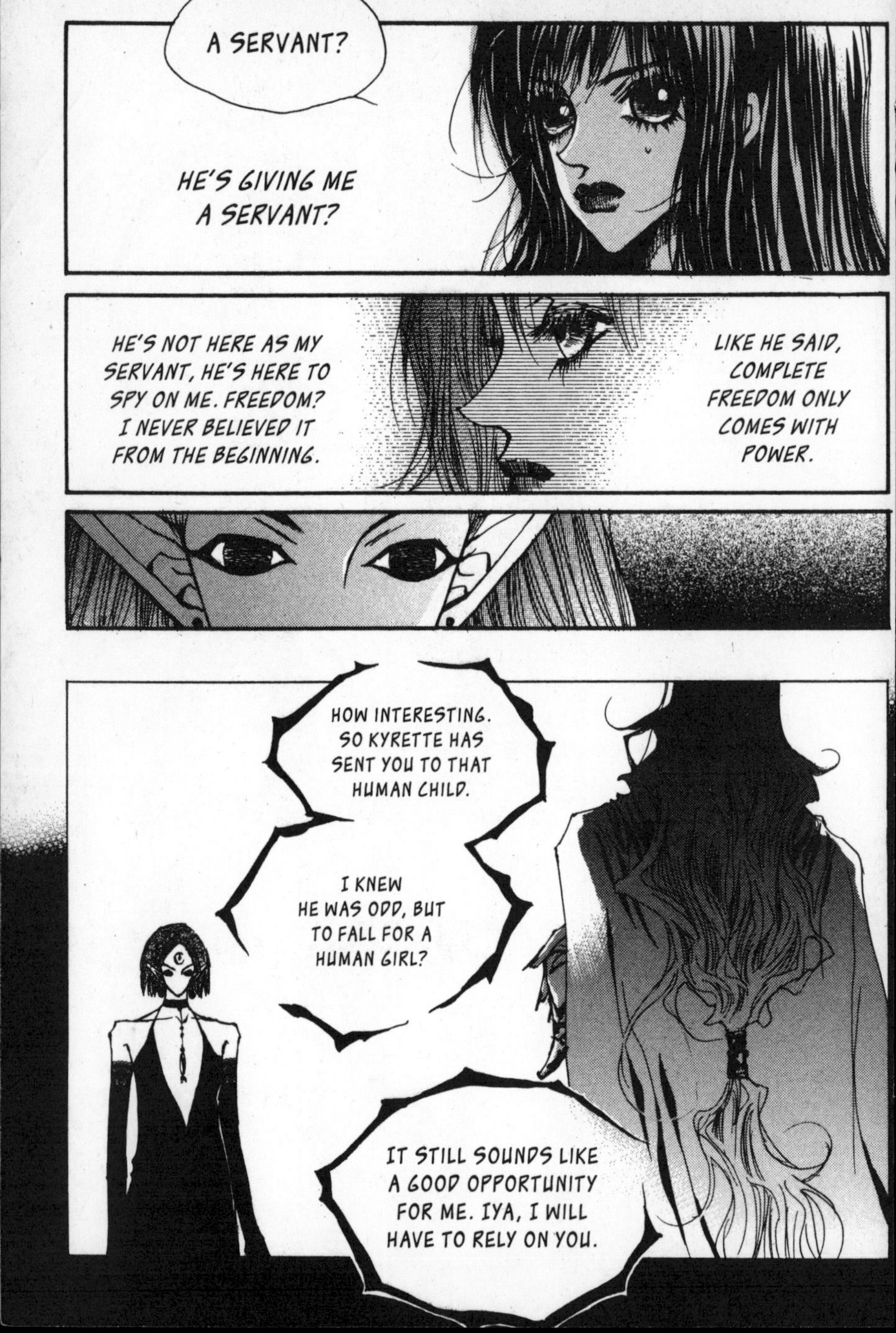
A SERVANT?
HE'S GIVING ME A SERVANT?
LIKE HE SAID, COMPLETE FREEDOM ONLY COMES WITH POWER.
HE'S NOT HERE AS MY SERVANT, HE'S HERE TO SPY ON ME. FREEDOM? I NEVER BELIEVED IT FROM THE BEGINNING.
HOW INTERESTING. SO KYRETTE HAS SENT YOU TO THAT HUMAN CHILD.
I KNEW HE WAS ODD, BUT TO FALL FOR A HUMAN GIRL?
IT STILL SOUNDS LIKE A GOOD OPPORTUNITY FOR ME. IYA, I WILL HAVE TO RELY ON YOU.

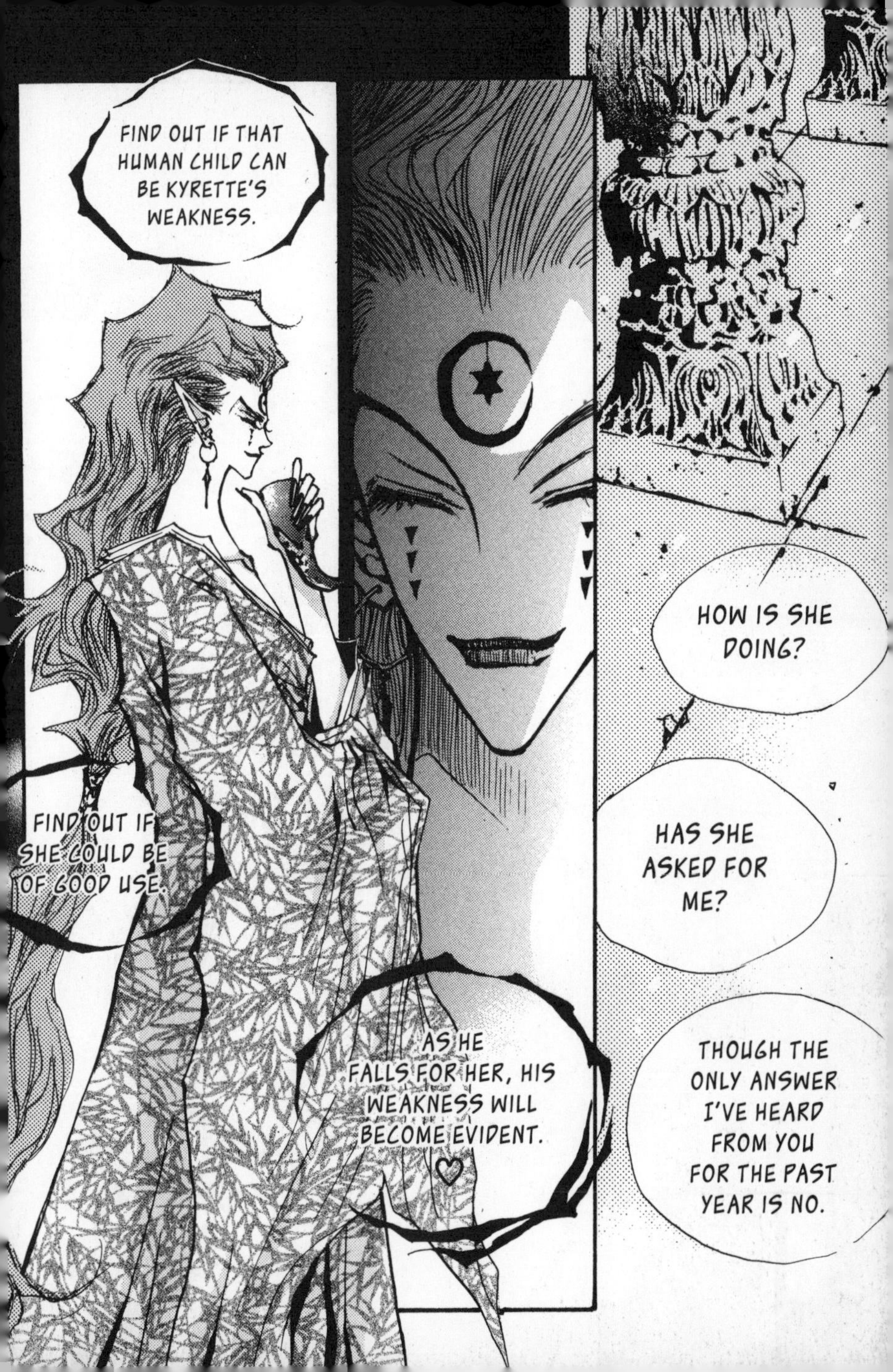
FIND OUT IF THAT HUMAN CHILD CAN BE KYRETTE'S WEAKNESS.
FIND OUT IF SHE COULD BE OF GOOD USE.
AS HE FALLS FOR HER, HIS WEAKNESS WILL BECOME EVIDENT. ♡
HOW IS SHE DOING?
HAS SHE ASKED FOR ME?
THOUGH THE ONLY ANSWER I'VE HEARD FROM YOU FOR THE PAST YEAR IS NO.

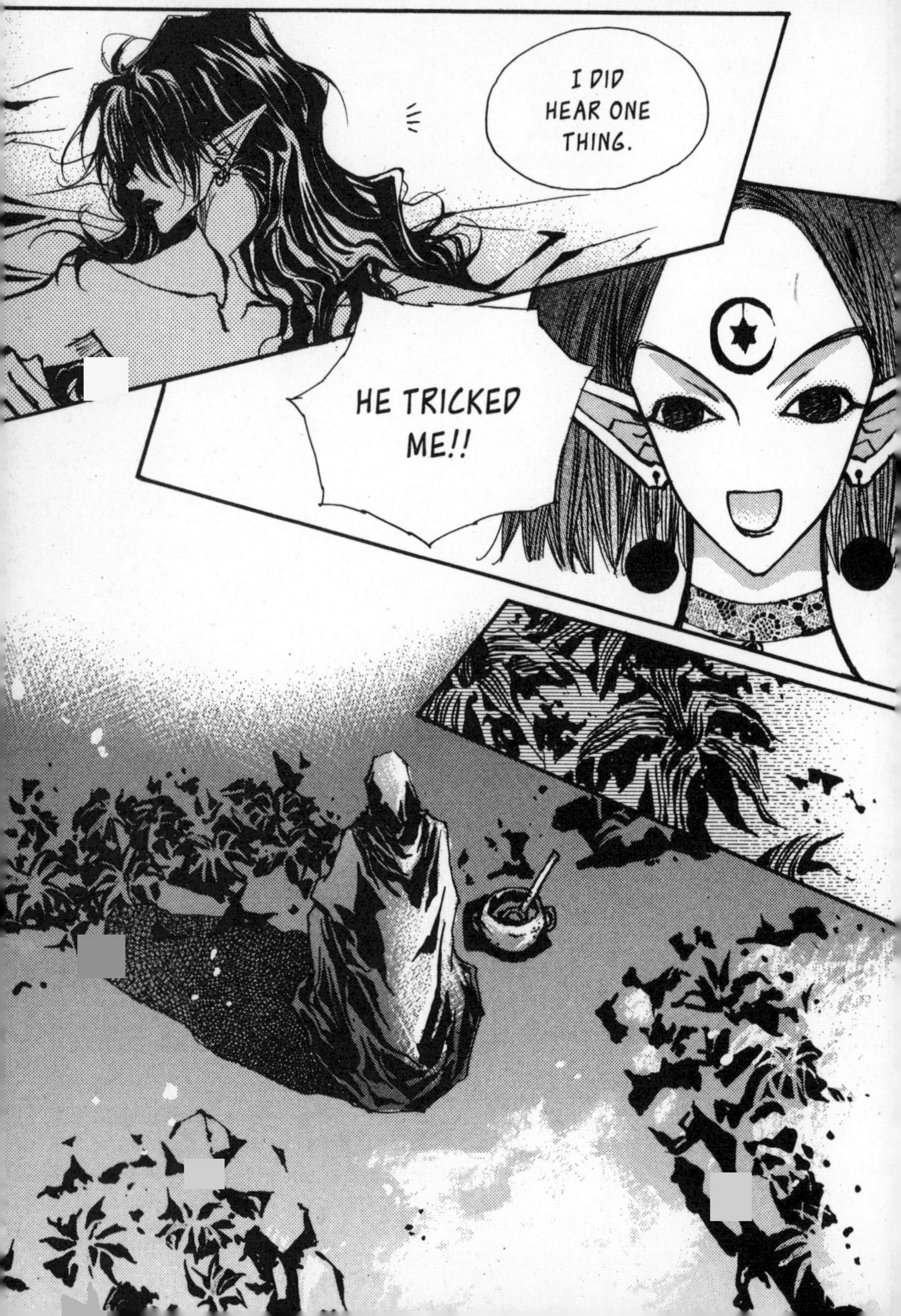
I DID HEAR ONE THING.
HE TRICKED ME!!

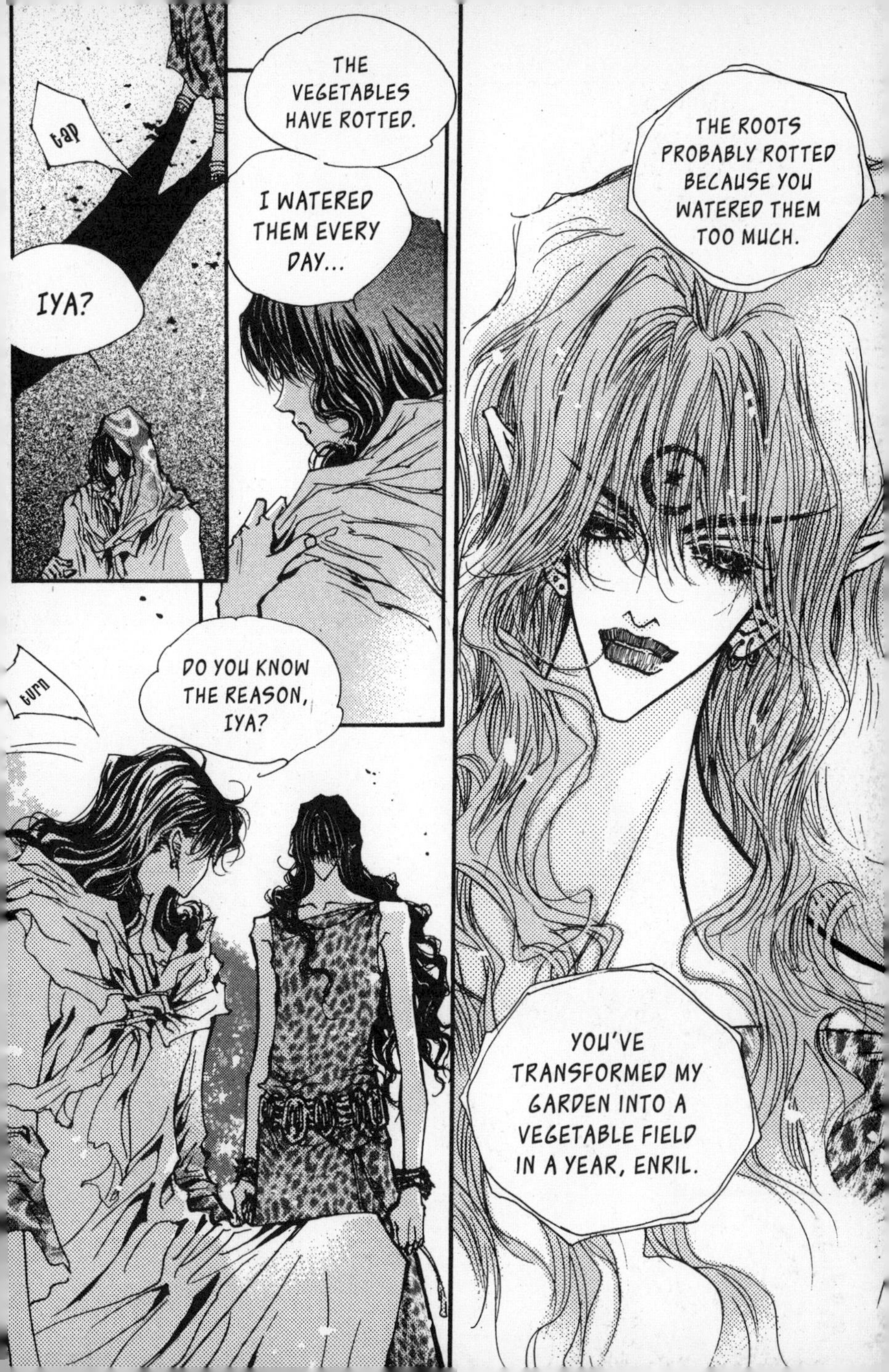
tap
IYA?
THE VEGETABLES HAVE ROTTED.
I WATERED THEM EVERY DAY...
turn
DO YOU KNOW THE REASON, IYA?
THE ROOTS PROBABLY ROTTED BECAUSE YOU WATERED THEM TOO MUCH.
YOU'VE TRANSFORMED MY GARDEN INTO A VEGETABLE FIELD IN A YEAR, ENRIL.

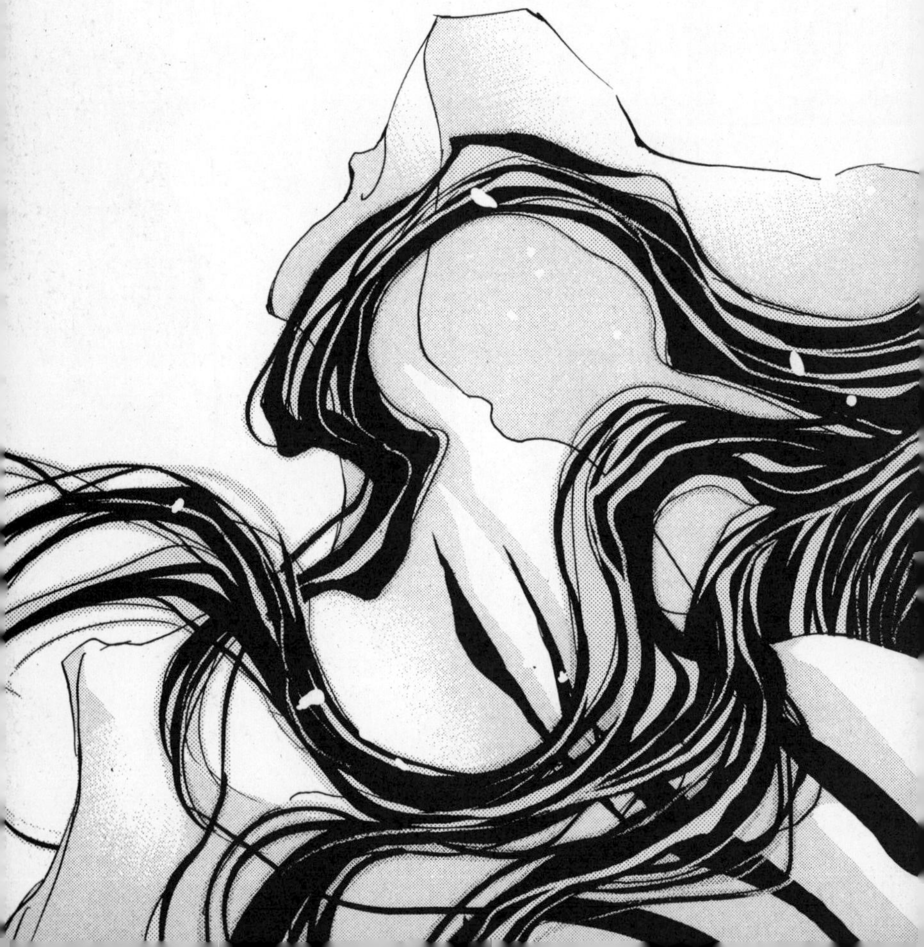

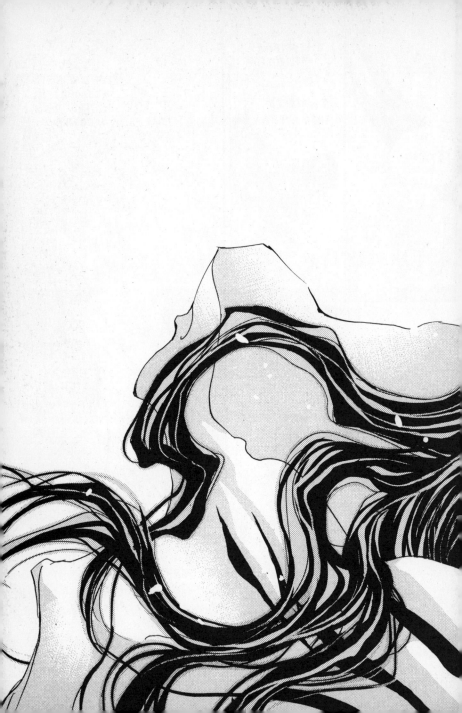

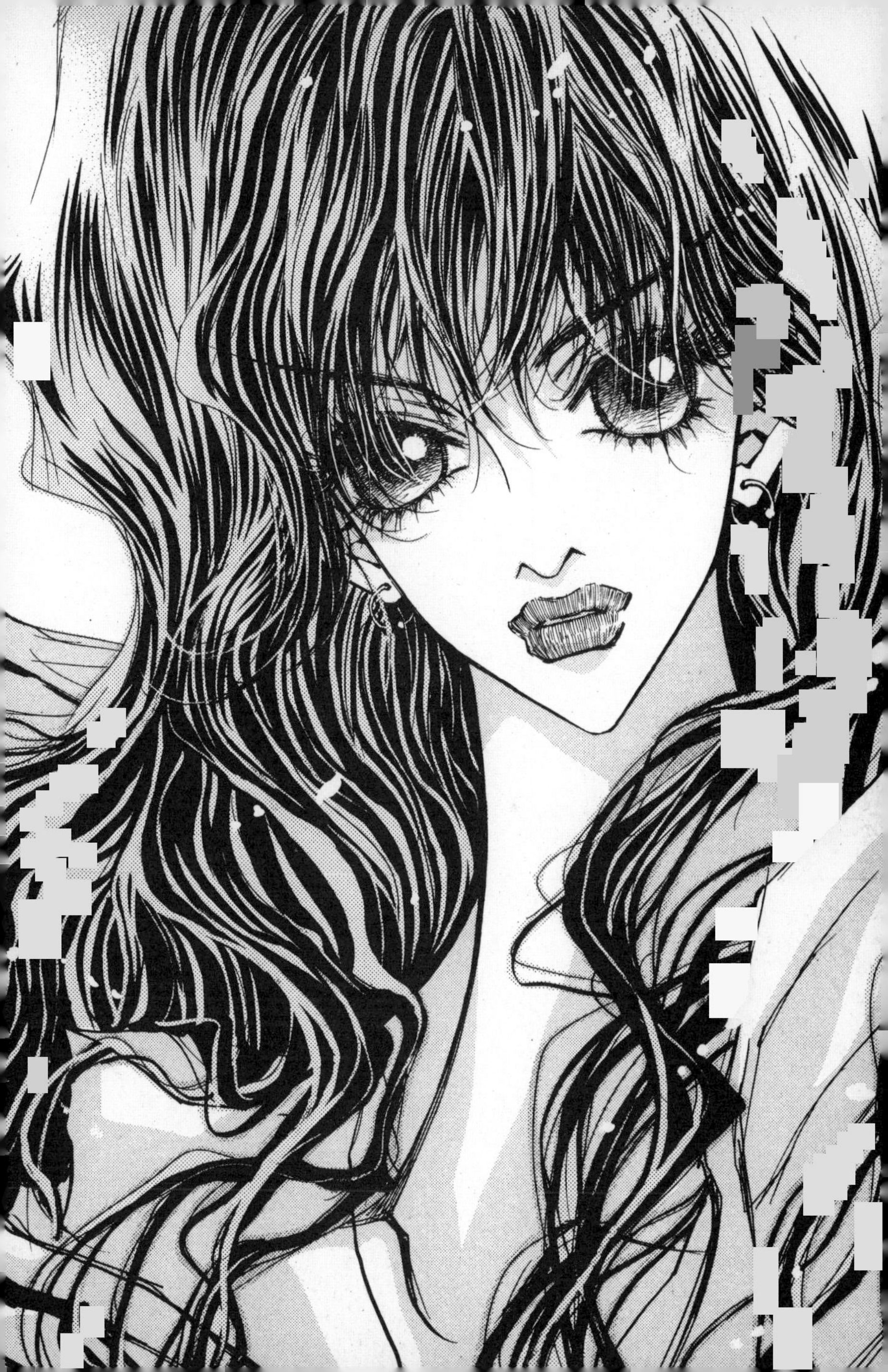

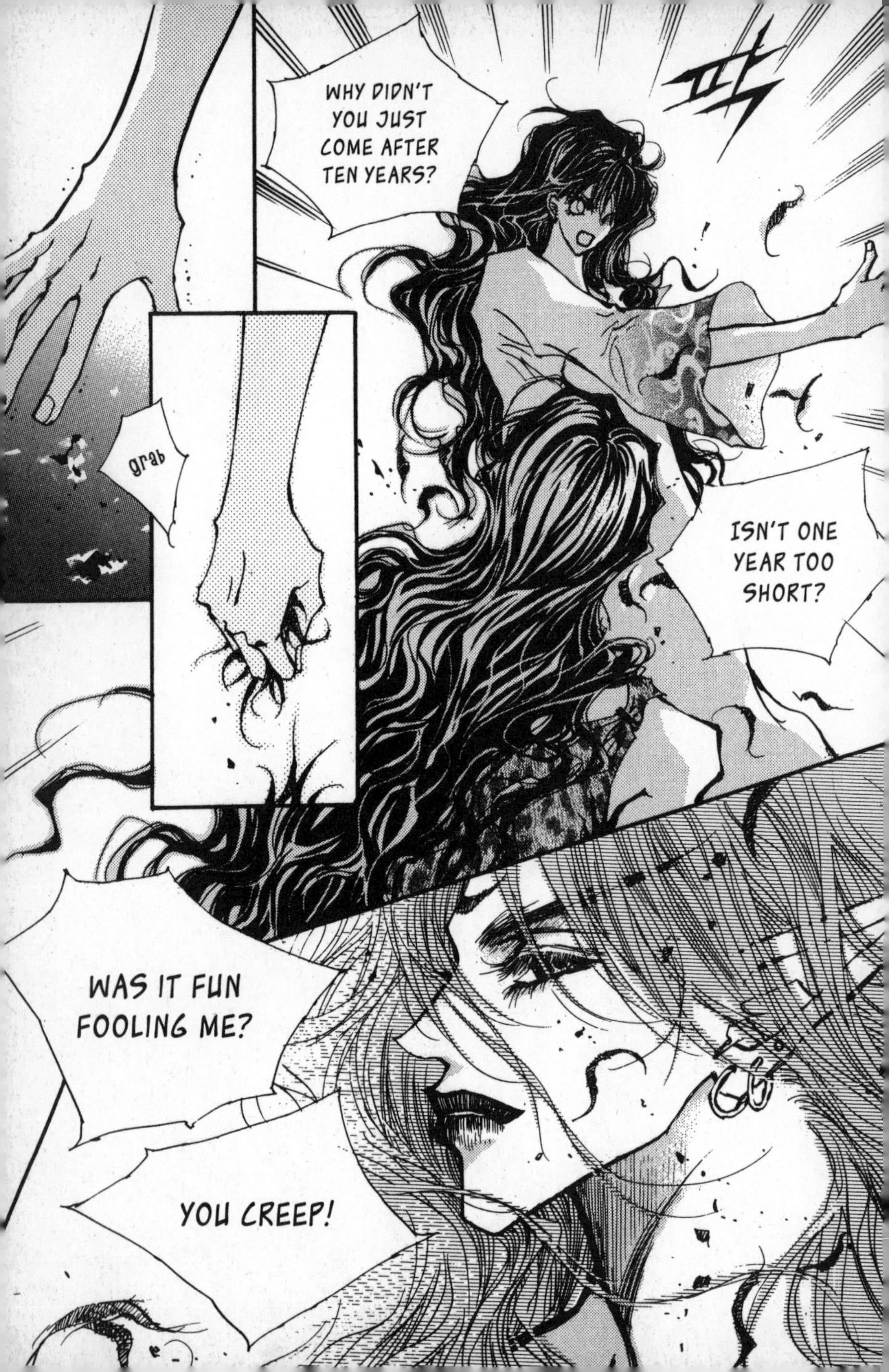
WHY DIDN'T YOU JUST COME AFTER TEN YEARS?
ISN'T ONE YEAR TOO SHORT?
grab
WAS IT FUN FOOLING ME?
YOU CREEP!

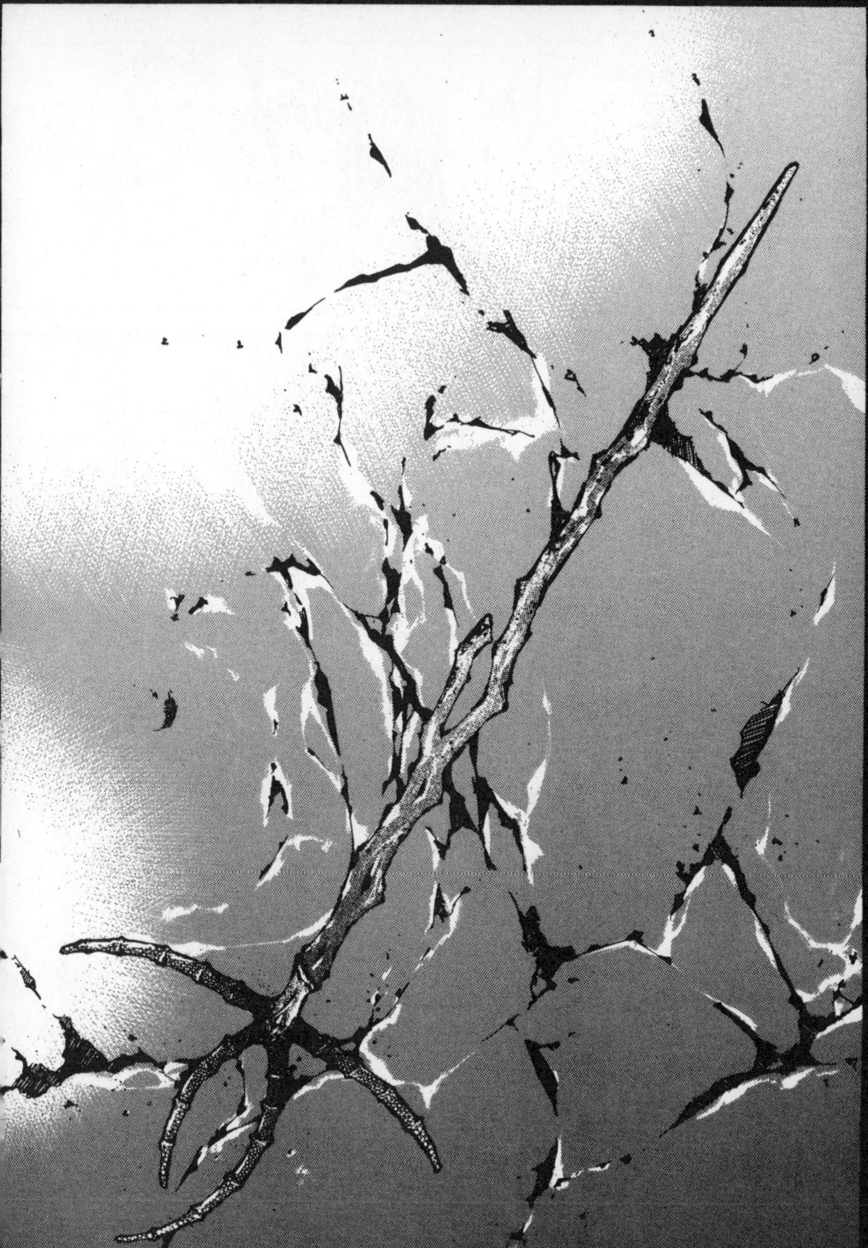

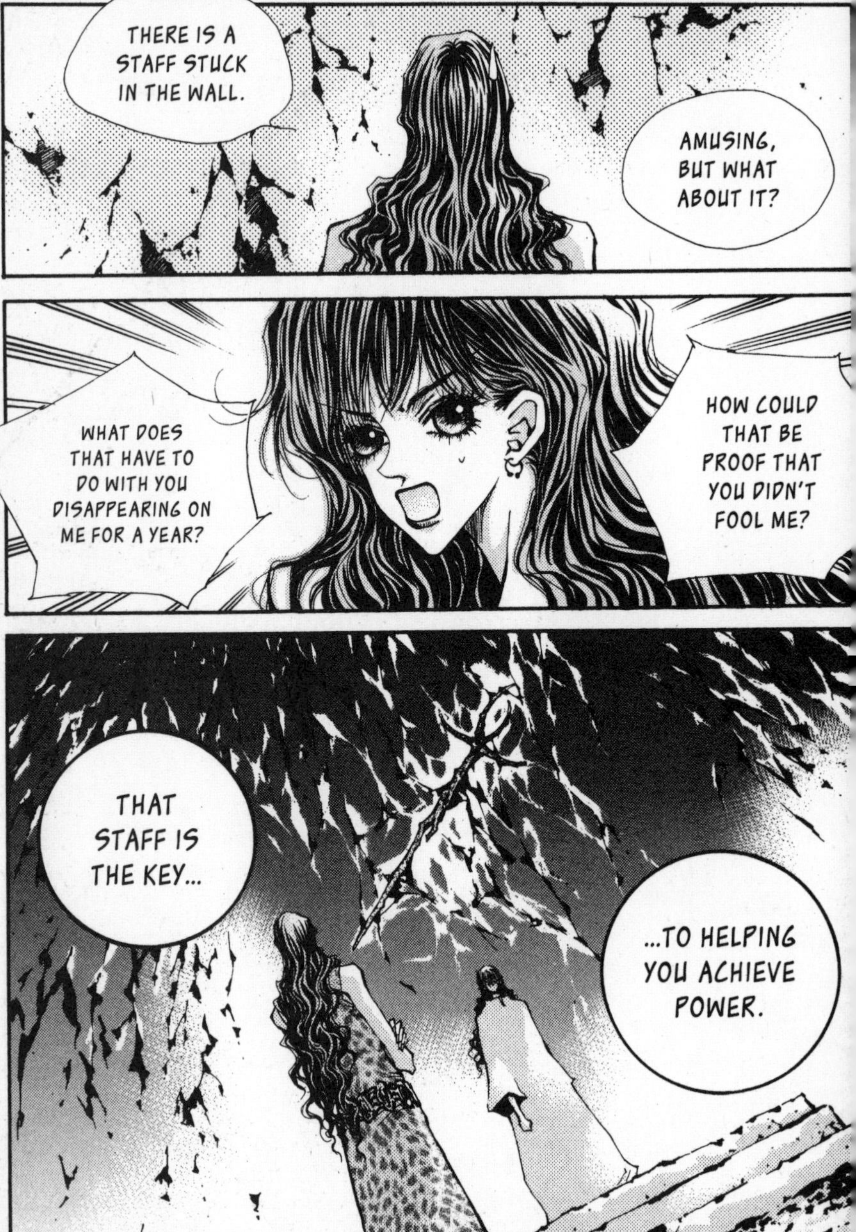
THERE IS A STAFF STUCK IN THE WALL.
AMUSING, BUT WHAT ABOUT IT?
WHAT DOES THAT HAVE TO DO WITH YOU DISAPPEARING ON ME FOR A YEAR?
HOW COULD THAT BE PROOF THAT YOU DIDN'T FOOL ME?
THAT STAFF IS THE KEY...
...TO HELPING YOU ACHIEVE POWER.

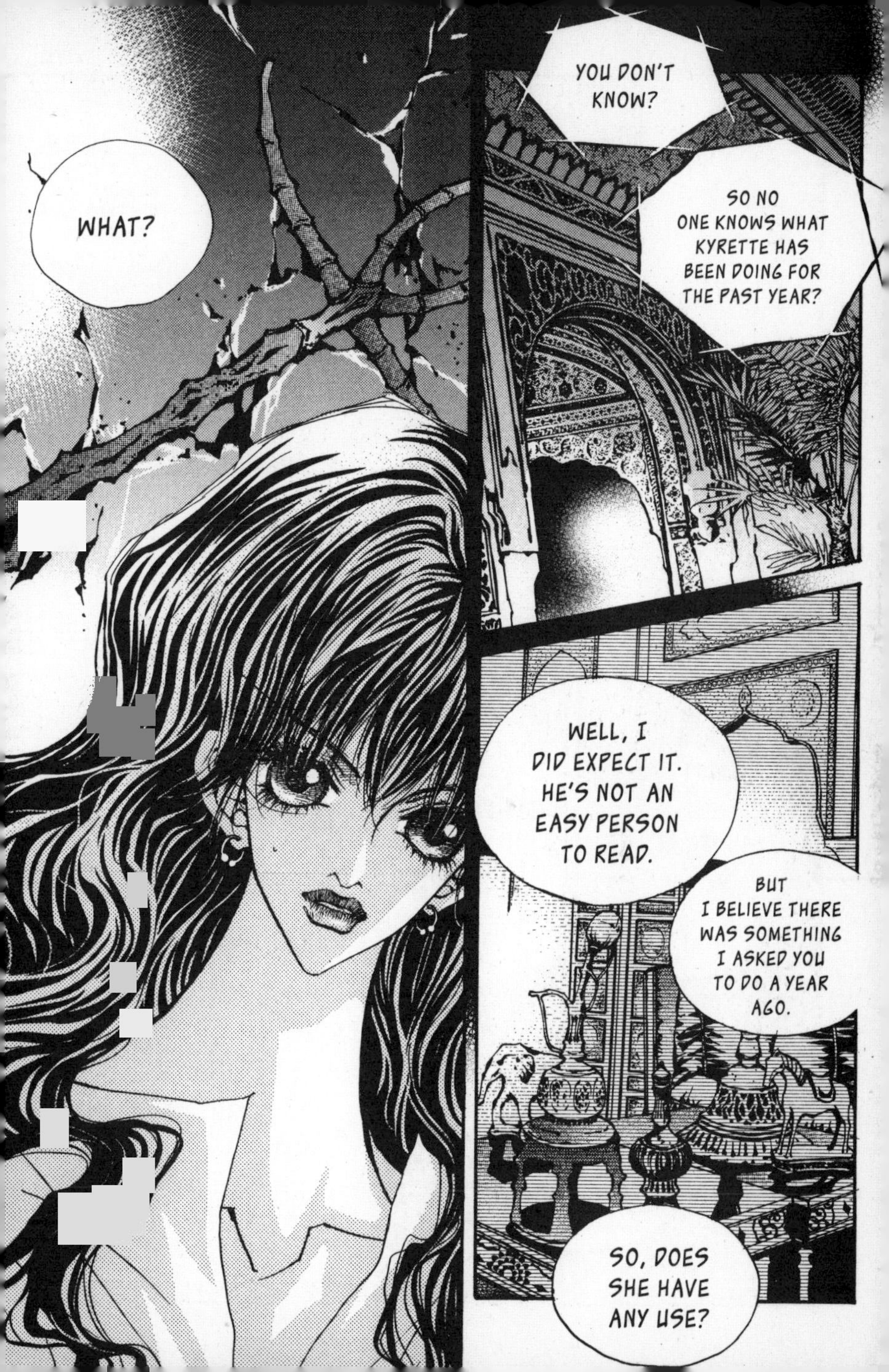
YOU DON'T KNOW?
SO NO ONE KNOWS WHAT KYRETTE HAS BEEN DOING FOR THE PAST YEAR?
WELL, I DID EXPECT IT. HE'S NOT AN EASY PERSON TO READ.
BUT I BELIEVE THERE WAS SOMETHING I ASKED YOU TO DO A YEAR AGO.
SO, DOES SHE HAVE ANY USE?
WHAT?

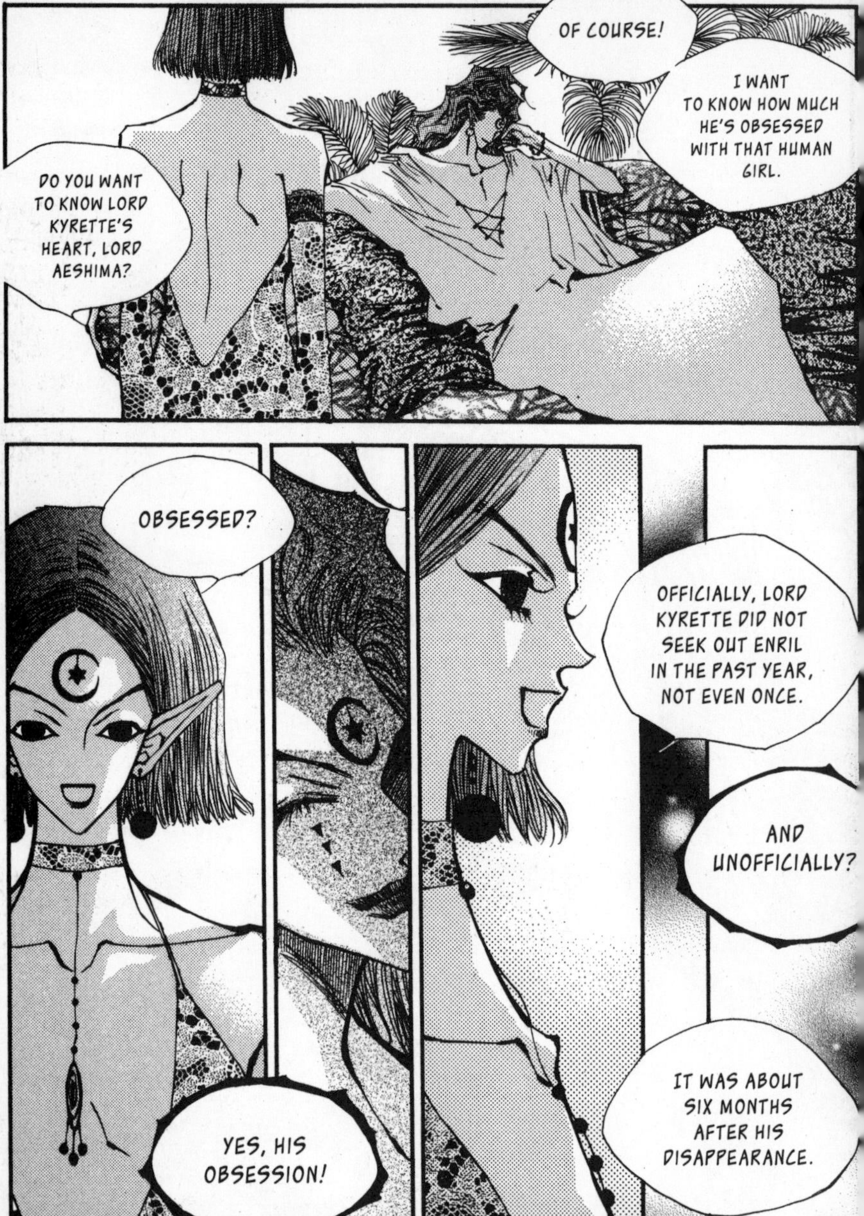
DO YOU WANT TO KNOW LORD KYRETTE'S HEART, LORD AESHIMA?
OF COURSE!
I WANT TO KNOW HOW MUCH HE'S OBSESSED WITH THAT HUMAN GIRL.
OBSESSED?
YES, HIS OBSESSION!
OFFICIALLY, LORD KYRETTE DID NOT SEEK OUT ENRIL IN THE PAST YEAR, NOT EVEN ONCE.
AND UNOFFICIALLY?
IT WAS ABOUT SIX MONTHS AFTER HIS DISAPPEARANCE.

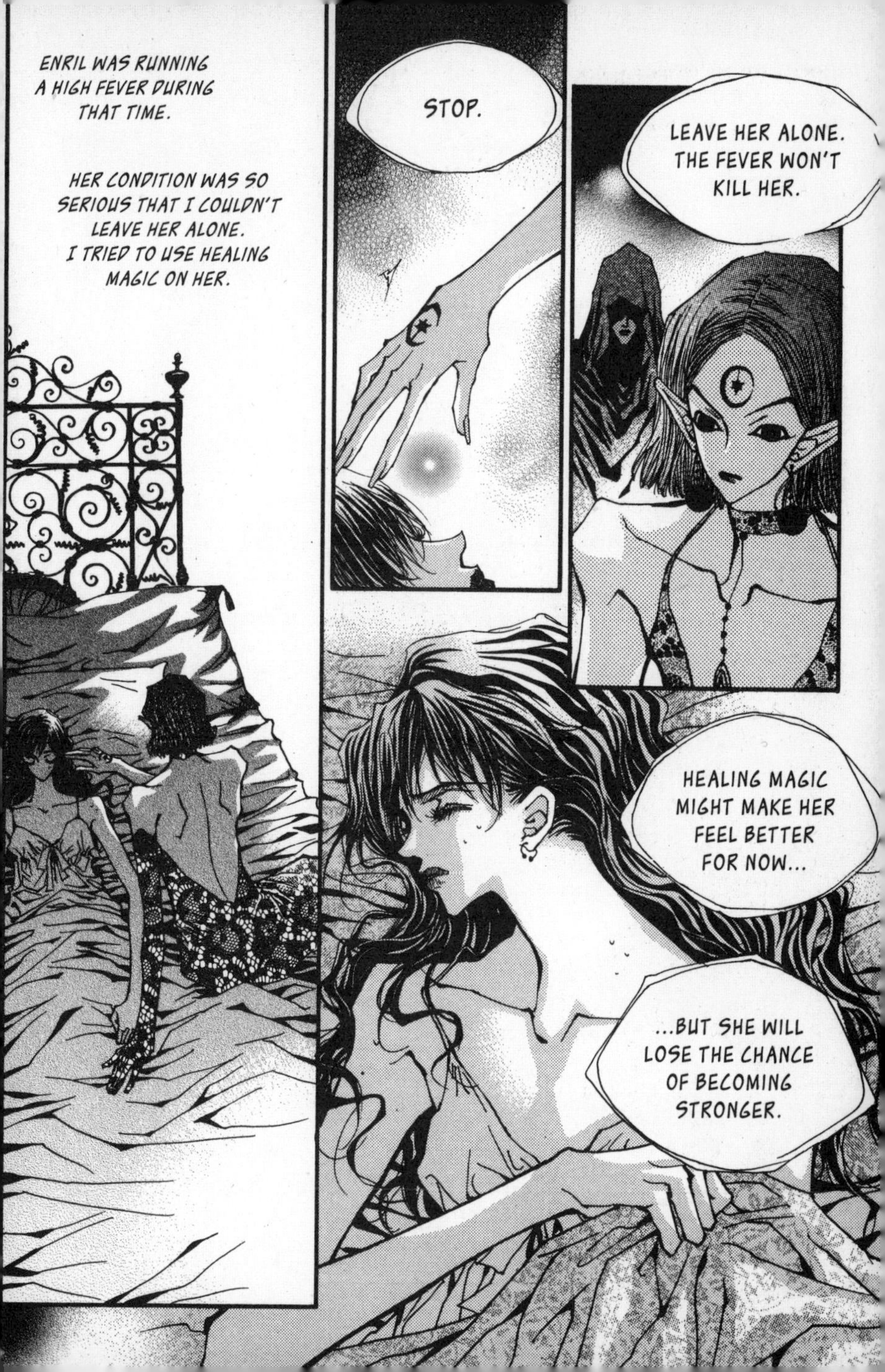
ENRIL WAS RUNNING A HIGH FEVER DURING THAT TIME.
HER CONDITION WAS SO SERIOUS THAT I COULDN'T LEAVE HER ALONE. I TRIED TO USE HEALING MAGIC ON HER.
STOP.
LEAVE HER ALONE. THE FEVER WON'T KILL HER.
HEALING MAGIC MIGHT MAKE HER FEEL BETTER FOR NOW...
...BUT SHE WILL LOSE THE CHANCE OF BECOMING STRONGER.

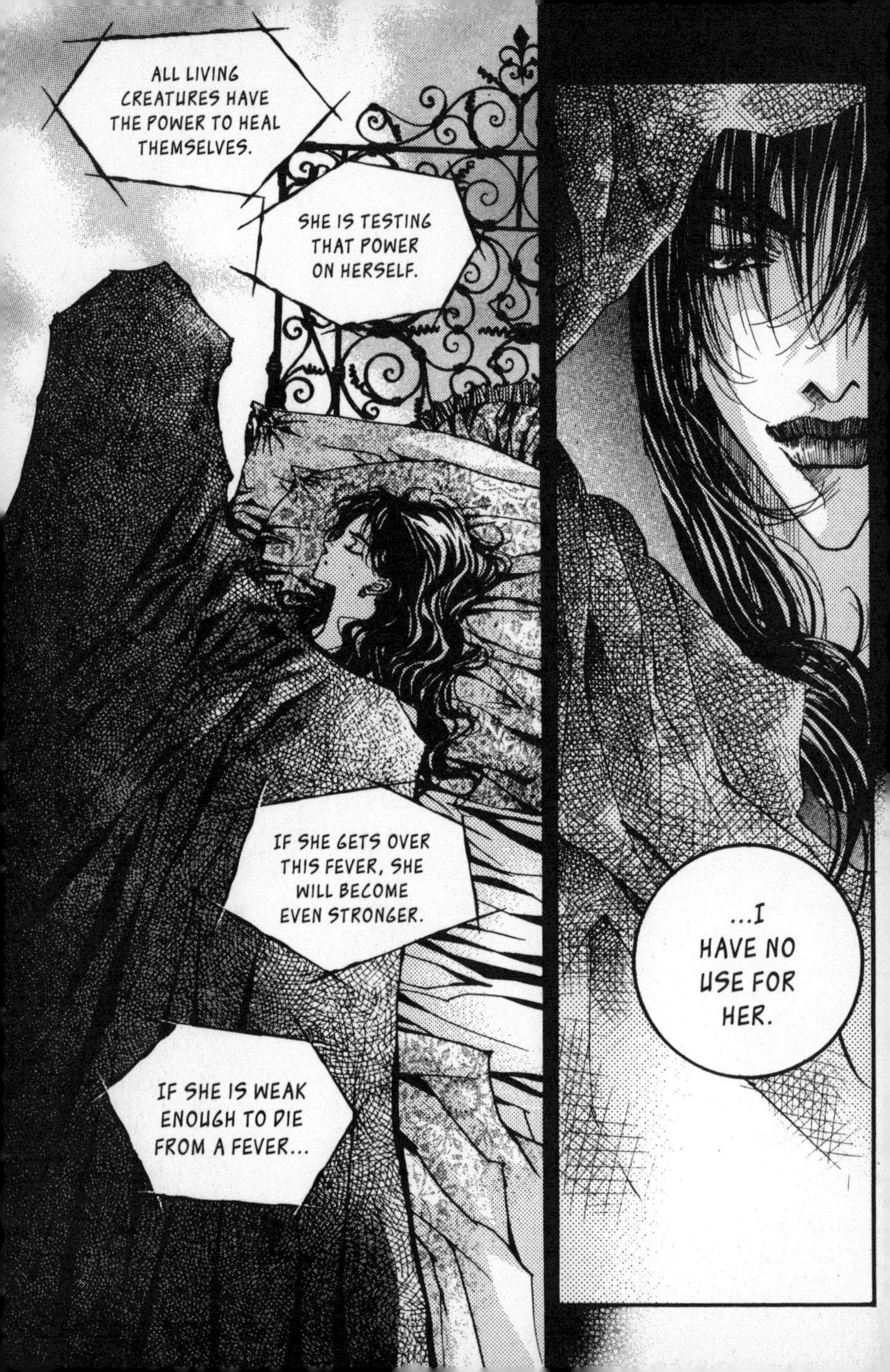
ALL LIVING CREATURES HAVE THE POWER TO HEAL THEMSELVES.
SHE IS TESTING THAT POWER ON HERSELF.
IF SHE GETS OVER THIS FEVER, SHE WILL BECOME EVEN STRONGER.
IF SHE IS WEAK ENOUGH TO DIE FROM A FEVER...
...I HAVE NO USE FOR HER.

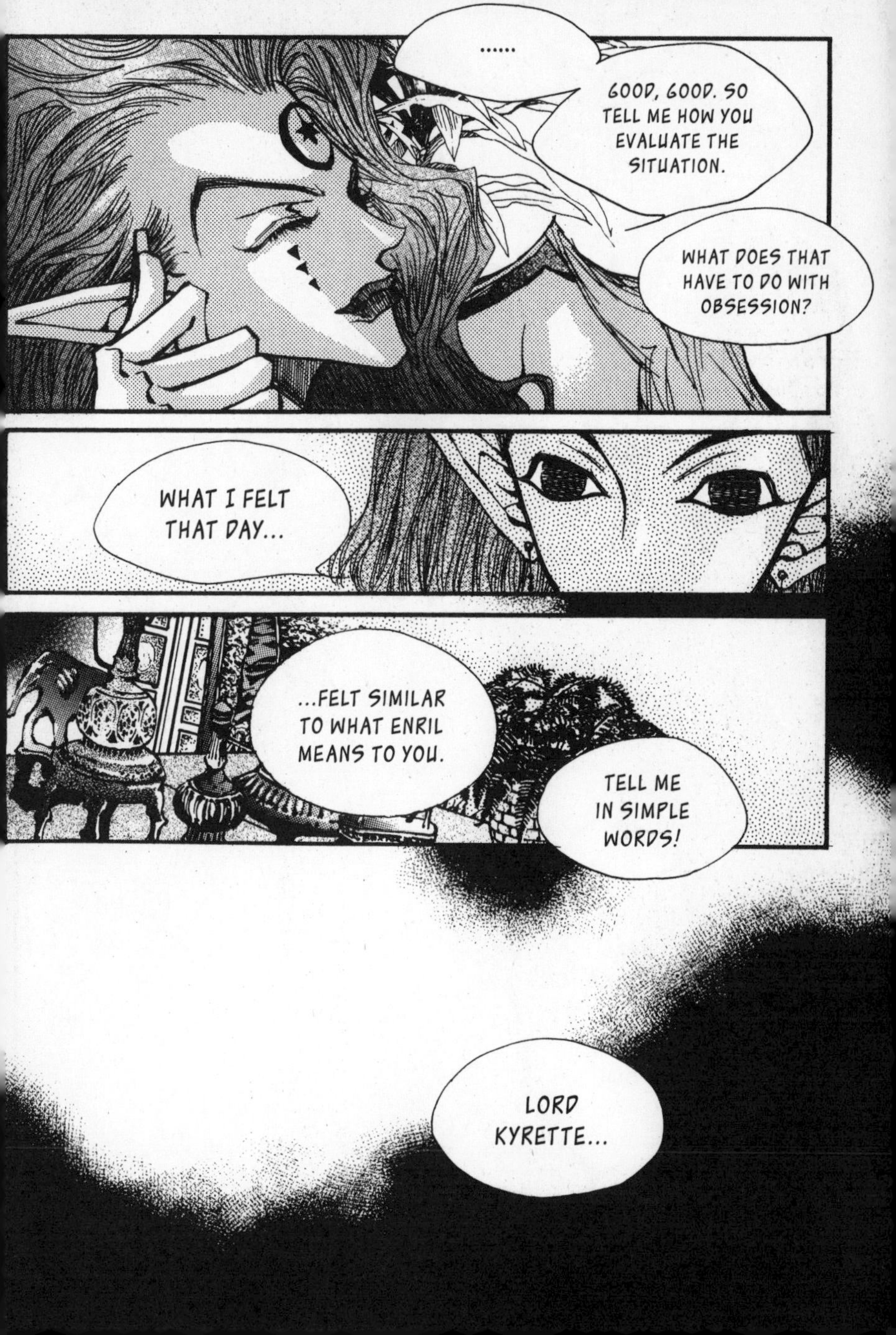
......
GOOD, GOOD. SO TELL ME HOW YOU EVALUATE THE SITUATION.
WHAT DOES THAT HAVE TO DO WITH OBSESSION?
WHAT I FELT THAT DAY...
...FELT SIMILAR TO WHAT ENRIL MEANS TO YOU.
TELL ME IN SIMPLE WORDS!
LORD KYRETTE...

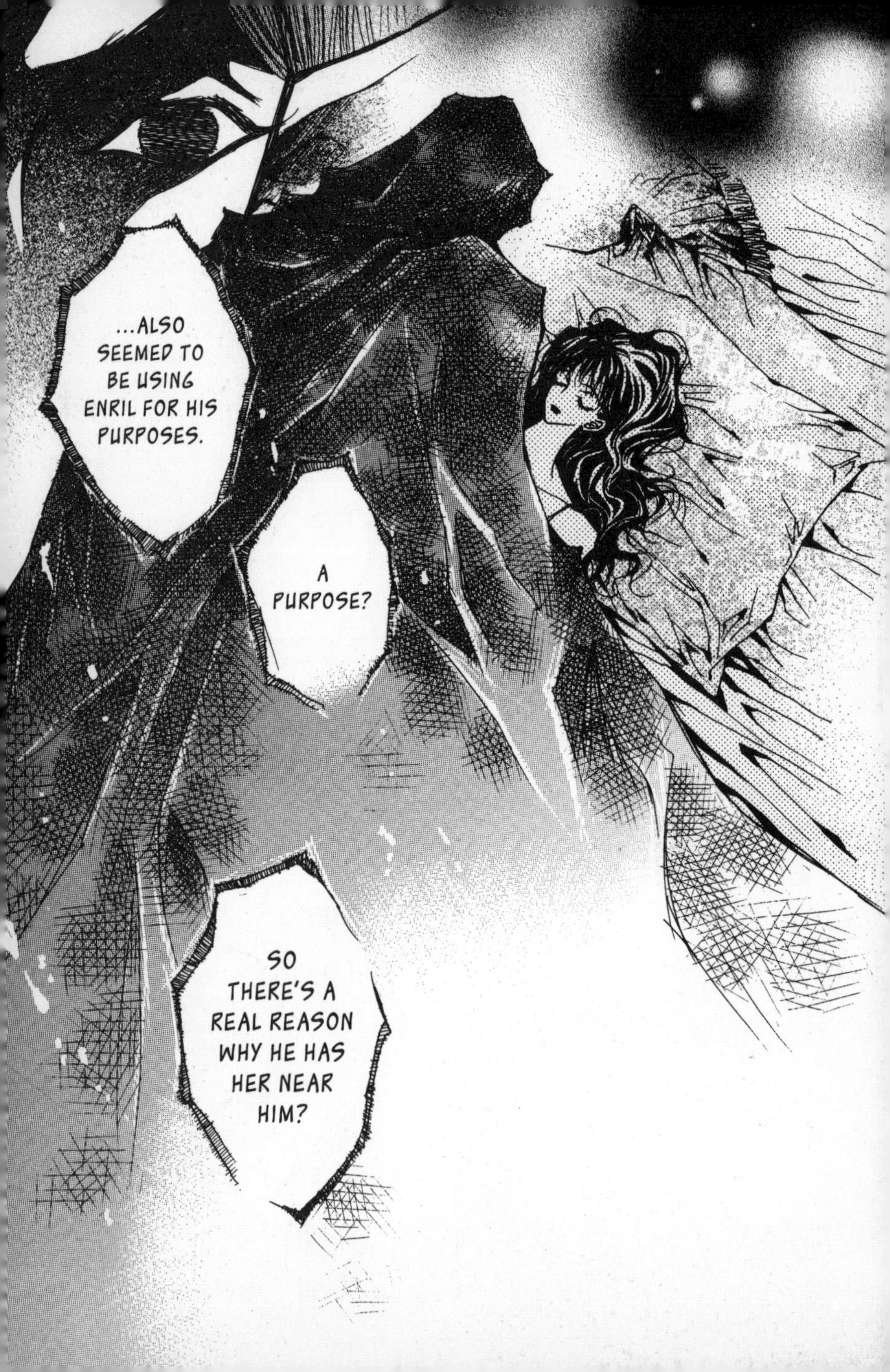
...ALSO SEEMED TO BE USING ENRIL FOR HIS PURPOSES.
A PURPOSE?
SO THERE'S A REAL REASON WHY HE HAS HER NEAR HIM?

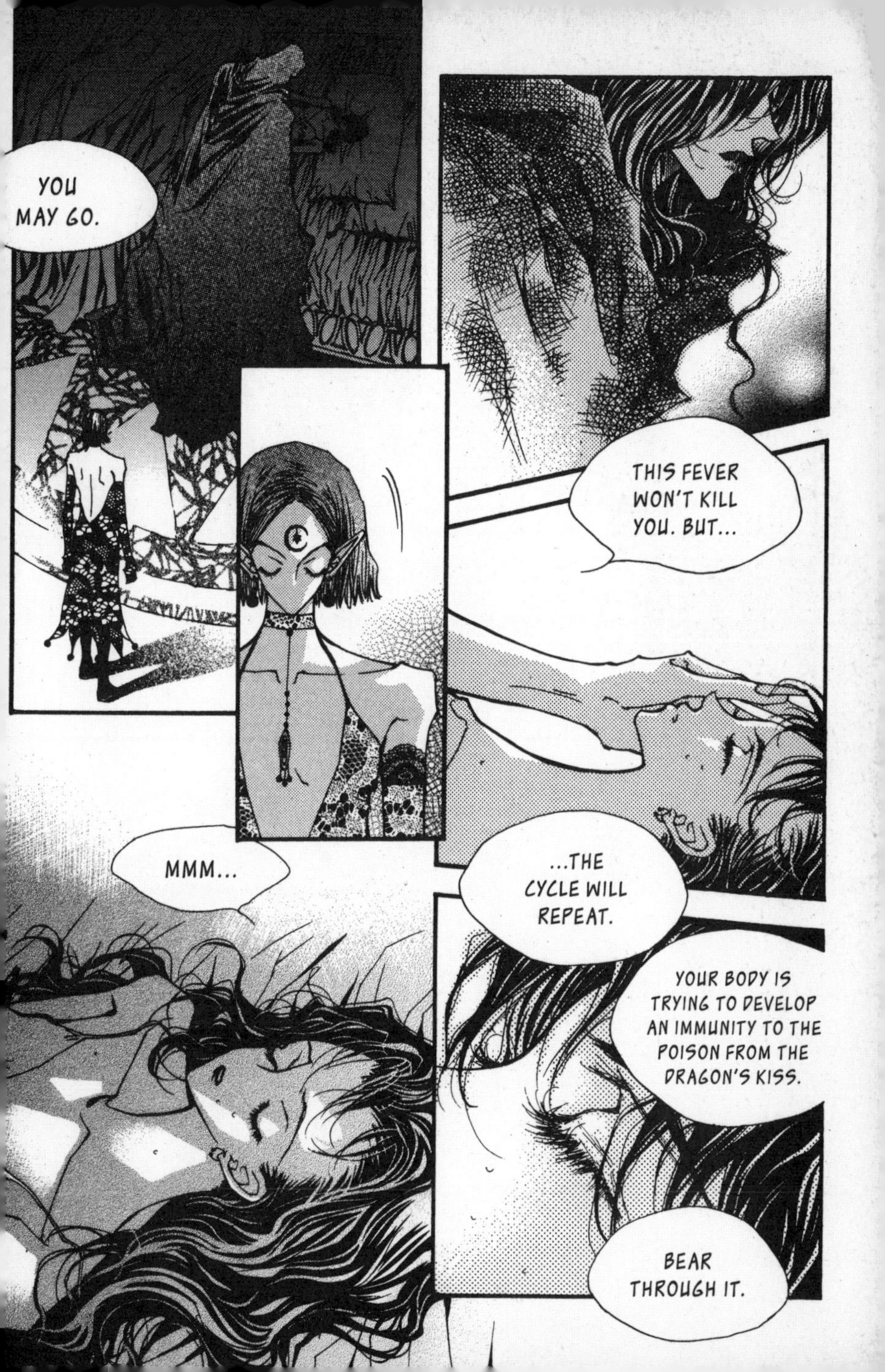
YOU MAY GO.
THIS FEVER WON'T KILL YOU. BUT...
...THE CYCLE WILL REPEAT.
YOUR BODY IS TRYING TO DEVELOP AN IMMUNITY TO THE POISON FROM THE DRAGON'S KISS.
BEAR THROUGH IT.
MMM...

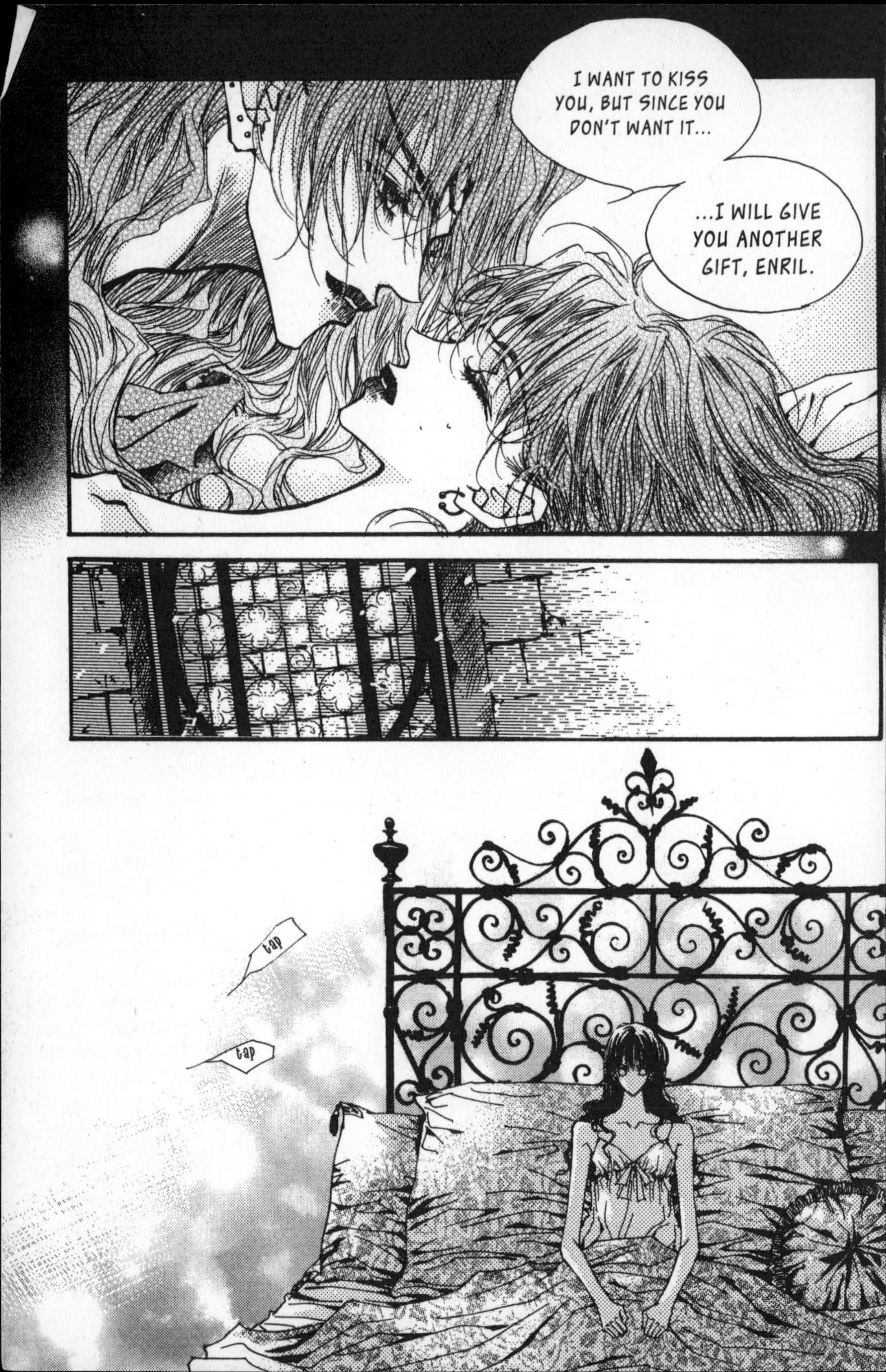
I WANT TO KISS YOU, BUT SINCE YOU DON'T WANT IT...
...I WILL GIVE YOU ANOTHER GIFT, ENRIL.
tap
tap

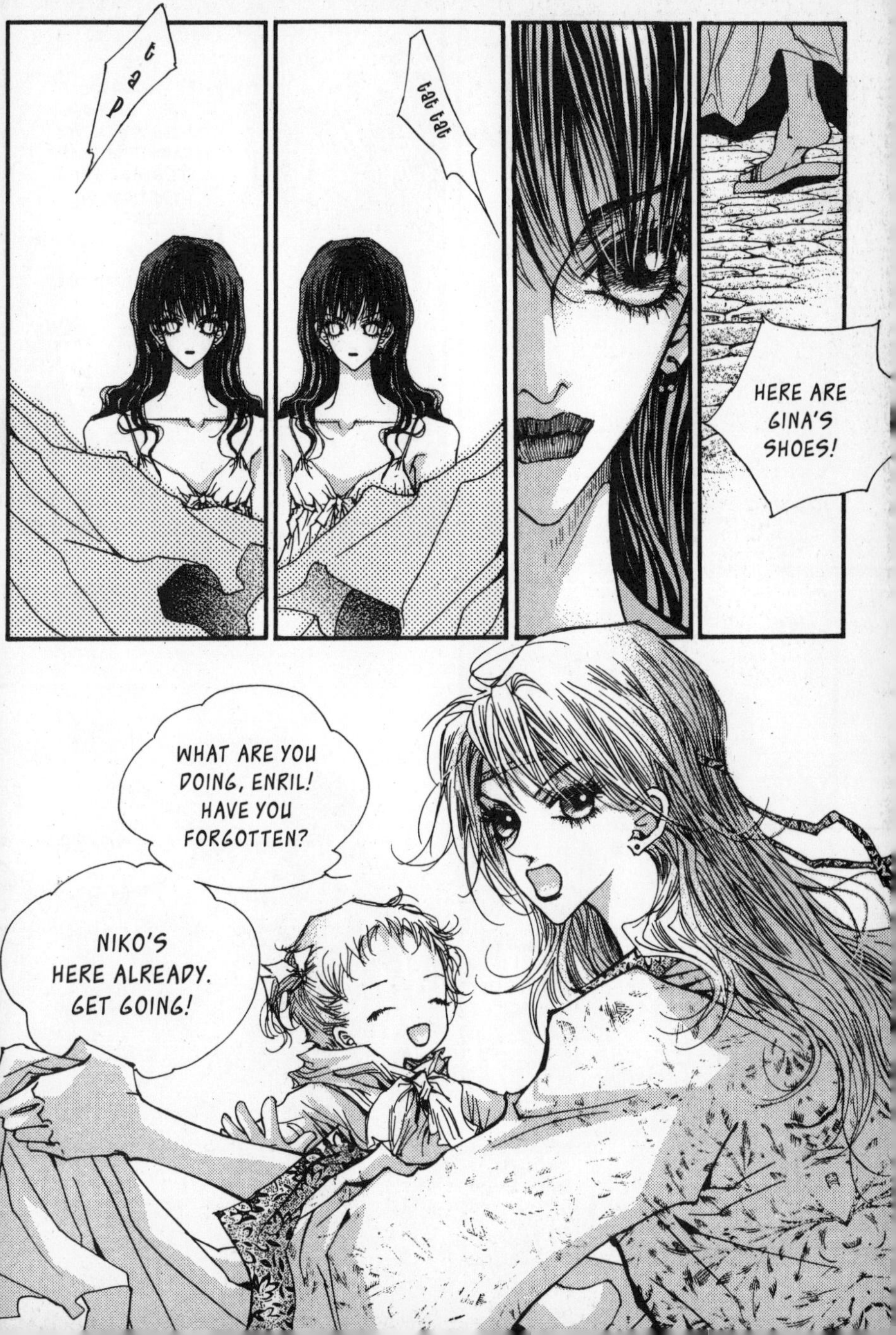
tap
tat tat
HERE ARE GINA'S SHOES!
WHAT ARE YOU DOING, ENRIL! HAVE YOU FORGOTTEN?
NIKO'S HERE ALREADY. GET GOING!

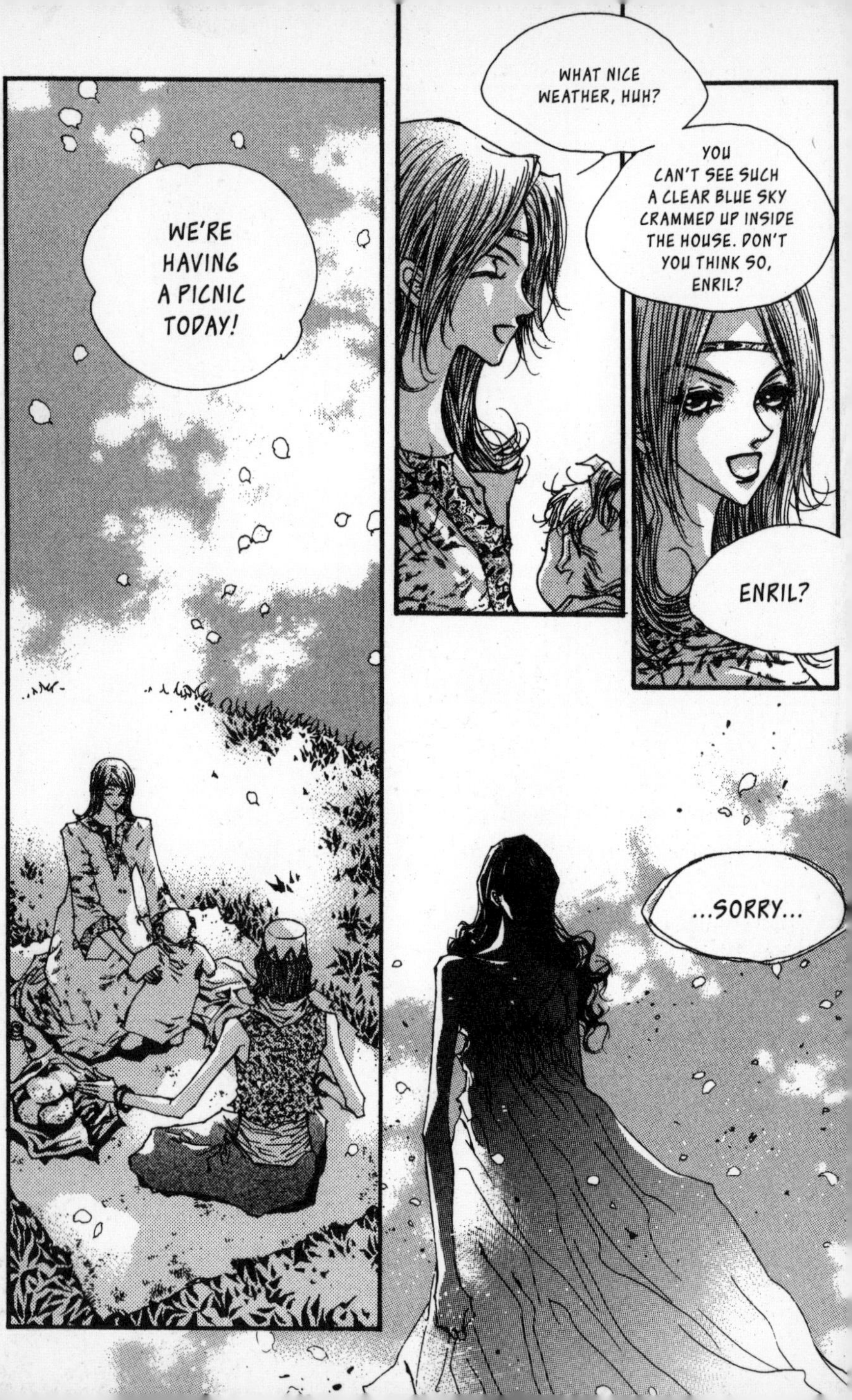
WE'RE HAVING A PICNIC TODAY!
WHAT NICE WEATHER, HUH?
YOU CAN'T SEE SUCH A CLEAR BLUE SKY CRAMMED UP INSIDE THE HOUSE. DON'T YOU THINK SO, ENRIL?
ENRIL?
...SORRY...

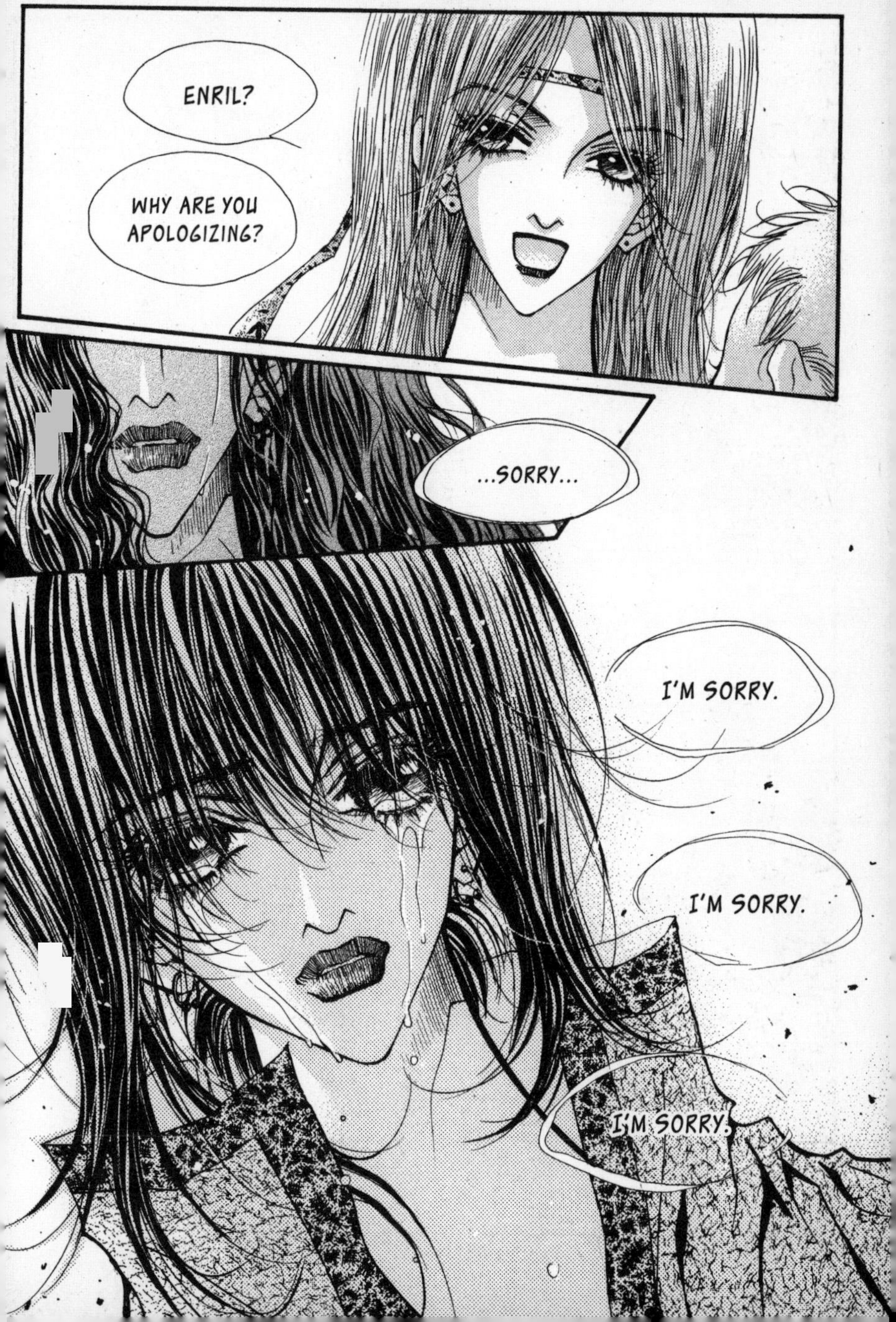
ENRIL?
WHY ARE YOU APOLOGIZING?
...SORRY...
I'M SORRY.
I'M SORRY.
I'M SORRY.

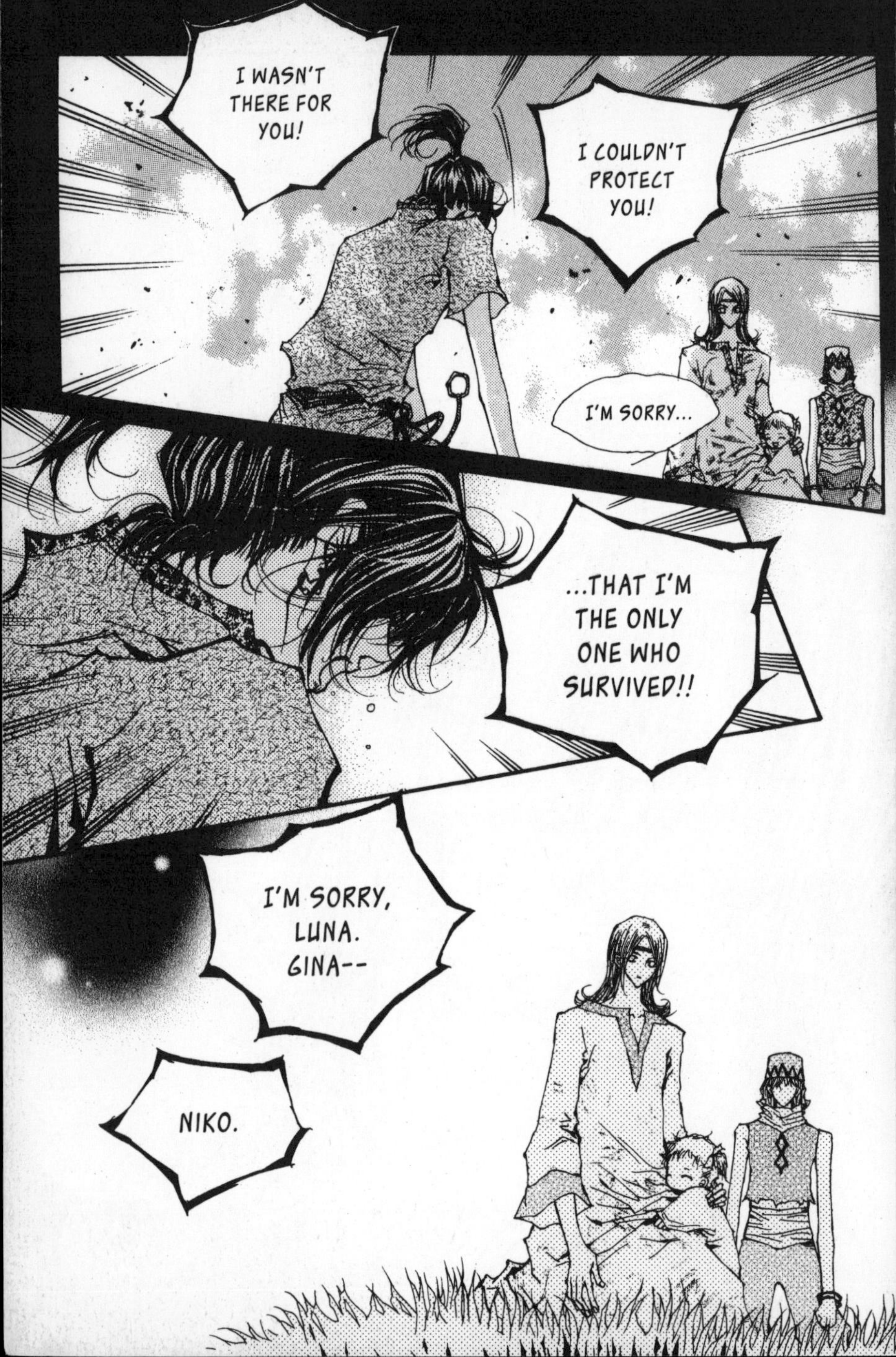

I COULDN'T PROTECT YOU!
I WASN'T THERE FOR YOU!
I'M SORRY...
...THAT I'M THE ONLY ONE WHO SURVIVED!!
I'M SORRY, LUNA. GINA--
NIKO.

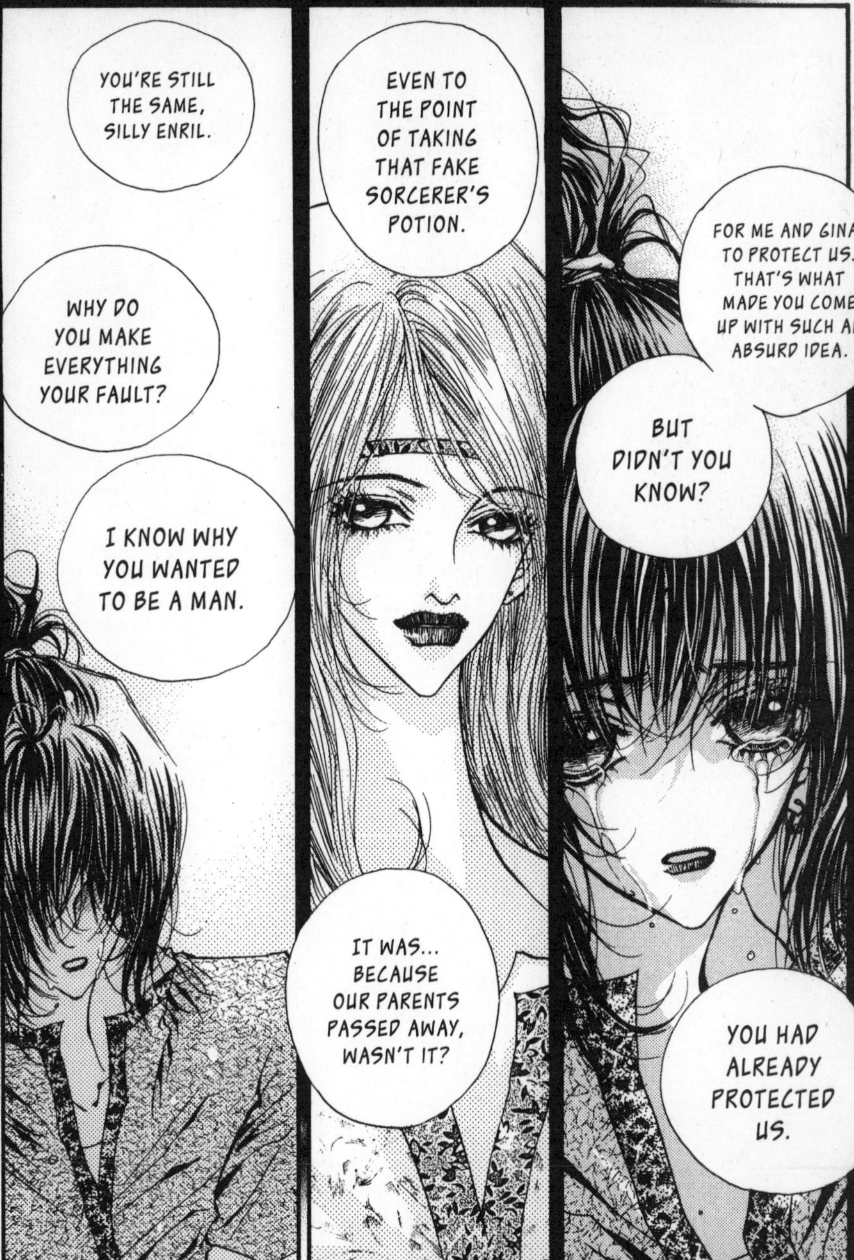
YOU'RE STILL THE SAME, SILLY ENRIL.
WHY DO YOU MAKE EVERYTHING YOUR FAULT?
I KNOW WHY YOU WANTED TO BE A MAN.
EVEN TO THE POINT OF TAKING THAT FAKE SORCERER'S POTION.
IT WAS... BECAUSE OUR PARENTS PASSED AWAY, WASN'T IT?
FOR ME AND GINA. TO PROTECT US. THAT'S WHAT MADE YOU COME UP WITH SUCH AN ABSURD IDEA.
BUT DIDN'T YOU KNOW?
YOU HAD ALREADY PROTECTED US.

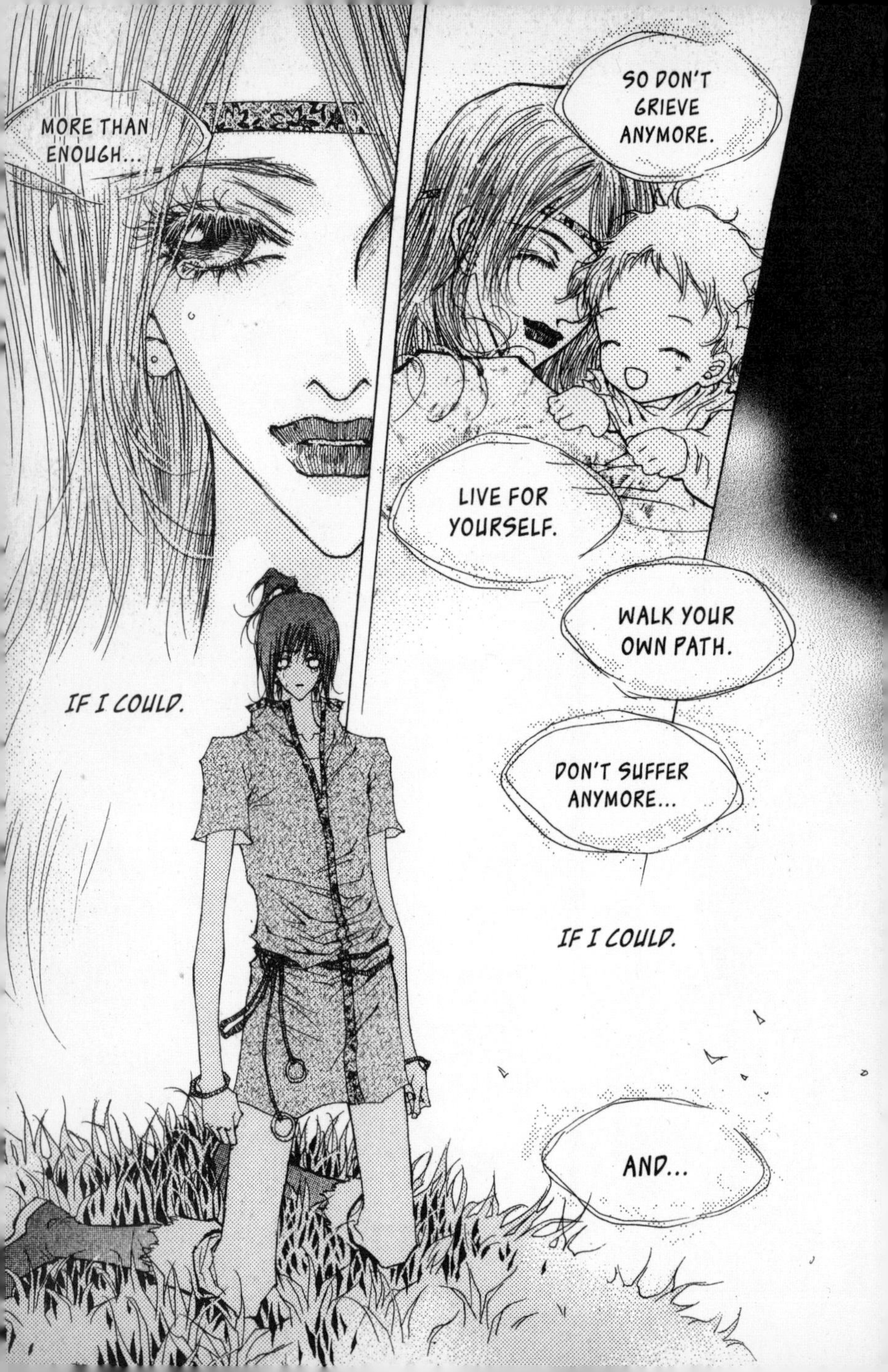
SO DON'T GRIEVE ANYMORE.
LIVE FOR YOURSELF.
WALK YOUR OWN PATH.
DON'T SUFFER ANYMORE...
MORE THAN ENOUGH...
IF I COULD.
IF I COULD.
AND...

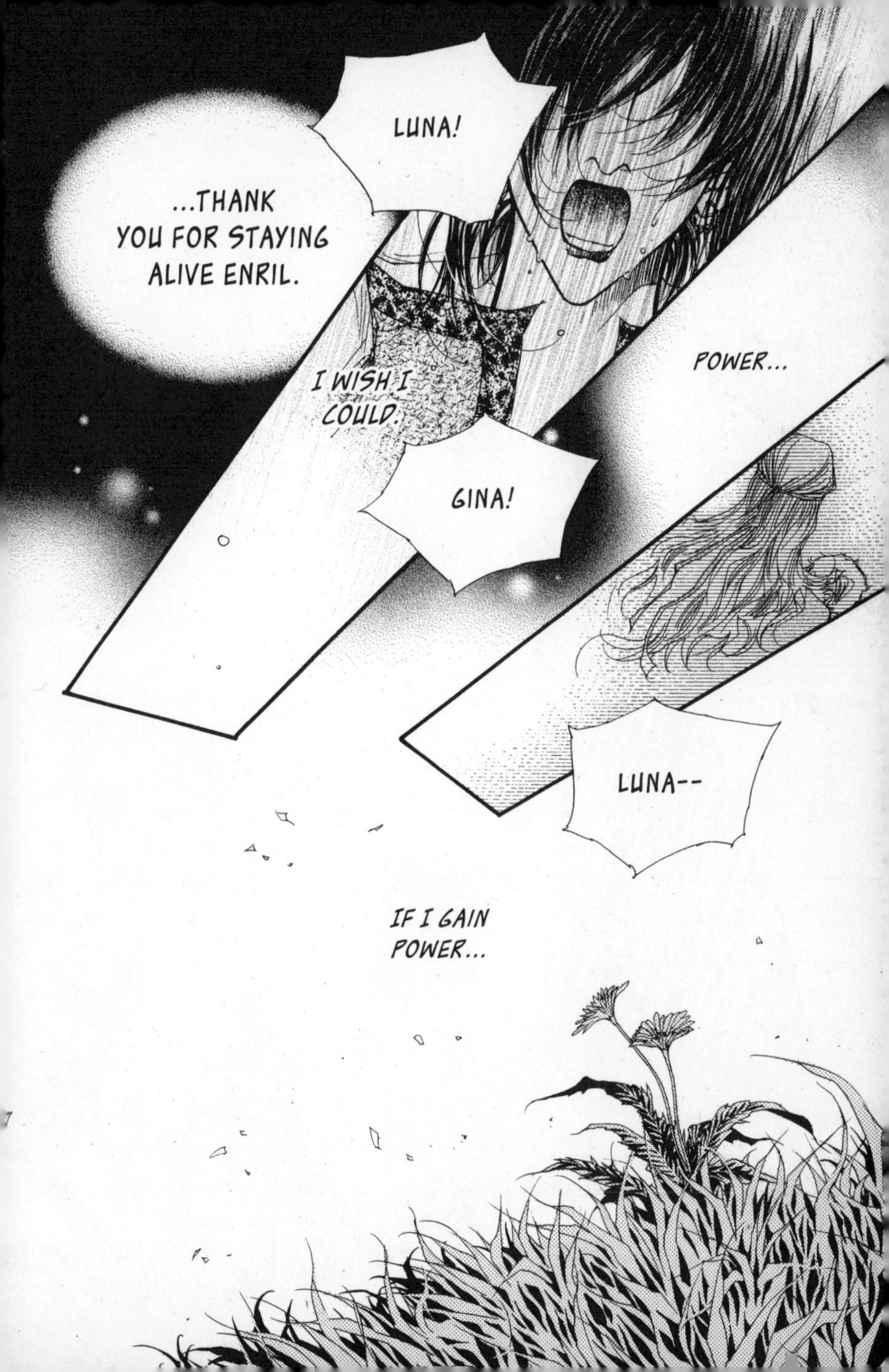
LUNA!
...THANK YOU FOR STAYING ALIVE ENRIL.
POWER...
I WISH I COULD.
GINA!
LUNA--
IF I GAIN POWER...

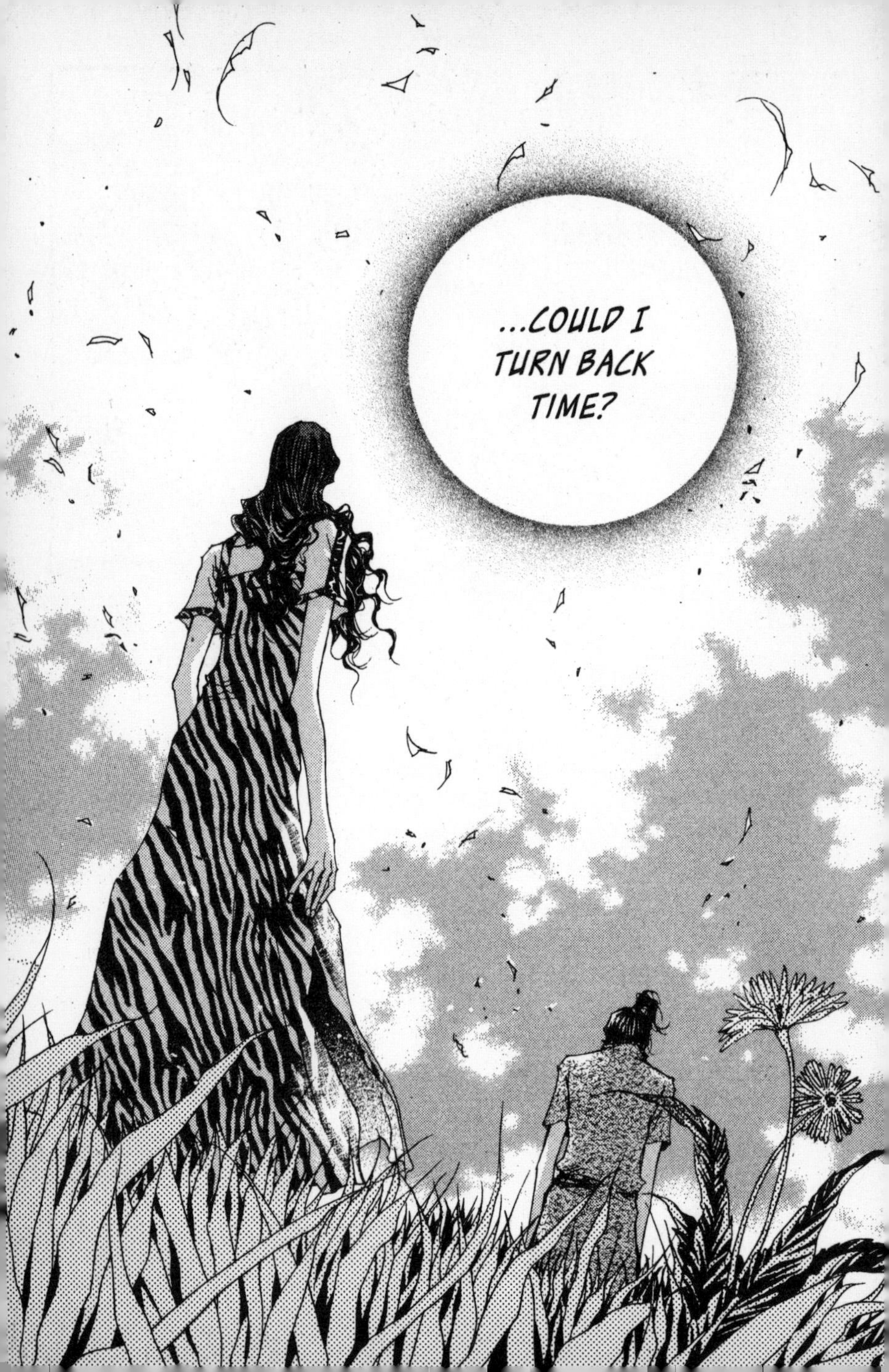
...COULD I TURN BACK TIME?

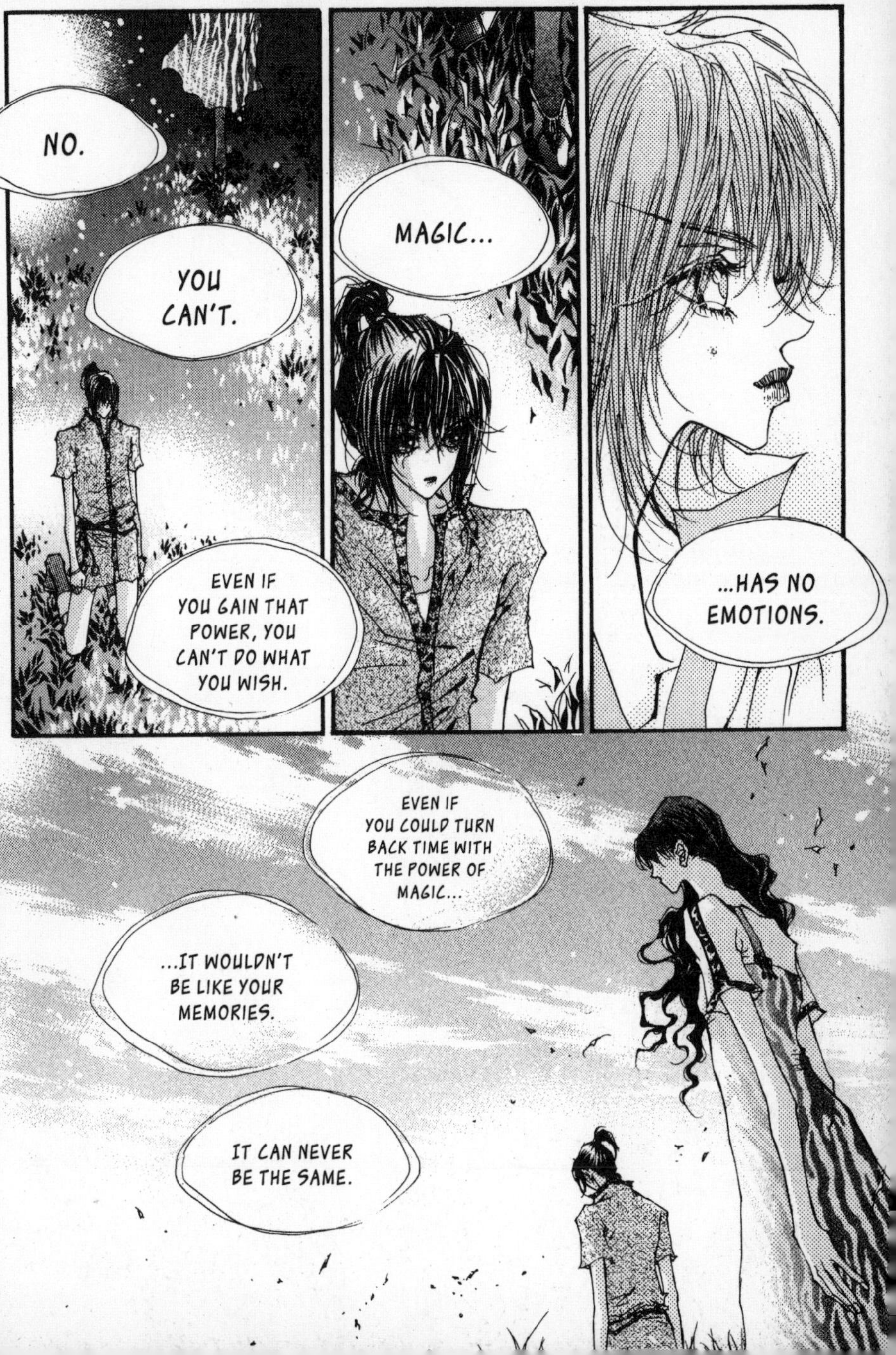
NO.
YOU CAN'T.
EVEN IF YOU GAIN THAT POWER, YOU CAN'T DO WHAT YOU WISH.
MAGIC...
...HAS NO EMOTIONS.
EVEN IF YOU COULD TURN BACK TIME WITH THE POWER OF MAGIC...
...IT WOULDN'T BE LIKE YOUR MEMORIES.
IT CAN NEVER BE THE SAME.

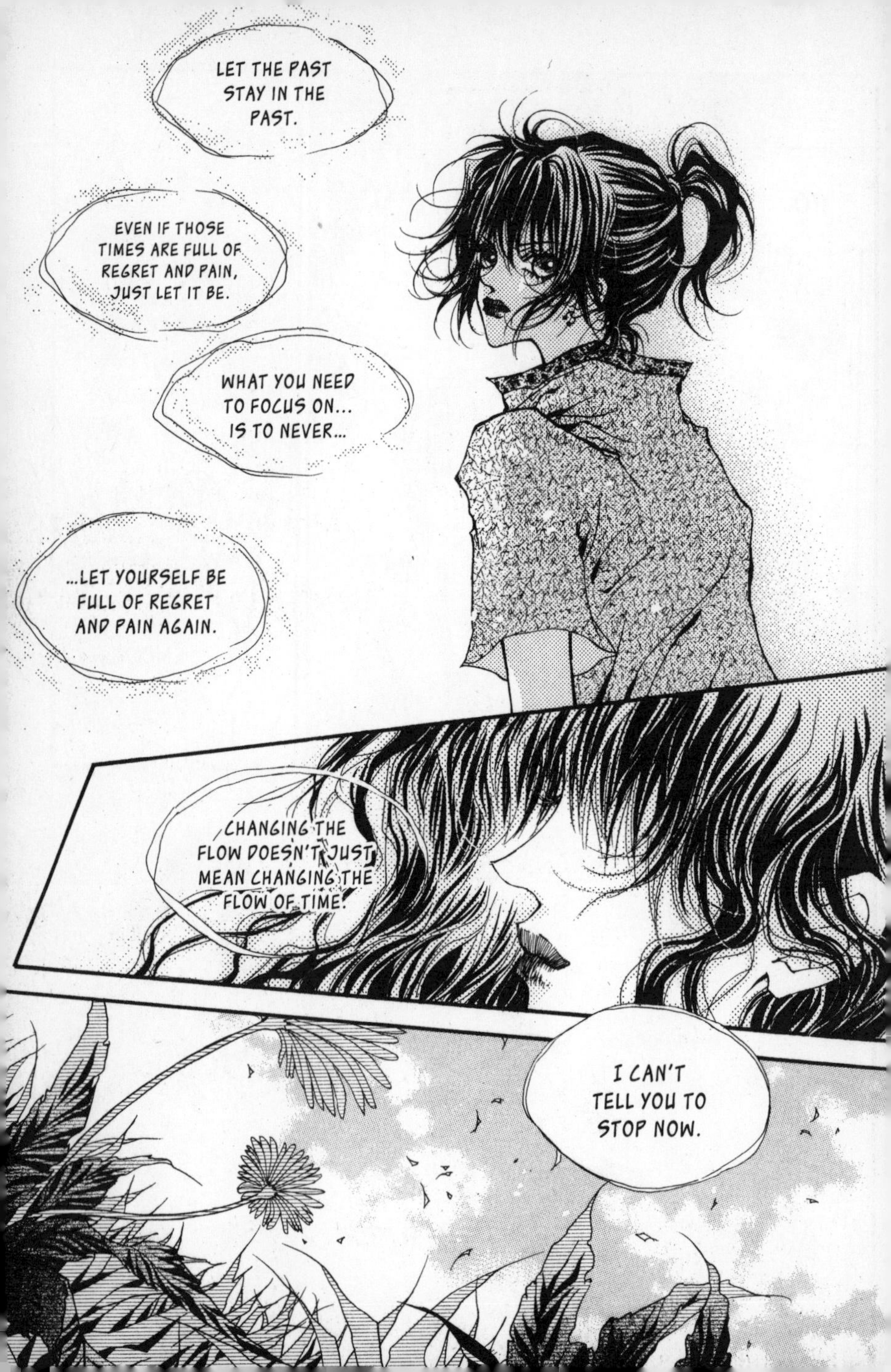
LET THE PAST STAY IN THE PAST.
EVEN IF THOSE TIMES ARE FULL OF REGRET AND PAIN, JUST LET IT BE.
WHAT YOU NEED TO FOCUS ON... IS TO NEVER...
...LET YOURSELF BE FULL OF REGRET AND PAIN AGAIN.
CHANGING THE FLOW DOESN'T JUST MEAN CHANGING THE FLOW OF TIME.
I CAN'T TELL YOU TO STOP NOW.

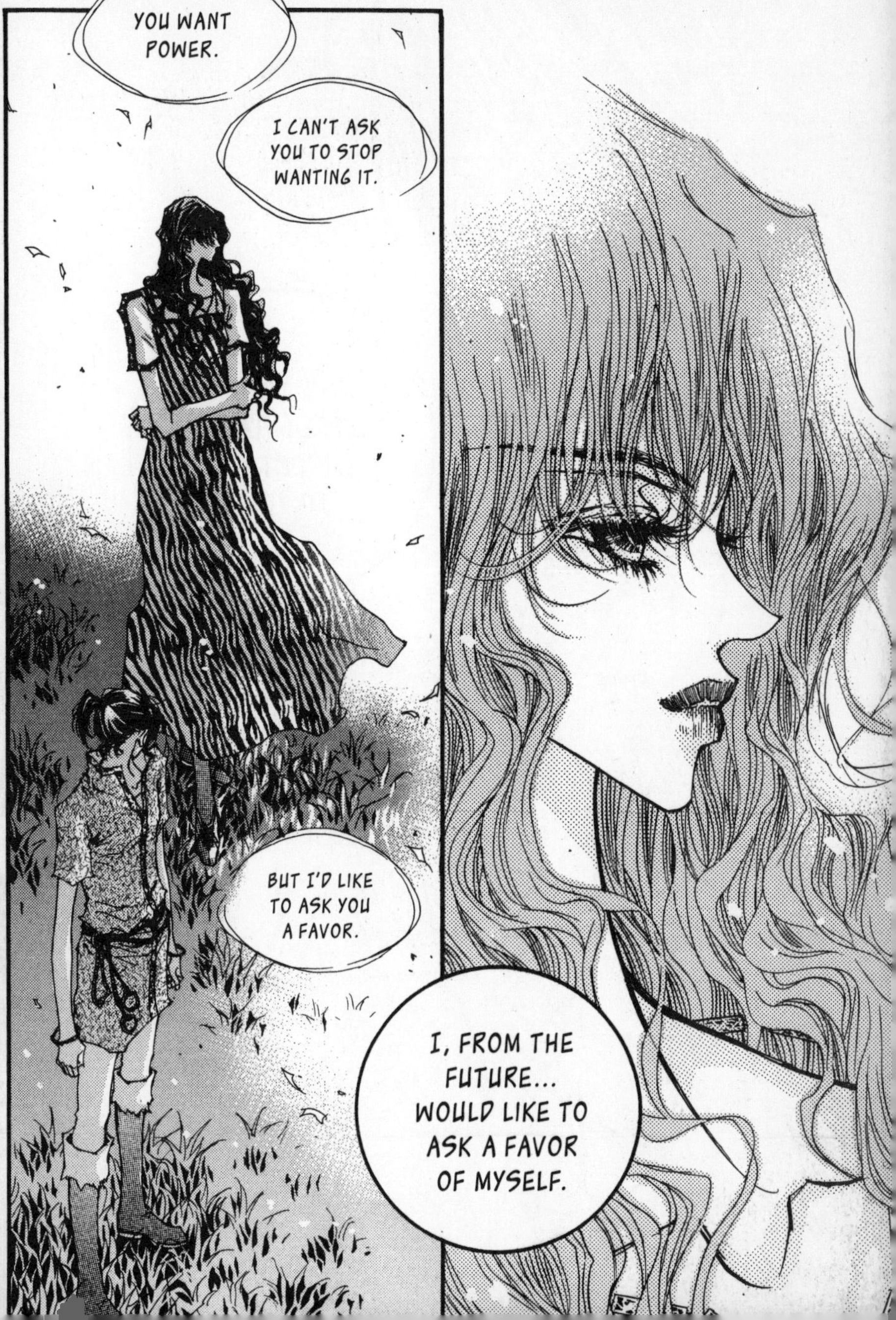
YOU WANT POWER.
I CAN'T ASK YOU TO STOP WANTING IT.
BUT I'D LIKE TO ASK YOU A FAVOR.
I, FROM THE FUTURE... WOULD LIKE TO ASK A FAVOR OF MYSELF.

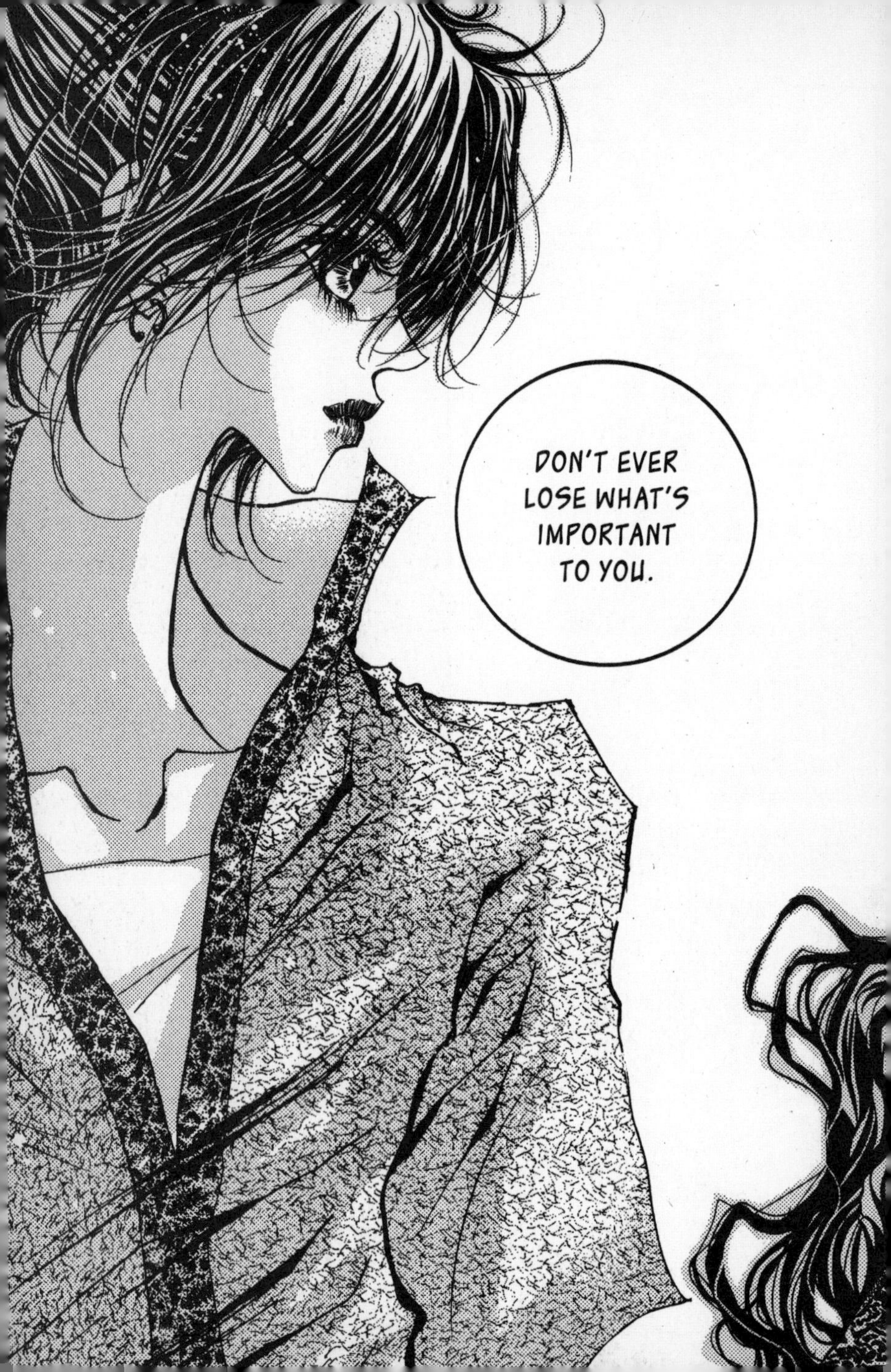
DON'T EVER LOSE WHAT'S IMPORTANT TO YOU.

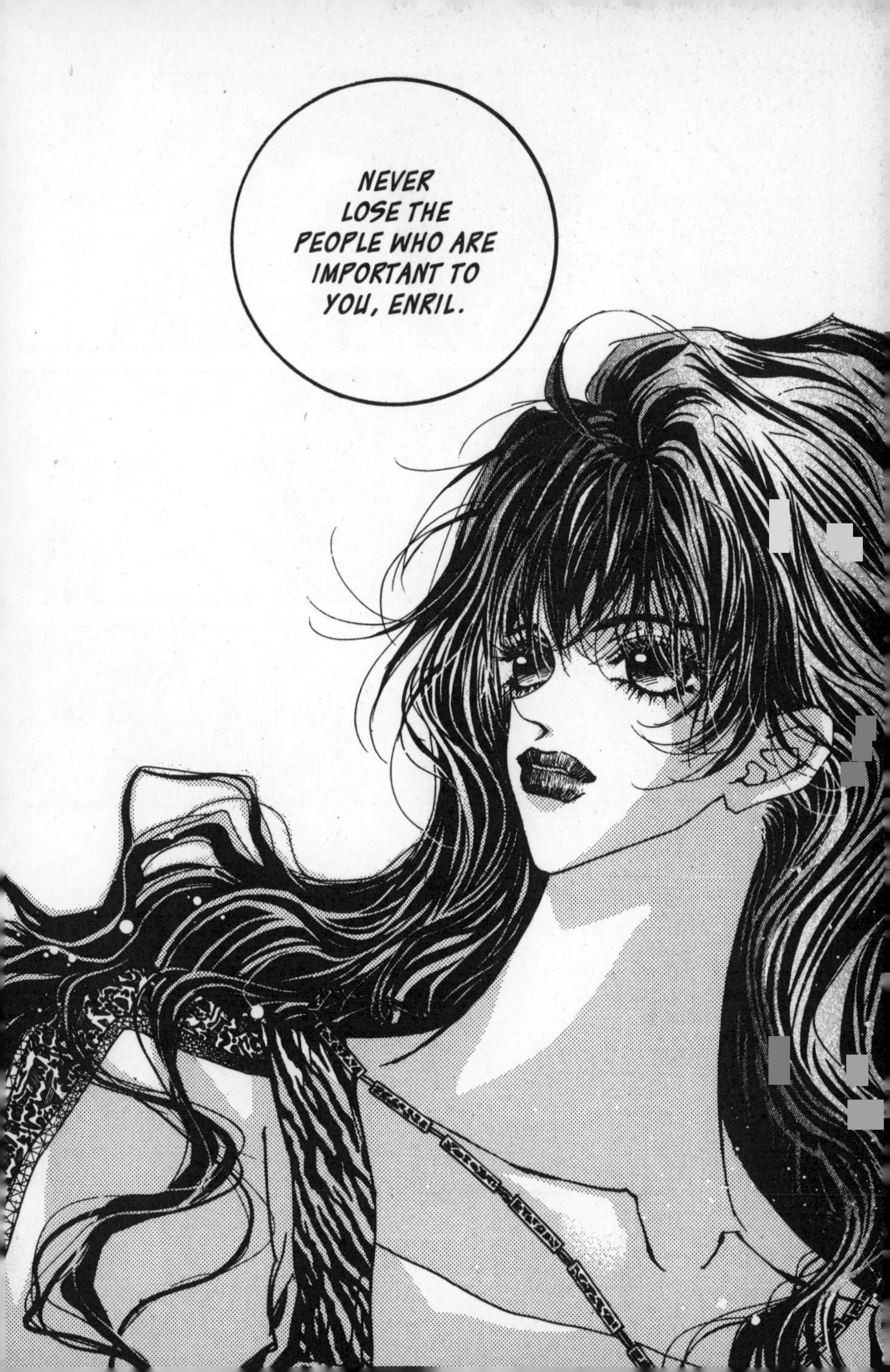
NEVER LOSE THE PEOPLE WHO ARE IMPORTANT TO YOU, ENRIL.

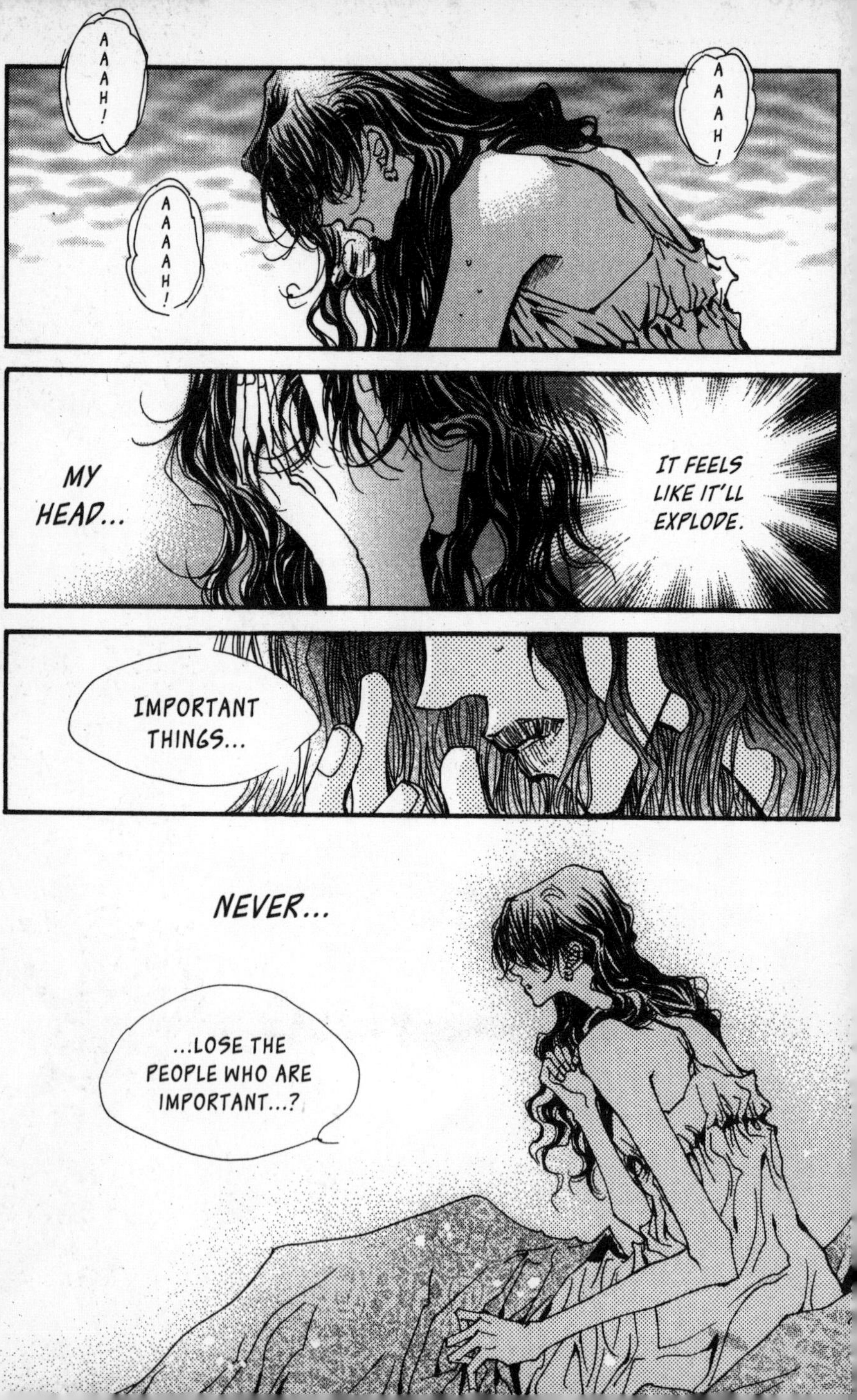
AAAH!
AAAAH!
AAAH!
MY HEAD...
IT FEELS LIKE IT'LL EXPLODE.
IMPORTANT THINGS...
NEVER...
...LOSE THE PEOPLE WHO ARE IMPORTANT...?

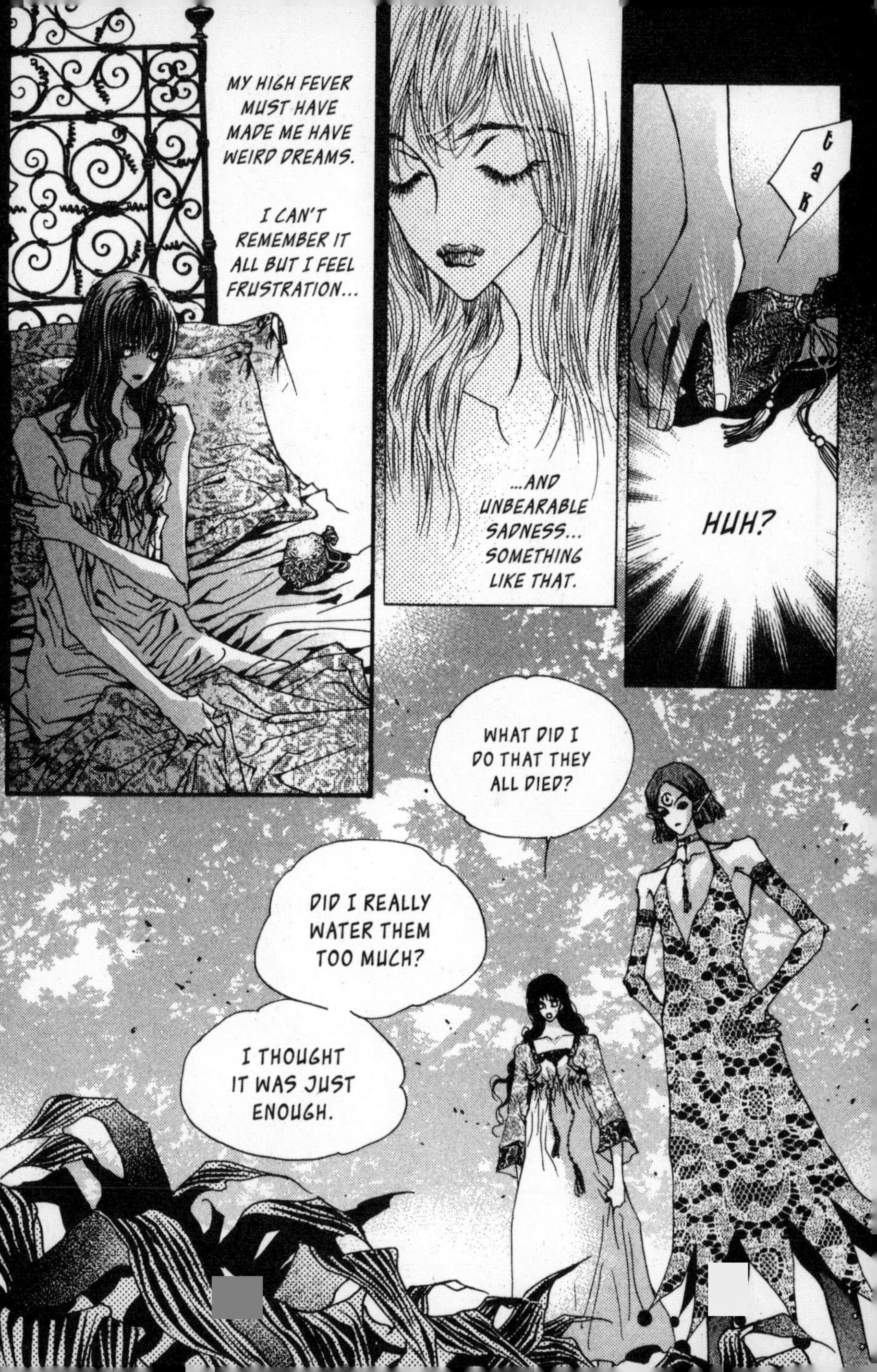
MY HIGH FEVER MUST HAVE MADE ME HAVE WEIRD DREAMS.
I CAN'T REMEMBER IT ALL BUT I FEEL FRUSTRATION...
...AND UNBEARABLE SADNESS... SOMETHING LIKE THAT.
tak
HUH?
WHAT DID I DO THAT THEY ALL DIED?
DID I REALLY WATER THEM TOO MUCH?
I THOUGHT IT WAS JUST ENOUGH.

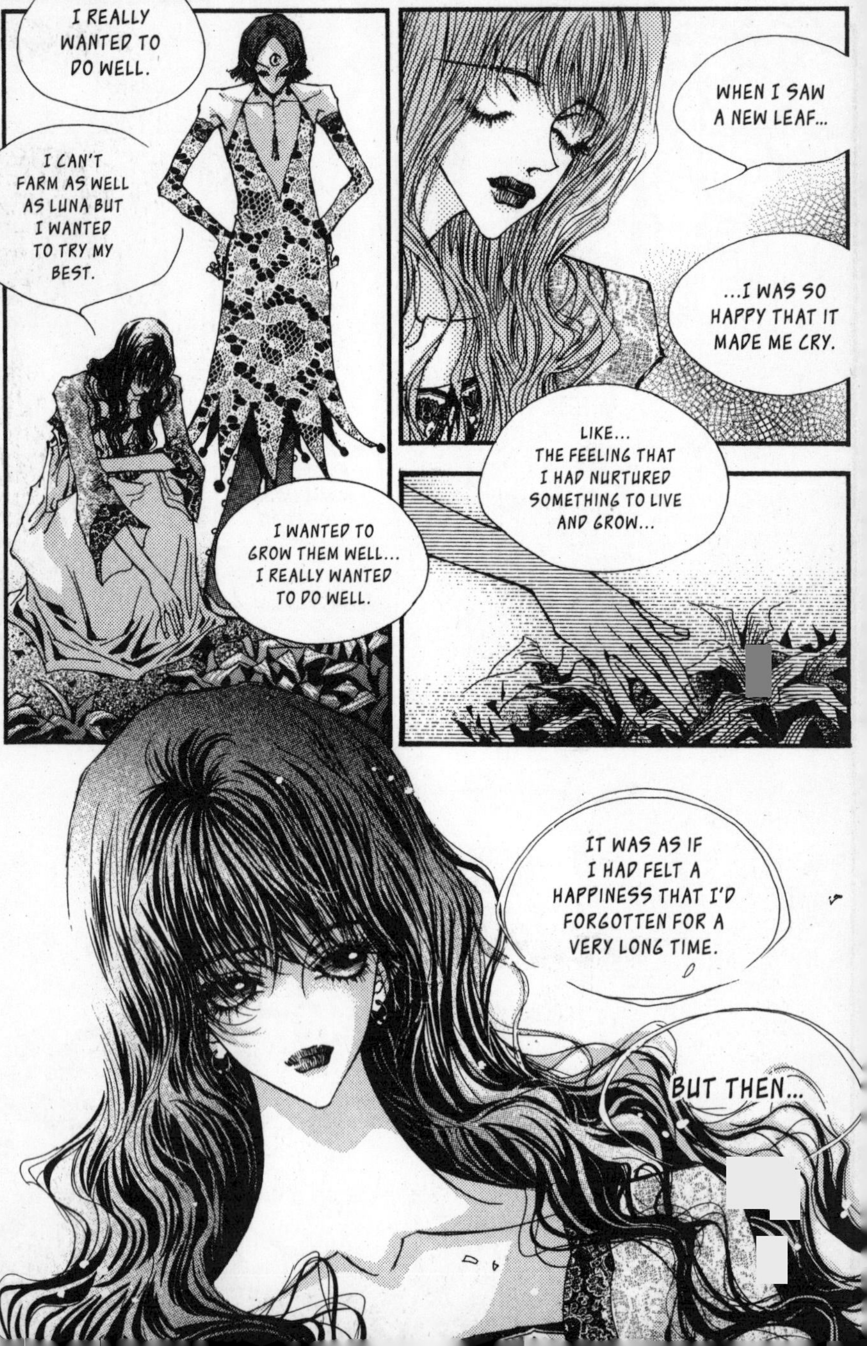
I REALLY WANTED TO DO WELL.
I CAN'T FARM AS WELL AS LUNA BUT I WANTED TO TRY MY BEST.
I WANTED TO GROW THEM WELL... I REALLY WANTED TO DO WELL.
WHEN I SAW A NEW LEAF...
...I WAS SO HAPPY THAT IT MADE ME CRY.
LIKE... THE FEELING THAT I HAD NURTURED SOMETHING TO LIVE AND GROW...
IT WAS AS IF I HAD FELT A HAPPINESS THAT I'D FORGOTTEN FOR A VERY LONG TIME.
BUT THEN...

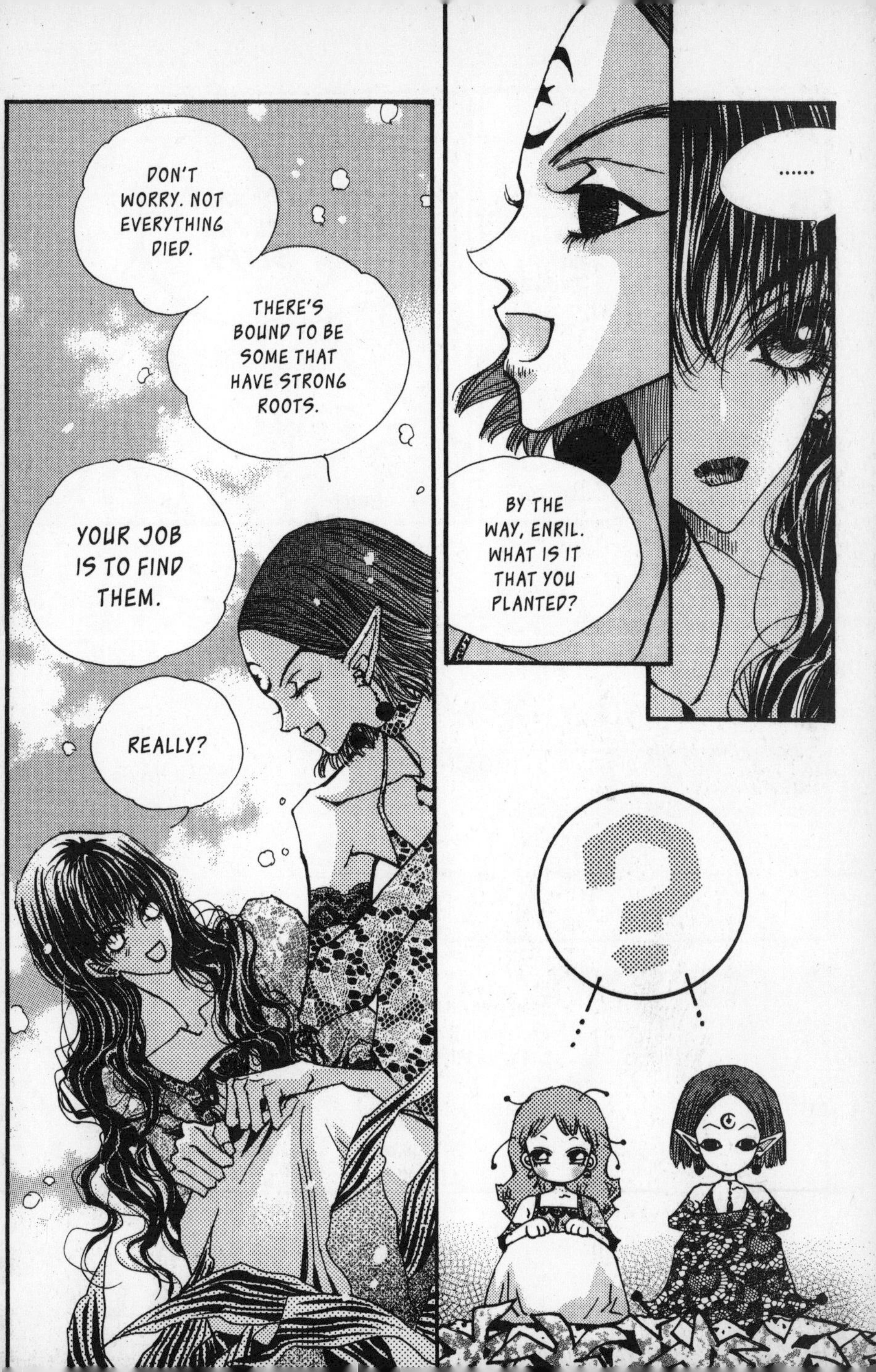
DON'T WORRY. NOT EVERYTHING DIED.
THERE'S BOUND TO BE SOME THAT HAVE STRONG ROOTS.
YOUR JOB IS TO FIND THEM.
REALLY?
......
BY THE WAY, ENRIL. WHAT IS IT THAT YOU PLANTED?
?

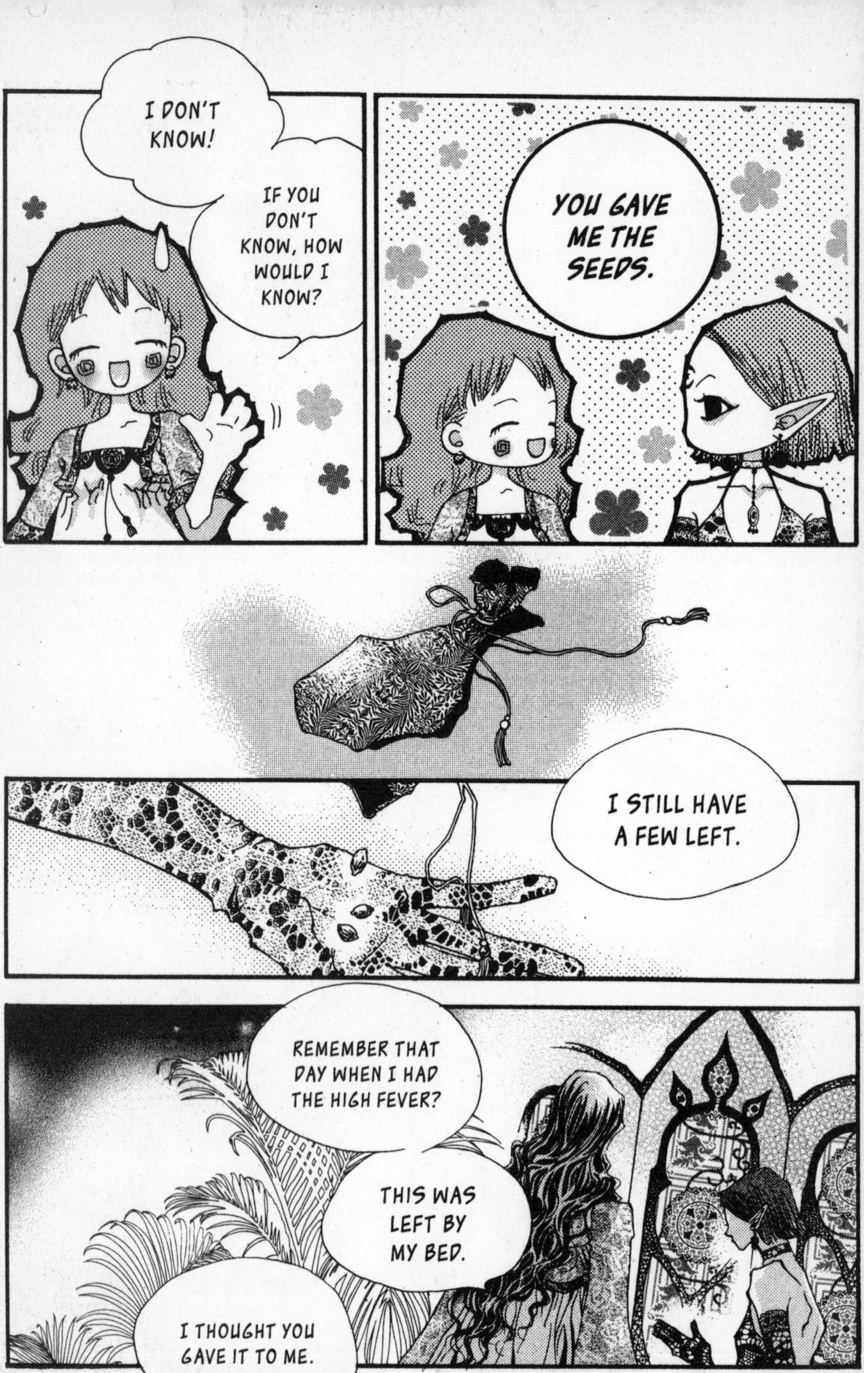
I DON'T KNOW!
IF YOU DON'T KNOW, HOW WOULD I KNOW?
YOU GAVE ME THE SEEDS.
I STILL HAVE A FEW LEFT.
REMEMBER THAT DAY WHEN I HAD THE HIGH FEVER?
THIS WAS LEFT BY MY BED.
I THOUGHT YOU GAVE IT TO ME.

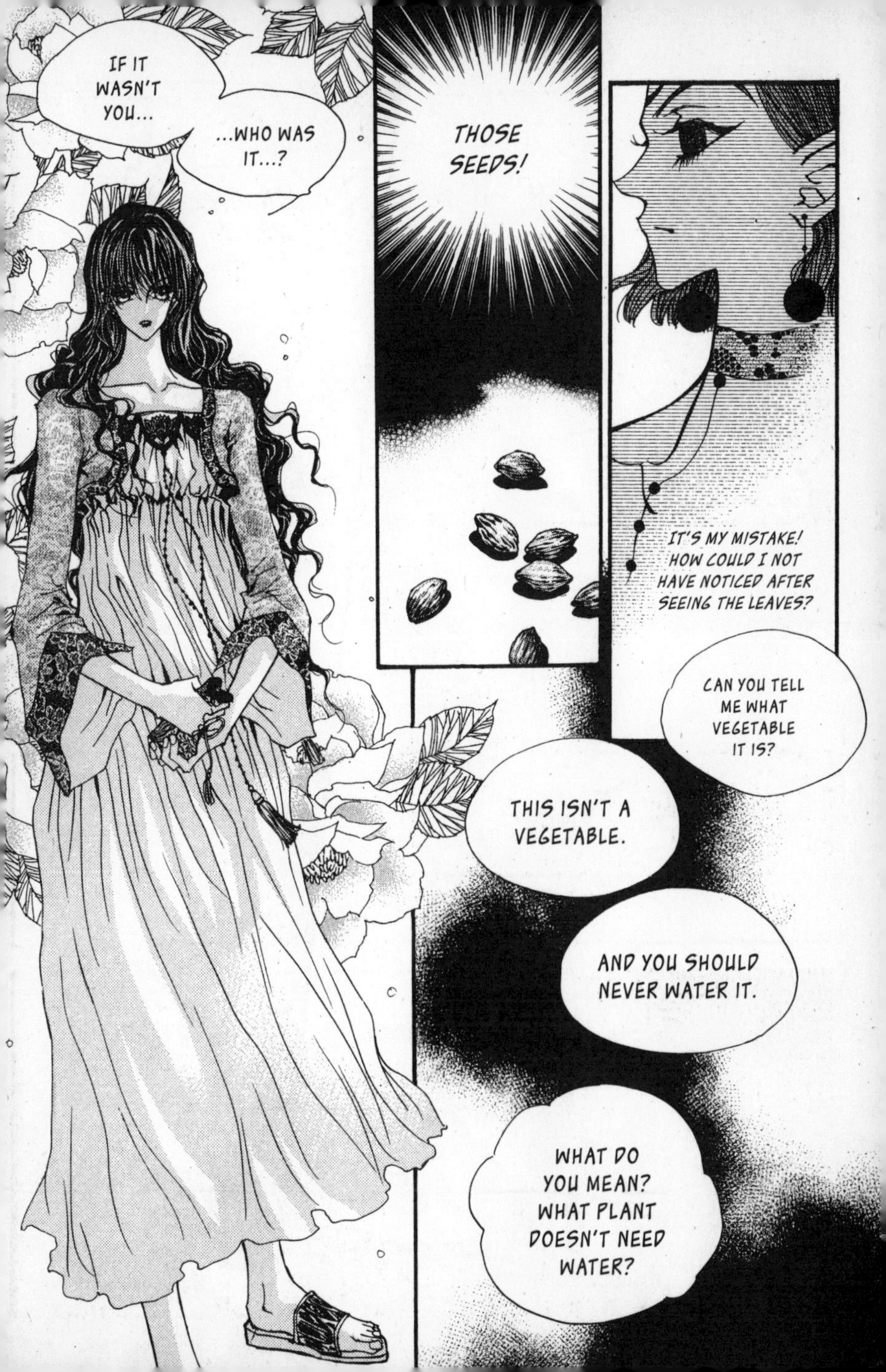
IF IT WASN'T YOU...
...WHO WAS IT...?
THOSE SEEDS!
IT'S MY MISTAKE! HOW COULD I NOT HAVE NOTICED AFTER SEEING THE LEAVES?
CAN YOU TELL ME WHAT VEGETABLE IT IS?
THIS ISN'T A VEGETABLE.
AND YOU SHOULD NEVER WATER IT.
WHAT DO YOU MEAN? WHAT PLANT DOESN'T NEED WATER?

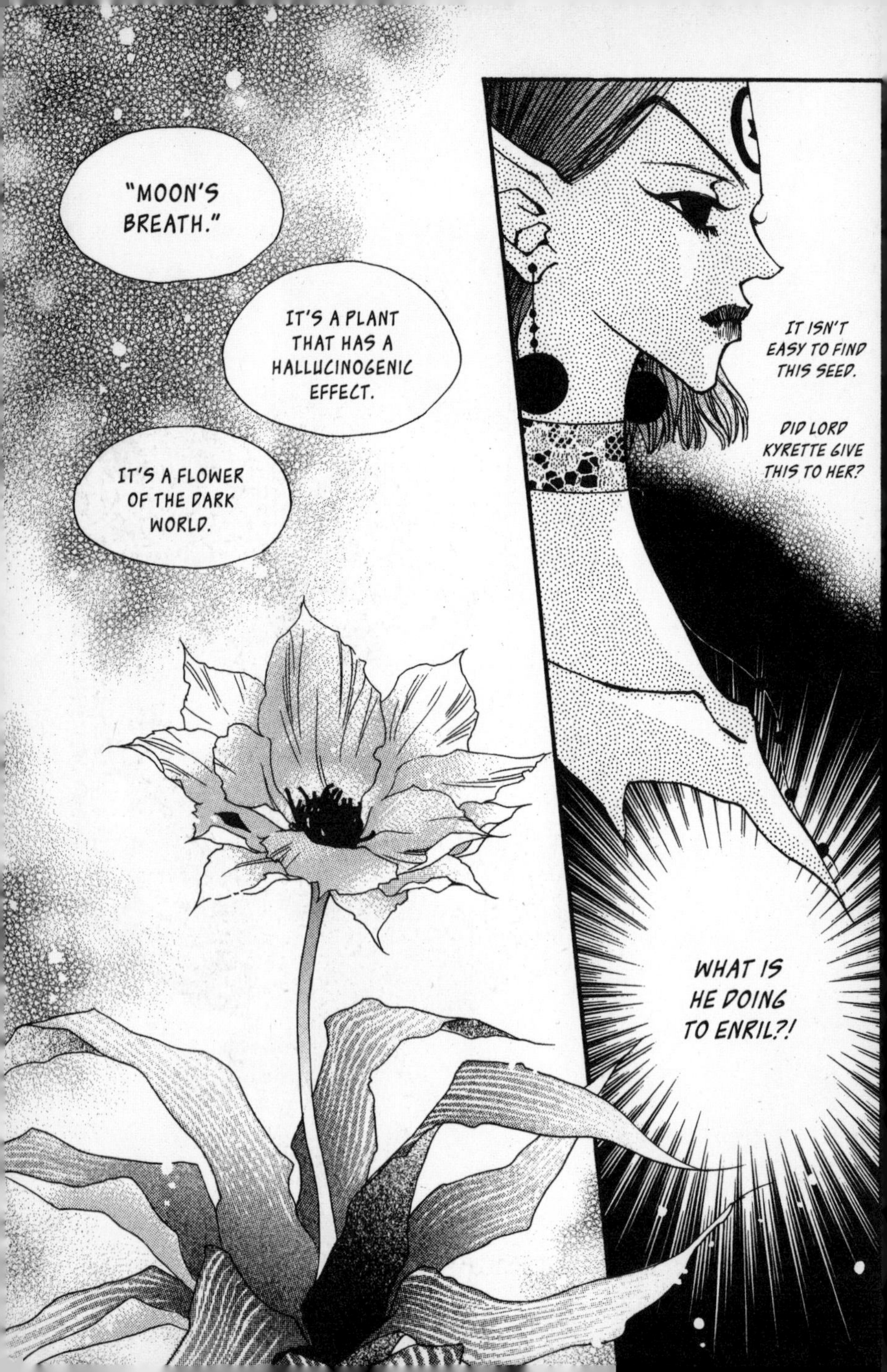
"MOON'S BREATH."
IT'S A PLANT THAT HAS A HALLUCINOGENIC EFFECT.
IT'S A FLOWER OF THE DARK WORLD.
IT ISN'T EASY TO FIND THIS SEED.
DID LORD KYRETTE GIVE THIS TO HER?
WHAT IS HE DOING TO ENRIL?!

TO BE CONTINUED IN ARCANA VOLUME 8! ♥

THE QUEST CONTINUES IN

VOLUME 8

IN THE CONTINUING STORY OF ARCANA'S
PAST -- THE TALE OF ENRIL -- WE WITNESS A
DARK PLAN UNFOLD. KYRETTE HAS PLOTTED
ENDLESSLY TO ACHIEVE HIS DARK GOAL
THROUGH ENRIL. BUT HIS MACHINATIONS
NEVER ACCOUNTED FOR SOMETHING AS
UNPREDICTABLE AS HUMAN EMOTIONS. AS
CLEVER AS HE IS, IT MAY PROVE TO BE HIS
UNDOING...

THERE'S INTRIGUE AND ADVENTURE IN
EVERY PAGE OF THE NEXT VOLUME OF
ARCANA!

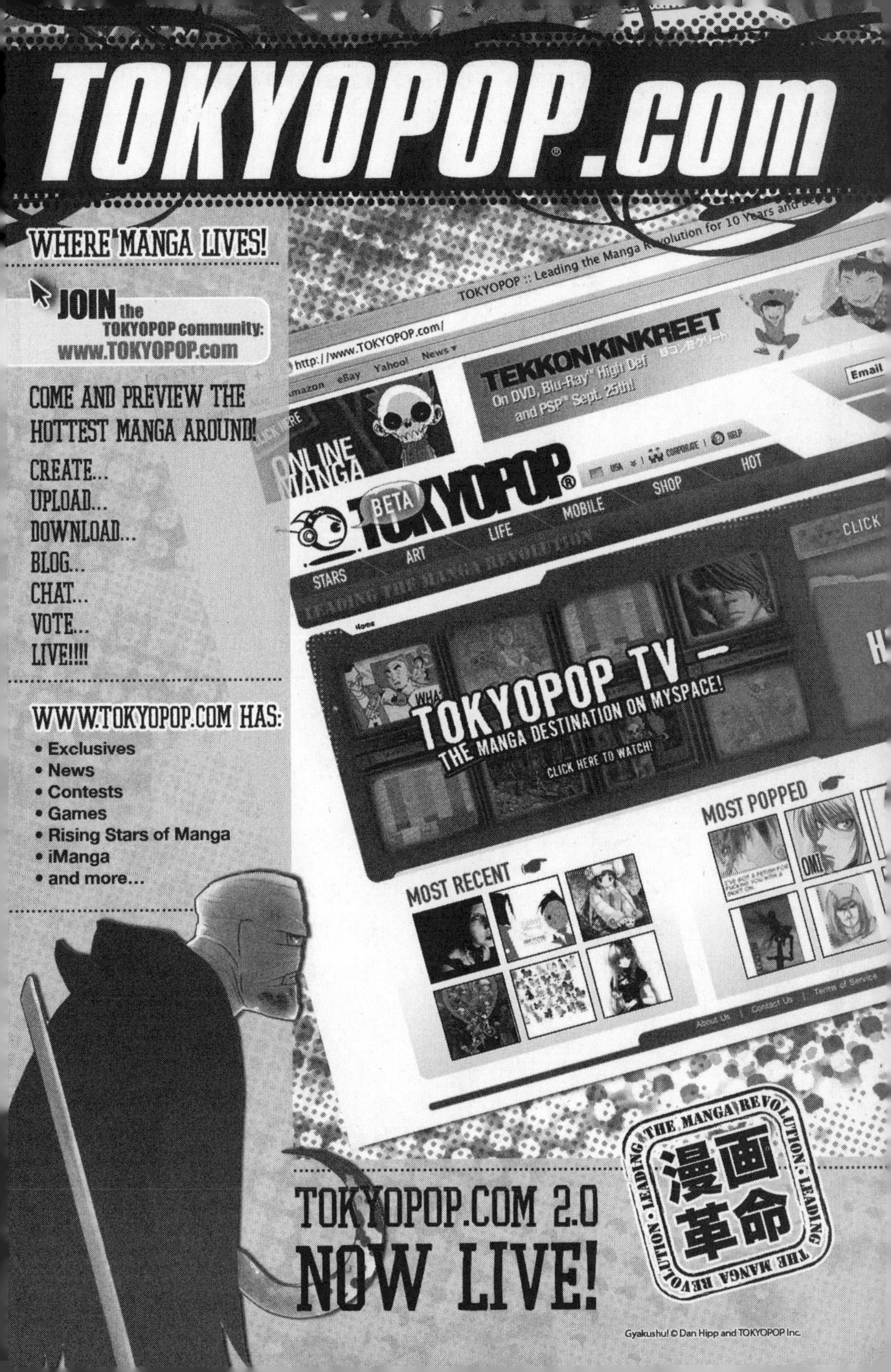
TOKYOPOP.com
WHERE MANGA LIVES!
JOIN the TOKYOPOP community: www.TOKYOPOP.com
COME AND PREVIEW THE HOTTEST MANGA AROUND!
CREATE...
UPLOAD...
DOWNLOAD...
BLOG...
CHAT...
VOTE...
LIVE!!!!
WWW.TOKYOPOP.COM HAS:
• Exclusives
• News
• Contests
• Games
• Rising Stars of Manga
• iManga
• and more...
TOKYOPOP :: Leading the Manga Revolution for 10 Years and Beyond
http://www.TOKYOPOP.com/
TEKKONKINKREET
On DVD, Blu-Ray™ High Def and PSP™ Sept. 25th!
ONLINE MANGA
TOKYOPOP
BETA
STARS
ART
LIFE
MOBILE
SHOP
HOT
TOKYOPOP TV
THE MANGA DESTINATION ON MYSPACE!
CLICK HERE TO WATCH!
MOST POPPED
MOST RECENT
TOKYOPOP.COM 2.0 NOW LIVE!
LEADING THE MANGA REVOLUTION
漫画革命
Gyakushu! © Dan Hipp and TOKYOPOP Inc.

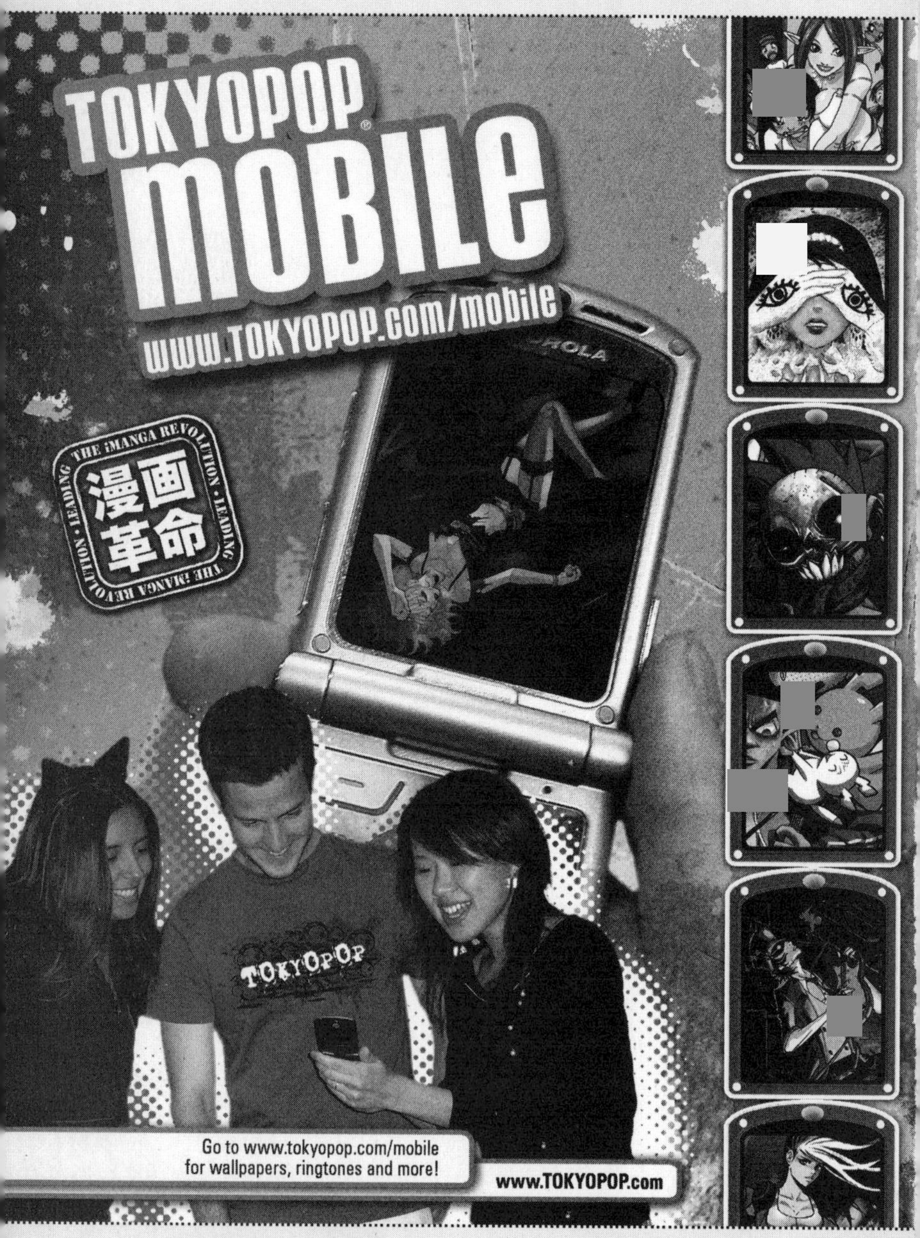
TOKYOPOP® MOBILE
www.TOKYOPOP.com/mobile
THE iMANGA REVOLUTION • LEADING
漫画革命
TOKYOPOP
Go to www.tokyopop.com/mobile
for wallpapers, ringtones and more!
www.TOKYOPOP.com